Roanoke, Virginia,
1882–1912

Roanoke, Virginia, 1882–1912

Magic City of the New South

Rand Dotson

[signature]

10.21.08

The University of Tennessee Press / Knoxville

Copyright © 2007 by The University of Tennessee Press / Knoxville.
All Rights Reserved. Manufactured in the United States of America.
Cloth: First printing, 2007.
Paper: First printing, 2008.

This book is printed on acid-free paper.

Library of Congress Cataloging-in-Publication Data

Dotson, Rand, 1967–
  Roanoke, Virginia, 1882-1912 : magic city of the new South / Rand Dotson.
– 1st ed.
      p. cm.
  Includes bibliographical references and index.
  ISBN-13: 978-1-57233-643-8
  ISBN-10: 1-57233-643-9

  1. Roanoke (Va.)–History.
  2. Roanoke (Va.)–Economic conditions–19th century.
  3. Roanoke (Va.)–Economic conditoins–20th century.
  4. Industrialization–Virginia–Roanoke–History.
  5. Railroads–Virginia–Roanoke–History.
  I. Title.

  F232.R6D68 2007
  975.5'791–dc22   2007002616

For my parents
Paul & Carol Dotson

Contents

Figures

Maps

Acknowledgments

I have been fortunate enough to have had generous advice on this project from several scholars whose work I admire. Gaines Foster, who patiently supervised a previous iteration of this study, is both a mentor and a friend whose wise guidance over the years made me see at least some of the complexities and ambiguities in Roanoke's history. Earlier readings by Charles Royster, Chuck Shindo, and John Rodrigue at LSU were also particularly helpful. Ann Field Alexander, whose excellent work on the Roanoke Riot of 1893 guided my subsequent investigation of that episode, kindly read this entire study and offered invaluable comments on it. Gordon B. McKinney and Louis M. Kyriakoudes, the outside readers for the University of Tennessee Press, provided abundant suggestions that have also proven enormously useful. It was in one of Crandall Shifflett's graduate seminars at Virginia Tech where I first pondered the early history of Roanoke; his subsequent encouragement and friendship over the years have been all a former student could hope for. Thanks also to John Selby at Roanoke College.

The goodwill of archivists and institutions contributed enormously to this book. Elaine Powers, former librarian of the Virginia Room in the downtown branch of the Roanoke City Public Library, gave me unlimited access to the Virginia Room's rich collection one summer when the library was undergoing renovations. Kent Chrisman, chairman of the History Museum and Historical Society of Western Virginia, likewise did all he could to make the museum's vast collection accessible. George Kegley, longtime student of Roanoke's history and editor of the Historical Society's journal, helped track down some of the images that appear in this book and answered questions about the Magic City that no one else likely could. The Virginia Historical Society in Richmond graciously provided an Andrew W. Mellon Research Fellowship that permitted an extended sweep through its superb collection. The exceptional VHS archives and library staff made that visit extremely profitable. Nelson Lankford, editor of the VHS's *Virginia Magazine of History and Biography,* published some of my earlier work and later offered comments on a portion of this study at the first annual "Virginia Forum." (Thanks to Brent Tarter and Warren Hofstra for the invitation to participate in that conference.) The

Special Collections staffs at Virginia Tech, the University of Virginia, and the Library of Virginia were likewise exceedingly helpful. The Interlibrary Borrowing Department at Middleton Library here at Louisiana State University corralled about a mile of newspapers on microfilm from libraries around the country, and a Graduate School Fellowship from LSU provided funds for nearly a year of writing. Scot Danforth, my editor at the University of Tennessee Press, has been a model of patience, thoughtfulness, and kindness that I have learned from. Thanks also to Stan Ivester, managing editor at UT Press, and to Evelyn Schlatter, who copyedited this book.

Over the course of writing this book, I had all the unfair advantages that accompany the clever counsel and skilled camaraderie of Courtney P. Carney, James A. Burtch, and Michael K. Steinberg. A fellow could not ask for a better set of lads, nor a more talented bunch of friends. Other comrades deserve mention as well. At LSU: Heather Morrison, Benjamin Cloyd, Mathew Reonas, Christopher Leahy, and John Sacher. At Virginia Tech: Sabrene Blevins, Sarah Cotton, and Christopher Curtis. In Roanoke: Christine Hastings, Jill Carter, Steven Sellers (now of Wilmington, North Carolina), and my former colleagues at the late great Books, Strings & Things on Market Square. Thanks also to my colleagues at LSU Press, and especially to MaryKatherine Callaway, John Easterly, Alisa Plant, and Kerry Webb.

My family–Brett, Kathy, and Roxy Blue Dotson of Nevada City, California; Liza, Neil, Hayden, and Blake Conner of Salem, Virginia; Florence Wyatt of Salem; and my parents Paul and Carol Dotson of Salem–could not have been more supportive. I dedicate this book to my folks, who more than anybody else are responsible for whatever good it contains.

Spanish Town
Baton Rouge, Louisiana
December 2006

Introduction

In the 1880s, no city in the South grew faster than the railroad hub of Roanoke, Virginia. Located in a valley of the Appalachian Mountains in the southwestern portion of the state, Roanoke had been the Town of Big Lick—a tobacco depot with about a thousand residents—until 1882, when a group of native businessmen used tax breaks, cash bonuses, and land grants to convince a Philadelphia investment firm to select the place as the junction, headquarters, and machine shops for its Norfolk & Western and Shenandoah Valley railroads. In the aftermath, skilled workers from the North and rural migrants from the Virginia countryside arrived by the thousands to take jobs in the city's burgeoning industries. By 1890, Roanoke had become the fifth largest municipality in Virginia; a decade later, it was the state's third biggest city and home to the largest locomotive manufacturing plant in the South. Regional boosters, encouraged by the town's seemingly spectacular rise from nowhere, declared it the "Magic City of the New South" and guaranteed that Roanoke would eventually become the Atlanta of Virginia—a sister city to the region's most heralded post–Civil War success story.

Roanoke's progress, while perhaps stunning for a time, never quite measured up to the inflated rhetoric heaped upon it by New South prophets, who promised the nation's most deprived region unparalleled growth and modernization—adjuncts of blind adherence to a creed that put economic development above all other concerns. By the early twentieth century, Roanoke's industrial and demographic expansion had leveled off, and over the following hundred years, the city tumbled back down the list of Virginia's most significant municipalities. For a time, however, the Magic City seemed poised to prove southern boosters correct. This book is a history of that period.

It begins in the 1870s, when harvesting natural resources in Appalachian Virginia set in motion the processes that resulted in the rise of Roanoke, continues through the 1880s and 1890s, when residents tried to solve myriad social and infrastructure problems associated with the city's chaotic origins, and ends in the early twentieth century, when civic reformers led a crusade to recast the town and its people in ways that would make the place more attractive to potential investors. To understand that history without allowing its cacophony of events and voices to become overwhelming, this analysis uses class, community, and reform as points of departure. It does so in ways that puts the desires and expectations of the city's people at the fore of the story, and with a deep appreciation for the richness and diversity of their experiences. Rather than simply viewing the city as a static entity, this study also considers Roanoke and its people as part of an ongoing process—one laden with a multiplicity of unintended consequences, uncertain outcomes, and ambiguous conclusions.

Those processes began when a group of Big Lick's merchants persuaded a Philadelphia investment firm to make their town the base of operations for its recently acquired railroads. These Big Lick natives, albeit with a helping hand from their northern benefactors, were primarily responsible for the intense industrial and demographic development that accompanied the arrival of the railroad. They were also the residents who reaped the most significant economic rewards in the land booms and manufacturing investments that followed. Unlike other natives trapped in industrializing Appalachia's colonial economy, these men not only courted and welcomed northern-owned extractive industries, they also shepherded them into place, served on their boards of directors, and mitigated conflicts between them and the municipality's inhabitants or elected officials. Having nearly abolished corporate taxes and guaranteed all new enterprises an accommodating and obsequious government in order to get manufacturers to locate in Roanoke, they also strapped the place with a chronically under-funded government, chaotic growth pattern, company-town appearance, and boomtown ethos.

During this initial period of haphazard expansion, the city's infrastructure failed to keep pace with the influx of new residents. Its dirt streets became impassable mud bogs after a rain, and its stagnant streams served as open sewers, which, coupled with a complete lack of sanitation, produced frequent outbreaks of cholera and typhoid. Furthermore, migrants from the countryside arrived with rural customs unsuited for urban living, which only exacerbated the situation. Political and social conflicts between native southerners and northern newcomers divided the town for a time. And even though the arrival of the railroad generated massive development, most of it occurred well to the east of the original settlement of Big Lick, in a place natives dubbed "New Town"—a semi-private neighborhood where the paternalistic hand of the railroad ameliorated Roanoke's frontier conditions with macadamized streets, drainage improvements, running water, a private police force, and gas lighting.

After the dust of the city's initial industrialization process cleared, natives for a time became even more suspicious of their northern neighbors, especially since most of them were Republicans, who, with the support of African American residents, threatened the hegemony of local Democrats. Very quickly, however, most white residents, no matter what their geographic origins or political affiliations, found common ground in pushing the municipality to fund modest infrastructure improvements.

The city's African Americans, who never received anything close to a fair share of public funding, fought the appropriations, and in the process alienated their Republican allies. Whites also coalesced around a variety of law-and-order issues—primarily in a crusade against black saloons or in quests to hunt down African American men suspected of capital crimes. In addition, they unified behind efforts to fill in gaps in public services by staffing volunteer fire brigades and militias or by contributing to charities or the campaign for a public hospital. While these combined efforts bridged many of the initial rifts between natives and newcomers, they also generated a deep racial divide that relegated black residents to the margins of the larger community.

The natives most responsible for the rapid industrialization of Roanoke quickly became its most affluent and influential citizens. They worked hand-in-glove with the municipality's new corporate parents, instigated additional economic development, and eventually started their own successful enterprises. These local business boosters were also the primary players in a land speculation frenzy that swept Southwest Virginia in the late 1880s—men responsible for millions of dollars of investments by northern and European real estate speculators. Though Roanoke's dismal urban environment stood in marked contrast to boosters' propaganda, its business leaders adhered steadfastly to a creed that put further industrialization above all other concerns. As a result, the city continued offering tax exemptions, free lots, and municipal stock subscriptions to any outside corporation that agreed to locate there, and it did so at the expense of making significant infrastructure improvements or providing adequate public services.

The society that emerged in the Magic City was deeply divided by class and race. White migrants from the countryside and working-class residents from the North existed in one world, upper-class natives and newcomers in another, and black residents in yet one more. Most of the town's white working classes lived in company-owned housing, frequented the city's thriving saloon district, and patronized its lowbrow culture of street carnivals, traveling museums, and bawdy theaters. Native and newcomer elites, by contrast, resided in Queen Anne mansions on the outskirts of town and lived in a world of exclusive societies, fraternal orders, civic associations, and patrician clubs. They patronized highbrow entertainment, such as opera or drama, in the Academy of Music, a venue clearly demarcated as the space of Roanoke's privileged classes. African Americans—nearly a third of all residents—lived in a world of exclusion, almost entirely outside white society. They resided in a completely separate section of town, where they created a flourishing culture of dance halls, eating houses, and saloons that white inhabitants rarely frequented. Roanoke's three distinct subcultures, although for the most part completely divided, occasionally came together in ways that helped foster a civic identity. They cheered on local baseball teams, patronized circuses and fairs, and participated in citywide celebrations, all of which created a sense that they were "Roanokers."

In the 1890s, nevertheless, stark divisions opened up between white residents. Part of the divide stemmed from Evangelicals' attempt to impose prohibition on working-class residents; some of it was the consequence of authorities' failure to hold blacks accountable for their supposed crimes at a time when lower-class whites' predilection for vigilante justice was at an all-time high. A catastrophic economic depression and Roanoke's primitive conditions made these class tensions worse, and in 1893, when municipal leaders refused to hand over an African American who stood accused of assaulting a white female, an underclass mob ignited one of the worst lynch riots in Virginia's history. By the time it ended, the local militia had killed eight white citizens, the black prisoner had been dragged through the streets and burned in front of thousands of cheering residents, and the city's mayor had fled for his life. In the aftermath, business boosters and municipal authorities, well aware that the reputation of the Magic City was in shambles, responded with calls for increased law enforcement, prompt punishment of rioters, and a public relations campaign touting Roanoke as moral, progressive, and business friendly. In the end, their efforts removed lynching from the canon of extralegal punishments available to under-class whites, erased much of the riot's public memory, and at least partially rehabilitated the city's standing.

Having mitigated the damage from the 1893 revolt, Roanoke's boosters next shepherded the city through the decade-long national depression that followed—an economic downturn that threw scores of local laborers out of work, drove the Norfolk & Western (N&W) into bankruptcy, and financially destroyed many of the city's most successful natives. During the crisis, a second generation of promoters with fewer overt ties to the N&W emerged to champion a plan to bring in another railroad to lessen the damage done by the economic downturn and end the N&W's monopoly on local rail access.

When the depression finally ended, indigenous enterprises, such as the Virginia Brewing Company and the Stone Printing & Manufacturing Company, rose to prominence and offered striking counterexamples to notions that Roanoke was solely a railroad town. The men behind these and other new corporations boosted their municipality like never before in the early 1900s, using its Board of Trade and Chamber of Commerce as promotional machines to draw in dozens of new heavy industries and diversify the local economy. While still offering an array of corporate bonuses to any potential new enterprise, these boosters also pointed to Roanoke's abundant and tractable Anglo Saxon labor force as a key selling point. Most local workers belonged to unions but rarely challenged corporate authority. Company paternalism, relatively high wages, corporate welfare, a stridently pro-business local government, and the isolation of Southwest Virginia all contributed to workers' submissiveness.

Roanoke's business boosters—the men who successfully promoted the city to outside investors and industries—had an almost blind faith in economic development as a panacea for all the town's problems. In the end, however, their faith failed to shape the city in the fashion they expected. As a result, by the turn of the century, the town still seemed more Big Lick than Roanoke. It still sported numerous dirt streets, hundreds of free-ranging cattle, a polluted farmer's market, few enforced health regulations, a rowdy saloon and brothel district, overcrowded and dingy schools, and no public parks or library. In addition, racial conflicts over politics or public space continued to generate anxiety among most whites.

Eventually, local business leaders, Evangelicals, and clubwomen stepped forward to attempt to remedy these and other issues. While the city's reform-ers often clashed over how best to recast the town, they had a remarkably similar goal: reorder Roanoke in ways that would ensure continued economic modernization, promote healthiness, and facilitate social stability. Each group sought distinct means to remedy the problems they perceived, but their methodology was usually hierarchical in orientation and their solutions gener-ally aimed at residents who either cared little about the issue or opposed the

Oxcart in front of Roanoke Real Estate Exchange, early 1890s. History Museum and Histori-cal Society of Western Virginia, Roanoke.

change. In spite of their different techniques, the city's "progressive reformers" were uniformly conservative in their outlook—they did not advocate social justice, were not interested in social uplift, and never doubted the absolute suitability of Roanoke's economic and racial order.

The rapid urbanization and industrialization of Roanoke is but a brief chapter of the overall story of modernization taking place in the late-nineteenth-century South. Elsewhere in the region, a few older towns experienced similar growth and some other new cities also seemingly sprang from nowhere. In these urban places, a different kind of South was coming into existence—one marked by a mixture of old and new: industrial labor, cash exchange, class stratification, racial segregation, rapid transportation, modern communication, and mass culture. It was in southern towns and cities that the region's Antebellum political and economic leaders were supplanted by a new generation of urban entrepreneurs, businessmen, and boosters—men who clung to a belief that the New South creed would put the region back on the path to national supremacy. With little capital at their disposal, they turned to northern financiers and welcomed the creation of a "colonial economy" in which the South traded its natural resources for extractive industries and northern-produced factory goods. They were also in the fore of a movement to subjugate African Americans through the creation of an elaborate racial caste system that used disfranchisement and segregation as the primary means to end racial turmoil. While all these processes were taking place throughout the South, most either originated or came into sharpest focus in the region's urban spaces and especially in its newly emerging cities, company towns, and mill villages.[1]

Historians of the New South generally point to Roanoke as an extreme example of the phenomenal change that occurred in some parts of the region. Most place it alongside Birmingham, Alabama—another so called "Magic City"—and suggest that each was a New South boomtown. Since almost all southern cities lagged far behind their northern counterparts in terms of demographics, infrastructure, per capita income, and factory output, most of the overblown rhetoric about the existence of a New South rested on exceptional instances of growth and industrialization that happened in a region where the vast majority of the population continued to live in poverty- stricken rural areas, dependent on a stagnant agricultural economy.[2]

In the 1880s and 1890s, southern business leaders pointed to Birmingham's steel mills and Roanoke's railroad industries as beacons of progress. In Appalachia, most boosters extolled Roanoke's emergence as well. For unlike most new mountain towns, which were generally the base of operations for extractive industries and typically owned by northeastern capitalists, Roanoke was an independent municipality largely under the control of natives, where manufacturing was the main source of employment.[3]

Visitor after visitor to Roanoke in the 1880s and 1890s described the place as an odd industrial outpost on the Appalachian frontier. Most assumed it was a company town, owned and managed by the N&W Railroad, and time after time, they claimed it looked more like a New England factory village than a southern city. Many noted a "peculiar" civic spirit among its businessmen, explaining that nearly every Roanoker they encountered was in some way connected to a local booster club, had a stake in one or more land companies, was invested in various commercial schemes, and was more than happy to offer outsiders speculation in these and other business ventures at bargain prices. What may have seemed striking to visitors was no accident. Roanoke, a city born in a business deal and built up on former cow pastures, had a population hell bent on turning a fast buck, and it was just what regional boosters had promised—*the* New South.

Chapter 1

From Big Lick to Boomtown

In the 1880s, the promise of a New South rising out of the ruins of the former Confederacy looked hollow to all but the most devout adherents of that vision. Evidence of modernization in the form of industrialization and urbanization was especially hard to find, which made the unexpected emergence of Roanoke, Virginia, in 1882 as the junction, headquarters, and machine shops for two Philadelphia-owned railroads all the more astonishing. Opportunity in the town attracted thousands of highly skilled northern laborers and scores of new residents from the surrounding mountains and countryside, and over the next eight years, its population increased at a rate that far surpassed any other southern city. By 1890, it had become Virginia's fifth largest municipality and regional boosters were heralding it widely as the "Magic City of the New South."[1]

The intensive growth initially turned Roanoke into a "boomtown," with all the haphazard development, infrastructure problems, and social disorders common to such places. Homes went up in what had recently been cow pastures or wheat fields, and a downtown of false-fronted stores and saloons emerged amidst bottomland bogs. The town had illogically arranged dirt or mud streets, creeks for sewers, no running water or gas lighting, no systematic method of drainage, inadequate schools, and an understaffed police force. Incidents of public drunkenness, raucous behavior, petty crime, prostitution, and gambling rose dramatically, as did natives' resentment of the railroad and toward the hordes of northern strangers and African Americans pouring into town. Many of Roanoke's newcomers, by contrast, had lived previously in the industrialized North and found the abysmal conditions and parochial atmosphere of their new home bewildering.

■■■

Although to many outsiders Roanoke seemed to have risen from nowhere, its origins were firmly rooted in what had until 1882 been Big Lick, a town that emerged in the 1850s next to the tracks of Southwest Virginia's first railroad. "Big Lick" had been one of the names of a brackish marsh nearby, and the town that inherited the name was situated on a lowland plateau in a wide valley of the Blue Ridge Mountains not far from the banks of the Roanoke

River. The area had first been settled in the late 1750s, when homesteaders built a mill along a nearby creek. Located then in sprawling Botetourt County near the junction of the "Great Road" (a north-south route from Philadelphia to Yadkin) and the "Carolina Road" (an east-west route to the Cumberland Gap), the mill went on to become a trading post for farmers scattered about the valley floor as well as the location for a tavern serving waves of settlers traveling along the nearby wagon paths.[2]

In the early 1830s, land speculators purchased the mill and the surrounding property and laid out 120 lots on the Great Road for a development they called "Gainesborough." The men sold dozens of lots to settlers, merchants, and investors, and within a year enough residents had moved into Gainesborough to petition the state for township status.[3] The Virginia General Assembly carved Roanoke County out of Botetourt County a few years later, and for at least a moment the centrally located Gainesborough was in the running for county seat.[4]

Local politicians, however, eventually selected Salem, an older and significantly larger town eight miles to the west on the Great Road.[5] In the ensuing decades, Gainesborough failed to evolve beyond a few hundred residents, three churches, a blacksmith shop, a tavern, and a couple of dry goods stores. In the early 1850s, after the Virginia & Tennessee Railroad built its tracks through Roanoke County roughly a mile to the south of Gainesborough, any chance for additional growth all but disappeared. Concerned more with building the cheapest roadbed possible than with passing through the various hamlets and villages in its path, the railroad positioned its tracks along the licks and built "Big Lick Depot" in the midst of corn and wheat fields next to a dirt road leading south into Franklin County.

The first train arrived in the fall of 1852, and at least a few of the numerous Gainesborough residents who turned out to see the wood-fired engine and three cars pass by understood the magnitude of the event and decided to relocate their businesses closer to the new depot.[6] Additional hotels joined "Trout House," a well-known inn on the road to Franklin County, just to the south of the tracks, and several general merchandise stores moved over as well. Not long after the railroad arrived, farmers in neighboring counties moved swiftly into tobacco production and began using Big Lick Depot, which was easily accessible via Franklin County Road, as a place to sell their harvests and stock up on supplies.[7] As a result, the village grew quickly into a small manufacturing center with the warehousing or production of plug and smoking tobacco as its core industries. On the eve of the Civil War, Southwestern Virginians were calling the area around the depot "Big Lick."[8]

The interruption of train service during the Civil War retarded Big Lick's initial growth. Even worse, in April 1865, federal cavalry raided the valley,

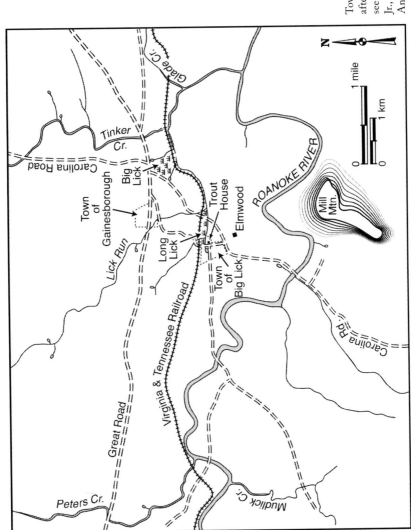

Towns of Gainesborough and Big Lick after the arrival of the Virginia & Tennessee Railroad. Map by Clifford Duplechin Jr., Cartographic Section, Geography & Anthropology Department, LSU.

ransacked the town, and burned its depot before destroying nearby railroad tracks and bridges.[9] In the aftermath of the war, Big Lick teetered on the edge of ruin. In 1868, according to one visitor, the once thriving tobacco hub resembled a ghost town.[10] A few years later, when Callowhill Turner opened a tobacco warehouse in the village, Big Lick had begun a sustained recovery and its population had rebounded to prewar levels. The "great big swamp" east of the station, Turner recalled, continued to menace locals with its mysterious miasmas and mosquito-borne diseases, and although some men hunted around the bogs, most residents considered them dangerous, since livestock that wandered into the marshes occasionally sank into the mud and disappeared below the water.[11]

By 1874, the community had grown large enough to petition the Legislature for township status. State Delegate Henry S. Trout, son of John Trout, the owner of Trout House, presented the bill, and in February, the General Assembly created the Town of Big Lick.[12] The new charter appointed Henry's father acting mayor and created boundaries a half-mile out from the depot, making Big Lick a half-mile square with the train station at its center. A spurt of development followed, and by 1876, the town had Lutheran, Presbyterian, Methodist, and Episcopal churches; seven general merchandise stores; five tobacco factories; three tobacco warehouses; a wagon and plow factory; a harness factory; two blacksmith shops; a flour mill; two photography shops; and three saloons.[13] The first formal census in 1880 counted 335 black and mulatto inhabitants along with 334 white residents. According to the Census, most of the town's workers were employed in its tobacco industries. Blacks or mulattos employed elsewhere tended to earn a living as farm laborers or domestic servants while whites otherwise employed worked as clerks, merchants, or tobacco salesman.[14]

The link to the Virginia & Tennessee Railroad that created and sustained Big Lick transformed the town again in the early 1880s, this time turning it into "Roanoke," a booming industrial city. Before it did, however, the Virginia & Tennessee Railroad would change ownership and another line, this one backed by northern capitalists looking to exploit the region's mineral wealth, would arrive. The process began in 1870, after "Redeemers" gained control of Virginia and the state rejoined the Union. The newly elected legislature authorized the consolidation of the Old Dominion's three major railways. Joined together that year, the Norfolk & Petersburg, Southside, and Virginia & Tennessee became the Atlantic, Mississippi & Ohio Railroad (AM&O) under the direction of former Confederate General William Mahone. Although Mahone won praise as a competent manager of the AM&O, the 1873 national economic depression caused the line to default on loans, and in 1875, courts placed the railroad in reorganization receivership.[15]

The depression also halted construction of the Shenandoah Valley Railroad (SVR), a line funded by Philadelphia investors that was being built along the Shenandoah River from Hagerstown, Maryland, to central Virginia. While the AM&O depended on passengers and agriculture for business, the backers of the SVR proposed to derive the bulk of their profits by transporting Southwest Virginia's coal and ore. The line was originally supposed to make an east-west link with the Virginia & Tennessee Railroad in Roanoke County, but in 1872, the company dropped that proposed terminus and selected a closer and significantly cheaper link with the Chesapeake & Ohio Railroad at Waynesboro, Virginia. Having barely begun surveying routes and starting construction by 1873, the ensuing financial panic halted significant progress on the SVR. By 1879, it consisted of only forty-two miles of track between Shepherdstown, Maryland, and the Shenandoah River.[16]

In June of that year, Enoch W. Clark & Company, a private Philadelphia banking house and rival of the firm that owned the SVR, purchased the struggling railroad. The Clark Company appointed junior associate and Philadelphia native Frederick J. Kimball head of the construction firm responsible for completing the line, and with the renewed financial support, tracks for the road again began moving north from Waynesboro and south from Hagerstown.[17] Like its previous owners, the Clark firm anticipated using the road to haul coal, iron ore, and lime.[18] Indeed, in its prospectus for the line, the new owners claimed the SVR would become "The great mineral railroad of Virginia." Not long after the purchase, the company decided that it needed a terminus further south or west of Waynesboro, and by 1881, its agents had surveyed several possible routes into Southwest Virginia and western North Carolina.[19]

Mahone's AM&O remained in receivership, and although it was turning a profit hauling cotton, cattle, tobacco, lumber, and grain, when it went up for auction in early 1881, Clarence H. Clark, president of Enoch W. Clark & Company, bought the line for $14,000,000. The purchase put the AM&O in the Clark Company fold, giving the firm an east-west trunk road through Virginia as well as an obvious junction line for its Shenandoah Valley Railroad. Clark changed the name of the AM&O to the Norfolk & Western (N&W), and a few weeks later, he and the other directors of the SVR appointed a "Committee on Construction" to find a terminus for the SVR with the N&W somewhere in the vicinity of Bonsack, Virginia. Although the firm appointed its railroad engineer, Frederick Kimball, president of the SVR and vice-president of the N&W, and created a board of directors for the N&W that overlapped the board of the SVR, the Clark Company maintained each of its lines as distinct corporations. The N&W's new managers expected it to continue hauling agricultural products, but proposed adding spur routes from the road into Southwest Virginia's coal beds as a way to boost business.[20]

The general location of the coal that the Clark firm anticipated hauling had been widely known for over a century, and from the 1840s onward, natives and outsiders alike knew the only hindrance to harvesting the minerals was gathering enough capital to construct a rail line into the Highlands. William Mahone's Richmond *Whig* had advocated development of the region since the early 1870s, and in the years that the SVR project had stalled, the coal belt had received even more attention. Indeed, a large audience had read about the area's potential in former Confederate Major Jedediah Hotchkiss's journal *The Virginias: A Mining, Scientific, and Industrial Journal Devoted to the Development of Virginia and West Virginia,* and in Charles R. Boyd's *Resources of South-West Virginia, Showing the Mineral Deposits of Iron, Coal, Zinc, Copper, and Lead.*

Boyd, a civil and mining engineer from Wytheville, Virginia, believed his book would "show up our resources in a proper manner; thus bringing in many men of capital to willingly help us not only bear our burdens, but create new facilities for making money."[21] Frederick Kimball studied Boyd's work closely and eventually purchased a hundred copies to distribute amongst Clark Company staffers and potential investors.[22] Access to the coalfields, Kimball speculated, would not only provide the coke necessary to fire iron furnaces in Virginia, it would also give the N&W and SVR a cheap source of fuel as well as a valuable cargo to ship North.

In the spring of 1881, Kimball went to the region with his wife and two Clark Company associates to find a rail route into the Highlands. The group rode horses into the backcountry of Tazewell County, Virginia, and after stumbling across a twelve-foot-wide outcropping of coal on Flat Top Mountain, they approved Mrs. Kimball's suggestion to name the deposit "Pocahontas" in honor of that Powhatan "princess."[23] Back in Philadelphia, dispatches from Kimball describing the seam jolted the Clark firm into action. In the months that followed, the firm purchased mineral rights for a hundred-thousand acres along the coal belt, bought out all existing railroad charters in the region, and established a leasing agency responsible for renting mining rights exclusively to operators who agreed to use the N&W. By August 1881, the N&W had begun construction on a seventy-five-mile spur line from Radford, Virginia, to Pocahontas, Virginia, a company town being built by the agency for use as its base of operations in the coalfields.[24]

News of the proposed SVR junction with the N&W in the vicinity of Bonsack spread to Southwest Virginia not long after Clark & Company purchased the AM&O, and towns that stood any chance of getting the junction initiated campaigns to lure the railroad. Salem, which had already been selected as a junction for the rival "Valley Railroad," sent a delegation that included the president of Roanoke College to meet with SVR officials. Later, the town convinced U.S. Senator William Mahone to petition the line for a terminus at Salem.[25] Lynchburg, already home to the AM&O's offices and machine shops as well as a junction with the Midland Railroad, also sent a prestigious delegation to confer with the officials.[26] The significantly smaller town of Big Lick assumed it was not in the running for the junction until a survey team for the railroad arrived and began plotting possible routes nearby. Residents "grew very much interested" after that, according to Henry Trout, and although the town lacked the budget of its larger rivals, it immediately instigated a modest campaign to make a case for the place.[27]

As part of that effort, the town's businessmen met to map a strategy for attracting the railroad. Although the citizens present expressed interest in doing what they could to get the line's attention, Peyton L. Terry, a wealthy tobacco merchant and dry goods store owner, told those gathered that he was afraid townspeople "were not sufficiently aroused to the importance of doing whatever necessary at once."[28] Members of the town's council seconded Terry's concern, and before the meeting ended, they appointed a committee to draft a formal address to Frederick Kimball "setting forth the advantages Big Lick offers as a terminus." The resulting "memorial" Kimball received therefore focused on the village's potential importance as a shipping center for tobacco and grain and let him know that Big Lick residents were "fully alive to the great benefits which would accrue to the town from this being chosen as the point." They also offered a lot for a depot and assistance to secure right-of-ways into town.[29]

When another team of surveyors arrived to inspect possible routes, the town's council interpreted the appearance as a sign that they were clearly in the running and dispatched a delegate to Philadelphia to meet with Clark Company officials.[30] The railroad, nevertheless, continued to survey numerous other possible routes, and in order to determine the potential cost of the various terminuses under consideration, it hired local right-of-way agents to secure options on possible roadbeds.

One of those employed was John C. Moomaw, a farmer and canning factory operator from neighboring Botetourt County. Though hired to explore several different routes, Moomaw wanted railroad access for his "Cloverdale Brand" of canned peaches, corn, and tomatoes, and thus was especially interested in pathways through the hamlet of Cloverdale into Salem.[31] His scheme, however, had problems: the original plan for a link at Bonsack was about seven and a half miles shorter and thus tens of thousands of dollars cheaper; the SVR was considering junctions at existing N&W depots in Big Lick, Buford's (present-day Montvale) and Ironville (present-day Villamont); and when Moomaw and Clark & Company agents visited Salem they encountered problems securing right-of-ways into town.[32] Having already sold the rights for a roadbed to the Valley Railroad, Salem residents were apparently less inclined to offer expensive incentives or cheap land to get a junction with the SVR.[33] Indeed, one resident recalled that "the Mayor and town council went hunting to avoid meeting the railroad men."[34]

Big Lick merchant Peyton Terry happened to be in Salem when the negotiations there faltered. Back in Big Lick, Terry relayed the news to a gathering of businessmen and suggested that it was now or never to do all they could to get the junction.[35] There is considerable debate about what happened next, but it seems likely that John Moomaw, on his way back to Lexington to confer with SVR officials, advised the businessmen gathered to offer the railroad a $10,000 "cash bonus" to secure right-of-ways into town. In the course of the next few hours, residents pledged the entire amount and likely convinced local officials to grant the railroad an acre of land and tax exclusion. Moomaw delivered their offer, and although the railroad did not immediately make public its intentions, it moved its entire survey team to Big Lick in early April 1881.

Townspeople assumed their village was to be the terminus, but did not know for sure until Frederick Kimball made the decision official in May.[36] Not long afterwards, he and other Clark & Company executives arrived in town to investigate the site. The "Big Lick Brass Band" met the delegation at the depot, and at a rally later in the day, the railroad men gave a series of rousing speeches to hundreds of residents who turned out to learn more about their apparent good fortune.[37] Although the town's tobacco industries set it apart from rural Southwest Virginia, its prosperity could not have impressed the visiting Philadelphians. At the time, according to one resident, there were "wheat and corn fields and meadow lands and wood lands that came to the edge of town."[38]

Over the next few days, Big Lick's businessmen watched as Kimball and the railroad men surveyed sites for a hotel, depot, and machine shop complex in cow pastures and wheat fields east of town. After Kimball paid Henry Trout $20,000 for a portion of his farm about a half-mile to the northeast, word spread that the railroad had no plans to build anything in Big Lick. Residents, Trout recalled, were bewildered and had him ask Kimball "not to put the hotel and depot down there, as we were afraid it would draw trade off of Franklin Road."[39] The town's council concurred and offered a suitable lot or $500 if the company would at least put its depot near the existing N&W station in the center of town.[40]

Both pleas failed, and over the next year, this decision and others combined to permanently alter future patterns of growth. For while Big Lick's "cash bonus" and tax incentives had solidified the deal, like the selection of railroad towns elsewhere in the country, the Clark Company made its decision based on the hundreds of acres of inexpensive farmland surrounding the town. Indeed, the Philadelphians selected Big Lick because it *was* a small town; the firm had

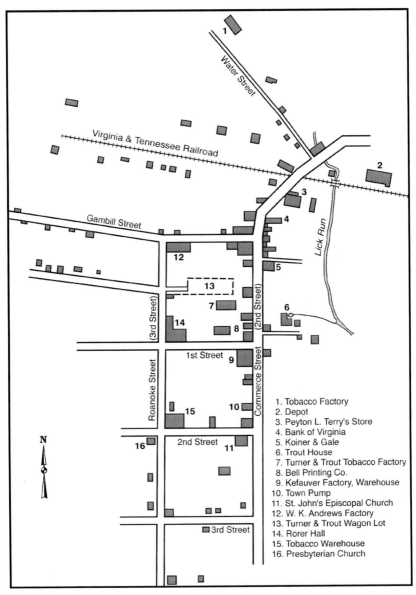

Town of Big Lick, c. 1880. Map by Clifford Duplechin Jr., Cartographic Section, Geography & Anthropology Department, LSU.

no plans to develop the place, but simply intended to use it as a temporary base of operations until its industries and company town went up nearby. Property left over, having increased phenomenally in value due to the new rail industries, could then be sold for ten to twenty times what the company paid for it.[41]

Shortly after the Clark & Company executives left, residents nevertheless voted to change Big Lick's name to "Kimball." "This has been done," John C. Moomaw informed their honoree, "to give evidence of the high esteem and appreciation you enjoy in the heart of these people on account of the improvements you are projecting in their midst . . . and to show that our people hold no unkind feelings toward the people of the North."[42] In his carefully worded response, Kimball declined the honor and informed townspeople that while he would "always remember this act of courtesy on their part," he preferred they change the town's name to "Roanoke," the appellation of the county and nearby river.[43] Residents, the *Big Lick Weekly News* observed, had expected Kimball to show just such "delicacy and good taste" in declining their original choice. Most believed Roanoke was "decidedly the prettier name for a town," and shortly thereafter voters approved it as the legal name for their home.[44]

The new town charter for "Roanoke" exempted capital invested in manufacturing enterprises from municipal taxation for the following ten years, limited property taxes to less than 1 percent of assessed value, and expanded the town's boundaries almost two and a half square miles, which absorbed the Town of Gainesborough along with land east of Big Lick recently purchased or optioned by the Clark firm. Although locals and outsiders alike began calling Big Lick "Roanoke" in the summer of 1881, it was not until February 1882 that the Virginia General Assembly approved the new charter and made that name official. "After the town is regularly laid off," the Big Lick correspondent of *The Salem Register* explained, "all enterprising men are invited to come and settle in our Embryo City of Roanoke."[45] Although little development occurred that summer, another newspaper was already predicting that "in two years this place will be as large as Lynchburg."[46]

■■■

While residents waited for the SVR construction teams to finish tracks into Roanoke, Enoch W. Clark & Company organized the additional corporations needed to transform the place into the base of operations for its railroads. In July 1881, the firm created "The Roanoke Land & Improvement Company" (RL&IC) as its real estate and development subsidiary, and a couple of months later, it organized the "Roanoke Machine Works" to manufacture and repair railroad cars and locomotives. The company appointed Peyton Terry, the merchant most responsible for brokering the junction deal, to the boards of directors of both new corporations, and it offered Henry Trout, the town's popular state delegate, the presidency of a newly organized local bank.[47] The RL&IC also paid Trout another $50,000 for the remainder of his farm, immediately making him one of Roanoke's wealthiest residents.[48]

When the Improvement Company laid out its property, it positioned workers' housing mainly to the northeast of Big Lick—adjoining the tract set aside for the Roanoke Machine Works—along new streets named for former Virginia Governors. "The town," a writer for the *Big Lick Weekly News* explained, "extends from Tinker creek on the east to Commerce street on the West, and from the village of Gainesborough on the north to Brook avenue . . . on the south."[49] In one of its first contracts for workers' cottages, the company called for the completion of three duplexes at $1,300 each and five "single homes" at $700 each by the end of 1881. Similar contracts followed, including one for twenty "single homes" at $1,100 each.[50] The company's town went up in former pastures or fields, and while this made the land relatively easy to develop, the stark landscape was so aesthetically displeasing that the company hired a landscape designer to plant close to one thousand shade trees. On the "bare hills" where the railroad's hotel was to go up, the designer put in "artistic landscape gardening" to provide the necessary "shading and ornamenting."[51]

Though there were abundant springs in Big Lick, residents relied on wells and cisterns for their water supply. Engineers for the RL&IC pushed immediately for a more modern system, and following their advice, the company purchased Elijah McClanahan's spring and mill at the base of "Mill Mountain." Assuming that Peyton Terry's six-hundred-and-fifty-acre farm southeast of the old AM&O depot would be good for "suburban residences," the company then spent $125,000 on that property, getting Terry's "Elmwood" estate and Mill Mountain—the peak above McClanahan Mill—as part of the deal.[52] Terry had paid only $800 for the entire tract five years earlier, and like the handful of other locals who sold what was once inexpensive farmland to the Improvement Company, he was suddenly rich beyond his wildest expectations.[53]

By the end of 1882, the RL&IC had purchased 1,152 acres in and around Roanoke. Reselling the land once it increased in value, the company's president J. B. Austin boasted, would bring "a handsome return for the capital invested in the enterprise." Realizing those profits, however, meant the firm would first have to transform "a tract of farming land into a busy city." That effort, Austin acknowledged, would be arduous "in a district remote from suitable supplies, destitute of skilled labor, and with an aggregated pressure of demand altogether unprecedented in this section of the country." Nevertheless, in 1882 alone, the RL&IC built one hundred and twenty-eight houses. It had planned sixty-two more but had been unable to find enough construction workers. The demand for dwellings, Austin told investors, "is constant, even in advance of the incoming mechanics soon to be employed by the Roanoke Machine Works."[54] Anticipating at least a few African Americans to be included in that total, the firm hired a local builder "to erect eight houses for colored people" at $350 apiece, specifying that the homes be constructed all "in one row."[55]

In what had been Peyton Terry's hilltop orchard—to the south of his former Elmwood estate—the Improvement Company started construction on a number of massive Queen Anne style homes for high-ranking railroad officials. These "villa residences," one paper argued, were proof that "our new residents have decided to stay, as they feel assured of the future prosperity of Roanoke."[56] Known before the project as "Orchard Hill" after a colony of executives moved in, locals renamed the spot "Officials' Hill."[57] The company also finished seventeen-thousand feet of streets, four-thousand feet of "plank side-walks," and, to eliminate "a possible cause of unhealthfulness," it straightened and deepened the channel of Lick Run that meandered through its land.[58]

The RL&IC finalized plans to construct a road up Mill Mountain, and after installing pumps and two miles of piping, the company began offering "its" side of town water from the spring at the base of that peak.[59] All in all, one reporter observed, the Improvement Company was responsible for "an astonishing metamorphosis." "The fields where husbandmen toiled and herds grazed," he explained, "are now broad-graded streets and rows of substantial pretty homes. Hills have been leveled and ravines filled in; bridges and substantial causeways [exist] where swamps and streams held sway."[60]

In the fall of 1882, workers completed the RL&IC's sixty-nine-room "Hotel Roanoke" on a hill overlooking the town. Philadelphia architect George Pearson designed the structure in Queen Anne style with thirty-four rooms, but before it was completed, company officials added a primitive-looking annex that doubled capacity.[61] The Queen Anne design that Pearson used was wildly popular in the late Victorian era, a period when elaborate ornamentation meshed with the gaudy ethos of the "Gilded Age." Paneled in heavily decorated wood with multiple gables and dozens of gigantic pressed-brick chimneys, the hotel featured hot and cold running water, glass doors opening onto verandas, interior paneling in oiled oak, ash, and cherry, a "large finely furnished bar room," a "Grand Dining Salon," and toilets that emptied into a nearby creek.[62]

The new "Union Depot" went up below the hotel, between the tracks of the SVR and N&W. Built in the same style, the station included a hundred-seat restaurant "finished in oiled woods and heated by hot air pipes" along with gender specific ticket offices and waiting rooms.[63] A "one thousand light gas machine" illuminated both new buildings and immediately made east Roanoke the most conspicuous part of town at night.[64]

Workers finished the railroad offices the following summer. Built of pressed brick but in the same Queen Anne design, the structure housed the bureaucracies of the SVR and N&W in forty-two rooms on its upper floors. The Improvement Company put its headquarters on the ground floor and

Hotel Roanoke in 1886, after other subsequent additions. Norfolk & Western Historical Photograph Collection (NS6024), Digital Library and Archives, University Libraries, Virginia Tech.

rented out other space there to various retail establishments.[65] East of the offices, contractors finished the massive Roanoke Machine Works. Pennsylvanian Samuel A. Crozier put his "Crozier Steel & Iron Company" next to the Works, and once in blast, his firm supplied the railroad shops with the ten tons of metal per day it needed to build locomotives and freight cars.[66]

Much as local businessmen had feared, the new industries and housing went up east of what had been Big Lick. The hotel, depot, and railroad offices were more than a half-mile away, and the machine shops, iron works, and company housing were a half-mile past that. Although a bottom area covered in woodlands and pastures initially separated what had been Big Lick from "New Town," the area developed by the RL&IC, a commercial and retail center eventually emerged between the settlements that linked them together. The Improvement Company owned most of the bottomland, and to facilitate growth there, it put in new roads, extended Railroad, Salem, and Campbell Avenues down from Big Lick, and channeled sections of the Long Lick bog running through the tract. Since most new businesses wanted spots convenient to residents in each section, they ignored the old business district on the portion of Franklin Road called Commerce Street and set up shop along the new roads in what was fast becoming downtown Roanoke.

Developing the town's new business district spurred additional growth, and by the time a writer for *The Bulletin of the Bureau of Immigration and Mining Intelligence* arrived in the fall of 1882, there were hundreds of jobs for masons, bricklayers, and house carpenters available along with numerous opportunities for enterprising businessmen. "While a number of mercantile houses have

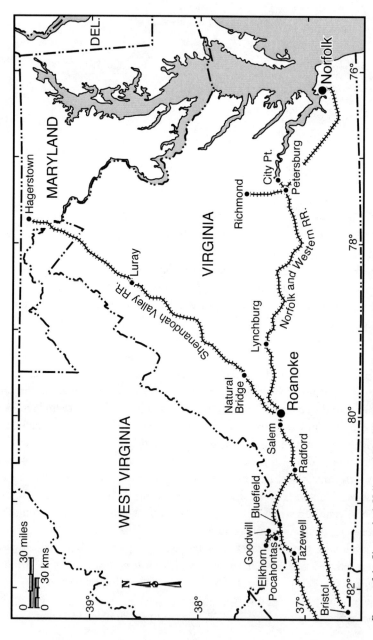

Routes of the Shenandoah Valley and Norfolk & Western Railroads in the 1880s. Map by
Clifford Duplechin Jr., Cartographic Section, Geography & Anthropology Department, LSU.

already been started," he reported, "there are still some branches of trade not represented and good openings awaiting skill, knowledge, and capital."[67] A commercial and retail boom followed; in 1882 alone, merchants increased from 15 to 83, lawyers from 0 to 9, hucksters from 1 to 32, and hotels and boarding houses from 2 to 57.[68] By the end 1883, grocery stores had risen from 1 to 23, 8 physicians had joined the 4 already practicing, residents had founded 4 more churches, and workers had completed 415 new homes along with 618 new buildings.[69]

Roanoke's emergence as an industrial center and boomtown attracted the notice of numerous journalists and writers. Many of them, especially New South boosters, were astonished by what they saw. "Had an old Virginian fallen asleep in 'Big Lick' last year to wake up to Roanoke today," *The Industrial South* exclaimed, "he would have been as much bewildered as Rip Van Winkle was when he awoke in the Kaatskills." Twelve hundred "engineers of all grades, and of all industries" had already arrived, the journal explained, and had turned Big Lick into a "bustling cosmopolitan town."[70] Roanoke, a *Richmond State* correspondent reported, "is 'booming' like a western city" and poised to become "the Atlanta of Virginia."[71] A reporter for the *Richmond Dispatch* was bewildered: "On every hand—on hillside and in dell, where last year the lowing herds found ample pasturage—now stand comfortable houses, broad streets, plank walks, and square after square of compact buildings, affording pleasant homes for upwards of three thousand persons who have collected here within less than a year."[72]

Northern writers were equally enthused. Roanoke's industries, a *New York Times* correspondent claimed, were in position to exploit the state's coal deposits and return Virginia "to something like its old position in the Union." The town, he reported, "has been built up by the Shenandoah Valley Road as a kind of Altoona or machine shop village . . . [and] has also attracted other manufacturers and mining companies until the town lots have risen in the last few years in the proportion of ten to one."[73]

In dispatches to the *Hartford Courant*, local-color writer Charles Dudley Warner described the place as rising from nowhere: "The noise of hammer and hauling filled the air; streets of temporary wooden shops and dwellings, drinking shops and 'hotels' with false board fronts hiding the upper half stories, and big letter signs, after the manner of the West, isolated dwellings on every hill and knoll, everywhere the debris of building and ditching and road-making."[74] On the train into town, another travel writer explained, "Roanoke blazes up ahead like an illumination; red-mouthed furnace-chimneys lift like giant torches above the plain; the roar of machinery, the whistle of engines, the ceaseless hum of labor and of life in the very heat of a quiet, mountain-locked valley."[75]

News of the growing opportunity brought hundreds of entrepreneurs hoping to turn a profit in the new boomtown. Two of the most influential arrivals were Fredericksburg mining engineer John H. Dunstan and Captain Samuel Seldon Brooke, the former editor of the Fredericksburg, Virginia, *Daily Star*. Together the men co-founded the Roanoke Steam Printing Company and began publishing *The Roanoke Leader*, a paper focused primarily on additional economic development, civic betterment, and social reform. Brooke, a Virginia Military Institute graduate, Civil War veteran, and University of Virginia-trained lawyer, put the paper's offices on Railroad Avenue in the new downtown district and published the first issue of the *Leader* in September 1882.[76]

Other commercial enterprises that started businesses downtown that month included: Teaford & Company Furniture, Woolford Hardware, Gravitt's Book & Music Store, and Willis Home Furnishing Goods, offering prices on glassware and furniture "as low as can be offered South of New York." Mining engineers and real estate firms put offices nearby, as did attorneys, insurance agents, druggists, and even a vocal and instrumental music instructor.[77]

E. H. Stewart & Co. Furniture was typical of the sixty-eight new merchants in town. In the spring of 1883, Erasmus Stewart found a spot for his business on Salem Avenue west of Jefferson Street, and by May, he and his wife Geraldine had relocated there from Culpeper County, Virginia. Geraldine was astonished. The town, she told kinfolk, "is beautifully located & the busiest place you ever saw. I couldn't tell you how many buildings are going up now; it is not more than two or three years old and has between four & five thousand inhabitants." She and her husband lodged over the store, she explained, but hoped to move "higher up in town" since their current quarters bordered the Long Lick bog and were "not considered healthy till this part of town in drained." In the distance, Geraldine reported, she could see "a very handsome & large Hotel on a high hill just out of town."[78] Erasmus began advertising the following month, letting locals know that he had an "$8,000 stock of furniture, carpets, oil cloths, mattings, curtains, wallpaper, chromos, oil paintings, [and] steel engravings," for sale "as low as any house in the state."[79] His was the only "first class" store of its kind in town, Geraldine reported, and it would, she predicted, "prove to be the very thing for him from present prospects; he hasn't opened a third of his stock & has sold a good many things."[80]

Perhaps not surprisingly, land speculation accompanied the rapid development. Ferdinand Rorer, owner of a huge tract of farmland in the northwest section of town, laid out streets on the property and began advertising "2,500 Town Lots For Sale!"[81] Peyton Terry also went into the real estate business; by early fall he had "Twelve newly built, nicely furnished, and well arranged

Shenandoah Valley Railroad General Office Building in 1886. Roanoke Land & Improvement Company Offices on first floor. Destroyed by fire 1896. Norfolk & Western Historical Photograph Collection (NS5791), Digital Library and Archives, University Libraries, Virginia Tech.

houses, with eight to ten rooms each" for sale along with fifty "choice building lots" on the newly completed Jefferson Street. "Several of our best citizens have already located there," he bragged, "and the neighborhood promises to be most agreeable."[82]

Outsiders invested as well. William Travers, general counsel for the SVR, joined three other railroad officials in contemplating a "scheme" to purchase seven acres in town from a dry goods merchant. "I was surprised," Travers recorded in his diary, "to find what rapid and intensive advances this place has made since I was here last July." The settlement, he went on, "has expanded over the hills surrounding the old portion of the town. New Houses have been erected and are occupied as soon as completed & often before. The estimate now is that there is a population of 3500 in the place." Although initially put off by the $17,000 asking price, the progress he saw convinced him to join the others in purchasing the tract.[83]

By early 1883, land companies had opened offices throughout town and local papers had added real estate supplements offering hundreds of properties to would-be investors.[84] The Reverend William C. Campbell, who had moved to Big Lick in the summer of 1881 to become pastor of its First Presbyterian Church, resented outsiders attempting to make a fast buck in town. Late in 1882, he recalled, was when "strangers began to flock in" and real estate values shot up: "From selling land by the acre they began to sell it by the lot and then by the front foot."[85] Practically nothing, however, was done to increase the value of most of the land. "Speculation in town lots," one resident observed, "was made without regard for present or prospective improvements; the sole object seeming to be that of buying property, and disposing promptly at an increased price."[86]

The promise of high wages, company housing, and opportunities for rapid advancement enticed scores of northern-born industrial workers to migrate to Roanoke in 1882, and by the end of 1883, over a thousand newcomers had found jobs in the town's burgeoning manufacturing enterprises. Crozier Furnace employed 125, the Machine Works hired 690, and the SVR signed on 262. Those employed were almost exclusively skilled laborers or clerical workers, and since the shops and railroad went out of their way to find family men, slightly over 45 percent of them were married.[87] Overall, at least 2,120 new residents arrived in Roanoke between 1881 and 1883. Almost all the newcomers were white and most were male. The town's 338 "new" black residents were mainly inhabitants of Gainesborough who had been absorbed into the new municipality, and although Big Lick had been nearly evenly divided by race, Roanoke was nearly 76 percent white.[88]

The largest group of black residents lived northwest of the tracks, in what had been Gainesborough but was now a section of Roanoke known as "Bunker Hill." Most blacks living south of the tracks had homes along one of the town's older roads west of Commerce Street, and only approximately 8 percent lived in housing developed by the RL&IC. Nearly 41 percent of whites, by contrast, lived in homes built by that firm. The largest concentrations of shop workers had houses on Gilmer or Patton Avenues in the Northeast, or in the southeast on lower Railroad Avenue, in a cheap row-style housing project

Sketch of Roanoke Machine Works and worker housing in northeast Roanoke. Roanoke Railway and Electric Company Photo Album, Norfolk & Western Historical Photograph Collection (RRE0038), Digital Library and Archives, University Libraries, Virginia Tech.

called "Brick Row." The rest of the town's white residents lived along older streets or on extensions of Salem and Campbell Avenues. Along with Commerce Street, these roads also tended to be home to those working in service- or retail-related businesses.

Occupational shifts from 1880 to 1883 due to the changing economic focus of the town benefited its black residents the least. Indeed, the closure of local tobacco factories to make space for the railroad's offices eliminated semi-skilled employment for 30 percent of African American females and 60 percent of African American males. Consequently, by 1883, almost all employed black women worked as domestic servants and close to 90 percent of employed black males worked as unskilled manual laborers. White men, by contrast, benefited the most from new industries, with employment for them in skilled labor more than doubling. Whites also maintained dominance of retail and commercial establishments.[89]

Those moving to Roanoke from rural areas encountered numerous difficulties adjusting to life in an urban setting. Like most urban areas in the South, the city attracted large numbers of impoverished migrants from the countryside who clung to rural customs.[90] Newly arrived farmers, for example, saw nothing wrong with letting livestock roam freely or with disposing of waste by simply throwing it outside. The local government attempted early on to end these and other practices, but as residents poured in, it found itself fighting a losing battle to turn Roanoke into something resembling a modern city. The town had no sewers, and although most residents used box privies, some newcomers dumped their waste into streams or yards.

In the spring of 1882, after receiving numerous complaints, the council passed a law requiring all residents to use box privies. The ordinance stipulated that the boxes be emptied beyond town limits at least twice a month but provided no municipal resources for this unpleasant chore.[91] In the fall, it also prohibited "owners of hogs from allowing them to run at large" and ordered all residents to place waste in barrels monitored by the town scavenger, imposing a fine of $5 to $10 on anyone caught dumping "soap-suds, slops, paper, straw, melon or rinds, or refuse matter in any form" on any land within town limits.[92]

In the months that followed, however, *The Roanoke Leader* reported that most rural newcomers continued to do as they pleased. Many had strung up barbed wire fences around their homes to keep livestock out and most, the paper complained, "are accustomed to throw the accumulations of both chamber and kitchen into their yards, while others dig holes in their yards and there deposit filth that causes stench that is offensive to the olfactories of the neighborhood and inimical to health." The paper's editor, S. S. Brooke, lectured the newcomers about the inappropriateness of barbed wire fences and encouraged the council to levy stiff penalties to "force them to have regard for the health of their neighbors, if they have none for their own."[93]

In the eastern section of the city, the Roanoke Land & Improvement Company used paternalism to push its residents to improve their section of town, offering monetary premiums to tenants with the "neatest & best laid out garden," largest and best blooms, and healthiest fruit or ornamental trees, shrubs, and vines.[94] The company also stepped in to supply amenities or services that Roanoke's under-funded municipal government was unable to provide. On a hill to the southeast of the Machine Works, for example, it laid out "Wood-land Park" as a recreation space for workers and their families. Clarence Clark, a member of RL&IC's board of directors, then donated "a very unique and novel school house" for shop workers' children.[95] Since many of those living in the company's cottages were Catholic, the firm provided an SVR passenger

Roanoke Machine Works employees, early 1890s. Norfolk & Western Historical Photograph Collection (NW3556), Digital Library and Archives, University Libraries, Virginia Tech.

car as a space for the town's first Mass and later donated a commanding hill behind the Hotel Roanoke for construction of a church. The Machine Works contributed a bell forged in its foundry to the project, and after construction ended, local Catholics christened their new brick chapel "Saint Andrew's."[96]

At least some RL&IC residents, nevertheless, resented the firm's monopoly on workers' housing and believed their rents—between $15 and $22 per month—were excessive. In early 1883, for instance, a Machine Works employee published a letter in the *Roanoke Saturday Review* accusing the company of extortion for charging his family rent that in five years would cover the cost of constructing their home.[97] In a sympathetic editorial that followed, the *Review* claimed that few men who earned a living by "daily toil" in the shops could afford the "exorbitant rents" of the RL&IC. The firm cared nothing about its white tenants, the paper complained, and had further alienated townspeople by building "Red Row," a cheap, frame, African American housing complex that was "one of the filthiest holes we ever saw." "This harlots' den," the *Review* observed, "is one of the blessings bestowed upon Roanoke by the Land and Improvement company."[98]

Throughout town, the number of establishments legally dispensing alcohol grew at a phenomenal pace, rising from two in 1881 to twenty the following year. Over the same period, sales of distilled spirits rose by 731 percent.[99] Perhaps not surprisingly in a town populated primarily by single working-class males, saloons outnumbered any other business in Roanoke's downtown district.[100] Most found lots on Railroad Avenue, the dirt road that paralleled the tracks of the N&W and SVR. The Morning Star Saloon, featuring "all kinds of mixed drinks prepared by skillful bartenders," started operations there in the fall of 1882, and the following spring, the "Great Liquor Establishment of David Lawson" began dispensing drinks a little farther up the street. Lawson's place claimed to have "the largest stock of Bottled Liquors of any house south of Baltimore" along with an attached saloon that "is justly regarded as the Fashionable Resort for gentlemen who take their 'Smiles' in Roanoke."[101] At night, a correspondent from the *Baltimore Sun* reported, "with the red-light beacons of the bar rooms all ablaze over the plank sidewalks, and the music of the violin and banjo coming through the open doors and windows, the town suggests a mining camp or a mushroom city of Colorado."[102]

Perhaps predictably, as single men arriving in town began congregating in its saloons, townspeople began to witness frequent episodes of alcohol-induced rowdiness. No night was now safe, one paper warned, noting that on a Monday evening three SVR employees, "fired with enthusiasm, bad whiskey, and contempt of law, turned themselves loose on Railroad avenue." The men kicked over a stove in the Relay House, tossed rocks through the windows of "Barry's bar room," burst into Gravatt's Bookstore and "used the most vulgar profanity and threatened to kick the window in," before assaulting several customers in Kimball House. Captured by police and thrown in jail, the trio "made the night hideous with yells and oaths" before two of the men escaped, releasing three black prisoners on their way out. The third "brawler," William McCaym—"too drunk to escape"—was arraigned before the Mayor in the morning and fined $10.[103]

Elsewhere in town, natives complained so loudly about "disorderly crowds" congregating at Union Depot that officials eventually assigned a special policeman to patrol the station.[104] On Railroad Avenue nearby, gunfights and "careless and dangerous shooting" from saloon patrons brought a torrent of calls for more police.[105] The entire area, according to one paper, was so "greatly infested" with "marauders" and "midnight prowlers" that law-abiding residents refused to venture there after dark unarmed.[106] In addition to the dozen or so taverns, bowling alleys, and billiard parlors aligning the road, Railroad Avenue was also home to several illicit "gambling dens" and was the favored location for the town's prostitutes.

To some natives, the rise in saloons and increasing lawlessness seemed a sure sign that their home had changed for the worse. Many, like William Campbell, pastor of the local Presbyterian Church, sensed a sea change in the morals of the community. In a letter to his wife, he bemoaned the turnout at a funeral he had just officiated. "It was the child of Hess the saloon keeper," he explained, "only 6 weeks old and died of whooping cough. It was a dismal funeral. Only 5 or 6 were present. No lady except for the mother and daughter." Clearly shaken by the experience, Campbell complained that "Roanoke is a hard place—one may die here and but few people know or care anything about it." This was all very different from the neighborliness he had witnessed in Big Lick, and in Campbell's mind, a stunning rise in immorality was to blame. Having accompanied the grieving Hesses to their quarters above the family business, the Reverend got a first-hand look at the problem: "The saloon Hess keeps is a horribly vile place. No wonder they are so dismal and forlorn."[107]

While some natives like Campbell bemoaned the rise of saloons, others worried about Roanoke's growing reputation for being uniquely unhealthy. Most of the town existed amidst bogs, cesspools, and polluted streams, and as a consequence, there were widespread rumors that the town was rife with typhoid, scarlet fever, smallpox, and a fictitious malady known as "Big Lick Fever."[108] Gossip about real ailments was worse. In early 1883, for example, newspapers throughout the state reported erroneously that smallpox was devastating Roanoke. Hoping to put an end to the story, the town issued a press notice for "parties who are unacquainted with the facts" which certified there had been no smallpox in Roanoke.[109] A few months later, exaggerated reports of sickness again made the rounds. This time it was scarlet fever. Although there were a couple "imported" cases, according to *The Leader,* "Every paper in the state has it that a malignant form of that disease prevails here."[110]

In the spring of 1883, after an enclave of black residents contracted smallpox and towns nearby banned Roanokers, residents had to deal with yet another wave of negative publicity.[111] William Campbell sent his wife and infant son to her parents' home in Harper's Ferry, West Virginia, to escape the contagion. Back in Roanoke, he reported, doctors had quarantined the infected but found other cases among blacks in Gainesborough.[112] "The negroes," Campbell reported, "are very much excited and do not want to go to the hospital. It seems that all who go there die."[113] The *Richmond State* listed upward of thirty cases of smallpox in Roanoke, and according to *The Leader*, there were "similar paragraphs in nearly every paper in the State." "Our contemporaries," S. S. Brooke complained, "exhibit a wonderful faculty for hearing anything that can injure Roanoke." Brooke's paper dismissed reports running elsewhere, informing a statewide audience that the few cases of smallpox in town "were colored." No whites had been sick, so there was no reason to be alarmed.[114] Hoping to quell additional cases, local authorities torched the "shacks" of those infected.[115]

Many natives blamed the periodic outbreak of smallpox on newly arrived blacks and worried about the increasing number of African Americans in their midst. Other locals, however, were gravely concerned about the takeover of much of their home by the railroad and the influx of newcomers from the North. Longtime resident Rush U. Derr, owner and editor of the *Roanoke Saturday News*—known previously as the *Big Lick Weekly News*—fostered localism by publishing inflammatory rumors and attacking natives he considered pawns of the Clark Company. In the spring of 1882, for example, his paper reported that "Upon unquestionable authority we are informed that employees of the Shenandoah Valley railway openly boast that the officials of that company and of the Roanoke Land and Improvement company are abiding their time and holding their views in abeyance, as it were, 'waiting until the works get in full operation and the Yankee boys will run the town.'" This scheme, Derr warned, was a matter of tremendous concern to "those who were born on this soil and whose inherent right would thus be wrested from them." Indeed, he predicted that "whoever comes here with the secret or avowed purpose of 'running the town' will find this an almost tropically warm climate and very unpleasant place to live."[116]

Roanoke's native businessmen were alarmed by what they read. Using "birth right" as the sole criterion for political power, one shop owner observed, would put "one or two white men and two or three Negroes" in charge of the town. The majority of natives, he insisted, welcomed "law-abiding" newcomers and would do all they could to guarantee them equal political rights.[117] Peyton Terry, editor and owner of the newly founded *Roanoke Commercial Advertiser* and the native who benefited the most from RL&IC real estate speculation, condemned Derr's story as "ill judged, intemperate, and uncalled for." Thus far, Terry testified, Roanoke's "Northern friends" had "spent much money, started large enterprises, built many homes, . . . in fact, have started our village on the high road towards being a large and important town."[118]

Stories in northern newspapers reprinted locally, however, added weight to Derr's accusations by intimating that Roanoke was a company town, created and owned by Yankee entrepreneurs. Enoch W. Clark & Company, the *Philadelphia Press* reported, had transformed a "rustic and rusty huddle of houses" in the wilderness of Southwest Virginia into a "suburb of Philadelphia" and "quickened energies and stimulated enterprises which would have lain dormant until the crack of doom."[119] The *Philadelphia Ledger* likewise ridiculed natives who "never dreamed of any enterprise beyond doing what their fathers did," giving sole credit for the "creation" of Roanoke to E. W. Clark & Company.[120] A correspondent for the *Baltimore Sun* went further, suggesting "Roanoke may be considered the property of the Roanoke Land and Improvement Company, from the overshadowing influence of that concern and its leadership in local enterprises, though the railroad company studiously preserves its control in this and all auxiliary concerns."[121]

The emerging sectionalism also bled into municipal concerns when the RL&IC—using the same mixture of paternalism and benevolence that marked improvement campaigns in its development—hired New York City "sanitary engineer" Randolph Herring to produce a comprehensive drainage and sewer plan. At the time, one resident recalled, navigating the town's streets after a storm was "like walking in a ploughed field after a heavy rain."[122] Even worse, residents continued to dump household waste in creeks flowing through downtown. After surveying these problems, Herring met with Roanoke's mayor and town council to explain the absolute necessity of his plan.[123] The RL&IC immediately implemented Herring's recommendations on its property, spending close to $3,000 on terra cotta piping, draining and filling three acres of marsh, and clearing a channel for Lick Run, but the municipal government claimed it was unable to afford such improvements.[124] Instead, it spent the little revenue it collected on far more basic and inexpensive enhancements. Unable to afford gas lighting or proper drainage, it approved funding for additional lampposts and kerosene lanterns along with plank sidewalks and stone curbing.[125] Crossing the street, however, remained an arduous experience and residents continued to use stepping stones to avoid losing shoes in the mud.

Although technically there were few funds in the town's treasury to spend on Herring's plan, the council's reluctance to initiate additional bond issues to cover the modest expense required suggests its hesitancy to invest in permanent improvements at a time when Roanoke's future was still somewhat uncertain. The town's mayor, Lucian H. Cocke, a lawyer and son of the founder of nearby Hollins Institute, and five of its six councilmen were longtime residents of Big Lick as well as members of its most well-established families. Indeed, with the exception of an assistant engineer for the SVR elected to council in the summer of 1882, the town's government was firmly in the hands of a conservative "old guard."[126]

A few months prior to Herring's arrival, the town's property owners—the only residents eligible to vote on funding initiatives—had approved some bond monies to better support the municipality, but the funds would not be available until July 1883 and only a small portion had been allocated for infrastructure needs.[127] In the meantime, financial support came solely from residential and commercial property taxes of fifty cents per hundred dollars of assessed value.[128] The failure to push for more money bewildered the Improvement Company's chief engineer, and when councilmembers refused to budge on the issue, he resigned his voluntary position as "Town Engineer."[129]

Roanoke's rapid growth and primitive conditions astounded visiting reporters. "The town," the *Philadelphia Ledger* explained, "with its wooden side-walks stretching over farm land and mass of incomplete homes, with hammer, trowel and saw hastily at work, rivals any mining settlement of mushroom growth the far West can show."[130] A reporter for the Pennsylvania-based *American Volunteer* found the place "a true type western town, grown up almost in a night, you might say." Roanoke's downtown, with its dozens of "irregularly built" businesses, he reported, was haphazardly constructed and had "a good-sized stream of water" running across its streets. What was more appalling, he noticed, was that the town had taxes enough to support only one school while its "saloons, which exist at every step, are well patronized."[131] Even an anonymous "Old Virginian" depicted Roanoke as "a queer place" that "might be likened to a great gypsy camp, with roughly constructed homes for tents." If this was progress, he went on, then the Old Dominion was in trouble: "The people looked like they had just got there and did not know whether to stay or not. The ungraded and treeless streets looked like a settlement of sappers and miners upset by an earthquake."[132]

The ridicule from outsiders coupled with the local government's refusal to implement Herring's plan infuriated S. S. Brooke, editor of *The Roanoke Leader*. The town's native-born leaders, he carped, were "a few narrow minds, wedded to old ways of doing things" who had ignored "the practical results of scientific investigation" because of "local prejudices and jealousies" against the RL&IC. The Improvement Company, he went on, had not only donated Herring's services but had implemented his suggestions on its property at no cost to townspeople. Its reward, Brooke pointed out, was a "perverse and narrow policy" that left "that stinking sewer" Lick Run flowing through downtown and then into RL&IC property.[133] Native editor Rush Derr, by contrast, praised the town's council for following the "voice of the people" over "interested parties." "Mr. Herring's report," Derr observed, "has not been acted upon simply because Mr. Herring was employed by and working in the interests of the Land and Improvement Company, and the council is not."[134]

Derr's efforts "to draw lines and make distinctions," Brooke retorted, were "worse than useless" since the interests of the town and the company were "identical and invisible." The debate, Brooke reported, had deepened the "sectional feeling and animosity in our city." Indeed, according to him, "There seems to be sentiment, which is somewhat encouraged, that the interests of the western part of the city are not identical with those in the eastern section."

The sentiment, he warned, had done much to alienate newcomers, almost all of whom "have become citizens and tax-payers, and who, as such, have a right to expect recognition from municipal authorities."[135]

The RL&IC did little to assuage the "sectional feeling" and even fueled further indignation by repeatedly referring to east Roanoke as "our town."[136] Justifiably or not, some natives held the company responsible for the abysmal conditions in the western part of Roanoke, or at the very least were jealous of the improvements they saw going on in the east. Indeed, in the midst of the debate over the Herring plan, *The Leader* reported that a gang of local "miscreants" had used the cover of night to pull up or break dozens of ornamental trees recently planted by the RL&IC.[137] Other residents circulated rumors that the Improvement Company owned Brooke's newspaper, and while not going quite that far, Derr's *Roanoke Saturday Review* accused him of being a major RL&IC stockholder. Brooke dismissed the accusations and pleaded again for unity in the effort to solve Roanoke's drainage problems so "that we may enter another summer proof against malarial or atmospheric detriment to public health."[138] Derr, nevertheless, continued to belittle Brooke as well as assail Herring and his fellow "prophylactic professors" as con artists "suffering from diarrhea of words and constipation of ideas."[139]

In early 1883, after the Improvement Company moved to secure a charter on the entire town's water supply, another sectional debate erupted when natives, weary of granting outsiders such a monopoly, demanded that the council fund a municipal reservoir instead. When the scheduled vote on the two options arrived, Henry Trout—a councilman and RL&IC executive—had the decision postponed so that representatives of the company could do some additional lobbying. The approval of such a delay, Rush Derr argued, was proof that local politicians were "obeying the beck and call of the Improvement company" as well as a sure sign that the firm was already "running the town."[140] After the council met again in a secret session and granted the firm a water franchise, Derr suggested that it had been done "in order to hurry the Land company's scheme through before the people found out what it was." The monopoly, he reasoned, was not only "shameful" and "disgraceful" but set residents up for extortion by "grasping corporations."[141]

Derr's continuing critiques infuriated Trout and Peyton Terry, the railroad's most influential native allies. Trout, incensed by Derr's allegations, stormed into Derr's office and threatened "a system of persecution" against the paper by the Improvement Company. Terry, a member of the RL&IC's board of directors, promptly withdrew his investment in the *Review* and cancelled his numerous advertising contracts. Derr nonetheless refused to back down, branded both men traitors, and vowed to continue "fighting for the people's rights." "Some rich people," he warned readers, "seem to think that their wealth should protect them from hearing unpleasant truths, but it will not with us."[142] Such talk was nonsense, according to S. S. Brooke, who accused the *Review* of clinging to "old Virginia fogyism" and misrepresenting local opinion. Letters to Brooke's paper backed the council as well: the truth, one local merchant complained, was that "We all owe our new found success to these new comers, and we do from our hearts, welcome them among us."[143] However, like Brooke and his supporters, newcomers tended to blame native leaders for the wretched conditions in some parts of town. One transplanted Yankee, fed up with inaction, savaged local officials for streets "ankle deep in mud" and suggested sending them to "some go ahead place for a week or two to see how other Councils run towns and cities."[144]

By the spring of 1883, when the effects of another national depression began to touch Roanoke, the town's growing atmosphere of dissension and abysmal environment had already generated a feeling of unease among many inhabitants. To numerous observers, the place had failed to measure up to the wild expectations heaped upon it, and the nationwide financial panic seemed a sure sign that the boom had gone bust. As a result, widespread gossip erupted about the looming collapse of land values, the railroad relocating, or the Improvement Company and Machine Works going bankrupt. "The air is rife with rumors of impending destruction," S. S. Brooke warned, "and every occurrence, connected even with the progress of events here, is distorted, magnified and greedily sent out." The town was doing well, he argued, so "the cranks had as well cease their croaking."[145]

Nevertheless, reporters' repeated focus on the similarities between Roanoke and "mushroom cities" of the West were far from an exaggeration. Most "instant cities" in Colorado or California lacked the small base of natives that were present in Roanoke but experienced the same period of intensive demographic growth coupled with haphazard structural development. Moreover, they also had the same abundance of cheaply built frame vernacular structures, similar wooden sidewalks aligning mud or dirt streets, lack of systematic sanitation, and numerous businesses using false fronts to camouflage their meager size or crude construction. Since a gold or silver vein could dry up at any moment, their residents, like Roanoke's inhabitants, were less likely to gamble on expensive brick buildings. They were also not overly concerned about municipal services because their long-term residency was questionable. In this "camp phase" of development, land companies, saloons, gambling houses and brothels usually outnumbered dry-goods stores, churches, restaurants, or schools, and most inhabitants adopted a get-rich-quick mentality along with a somewhat disorderly "frontier ethos."[146]

The continuing comparisons between Roanoke and "company towns" were also unsettling to many residents. The town, of course, was not entirely developed, owned, or managed by the Clark firm—natives held onto most of the western section of the city, and the municipality had an independent government as well as numerous businesses not connected to the company. Nonetheless, the resemblance to a company town was striking. The RL&IC controlled almost all of eastern Roanoke, where most workers lived in company-owned cottages, and its paternalism was responsible for various civic improvements in that neighborhood. It owned the city's only potential water supply, developed nearly all of the property that was emerging as the central downtown district, and dominated holdings in local property and housing. The Roanoke Machine Works, the SVR, and the N&W were by far the municipality's largest employers, and the Clark firm was also a silent partner in several other local enterprises. Moreover, Clark & Company architecture—the Hotel Roanoke, the SVR Offices, the Union Depot, the massive shops, yards, and roundhouses—entirely dominated the local landscape. None of this, however, made Roanoke a company town. Instead, the city most closely resembled what one scholar has categorized as a "corporate town"—places where multiple enterprises and an independent government exist in a municipality originally planned and managed by a single industry. Roanoke, by this standard, had more in common with Manchester, New Hampshire, and Lowell, Lawrence, and Holyoke, Massachusetts, than with other Virginia cities.[147]

Roanoke Land & Improvement Company's 1883 "Brick Row" housing complex on east Railroad Avenue. Long abandoned by the time the photograph was taken in 1907. From John Nolen, *Remodeling Roanoke: Report to the Committee on Civic Improvement* (Roanoke: Stone Printing & Mfg. Co., 1907).

None of those northern metropolises, however, experienced anything close to the sort of intensive demographic shifts that occurred in Roanoke. Indeed, its population increased at least 416 percent from 1880 to 1883, another 579 percent from 1883 to 1890, and an additional 143 percent from 1890 to 1892.[148] The average rate of growth per year of roughly 290 percent far exceeds the contemporary 15 percent standard of increase used to define boomtowns. According to urban scholars, cities with rates in excess of 15 percent often suffer from "boomtown syndrome," a municipal malady characterized by the sort of severe institutional malfunctioning common in early Roanoke: municipal income shortfalls, strains on existing infrastructure, lack of adequate public services, sanitation problems, housing shortages, unattractive cityscape, excessive barren spaces, breakdown of informal social controls (caused by an influx of "strangers"), and increased incidents of alcoholism, rowdiness, crime, and vice. Moreover, Roanoke's longtime residents also reacted to the "boom" along the three distinct phases described in modern boomtown analyses: they were initially enthusiastic about the expected economic bonanza, they quickly became uncertain about the public services required of a city, and they were bewildered by revenue shortfalls.[149]

One of the main consequences of the syndrome in modern boomtowns is the occurrence of a variety of value conflicts between natives and newcomers. In Roanoke, much of the same discord emerged. Most obviously, locals' initial enthusiasm for the railroad turned to resentment when its workers, who paid few taxes on their rental homes, insisted that municipal funds be invested in what to natives seemed like "extravagant" improvements when the long-term status of the town was in doubt. Many locals were also suspicious of the RL&IC monopoly on the local water supply, and questioned the independence of their elected representatives. Most newcomers, by contrast, had relocated from established urban areas and found the primitive conditions, lack of public services, and parochial atmosphere they encountered in Roanoke perplexing. Many of them, however, perceived the place as only a temporary home, and as a result, they developed little identification with it or its inhabitants.[150] "Instant cities," one urban historian has suggested, did not always turn out "instant citizens." It was only those that did that emerged as metropolises; the others became ghost towns.[151]

■■■

By the end of 1883, Roanoke was a far different place than it had been just three years earlier. Newcomers outnumbered Big Lick natives by nearly three to one, industrial labor had supplanted tobacco manufacturing as the main source of employment, commercial and retail development had shifted east, and a paternalistic corporation managed part of the town. Local blacks, a slim majority in 1880, had become a distinct minority relegated to the margins of unskilled manual labor. The small cadre of local businessmen who lured the railroad to Big Lick made substantial profits when the company purchased their property, and they benefited the most from swift increases in demand for their products or services. Moreover, the railroad rewarded them with bank presidencies and appointments to its industries' boards of directors. In the process, it cultivated a strong and lasting alliance with the group that could most successfully mediate the periodic outbreaks of sectionalism between old Big Lick and New Town. In the years that followed, Roanoke continued to grapple with revenue short-falls and infrastructure problems, and residents continued to struggle to forge a community out of its diverse and divided population.

Chapter 2

Forging the Magic City

Roanoke's "boomtown" beginnings left a legacy of difficulties for the town and its citizens that ranged from severe infrastructure shortfalls and lack of municipal services, to sectionalism between natives and newcomers, to a rise in vice, hooliganism and crime. Having decided on the permanence of their city, residents in the 1880s turned to remedying these and other problems. In the process, they began fashioning a community out of the town's fractured population. First, however, they had to resolve deepening suspicions between residents of old Big Lick and New Town, which grew even worse when the city's African Americans teamed up with northern-born Republicans to threaten the longtime hegemony of local Democrats. One way whites found common ground was on the municipal level, where political discourse between them tended to coalesce around funding infrastructure improvements. The city's black inhabitants, in contrast, opposed improvement allocations because they rarely saw any municipal money spent on their neighborhoods. The issue eventually divided white and black Republicans, who, while agreeing on state and national politics, found themselves at odds over municipal spending for modernization.

The public crusade to turn Roanoke into something that more resembled a modern industrial city moved on other fronts as well. Local business boosters, politicians, and Evangelicals, aware that the town had a growing reputation as crime-ridden and debauched, eventually sought ways to curb behavior that they and other whites deemed immoral, which led to a crusade against African American "dives" in the city's saloon district. This process brought whites together in another common cause, but led to deeper fragmentation of the community along racial lines. Elsewhere in town, numerous brothels opened for business in working-class neighborhoods. Although popular with young men working in the industries nearby, families living in the area joined clergy in a campaign to drive the bordellos out of the area. When brothels continued to open in these neighborhoods, city officials respond by limiting prostitution in Roanoke to a de facto red light district in the African American section of town.

Residents who tired of complaining to elected officials about the city's lack of municipal services resorted to developing some themselves. Some organized militias to augment the town's chronically under-funded and tiny police force, others formed fire brigades to protect their homes from conflagration, and still others raised funds for a public hospital to provide healthcare for citizens in need. These various improvement crusades not only fulfilled longstanding municipal needs, they also functioned in ways that helped the white community coalesce around more common causes. Unfortunately, the more common ground that whites in town found, the more they pushed Roanoke's blacks to the margins of the community.

■■■

Along with northern-born Republicans, blacks from the countryside and poor whites from the mountains of Southwest Virginia poured into Roanoke in the 1880s. The later two groups also backed the GOP after the Civil War—as did most residents of Appalachian Virginia—and combined, the three factions of Republicans challenged Roanoke natives' longstanding support for "Conservatives" and "Bourbon" Democrats, turning the town into hotly contested political terrain.

Since Virginia's Republican Party had all but collapsed by the early 1880s, the factions did so mainly by backing what took its place—former Confederate General William Mahone's "Readjuster Party," which promised to downwardly "adjust" the state's massive Reconstruction debt, cut taxes, eliminate poll taxes, fund public schools, abolish the whipping post, and increase corporate taxes. Indeed, soon after winning the rail junction, native Democrats faced a coalition of black and poor white Readjusters and northern-born Republicans that swayed the town's vote in favor of sending Readjuster John S. Wise to Congress. Only a year earlier, when Big Lick's sole newspaper branded the newly created Readjuster Party an "unholy fusion between the worst and most unstable elements," such an outcome would have been almost unthinkable. The results stunned Democrats and generated even more resentment toward newcomers in town. Since local "Conservatives" assumed mountain whites could be peeled away from the Readjusters over race issues, they focused their wrath mainly on northern-born newcomers and blacks.[1]

In statewide elections a year after the Readjusters' victory, Roanoke's Democratic Party rebounded by calling for white unity in the aftermath of what became known as the "Danville Race Riot." In nearby Danville, black Readjusters and white Republicans had gained control of local government but afterwards faced relentless attacks from Democrats, who issued a widely circulated broadside accusing the "mongrelized" city council of humiliating whites by inspiring contemptuous public behavior among African Americans, thus threatening Anglo-Saxon superiority. Just days before the 1883 election, Democrats in Danville instigated a race riot and used the occasion to overthrow the municipal government. In the aftermath, Readjusters lost support among poor and working-class whites, and the party suffered catastrophic defeat everywhere in the state. Roanoke's firmly Democratic press gave the racist Danville broadside front-page coverage and played up the resulting riot as a precursor to an all-out race war. Whites in town abandoned the Readjusters in droves, and as a result, the party garnered votes almost exclusively from black residents, pulling in only about 38 percent of ballots cast.[2]

The overwhelming majority of newspapers published in Roanoke were stridently Democratic. The *Roanoke Saturday Review* and *The Roanoke Leader* were two of the first, and when they folded, the *Roanoke Daily Times*, *The* (Roanoke) *Evening Telegram*, *The* (Roanoke) *Evening World*, and *Cosmocrat* carried on in their stead. The town's first GOP newspaper emerged in the latter months of James G. Blaine's 1884 Presidential campaign, when northern-born Republicans in the Third Ward began publishing *The Roanoke Telegram*. The Third Ward voted a straight Republican ticket in that contest, but Wards One and Two in the older sections of town swayed the city to Grover Cleveland. African American voters turned out in force for Blaine and the GOP as well. Indeed, according to one black schoolteacher, African American residents welcomed the increased political competition among whites because they believed the Republican Party "was the voice of God" and that Democrats stood for "Human slavery, oppression, ignorance."[3] In the aftermath of Blaine's defeat, the *Telegram* folded and the *Roanoke Weekly Sun* took its place as the town's sole Republican newspaper until 1891, when African American businessman John H. Davis began publishing the Roanoke *Press*, a black GOP paper.[4]

In 1885, local Democrats, "never in better trim," gathered at the Planter's Warehouse downtown to endorse former Confederate cavalry officer Fitzhugh Lee—the grandson of "Light Horse Harry" and nephew of Robert E. Lee—as their party's candidate for governor.[5] The state's Republican Party, which absorbed the Readjuster Party after the 1883 elections, picked former Readjuster Congressman John S. Wise to be his opponent. Democrats elected S. S. Brooke, editor of *The Roanoke Leader*, secretary of the local party. Not long afterwards, Brooke began filling the pages of his newspaper with lengthy diatribes against Wise. His coalition party, Brooke railed, was in fact no party at all but rather "the spawn of political prostitution" whose only hope was to attract "insatiate spoils seekers, ballot box stuffers, political renegades and shameless demagogues."[6] Nevertheless, when Wise came to town in September, a racially mixed crowd of over five hundred turned out to hear him speak.[7]

Democrats staged a massive rally for Fitz Lee the next month, sending a column of two hundred and fifty men on horseback to escort him and Jubal Early on a parade down Salem Avenue. Lee spoke at the baseball grounds that night under fireworks and in front of scores of fanatical followers.[8] Local Democrats predicted another landslide victory, but on Election Day, Lee and his party polled only about 10 percent better than Wise and the Republicans. The Third Ward voted a straight Republican ticket and the heavily black Second Ward cast over 46 percent of its ballots for Wise. It is entirely possible that the GOP would have done even better if poll workers affiliated with the Democrats had not turned away scores of African Americans who attempted to cast votes. In the aftermath of the Readjusters' 1883 defeat, the Virginia Democrat Party seized control of the election apparatus, and in most elections that followed, there were widespread charges of fraud.[9]

Unlike most other white Virginians, Roanokers of all political affiliations tended to support the Republican-initiated federal tariff on imports because it protected local industries. The Norfolk & Western Railroad backed the tariff as well, but on the state level provided financial support for Democrats, who opposed regulating railroads and were soft on corporate taxes. Attempts by President Cleveland to reduce the tariff gave the GOP and its candidate for governor—former U.S. Senator William Mahone, head of the state's Republican Party—a hot issue for the 1889 race. Philip McKinney, the Democratic nominee, countered Mahone by focusing on threats to Anglo-Saxon control of the Old Dominion by "mongrelized" Republicans.[10] Moreover, Mahone had by then alienated many party operatives with his dictator-like control of the organization.

David F. Houston, head of Roanoke's Crozier Iron Works and chairman of the Virginia Republican Executive Committee, had been elected to the state senate in 1887, but soon after, he joined John S. Wise in bolting the "Boss Mahone" machine to form a splinter faction of the Republican Party.[11] Local party worker William A. Pattie, who lost appointment as Roanoke's postmaster in an ugly GOP patronage battle, also turned against the "old despot," and like most anti-Mahone Republicans, he chose to "go a 'fishin'" on election day rather than vote against the Democrats.[12] Mahone lost in a landslide statewide and by 20 percent locally in one of the Virginia's most vicious and controversial elections. The city's "white people," the *Roanoke Daily Times* boasted afterwards, were ecstatic "over the downfall of 'Mahoneism' and in the triumph of the Anglo-Saxon race." The town's "colored men," it noted, "as a rule seemed disgusted with the result."[13]

Roanoke voters were politically divided over state and national politics, but on the municipal level, political campaigns eventually served as a means to unite much of the white community around the common cause of modernizing their city. In late 1883, residents interested in changing the course of the town met to discuss drafting a new charter and petitioning the state for city status. The group, comprised mainly of professionals, doctors, and lawyers had pressured Roanoke's mayor and town council for a revised charter months earlier, but saw so little progress on the matter that they decided to act on their own.[14] A few weeks later, the "Citizens' Committee" agreed to mesh its charter with one drawn up by local officials, and not long after that, residents approved it.[15] The city charter left Roanoke's fifteen-year tax exemption for new manufacturers in place but also authorized a large bonded debt specifically to rectify municipal ills.[16]

Gaining an official "city" designation, however, proved problematic when the town's December 1883 internal census listed a population of only 2,789 inhabitants, falling far short of the 5,000 residents required by the state to attain "city" status. In a move to bolster Roanoke's sagging reputation, local leaders passed on a figure of just over 5,000 residents to the General Assembly anyway, and in January 1884, Roanoke officially became a city. Misleading the Virginia Legislature with a wildly inaccurate population report had been the contingency plan all along, according to local printer Edward Stone, who remembered that "it was rumored that it might be necessary to 'stuff the ballot box' to secure the required population."[17]

The new charter left Mayor Lucian Cocke and the town council in place until July 1884 but scheduled city-wide elections that May. Although the local government had previously been hesitant to push for extensive improvements, that April it approved a bond initiative specifically to address sewer problems and called on property owners to endorse it. The bond measure, designed in part to bolster the standing of Cocke and the council before the upcoming election, was hotly debated in the weeks leading up to the vote. Previous bond monies had gone to macadamize a few streets and channel Lick Run but severe drainage problems remained and Lick Run, though now walled, continued to serve as an open sewer. In the pages of *The Roanoke Leader,* S. S. Brooke damned the measure as the last desperate act of a government incapable of "remedying our present filthy condition—a condition that has come upon us by almost criminal neglect of our authorities to enforce plain, needful and most apparent sanitary regulations." In the vote that followed, 72 percent of freeholders listened to Brooke and rejected the bond.[18]

In the municipal elections that followed, Roanoke's "old guard" faced challenges from a slate of newcomers. John H. Dunstan, S. S. Brooke's business partner, ran for mayor against incumbent Lucian H. Cocke. Dunstan, a mining engineer from Fredericksburg, had arrived in town two years earlier, and besides co-owning *The Leader,* he had invested in several local businesses, including the Roanoke Gas Company, of which he was secretary-treasurer. Dunstan campaigned on a promise that he was not a speculator, and he pointed to his stake in numerous "permanent improvements to the town" as proof. Playing up his role as a town booster, he also claimed that his newspaper had "probably done as much, if not more, than any other in bringing before the world at large the advantages and benefits of this place." Not long after entering the race, however, widespread rumors circulated that he was secretly "connected" to the Roanoke Land & Improvement Company. In campaign ads, Dunstan denied any legal association with the firm but admitted to being an intimate friend of the company's president.[19]

In the election, Dunstan beat Lucian Cocke, and residents voted in ten different council members, six of whom were newcomers. The results marked an important transition from a government of native elites with a fiscally conservative outlook to a government comprised mainly of newcomer elites interested in boosting Roanoke's chances for continued growth through professional city planning and improvements.[20] The northern workers clustered in the Third Ward elected four Republicans to council, including David F. Houston, superintendent of the Crozier Iron Works. Voters in Wards One and Two in the older sections of town elected six Democrats, including the only two incumbents who ran for re-election, along with one independent and one Republican. Furniture store E. H. Stewart, who like Dunstan had moved to town only two years earlier, won a seat in the Second Ward. Also on the ticket from Ward Two was the lone African American candidate for office—John H. Davis, who ran for council on the GOP ticket and received about 6 percent of the vote.[21]

Once in office, Mayor Dunstan advocated an aggressive agenda of improvements and economic development. In his first address to the City Council, he argued that the town needed a new jail, a market house, a new city hall, a firehouse, a new white school for workers' children in east Roanoke, and a new black school for the city's African American children. He also called for a diversification of local industries, advising the council to "offer any parties starting a manufacturing enterprise different from any now operation here, a bonus of a free site."[22]

That fall the new government passed the city's first comprehensive set of general ordinances. Most of the new laws addressed "problems" created by inhabitants who had refused to conform to the etiquette of life in an urban setting. They banned bathing in streams, damaging trees, firing guns, creating "noise," putting "filth" in creeks, laboring or drinking on Sunday, storing hay inside homes, and tying livestock to lampposts. They outlawed vagrancy and called on police to put anyone in the city without visible means of support on the chain gang. In an attempt to ameliorate Roanoke's frontier-town appearance, the new laws prohibited the construction of wooden buildings in the downtown district. They also created the Roanoke Board of Health to regulate "infected persons," monitor the sale of food, and levy fines on residents with "cellars, yards, privies and other places which may be alleged to be offensive, or likely to become so."[23] Shortly after the Board took office, S. S. Brooke directed them toward several neighborhoods where residents created "an abomination to the eye and nose" by dumping "slops" into their yards. The resulting odors, he argued, "ought to warn every healthful person of the malarial influence breeding there, to break out eventually in fevers and diphtheria."[24]

Lack of sewers, primitive drainage, and stagnant marshes all bred disease, and as the population increased, deaths from pathogens skyrocketed. By 1885, the city's death rate of over thirty-one persons per thousand had even far surpassed the rate for New York City.[25] "A good many deaths" that year, according to one resident, had come from widespread outbreaks of "diphihery" and "colry."[26]

Dr. George S. Luck, head of the board of health, attempted to remedy the situation by insisting that residents use disinfectants regularly and "exercise unusual diligence in maintaining their premises in a cleanly condition."[27] Sickness from disease, however, continued unabated, as did persistent rumors about dangerous health conditions in Roanoke. Local writer Thomas Bruce, like other residents, resented the published reports of sickness and death in town. "Some people," he protested, "are disposed to cavil as to Roanoke's health, but we who have lived and resided here enjoy the same health as other people." Yes, people died there, Bruce explained, "but not in greater numbers than elsewhere, and considering the number of excavations going on for new buildings in the city, we wonder that, without a proper sewerage system, it should be so healthy."[28]

Dunstan and the new city council moved to remedy sewer and drainage problems by reviving the $60,000 bond initiative for municipal improvements along with a new courthouse and market house that had been voted down three months earlier.[29] Although this time property holders overwhelmingly endorsed the measures, debate on how exactly to spend the money broke out soon thereafter.[30]

Among the first to criticize plans for the bonds was influential contractor Daniel C. Moomaw, who argued in a letter to the editor that the plan to channel and cover Lick Run but continue to use it as a primitive sewer system for the city was misguided and shortsighted. The complete allocation, he suggested, should go toward the construction of a modern sewer system and to macadamize the "impassable bogs" that the city used for roads.[31] S. S. Brooke condemned the plan as well, suggesting in an editorial that covering Lick Run "will make matters worse that they are at present."[32] Newly elected councilman E. H. Stewart concurred and argued for implementing Randolph Herring's 1882 drainage and sewer plan. The council agreed, and that winter it approved a vote on combining all the bonds into a single fund to construct sewers and improve roads.[33] The proposal, however, failed to garner the necessary two-thirds vote, leaving the council no choice but to fund the original plan.[34]

Even that, however, proved problematic. The lingering 1883 nationwide depression hit Roanoke especially hard, throwing hundreds of machinists out of work at the Machine Shops and forcing dozens of merchants to close their businesses. Scores of residents left town in search of opportunity elsewhere. As real estate values plummeted, widespread rumors surfaced that the railroad would never recover. The financial panic drove away potential investors in the municipality, and as a result, the city was only able to sell $16,000 worth of bonds. Work on some of the improvement projects went on anyway, and the city ran up a $9,000 deficit in the process. As a result, Dunstan called for an end to all street and drainage work except for that conducted by the chain gang, a reduction in the already tiny police force, and the elimination of the city solicitor position held by former Mayor Cocke.[35] S. S. Brooke blamed E. W. Clark & Company for the shortfall, informing readers that "certain Philadelphia parties" had promised to purchase the entire allotment of bonds but had bailed out when the depression set in.[36] A clearly disillusioned Dunstan bailed out as well, resigning as mayor a short time later to "pursue mining interests" in South America.[37]

In the first few years of its existence, the city's municipal government was nearly evenly split between Democrats and Republicans. In the spring of 1885, however, the GOP lost three of its five seats. The bond funding debacle and continuing accusations of mismanagement or malfeasance hurt all incumbents but was especially devastating to Republicans, since it gave Democrats a temporary wedge issue in the Third Ward. Moreover, before the vote, GOP leaders outraged blacks by ignoring their request that John H. Davis be nominated for the council in the Second Ward. Afterwards, the town's African Americans bolted the party and placed S. A. Ricks on the ballot as their black Republican nominee for city constable. Ricks, who garnered no support from white Republicans, lost decisively in the heavily white and mostly GOP Third Ward and polled significantly below all Republican candidates in Wards One and Two. "The Republicans," S. S. Brooke boasted after the split, "have lost the only opportunity that will ever be afforded them to control municipal affairs."[38]

The following spring, an anti-liquor party ousted two Democrats in the Second Ward and the Republicans lost another seat in the Third. Blacks, increasingly at odds with the city's Republican leadership, had run schoolteacher Zachariah Hunt for constable and endorsed Democrats in the other citywide races. Hunt polled only 1 percent of the vote, and the Democrats easily defeated the other Republican nominees. Democrat William Carr, who had moved from West Virginia in 1883 to take a job in the Machine Shops, won the mayor's race.[39]

Although the city eventually found funds to carry out all the initial infrastructure work approved in 1884, sanitation, drainage, and road problems went largely unaddressed until the end of the decade. The board of health's campaign against unsanitary practices was finally having an effect by then, its head physician reported, since most citizens devoted "more attention to the cleanliness of their own premises than formerly." As a result, he boasted, the city was "never cleaner than now."[40]

The campaign against unsanitary homes and yards, however, did not stop. The day after this announcement the board had twelve black residents arrested for "neglecting to keep their premises clean."[41] Elsewhere in town, other sanitation problems emerged. At the newly constructed Market House, farmers had begun camping out in their Conestoga wagons. As a result, the *Roanoke Daily Times* reported, "wherever these wagons have stood, there is left piles of garbage, and there it lies nearly everyday, festering in the sun and breeding disease."[42] The limited number of stalls in and around the market building forced hucksters to park their horses and carts along nearby streets, and the lack of systematic sanitation or restroom facilities meant that animal manure and wagon "slops" mingled with spoiled meat and rotten produce in and around Market Square. Authorities were well aware of the "fever-breeding odors" caused by the farmers, the paper reported, but had done nothing to regulate the place.[43]

1886 Market House on west side of Market Square in 1889. Second floor is Roanoke "Opera House" with entrance on Salem Avenue. Norfolk & Western Historical Photograph Collection (NS5761), Digital Library and Archives, University Libraries, Virginia Tech.

An anonymous "Sufferer" also blamed elected officials for the situation, relaying in a letter to the editor that the lane in front of the Market House was "as bad if not worse than any swamp, and the stench can now be compared to a glue or guano factory."[44]

Chronic street and drainage problems continued to plague city fathers as well. Like almost all southern cities at the time, Roanoke had few macadamized or paved roads and a municipal government hesitant to allocate funds for street improvements.[45] Freeholders approved bonds for modest sewer improvements in 1888 and for three bridges over railroad tracks in early 1890, but were not given a chance to vote on bonds for street work. Moreover, in 1890 the town annexed land surrounding the city that nearly doubled its size, added even more roads to maintain, and pushed the town's population over sixteen thousand. Funds for upgrading streets and building additional sewers did not exist, but that did not stop residents from insisting that authorities address these issues.

Railroad Avenue, the first street visible from the depot, was not macadamized, and after even a light rain, it turned to mud. The situation, one entrepreneur reasoned, was bad for business since any capitalist passing through the city was "not likely to be favorably impressed."[46] In the spring of 1890, a hundred and fifty residents, concerned about miasmas from a "marshy bottom" along Commerce Street, signed a petition demanding that officials do something. The *Roanoke Daily Times* endorsed their request and pointed out the danger posed by a "chain of mud-puddles" on Salem Avenue: "Every time it rains they are refilled and stand festering in the sun with the winds blowing their fetid breath up and down the city."[47] By summer, the paper argued, the streets of Roanoke were "in worse condition than those of any city in the country."[48] The roads looked dreadful, threatened the health of the municipality, and even endangered those walking downtown, since horses and wagons speeding along them inevitably splashed "helpless pedestrians" on nearby sidewalks with mud and stagnant water.[49] Even worse, residents in "thickly populated" areas continued to drain kitchen or bath water and "slops" onto nearby roads, rendering streets in some parts of town little more than cesspools.[50]

Officials and the board of health did what they could, ordering the chain gang to fill potholes and cover the streets with lime, but the city lacked the funds to make permanent improvements. The situation grew worse in the winter of 1890, when nearly three feet of snow from a winter storm began to melt. Overloaded coal wagons cut deep ruts in the town's flooded roads and eventually the situation grew so bad that residents placed stakes around especially large mud holes to warn buggy drivers. "Most of the streets," *The Times* reported, "look more like liquid lakes of mud than thoroughfares of a city." Residents had "besieged" the city engineer with complaints, and all over

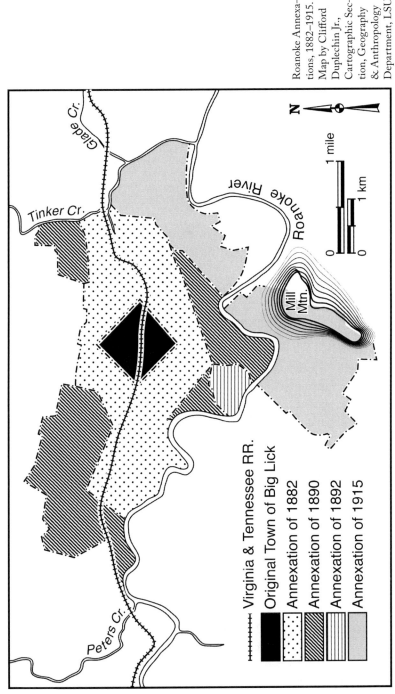

Roanoke Annexations, 1882–1915. Map by Clifford Duplechin Jr., Cartographic Section, Geography & Anthropology Department, LSU.

N

1 mile

1 km

0

0

Glade Cr.

Tinker Cr.

Peters Cr.

Roanoke River

Mill Mtn.

Virginia & Tennessee RR.
Original Town of Big Lick
Annexation of 1882
Annexation of 1890
Annexation of 1892
Annexation of 1915

town, the paper explained, "ladies fill the air with railings against the street committee and City Council."[51]

Other municipal problems came to a head as well; the new courthouse was far too small and the new jail, which was literally falling apart, had been plagued by an utter inability to contain prisoners.[52] The council took the blame for these problems too, and in early 1891, after receiving blistering criticism from residents, it approved bond issues totaling $360,000 to address the city's various needs. If endorsed by freeholders in early March, streets and sewers would get a $300,000 upgrade, the Northeast would get a new firehouse, the city would get a fire alarm system, the courthouse would get an addition, Roanoke would have a new jail and its first official map, and public school students would get additional space.[53]

In the weeks leading up to vote, debate raged over the appropriateness of approving the bonds. The town's press endorsed all the issues, but many residents were far less enthusiastic. African Americans, then about 30 percent of the population, opposed the courthouse addition, new fire station, and sewers on the grounds that they were unnecessary or were improvements that benefited white neighborhoods exclusively. Previous bond allocations, while providing a schoolhouse, had not been spent on improving African American sections of town. As a result, black ministers and political leaders organized mass meetings to rally voters against further allocations unless the council guaranteed them a "proportionate share."[54]

Some city fathers ignored their request; others reacted with hostility. A Third Ward councilman, for example, blasted the notion of blacks "combining" against the appropriation and turning it into "a regular race issue," while another predicted the bond vote would be carried explicitly because "the negroes have expressed themselves against it."[55] After hearing these reactions, Richard R. Jones, pastor of the city's black First Baptist Church, told those gathered at another rally that the time had come to demonstrate African American disapproval by rejecting the bonds.[56] Black voters, however, made up only about 25 percent of the electorate and posed no real threat unless a significant number of whites joined them.[57]

Roanoke's white voters, by contrast, pushed for postponing the bond vote until after citizens elected a new council or the current council appointed an independent "advisory board" to oversee funding for projects. When officials refused to delay the vote and claimed that the city charter did not permit an advisory board, numerous business leaders spoke out against endorsing the bonds. The president of the Roanoke Real Estate Exchange blasted the decision and accused the street committee of misappropriating previous funds. Peyton Terry argued that thousands of dollars had already "'been largely wasted'" by the current municipal government. Tipton T. Fishburn, president

Looking north on Jefferson Street from corner of Campbell Avenue, c. 1890. Norfolk & Western Historical Photograph Collection (NS5716), Digital Library and Archives, University Libraries, Virginia Tech.

of Roanoke's National Exchange Bank, even suggested that an influential member of the street committee had used past allocations to improve streets only in his ward.[58] In the vote that followed, however, the town's volunteer firemen crowded the polls to encourage voters to endorse the firehouse appropriation along with the other bonds, and few property holders dared ignore them. Black voters' attempt to kill the appropriations fell flat, and most of the issues passed with at least 80 percent of the vote.[59] The approval, one paper reflected later, ushered in an "era of extensive improvements" and showed the rest of the state that Roanoke "had ceased to be a large country town."[60] In the municipal elections that followed two months later, all the candidates who had spoken out against the advisory board lost their seats.[61]

The city adopted another new charter in early 1892 that carved two new wards out of the 1890 annexations and created a board of public works to oversee improvement projects. It also abolished its board of police commissioners—created in 1884 to manage the department—and returned complete control of the force to the mayor. Work on installing sewers started that spring, as did grading, macadamizing, and bricking central roads and systematizing the town's jumbled and confusing street names.[62] The board of health's campaign against unclean premises continued as well, and in the summer of 1892, the council authorized the systematic inspection of all homes in "certain districts." Those found "unsanitary" had twelve hours to fix the problem or face arrest. The campaign worked, according to most physicians, who by fall deemed the sanitary condition of the city "better at present than it has been at any time."[63]

In the municipal elections stipulated by the new charter, voters had to fill all government positions and elect an entirely new council. Republicans, energized by the state GOP convention held in Roanoke a few weeks earlier, nominated a solid Republican ticket for the Third Ward and put up a candidate for mayor for the first time. Local party leaders had reached out to black voters in the days before the statewide caucus, appointing a mixed delegation to the convention that included some of the city's most influential African Americans.[64] Democrats, by contrast, were widely accused of "machine" politics after party bosses handpicked all the nominees for office. Indeed, *The Roanoke Times* blasted the maneuver and called on voters to "pulverize the machine out of recognition" by electing two independent candidates for council from the Second Ward instead of men "who are Democrats 'for revenue only.'"[65]

In a reversal of its usual partisan stance, *The Times* also suggested that voters ignore political affiliations and elect a council based solely on its ability to manage the city and implement the remainder of the improvement bonds. The paper accused Roanoke's "Tammany-aping politicians" of already spending over $100,000 of the recently approved bonds on a variety of projects that had done little to improve the city. It also accused them of mismanaging the police force in the wake of revelations that numerous officers had been found asleep or drunk on duty and others had been charged with assault or embezzlement.[66]

Republican officials speaking at the "Young Men's Republican League, Colored" concurred with the paper and told the 250 in attendance that the Democratic machine was out of control.[67] In the election, Henry S. Trout, the Democrats' nominee for mayor, pulled in 61 percent of the vote, and although Democratic incumbents nominated by the "machine" beat the two independent candidates, most of the party's fifteen councilmen were new to elected office. Republicans carried all races in the Third Ward as well as one council seat in the 30 percent black Fifth Ward.[68] It was not exactly the victory *The Times* asked for, but it was nonetheless a "clean sweep" of most incumbents by candidates pledged to reform the "un-business-like methods" of the former council.[69]

Trout and the new council took the reins in July. In one of his first actions as mayor, Trout called the entire police force into City Hall and made them pledge to follow his revised behavior guidelines, which banned sleeping, drinking, and consorting with prostitutes while on duty.[70] He and the council also made management of bond spending more transparent, offering residents semi-annual updates on funds spent and improvements carried out. By fall, the new jail and firehouse were going up, work on the addition to the court-house was under way, bridges approved in 1890 were open over Randolph, Park, and Henry Streets, nearly eight miles of streets had been macadamized or covered in vitrified brick, contractors were finishing drains for the sewer, and two new schools had been built.[71] These improvements finally solved most of the city's chronic infrastructure needs. The cost of the projects and the lack of tax revenue from local industries, however, saddled the city with a massive municipal debt. Funding the improvements, nevertheless, showed that natives and newcomers alike were prepared to accept the permanence of their home and were willing to work together to make it a decent place to live.

■■■

Solving the "Magic City's" myriad street, sewer, and drainage problems was only one component of a multi-faceted municipal improvement campaign. By the time residents approved the funds necessary to correct infrastructure prob-lems, the city had developed a widespread reputation as particularly lascivious, crime-ridden and violent. Robbery, theft, and assault all rose dramatically in the 1880s, as did prostitution. "Roanoke in its morals," Presbyterian minister William Campbell observed, "for a time sadly deteriorated." He blamed the decline on the rise of dozens of "barrooms with their baneful influence" and on the influx of a large and "dangerous" population "inclined to do as they pleased in a new place."[72] By the early 1890s, clergy and residents alike sensed a wave of lawlessness emerging around them. White citizens blamed much of the lawbreaking on newly arrived blacks, and in conjunction with elected officials, they began grappling with ways to restore civic and racial "order" by disciplining real and perceived offenders in their midst.

Much of the racial tension had roots in an unsolved murder from 1884, when white residents suspected two black men had brutally assaulted, raped, and killed Lizzie Wilson, a fourteen-year-old white girl. According to a state-ment from Wilson's younger sister, the siblings had been walking home in the Northeast part of town after dark when two African American men abducted Lizzie. Wilson's screams for help and the hysterical account of the kidnap-ping from her sister threw the entire neighborhood into a panic. Armed men scoured the woods nearby and eventually found Lizzie not far from where she had been abducted, her throat slashed ear to ear and her clothing torn into tat-ters. As news of the murder and suspected rape spread, hundreds of residents descended into the neighborhood to search for suspects. Had any been found, *The Roanoke Leader* surmised, "in all probability they would have been lynched immediately under the excitement of the moment."[73]

In the days that followed, the city council put up a reward for information and hired three Pinkerton Detectives to work the case. Business leaders and clergy also got involved by organizing a "Citizens' Committee" to assist with the investigation and add to the reward.[74] In the meantime, William Campbell and the Wilson family buried Lizzie in a plot at the city cemetery donated by the municipal government. Newspaper accounts in the days that followed played up Wilson's working-class origins, six siblings, and impoverished parents, rendering the killing all the more heartbreaking. Looking to better their life in the "Magic City," the Wilsons had migrated to town in 1883 and rented a room in the Brick Row housing complex in the southeast section. Mr. Wilson worked in one of the nearby industries, his wife and children labored in odd jobs, and by 1884, the family had saved enough money to rent a Roanoke Land & Improvement Company home on Madison Avenue in the Northeast section. Not long after making the move, Lizzie found work in a bakery. She had been returning home from that job when the assault took place.[75]

In the days after the murder, Campbell recalled, most residents were "completely terrorized" and "afraid to leave their homes after dark."[76] Rumors about the identity of Wilson's killers were rampant, but in the weeks that followed, police made no arrests. In an editorial in *The Leader*, S. S. Brooke encouraged responsible white men to have shotguns and pistols at their disposal and to be fully aware of the numerous tramps and "suspicious persons prowling around our city." The town's women, he went on, were "very much frightened" and in need of vigilant protection.[77] The city was "wrapped in gloom" for weeks, according to another resident, and as frustrations and fears mounted, dozens of men joined posses to conduct extralegal investigations.[78] Police exonerated everyone they brought in, and in one case, the "Citizens' Committee" even published a notice chastising the vigilantes for "arresting" an innocent man, noting afterwards that "his reputation has been sullied, his business injured and a great wrong done him."[79]

Over the next several months, much to the horror of white residents, investigators failed to pin the crime on anyone. The following spring, however, police in Salem reported that Wilson Steptoe and Lewis Watkins, two black men who had been charged there with attempted rape, had bragged about killing Wilson.[80] Roanoke investigators immediately charged the men with murder. In their subsequent hearing, however, the jury hung along racial lines, with seven white votes for guilty and five black votes for not guilty. "Popular indignation was so fully aroused by the verdict," one journalist reported afterwards, "that serious apprehension was entertained that the prisoners would not be allowed to live to have a second trial." Indeed, the situation grew so tense that the presiding judge had the men rushed by train to Wytheville in order to prevent a riot.[81] When authorities brought Steptoe and Watkins back to Roanoke for their retrial, mobs of white men gathered outside the jail and talked openly, according to one reporter, "that the prisoners may be lynched at any moment." That night, a crowd of about two hundred black residents surrounded the prison to protect the men and refused to leave until authorities convinced them that the situation was under control.[82] Having given up on any hope of an impartial jury from the city, the presiding judge had jurors selected from Roanoke County, but when they also deadlocked by race, he dismissed the case.[83]

White resentment over the outcome of the trail generated racial hostility as well as a growing mistrust of local authorities' ability to protect citizens and punish lawbreakers. Although crime in the city was hardly confined to one area, most middle- and upper-class whites joined the press in focusing their ire on the saloon district along Railroad Avenue.[84] Police had made numerous arrests for gambling, drunkenness, fighting, and discharging handguns in the area, and by the mid 1880s, muggings and robberies there were commonplace.[85] The area attracted a diverse clientele of mainly poor and working-class whites and blacks. Like the rest of the town, the saloon quarter was informally segregated, with African Americans tending to frequent black-owned bars and "snack shacks" along a portion of the district between Jefferson and Henry Streets that authorities dubbed "hell's half acre."[86]

Newspaper accounts of mayhem and violence on Railroad Avenue appeared in a steady stream throughout the 1880s and reached a crescendo in 1890. That February, for example, police found a well-dressed visitor unconscious in an alley behind one of the saloons. Swindlers had drugged and robbed him, a tactic used frequently on out-of-towners who wandered into the area. "This part of the city," one paper warned, "is becoming very obnoxious to all respectable citizens and a person carries his life in his hands who ventures there in the night time."[87] A few days later, at a black-owned establishment called Charlie Morton's, an intoxicated "notorious negro" hurled an oil lamp at a female bartender, setting her clothing on fire and sending her into a "frenzy" before she extinguished the flames in a mud-hole outside.[88] The next month, three men attacked a patron exiting a bar, broke his jaw and robbed him, and in early summer, a group of "colored boys" bashed a drunken Crozier Furnace employee in the head with rocks.[89] A few weeks later, a drunken white man in Wilmeth's Barroom stabbed a black patron in the heart, and in early fall, a group of thugs waylaid and robbed a businessman from Pennsylvania.[90] In October, police reported that men renting rooms above the bars regularly urinated out windows into the street, and later that month, "negroes using brass knucks liberally," battered a policeman who ventured into an African American saloon.[91] Most "idle and dissolute negroes" in the district, one paper reported, carried pistols, razors, or other concealed weapons, and few were hesitant about using them on local police.[92]

Railroad Avenue is on the left, early 1900s. Norfolk & Western's 1882 Union Depot in center of tracks. Second N&W General Office Building is in the distance on the right. Norfolk & Western Historical Photograph Collection (NS381), Digital Library and Archives, University Libraries, Virginia Tech.

Although middle- and upper-class whites were critical of Railroad Avenue, a serious campaign against crime there did not begin until December 1890, after black men stood accused of brutally assaulting and robbing Thomas Massie, a sixty-year-old real estate agent. Massie, according to police, had been walking in the "West End"—far from Railroad Avenue—when attacked. Although it had been dark and Massie did not get a good look at his assailants, police immediately charged two African American restaurant owners from "hell's half acre" with the crime. John Redd and Rufus Williamson, the men in custody, had paid Massie their rent only hours before he was assaulted, which to the city's incompetent police, was proof enough of their culpability in the matter. That such an attack could occur in a "respectable" part of town stunned white residents, and the following day the mayor and a citizens' council placed a substantial reward for information about the crime. "It is evident," *The Roanoke Times* reported, "that there is a lawless element gathering here from other points which has got to be stamped out with a heavy foot."[93]

Numerous witnesses supported alibis offered by Redd and Williamson at their preliminary hearing, but when Massie died of cerebral hemorrhage, prosecutors charged the pair with murder. Roanoke's Chief of Police informed the press that the two men were guilty, and as news of Massie's death spread, crowds of white men began gathering downtown, where, according to a reporter on the scene, "there were many strong threats of lynching."[94] *The Roanoke Times* reminded residents that Lizzie Wilson's killers "had gone unhanged" and reported that as a result most citizens now favored "a summary dealing out of justice at the hands of the people" by "invoking lynch law."[95] Blacks in the community, the paper observed, "are much excited and worked up in the matter, and almost as a whole believe that Redd and Williamson are innocent." African American ministers certainly did, the story noted, but most, like the pastor of High Street Baptist who told his congregation that "'the law is in the hands of those whose hands they are in, and we can do nothing but pray that they may get justice,'" expected the worst.[96]

In the days that followed, the city bristled with racial animosity. Authorities placed the "Roanoke Light Infantry" militia on alert for a lynching attempt by whites or rescue effort by local blacks.[97] From his cell, Rufus Williamson pleaded with residents to stay calm and not to assume he was guilty "until I am given a chance to prove I am innocent."[98] Police and prosecutors found no evidence linking either of the men to the murder, eventually dropped all charges, and finally tried to prove that a mulatto vagrant already in custody for an unrelated offense had murdered Massie. Edward Daniel, alias William Hazelwood, whose three sisters were Railroad Avenue prostitutes, had shoveled snow for Massie, was in the "West End" begging for money in the days leading up to the attack, and had supposedly bragged about the murder to a cellmate in the Roanoke Jail.[99] In the subsequent trial, however, authorities failed to come up with enough other evidence to convict him.[100]

In the aftermath of the Massie murder, white residents and the press called for action. The city, William Campbell warned his congregation, was "in the midst of a carnival of crime" and authorities had done little to remedy the danger.[101] Black "resorts" on Railroad Avenue were "infested with desperadoes," one paper observed, noting that local sentiment had finally been "roused to a determination that those dens of iniquity shall be destroyed and their denizens either brought to justice or driven back to the places whence they came."[102]

A few days later, police conducted early morning raids on African American saloons in "hell's half acre" and arrested over a dozen black bar owners. *The Roanoke Times* praised the roundup as "the first chapter in the good work" and insisted that the mayor, chief of police, and "People of Roanoke" all agreed: "The negro dives on Railroad avenue must go!" Everyone was aware, the paper continued, that these saloons were "infested with the vilest of human beings" or with "breeders of disease," and respectable residents wanted the places "annihilated." A reporter covering the story concurred, explaining that once authorities kicked in the door of Charlie Morton's "den" and went inside they found the place so "unspeakably filthy and pestilential" that many of them "could almost see the grim form of disease rising from the place, and with his skeleton-like fingers spreading the black mantle of disease over the city."[103] The mayor fined all those arrested and ordered three suspicious women caught in the roundup to leave town.[104]

Crime on Railroad Avenue, however, proceeded unabated. Indeed, only weeks later *The Times* complained about a "notorious gang of thugs" and "cut-throats" who had been assaulting and robbing whites in "hell's half acre." The group preyed on intoxicated white men and had just attacked a Norfolk & Western brakeman who had been "carousing about" the avenue before being "seized by the hustlers and hurried back into an alley where he was knocked in the head" and relieved of forty dollars.[105] Another white man, "so drunk that he hardly knew where he was," remembered a "crowd of negroes gathering around him" before he passed out behind Morton's saloon and woke up missing twenty dollars.[106] A few weeks later, a Machine Works blacksmith was stumbling down Railroad Avenue when a gang of black toughs in front of Murray King's "dive" attacked him, stabbed him, and robbed him.[107] Similar assaults and robberies continued in spite of other periodic roundups. By 1893, Roanoke's Evangelicals were citing saloons in the district as one of the main reasons voters should endorse prohibition.

A growth in prostitution in Roanoke paralleled the rise in crime on Railroad Avenue. By 1890, there were dozens of brothels operating openly in poor or working-class white neighborhoods in the southeast part of town and in black sections of Gainesborough. For many women, whether never married, abandoned by their husbands, or widowed, prostitution was simply a way to better themselves economically. Indeed, in places with an abundance of single males like Roanoke, prostitutes could earn ten times the weekly wage of "legitimately" employed females.[108] As a result, arrests for "keeping a house of ill repute," "trolling the streets at an unseemly hour," or being "disreputable" all increased in the 1880s. Most of the women taken into custody faced only a small fine, and police rarely arrested prostitutes conducting business near the city's saloons or in black neighborhoods.[109] Though prostitution was technically illegal, municipal authorities in Roanoke—and in most American cities—preferred to regulate and control a vice that they perceived as inevitable. Fines therefore served as a way to collect taxes on the trade, and only "disorderly" or unsuitably located brothels were singled out for closure.[110]

Most brothels in town were race-specific, with white or black females running houses inhabited exclusively by white or black prostitutes, but in at least a few cases, white "landladies" managed all black or "octoroon" "bagnios" in Gainesborough. The bordellos recruited "inmates," according to one reporter, by preying on females traveling aboard trains alone or by offering single women new to the city a free place to stay.[111]

Although Roanoke papers published the names of women arrested for prostitution, they seldom bothered to include details about them unless they could do so as a warning. When women working in bordellos killed themselves, for example, local editors usually put a sensationalistic account of the event on their front pages. After Nellie Hendricks, an "inmate of a disreputable house," shot herself in the head after a fight with her lover, *The Roanoke Times* reported that she was from Campbell County, Virginia, and had been married and living in Jacksonville, Florida, before supposedly deserting her husband and moving to Alum Springs in Bedford County, Virginia, where "she began to sink lower in the scale of humanity" and ended up in a Roanoke brothel.[112]

A campaign against some of the bordellos began in earnest in late 1889, after working-class residents in the southeast petitioned Mayor William Carr to shut down seven "houses of prostitution" operating on Holiday Street. Carr, a member of William Campbell's congregation, served notice to landlords renting the properties that they had a week to eject the occupants or face charges of "keeping a house of ill repute." Real estate agent J. R. Hockaday, owner of several of the houses in question, was furious over the implication and confronted Carr on Salem Avenue before slapping him in the face. The mayor responded by bashing his cane over Hockaday's head, and the two men wrestled on the sidewalk before bystanders broke up the fight. The other landlords, however, quickly complied with Carr's order and evicted the accused women.[113]

A few months later, a mob of working-class residents in the southeast, upset about "immorality" and "determined to make their indignation felt," smashed windows in a section of Brick Row that was used by prostitutes.[114] In the weeks that followed, according to the chief of police, mothers in the neighborhood demanded that he shut down other brothels nearby and "lodged complaint after complaint that their sons were being ruined in them."[115]

The women kept up their campaign. When authorities failed to meet their demands, they continued to act on their own. In July 1892, a rock- and brick-throwing mob staged a "midnight attack" on a bordello run by Nora Heath. "Respectable families," the attackers reported in a letter to the paper, had been subjected almost daily to "disgraceful scenes" in their neighborhoods. Even mothers and children returning from Sunday school had seen "lewd women and their lovers" frolicking in Heath's front yard. Conscientious citizens had finally chosen to act, they explained, "for the protection of God, home, respectable women and helpless children."[116] The day after the attack, over a hundred southeast area residents gathered in a mass meeting and signed a petition asking newly elected Mayor Henry S. Trout to evict Heath and her "prostitute companions" along with the "inmates" of several other bordellos nearby.[117]

Trout promptly ordered the women out of the neighborhood and then had police investigate their landlords. The mayor, *The Roanoke Times* surmised, "has commenced a war against the disorderly houses situated in the south-eastern portion of the city."[118] More evictions followed, and eventually Trout even began jailing those who refused to relocate.[119] Although local clergy and Evangelicals railed against the city's "social evil," the prostitution "problem," as officials interpreted it, existed only because bordellos were operating in a white neighborhood. To remedy the problem, they simply evicted brothel operators in the southeast and left similar houses near Gainesborough unmolested. Bordello managers and prostitutes got the message. By 1893, city authorities had confined most brothels to an unofficial red light district in the heavily black northwest section of town.[120] This solution mirrored the remedies of countless municipal authorities elsewhere in the nation, who also created segregated brothel districts to limit vice to acceptable areas.[121] During the remainder of the decade, arrests for "keeping houses of ill repute" declined significantly in Roanoke, and it was not until the early 1900s, after Evangelicals and their ministers began a crusade against the northwest's unofficial brothel district, that politicians had to confront the issue again.[122]

■■■

Although the municipal government found ways to create a semblance of law and order, its chronic lack of tax income meant that it could support only the barest of public services. As a result, residents instigated civic reforms to fill in the gaps. The police force was woefully undermanned, so citizens concerned about the rise in crime organized private militias. In the early 1880s, Henry Trout and dozens of other prominent businessmen established the "Kimball Rifles"—named in honor of the man "who has done so much to promote the prosperity of Roanoke"—and theirs was but the first of numerous units organized throughout the decade.[123] Indeed, when civil unrest loomed, Roanoke's municipal government had several militias available to respond.

Residents also moved to provide fire protection for their largely wooden city. Without a fire brigade, S. S. Brooke pointed out, all inhabitants risked a "destroyed city, ruined businesses and homeless population." Ambivalence over the danger, he argued, was not "in keeping with the business-like spirit evinced in every other direction by the people of Roanoke."[124] The Machine Works and Hotel Roanoke already had volunteer hose companies, and not long after Brooke's harangue, other men organized the "Vigilant Fire Company" to protect the downtown. The municipal government purchased a used, horse-drawn "pumper" for the Vigilants and rented fire hydrants owned by the Roanoke Land & Improvement Company. The fire brigade used a storehouse for its station until the spring of 1886, when it moved into quarters in the new Market House. The relocation, however, proved problematic, as congestion around the building and muddy streets nearby regularly impeded its wagons. Freeholders eventually approved bonds for a new firehouse, and in 1888, the Vigilants moved into a two-story brick building on Jefferson Street and Kirk Avenue.

In west Roanoke, residents organized the "Junior Fire Company," and in the east, shop and railroad workers put together the "Union Fire Company."[125] The city provided some financial assistance for those units as well, but the brigades operated mainly on membership dues and on money raised at "Fire Laddy Fairs" organized by local women. In the early 1890s, for example, a "board of lady managers" supervised a two-week fair at the firehouse of "Friendship Fire Company" in the Northeast. The women decorated the station, sold food and drinks, and chaperoned dancing. The Roanoke Machine Works Orchestra provided the music and nearly two hundred women turned up every night to dance with firemen decked out in red dress uniforms. When it was over, the group had raised over a thousand dollars for the Company.[126]

Friendship Fire Company and Firehouse, northeast Roanoke, 1890. Norfolk & Western Historical Photograph Collection (NW3579), Digital Library and Archives, University Libraries, Virginia Tech.

Creating volunteer fire brigades to protect the city from conflagration, while an important municipal reform, was but one of the ways residents responded to the city's needs. They also funded the construction of a city hospital after physicians on Roanoke's Board of Health deemed such a facility a necessary adjunct of modernization. The need was especially acute in Roanoke, they argued, because local industries churned out waves of horrifically injured workers who had no decent place to receive professional care or to recuperate.

As a result, one doctor recalled, those injured "were frequently operated on in oil houses or other premises of the railroad company, or on a pile of crossties." Even worse, he explained, most of those injured were young and new to town, living away from their relatives in local boarding houses, which meant they had no family to care for them or to help with expenses.[127]

Industrial accidents began as soon as Roanoke's industries started operations. By 1890, they had reached appalling levels. Early that year, for example, a railcar crushed the foot of a fourteen-year-old working at the Machine Works, another employee caught his hand in a milling machine and had it "literally chopped to pieces, no part of it being left except the thumb," a Shenandoah Valley Railroad worker was hit by a train in the rail yard and "cut entirely in two," while another railroad worker was crushed to death while he was unloading lumber. In the spring, an exploding steam hammer killed a shop worker, another employee was smashed between two railcars and lost an arm, and the assistant yardmaster misjudged his jump onto a passing locomotive and lost a leg. In the summer, a yard worker died after being "horribly mangled" under a passing train, an N&W brakeman died after having his "head broken" by a railcar, a Crozier Furnace worker "met with a horrible death" after being struck by a train and "entangled in the machinery," while another N&W employee fell under a passing locomotive and had his legs "crushed to jelly" and intestines "torn out." In the fall, an N&W brakeman was "killed instantly" after being caught between two railcars, an SVR hostler was hit by a locomotive and killed, and an N&W switchman lost a leg after getting it caught between two railcars.[128]

Roanoke's pedestrians fared only slightly better. There were few bridges over the town's seven rows of railroad tracks and neither railway used crossing guards to warn residents about approaching locomotives. Worse, since the Union Depot was between the rails of both lines, inhabitants and visitors alike had to cross numerous sets of tracks to reach the station. Horrific stories about trains running over pedestrians appeared regularly in newspapers. In February 1890, for example, *The Daily Times* reported that Sarah Hogan was crossing the tracks near the depot when an SVR locomotive ran into her: "She was struck by the tender and hung on tenaciously to an iron bar, but the wheel caught her foot and compelled her to let go her hold, crushing her left leg from the knee down." She "cried piteously for help" from under the locomotive, the paper explained, "but her position was such that the engine had to be moved again, during which her cries were terrible to hear." Bystanders carried Hogan home, where she died shortly after doctors declared her injuries untreatable.[129]

In the spring, residents found a mangled furnace worker on the rails: "The head, both arms and both legs severed from the body and the sight was a horrible one."[130] In June, Joseph Kelly, an SVR clerk, tripped on the tracks in

front of a locomotive and lost both legs, and in October, a train hit a black resident at the Commerce Street crossing. Police found him, a reporter explained,
"with his head severed from the body and mashed almost to a jelly."[131]

The horrendous injuries to workers and pedestrians alike eventually led
female church groups to get involved in local healthcare issues. In the late
1880s, the various members of the multi-denominational "Circle of Charity
of the King's Daughters" opened a six-bed "Home for the Sick" as a place for
the injured to convalesce. Their Home did not have operating facilities and,
according to physicians, was "totally inadequate as to capacity."[132]

As a result, not long after it began operations, Tipton T. Fishburn, the
president of Roanoke's National Exchange Bank, organized the Roanoke Hospital Association to begin a fundraising campaign for a municipal medical facility. In early 1890, the Association asked freeholders for bond money to augment their fundraising. Property holders, however, rejected the plea.[133] The
vote disappointed local editors, and many of them bemoaned the slow pace
of the campaign. *The Roanoke Daily Herald,* like the other papers, called on
women to get more involved: "If our gentle ladies could only witness the scenes
of suffering which come so frequently under the notice of surgeons and reporters; could see the maimed wrecks of humanity moaning and writhing in mor-
tal agony; . . . the hospital fund would be doubly made up within twenty four
hours."[134] The appeal worked, and several female benevolent societies added
the hospital campaign to their other fundraising drives. By summer 1890,
Fishburn and the other business leaders in the Hospital Association had raised
half of the $25,000 needed to complete the structure.[135]

In the fall of 1890, the organization redoubled its appeal for donations
so that "strangers within our gates stricken by sickness, the toiling artisan,
or the humble laborer, the victims of accident, or whomsoever overtaken by
those of ills of life" would have a facility in which they could be professionally
cared for.[136] Roanoke's papers continued to strongly encourage contributions
and began publishing lists of those who gave to the cause. It took two more
years, however, to raise the additional funds. By then, the Roanoke Land &
Improvement Company and Roanoke Machine Works had donated a lot for
the facility near Crystal Springs. Shortly after contractors had completed the
exterior of the building, however, another nationwide depression crippled the
ability of citizens to fulfill their subscription commitments and construction
ground to a halt. Freeholders subsequently voted down a $10,000 bond to
complete the structure, and for the following six years, the building was not
finished.[137]

In the meantime, the council finally moved to protect pedestrians by nar-
rowly passing an ordinance requiring the N&W to install crossing guards and
limit the speed of its trains passing through Roanoke. Mayor Trout, citing

potential damage to the railroad's business, vetoed the bill, and in the heated debate that followed, councilmen backing him claimed that the ordinance would drive the N&W out of town. Democrats statewide and in Roanoke received financial backing from the railroad, and perhaps not surprisingly, they generally opposed any form of regulation on the industry. James Pattie, a Republican from the Third Ward, blasted Democrats' attempts to deny residents the protection they required, but he and the four other GOP councilmen lacked the votes to keep the issue from being buried in a Democratic-controlled railroad committee.[138]

■■■

By the early 1890s, Roanoke looked more like a city than an evanescent boomtown. The municipal government had finally solved chronic sewer, street, and drainage problems, and the board of health had curbed some of the unsanitary conditions that had plagued the town in its early years. A real city hall had replaced Ferdinand Rorer's storehouse, a market building had gone up downtown, and residents had instigated the town's first civic reforms to fill voids in municipal services. Over thirteen thousand newcomers arrived during the 1880s, and by the end of the decade, Roanoke was Virginia's fifth largest city. The common adjuncts of urbanization arrived as well, with assault, robbery, murder, and vice becoming commonplace by the middle of the decade. By then, the concept that Roanoke was divided into old and new sections had been replaced by resentment between whites and blacks or between the forces of "morality" and those deemed "immoral."

Much of Roanoke's white community found common ground in modernizing their homes, adding civic institutions, quashing "immorality," and demanding that blacks be punished for real or imagined crimes. These processes opened the door to reconciliation between natives and newcomers but contributed to growing resentment between the city's blacks and whites. Although politics generated some of the racial animosity, in the 1880s, northern-born Republicans had formed a coalition with native blacks to elect GOP candidates to local office. Occasionally these groups disagreed, but more often than not, they worked together to elect Republicans. In the rest of urban Virginia, African Americans stood largely alone as representatives of the GOP and experienced far less success. Funding municipal modernization, however, destroyed much of the city's Republican coalition since almost all whites, regardless of political affiliation, agreed on the necessity of neighborhood firehouses, sewers, and street improvements. The town's black residents, by contrast, saw no need to fund modernization unless they received some of the benefits. They therefore opposed most of the projects entirely.

Racial tensions also surfaced as the result of a growing belief among whites that African Americans were largely responsible for a fantastic increase in crime. Two sensational murders divided the community by race, nearly led to civil unrest, and fomented white demands for a crackdown on crime. The events created a bristling animosity between whites and blacks that showed no signs of dissipating by the early 1890s. Moreover, because authorities failed to provide the "justice" expected, white residents began to lose faith in the judicial process. In the years that followed, the increasing racial antipathy would combine with that lack of confidence to contribute to white residents extracting "justice" on their own.

Chapter 3

Industry, Business, and Boosterism

In the 1880s, during some residents' quest to improve and "moralize" their home, the City of Roanoke became a symbol of the sort of development that was possible in what regional business boosters were calling the New South. Roanoke's "rags to riches" story, replete with its supposedly impoverished origins, natives' initiative, and northern dollars, became a saga of progress that most spokesmen for the South referred to repeatedly. Northern papers likewise heralded the Magic City as an example of what was feasible when Yankee entrepreneurs used their acumen to liberate valuable minerals and natural resources that southerners had ignored for centuries. Under northern tutelage, they explained, natives had not only awakened to the possibilities offered by outsiders, they had even begun to participate in the harvest themselves, either by creating their own industries, speculating in land, or advertising the region to mesmerized financiers. In the Virginia Highlands and in Roanoke, a *New York Times* correspondent observed in 1887, "there is manifested now a spirit which calls for little more than constant pursuit to add materially to the strength, the influence, and the distinction of what is named 'the new South.'"[1]

The Norfolk & Western Railroad was largely responsible for the transformation, having opened the entire region up for industrialization by providing cheap access to iron and coal. The railroad lured thousands of investors into the mountains of the Old Dominion, and throughout the 1880s, mines, furnaces, and rolling mills sprang up along its tracks. Northerners and Europeans invested millions of dollars in these enterprises and speculated heavily in Highland and Roanoke property. These outside groups, however, did not develop the region alone; natives campaigned heavily for investments, courted financiers, and eventually began their own manufacturing enterprises. The role of insiders, especially in Roanoke, was every bit as crucial to industrialization as Yankee dollars.

Roanoke, as the only large city in Southwest Virginia, served as the headquarters for the region's extractive industries and as the epicenter of the coal, iron, and land booms that swept the area in the 1880s and early 1890s. Its residents successfully courted new manufacturers and convinced thousands of speculators to invest in local real estate schemes. Although the economic expansion ushered in a new wave of manufacturing enterprises and for a time bolstered natives' bank accounts, the vast majority of land speculations resulted in little actual development. Moreover, the boom did not solve Roanoke's chronic infrastructure problems. New industries not only received free land, but also paid no taxes, leaving the municipality with few of the funds necessary to address local needs. Mud streets and polluted creeks greeted visitors until the early 1890s, as did rumors that the town was particularly unhealthy and rife with disease. Optimists, undaunted, still billed their home as the Magic City, a metropolis that had risen up in cow pastures to take its place in the vanguard of the New South.

■■■

Before the economic boom hit Roanoke, the town and its industries had to deal with the impact of a national depression that began in 1883. The Roanoke Machine Works, having turned out eight coal hoppers or boxcars per day, completed nine locomotives, and repaired hundreds of old engines and railcars, had exceeded expectations. In 1884, once the depression set in, however, orders declined and the company reduced wages by 10 percent, cut hours from ten to nine per day, and ended Saturday work. The firm managed to continue full employment until the winter of 1885, when the deepening depression forced it to lay off hundreds of workers.[2] Other Clark Company subsidiaries had problems as well. In early 1885, the Shenandoah Valley Railroad defaulted on its loans, taxes, payroll, and invoices. Although the line continued in a receivership, eventually the mortgage company holding its notes filed suit for total liquidation of its assets. The Norfolk & Western Railroad, the majority owner of the line, fought a lengthy legal battle to halt the liquidation, and in 1890, it purchased the entire SVR for $4,500,000.[3]

Roanokers, one resident commented, were not accustomed to the "marvelous prosperity" they had witnessed before the depression, and as a result, most of them "had thought doubtless that the boom had come to stay."[4] The economic downturn hit the city's initial land speculators especially hard. "The bottom dropped out of everything in Roanoke," Reverend William Campbell recalled, "and there were neither rents nor sale of property."[5] Ferdinand Rorer, like most developers, lost everything. He closed his offices and left town, as did Roanoke's first mayor, Marshall Waid.[6]

Many of the laid-off shop workers packed up their families and left town amid widespread rumors that the Machine Works would eventually close for good.[7] In late 1885, however, the plant signed a contract with the New York, New Haven and Hartford Railroad for five hundred freight cars, albeit at a price far below what the Machine Works normally charged. Iron for the carriages and wheels came from the Crozier furnaces next-door and wood for the flooring came from thousands of White Oak trees harvested on the surrounding mountains. Not long after, the N&W put in an order for twelve heavy locomotives, and in the weeks that followed, most shop employees returned to work.[8]

Newspapers in the region saw the rehabilitation of the Machine Works as a clear sign that "the Magic City of the Southwest . . . has again recovered its usual business vim and enterprise."[9] By the time Shenandoah Valley Railroad lawyer William Travers visited in the fall of 1886, business in Roanoke had recovered from the depression. Its industries paid over $100,000 a month to employees, and most of the money, Travers explained, "is of course distributed in Roanoke." As a result, he reported, the town's stores were "bright and their owners cheery."[10] The Machine Works continued its recovery, and by the end of the decade, its workers had constructed forty-seven locomotives along with hundreds of freight cars and coal hoppers.[11] Monthly pay at the Works surpassed $65,000 in 1890, and a couple of years later, E. W. Clark & Company more than doubled the size of the plant and its workforce.[12] The Clark firm also put an addition on its Shenandoah Avenue railroad office that more than doubled its size and it added a thirty-six-room wing to the Hotel Roanoke. "We intend," N&W President Frederick Kimball explained, "to make the hotel one of the finest in every way in the South."[13]

Although its sister company the Shenandoah Valley Railroad went bust, the Norfolk & Western emerged from the depression largely unscathed. It increased the tonnage it transported out of the Pocahontas coal seam every year in the 1880s, and by the early 1890s, the railroad was moving close to three million tons of coal over the line. During the same period, the N&W purchased more than 300 locomotives, more than 5,000 freight cars, and more than 8,000 coal hoppers. It also horizontally integrated, absorbing other

First steam locomotive built at Roanoke Machine Works, c. 1884. Norfolk & Western Historical Photograph Collection (NS731), Digital Library and Archives, University Libraries, Virginia Tech.

Industry, Business, and Boosterism

railroads in Southwest Virginia and in Ohio and more than tripling its miles of track. In the early 1890s, the line sold over two million passenger tickets, and its gross earnings, which had increased throughout the 1880s, passed $10,000,000 for the first time.[14]

Much of the railroad's growth was a result of its efforts to generate additional industries along its tracks. To do this, it published a variety of booster guides, instigated town development, and brought in scores of outside investors to tour the region. In 1889, the railroad published its *Reference Book . . . Outlining the Condition of Progress in Mining, Manufacturers and Agriculture and the Undeveloped Resources of those Portions of the State of Virginia Traversed by its Line.*[15] The guide circulated widely in the North and abroad and contributed to the growth of iron furnaces in the Highlands. Indeed, one consequence of the rapid development of iron mills along the tracks of the N&W was an increase in production that moved Virginia from seventeenth in the nation in overall iron output in 1880 to sixth in 1890.[16] The N&W also built twenty-five hotels at its depots in Southwest Virginia as lodging facilities for a wide array of speculators and tourists, some of whom invested in the region's coal mines and iron plants.[17] Throughout the decade, the line invited scores of northern and European capitalists to tour the Virginia Highlands and Roanoke. High-ranking E. W. Clark & Company executives escorted the more eminent visitors, but no matter their statuses, native entrepreneurs solicited their assistance. In one typical tour, for example, Clarence Clark and Frederick Kimball escorted several dozen wealthy businessmen from New York, Philadelphia, and London on a stroll around town. The group, which had over $200,000,000 of capital at its disposal, arrived on a chartered N&W train, lodged at the Hotel Roanoke, and met with dozens of local business leaders before departing for the coal fields.[18]

These Yankee financiers and others, enticed by the prospects of inexpensive and unlimited access to the South's lumber, coal, and ore, were the men primarily responsible for funding temporary extractive industries near the region's natural resources. They also invested in manufacturing and management facilities on their periphery, in places like Roanoke and Birmingham. The "industrial invasion" of the 1880s and 1890s, while responsible for moderate urban growth, left much of the South that had been "touched by capital" with a colonial economy in which it exchanged raw materials generated in low-paying extractive industries for expensive finished goods manufactured in northern cities. While employment opportunities in mines, forests, and cotton mills did increase, the economic status of the average southerner, whether rural or urban, changed very little from 1880 to 1900.[19]

The middle-class boosters and town elite responsible for the "industrial invasion," by contrast, profited from industrialization and urbanization. Whether they were "new men" disconnected from the nexus of antebellum power or remnants of the old plantation gentry, they were the men who served as native agents and managers for northern corporations. Most also owned the general stores, distribution warehouses, construction firms, and commercial or retail establishments that benefited directly from the concomitants of modernization: transportation improvements, decline in self-sufficiency, growth of corporate power, emergence of a wage-earning population, and rise in consumerism.[20]

Those living in villages and towns along the N&W's tracks understood that Southwest Virginia's mineral wealth and natural resources combined with access to the railroad were attractive inducements for industries. Throughout the 1880s, local boosters and town councils published hundreds of surveys and information pamphlets that catalogued the advantages of the Highlands for a northern and European audience. Most of them linked Appalachian Virginia to modernization taking place elsewhere in the South and predicted that "miracle cities" like Roanoke would soon dot the landscape. They mimicked New South editors and spokesmen in arguing that industrialization and exploitation of the South's abundant natural resources were the keys to moving the impoverished region to a position of economic dominance within the United States. Outside ingenuity and investment meshed with southern autonomy, according to boosters, was the quickest means of accomplishing this feat. Like New South promoters elsewhere, they couched their appeal in the rhetoric of sectional reconciliation, racial harmony, economic and social order based on industry and science, and social Darwinism. Mountain boosters, however, also cast their plea in a vocabulary of benevolence that tied industrialization to the social uplift of a "strange land and peculiar people." Their efforts, and the fantastic increase in demand for iron and coal, led to a massive economic boom in the region that for a time, at least, seemed to offer the genuine promise of a New South.[21]

Although modernization offered many Southwest Virginia residents a way to transcend limited opportunities, some scholars insist that the process reduced once independent mountaineers to wage slaves in mines or mills, adrift in a colonial economy that left the region impoverished throughout the twentieth century.[22] Such a colonial model, however, breaks down entirely in cities like Roanoke, where natives sought outside capital, reaped substantial financial rewards and managed local industries, and where industrialization fomented civic progress, albeit at a slower rate than northern cities. Profits from the industrialization of Appalachia flowed not only to the Northeast, but also into towns like Roanoke on the periphery of the region's coalfields or timberlands. Many historians, nevertheless, downplay the significance of industrial-related urbanization, arguing that places like Birmingham and Roanoke were simply the base of operations for hegemonic northern industrialists. As a result, they tend to downplay the role that natives played in developing Appalachia's cities and towns, favoring instead a model that portrays the power dynamic between insiders and outsiders as one-sided and primarily in the hands of non-natives. Most deny natives' agency in the process, suggesting instead that Big Lick and Roanoke residents acquiesced to powerful northern industries and received few benefits for surrendering their bucolic village to industrial development.[23]

Contrary to the colonial economy model, Roanoke's middle-class businessmen were the main force behind luring the N&W and SVR to Big Lick as well as the primary group responsible for the numerous additional Yankee investments that followed later in the decade. Although the N&W clearly made such development possible, natives were largely responsible for bringing in the new industries. Northern capital had many friends in the city, the *Roanoke Daily Times* explained, noting that "while we honor the memories of those who fought and died for the Confederacy, . . . we have our faces toward the future and desire to reap all the advantages of a fully restored union." Like Atlanta's boosters, who played up that city's lack of antebellum history, local businessmen pushed Roanoke's disconnection to the Civil War in their campaign to lure northern investors.[24] The town's commercial leaders, one resident observed, had a "peculiar patriotic spirit" that made them natural boosters: "To anyone dwelling here the material advancement of the best interest of the place is the first consideration." As a result, if an industry showed interest in Roanoke, citizens asked no questions other than how they could make a "liberal subscription" and have "every impetus given to forward the undertaking."[25] Roanoke's "open for business" ethos resulted in a tax code that offered fifteen-year tax exemptions to new manufacturing facilities, free land for new industries, and hefty municipal stock subscriptions to worthy enterprises.

The northern press, which had branded Roanoke a ramshackle boomtown in the early 1880s, changed course once widespread industrialization began, and by the middle of the decade, Yankee reporters touted the city as an example of the area's unlimited potential. The *Manufacturers' Record* of Baltimore became one of the region's biggest boosters, with *The New York Times* not far behind.[26] It was mainly locals, the *Record* pointed out, who had ushered in the intensive industrial and demographic growth and made Roanoke "The Magic City," a place "teeming with wealth, culture, industry, energy, and vim." Its destiny, the journal promised, was "to be that of one of the largest manufacturing and industrial centers of the South."[27]

In 1887, a *Times* correspondent on a tour of the region stopped in Roanoke and declared it "perhaps the most remarkable exemplification of the possibilities in this Virginia district." Only five years earlier, he explained, the city was an "insignificant way-station" with a population that "had never a hint of what the bustle of trade or genuine industry was like. A whole dollar was a curiosity; a man who worked every day a phenomenon." Now, the place resembled a New England manufacturing town and its population was "busy, ambitious, pushing."[28] Dozens of other correspondents followed, including reporters working for *Frank Leslie's Illustrated Newspaper*, the Boston *Globe*, Philadelphia *Ledger*, Worcester *Telegram*, *New England Farmer*, and Baltimore *Morning Herald*.[29]

Although scores of Roanoke businessmen were responsible for the city's industrial boom, Big Lick natives Henry Shaver Trout and Peyton Leftwich Terry were the principal natives behind the development. Trout and Terry were not only dedicated and noteworthy boosters, they also managed several of the city's most important businesses and played instrumental roles in convincing dozens of northern industries to move to Roanoke. Henry Trout grew up in Big Lick, where he helped his father John manage the family farm and their Franklin Road inn, the Trout House. John Trout owned over twenty slaves in the 1850s, and in 1861, his nineteen-year-old son Henry withdrew from classes at Roanoke College to enlist in the Twenty-eighth Virginia Infantry. Peyton Terry moved to Big Lick from Campbell County, Virginia, in 1851, when he was just fifteen. Terry found work as a store clerk and became a merchant himself before he married Henry Trout's sister and enlisted in the Twenty-eighth Virginia as well. Trout and Terry both served in Pickett's Division, both fought at Gettysburg, and both were eventually captured and sent to Federal prisoner-of-war camps before returning to Big Lick. After the war, Trout went back to managing his father's farm and Terry returned to P. L. Terry & Company, his general store on Franklin Road. By 1868, Terry had done well enough to purchase the Elmwood estate, a Greek revival mansion and 625 acres south of Big Lick Depot. In 1874, the village's residents elected Trout as a state delegate and put Terry on the first Town Council. The brothers-in-law started a cattle business later in the decade, and by the early 1880s, both had also opened tobacco warehouses.

Trout and Terry held tightly to an unyielding and sanguine belief that an industrial city could rise in what had been their wheat fields and cow pastures. They were heavily involved in courting the SVR, and both profited from the line's decision to put its junction in Big Lick. In 1882, the Roanoke Land & Improvement Company bought close to 500 acres from Trout for $71,000, and after Frederick Kimball helped organize the First National Bank of Roanoke, he selected Trout as its president and put Terry on its board of directors. In 1881, Terry helped secure options on McClanahan Mill and Spring for the E. W. Clark & Company. In 1882, the Improvement Company bought his Elmwood estate for $125,000. The Clark Company also put him on the board of directors of the Roanoke Land & Improvement Company (RL&IC) and Roanoke Machine Works, and it appointed him president of the Roanoke Stockyards Company. In the spring of 1882, residents elected Trout to

Roanoke's first Town Council, and later that year, they selected him as their representative in the Virginia Senate.

In 1883, the two men joined Frederick Kimball in organizing the Roanoke Association for the Exhibition of Livestock. Later in the year, Terry founded the Roanoke Trust, Loan & Safe Deposit Company and moved the business into the ground floor rooms of the railroad office building. By 1886, the Clark firm had appointed Trout to the board of directors of the Roanoke Land & Improvement Company. It also made him a director of its Pocahontas Coal Company. Trout and Terry had helped organize the Roanoke & Southern Railroad that same year, and in 1888, Trout became president of the line. Both men were active in St. Mark's Lutheran Church, and eventually both helped found the Peoples Perpetual Loan & Building Association, the West End Land Company, the Crystal Springs Land Company, and the William Watts Camp of Confederate Veterans. By 1890, Terry was president of both the Roanoke Development Company and the Times Publishing Company, owner of *The Roanoke Times,* as well as vice-president of former Governor Fitz Lee's Iron Belt Building & Loan Association.[30]

Like boosters elsewhere in the South, Trout and Terry had much to gain in attracting business and securing a prosperous future for their community. They were the most significant local emissaries for the Clark Company, and although they received a significant boost from that firm, they acted largely on their own to develop other indigenous corporations, land companies, railroads, and investment houses. Trout and Terry were hardly the "new men" popularized in New South rhetoric, but they were close, and like most business leaders in up-and-coming southern cities, they had risen, albeit with assistance, from somewhat humble backgrounds to become the most well respected and wealthy men in town. Their booster spirit, optimism, and determination to reinvest capital at their disposal, and the similar ethos found in the seemingly united front of local business leaders, mirrors the boosterism and civic patriotism of places like Atlanta and Nashville, where a relatively new elite faced little opposition from an entrenched class of wealthy old timers opposed to industrialization and rapid urbanization. In long-established southern cities, like Mobile or Charleston, men like Trout and Terry would have faced tougher odds in rising beyond their original station, but in Roanoke, a town with no concretely established social caste and little real collective past to remember, they and dozens of men like them quickly emerged in the vanguard of the city's new bourgeoisie.[31]

Throughout the 1880s, Trout, Terry, and other local boosters convinced dozens of outside investors to open industries in Roanoke. The West End Iron Works and Roanoke Iron Company started operations, as did the American Bridge Works, the Roanoke Rolling Mills, the Roanoke Spike Works,

the Roanoke Mining Company, the Midland Iron Company, the West End
Brick and Tile Works, the Virginia Brewing Company, the Old Dominion
Phonograph Company, the Roanoke Black Marble Company, and the Adams
Brothers & Payne Brick Company. All told, *The Roanoke Times* reported, there
had been over $9,000,000 invested in manufacturing concerns and buildings.
The city's growth had been "so rapid," the paper boasted, "that, notwithstand-
ing the great influx of people, its population is not yet in proportion to the
manufacturing."[32] The *Baltimore Sun* concurred, insisting that Roanoke had
become "the Birmingham of the Old Dominion" and stood at the forefront of
"the race of progress upon which the South has entered."[33] None of the development would have occurred, however, had it not been for native boosters.

Employment opportunities in Roanoke's industries lured thousands of
skilled laborers and their families from the North. The city's iron furnaces and
machine shops required highly trained workers, and since Virginia had very
few men with such backgrounds, most of the best paying positions in local
industries went to migrants from Pennsylvania or Maryland. As a result, the
town's employment paradigm mirrored that of Birmingham—a city that also
seemingly sprang up from nowhere and lacked a skilled labor force.[34]

Employment for native whites was readily available, albeit in less skill-
oriented jobs. That opportunity, nevertheless, brought in thousands of new
residents from the surrounding countryside and mountains. Rural life in the
late nineteenth century, especially in Appalachia and the Virginia countryside, offered little prospect for advancement. As several scholars have pointed
out, wage labor positions in the region's emerging mining camps, towns, and
industrial cities quickly became attractive alternatives to the poverty, isolation,
and misery of tenant farming or sharecropping. Wage employment for single
white women, while almost nonexistent in the countryside, was available
in urban areas like Roanoke, which had numerous businesses that required
clerical workers. Jobs for African Americans in town, while also readily available, were limited almost entirely to domestic work for women and unskilled
manual labor for men. Indeed, while scores of blacks left tenant farming and
sharecropping in the Virginia countryside for a better life in Roanoke, most of
the newcomers landed in jobs so filthy and difficult that whites classified them
solely as "nigger work." While rural whites could expect to learn the skills
necessary to move up the pay scale in their jobs, African Americans were all
but cut off from significant advancement.[35]

Migration to the Magic City mirrored urbanization patterns throughout
Virginia, where the population of cities more than doubled from 1870 to 1900.
No urban area in the state, however, grew faster than Roanoke, which jumped
from Virginia's fifth largest city the first time its population was enumerated
in 1890, to third largest in 1900.[36] Although in 1890 boosters estimated that

Roanoke's population had grown to at least 20,000, the census that year placed the actual populace at 16,159. The figure, which represented a 579 percent increase from 1883 and a 3,472 percent rise from 1880, was nevertheless so disappointing that the *Roanoke Daily Times* declared it "nonsense" and demanded a recount.[37] Sixty-eight percent of the 13,370 new residents who arrived between 1883 and 1890 were white, and even though 4,256 new black citizens arrived as well, whites still comprised about 70 percent of the city's population. There were over six inhabitants for every house in 1890, and though by 1892 carpenters had built 578 more dwellings, 7,069 more newcomers had arrived, pushing the average number of inhabitants per home to over seven.[38]

The Roanoke Development Company, a firm co-owned by E. W. Clark & Company President Clarence Clark, fellow Philadelphian Arthur Deniston, Peyton Terry, and other local investors was responsible for about five hundred of the new residents. In 1891, the Development Company lured the Norwich Lock Factory, Duval Engine Works, Roanoke Iron Mills, and Bridgewater Carriage Company to its thirteen-hundred-acre tract west of the city. The industries built dozens of rows of identical cottages for their employees, and eventually the Development Company put a steel bridge over the river to induce investment in its holdings to the south of the mill village. The firm had lofty expectations for the neighborhood and zoned it "in order to avoid the erection of buildings which might prove out of character with the surroundings."[39] Lots sold briskly, and although papers predicted a "new city" would soon emerge and "knock at the doors of the corporation of Roanoke and ask admission," few other investors built anything.[40]

Native entrepreneurs did not rely exclusively on outside capital to create businesses in town, and throughout the decade, hundreds of them started indigenous enterprises. Peyton Terry helped found one of the first in late 1883, when he and the co-owner of *The Roanoke Leader,* John Dunstan, bought a utility franchise and founded the Roanoke Gas Company.[41] The council promptly approved funds for sixteen gas lamps at key intersections, but as one paper complained, they served mainly as "beacon lights to steer by" since one lamp came into view "about the time the other disappears in the rear."[42] The 1883 depression slowed the extension of gas mains and eliminated funding for more lamps. Indeed, when SVR lawyer William Travers arrived one night in the spring of 1887, he found downtown Roanoke so poorly lit that he made his way through the darkness only by dragging an umbrella along the sidewalk for guidance.[43] By the end of the decade, the Roanoke Water Works, a firm owned by Clarence Clark, Frederick Kimball, and other Clark & Company associates, had absorbed the struggling Roanoke Gas Company, a circumstance that once again put all the town's utilities in the hands of Philadelphians.[44]

Other natives fared somewhat better. Local entrepreneur Ferdinand Rorer, for instance, founded the Rorer Iron Company, bought the mineral rights to a deposit of ore on the west ridge of Mill Mountain, and constructed a narrow gauge railroad that linked the mines to the N&W.[45] Former Mayor Lucian Cocke, by contrast, attempted to profit from the city's muddy and poorly lighted streets by developing a mule car railway. He and other associates organized the Roanoke Street Railway Company in 1887. By the following year, their "hay burner" railroad operated on Jefferson and Commerce Streets as well as on Campbell and Church Avenues. The company added extensions that branched out from Salem Avenue. For a five-cent fare, residents and visitors alike could avoid the mud by taking a mule wagon to destinations throughout downtown. Tracks for the system rested on crossties that would sink, however, and as a result, cars occasionally bounced off and overturned in the street. This flaw and the unpredictability of the mules pulling the cars hurt business and eventually led the firm to modernize its tracks and install electric powered cars. The new line began operations in the summer of 1892 and had, according to *The Roanoke Times,* finally given Roanoke "that looked for, longed for, much to be desired adjunct to all enterprising cities—an electric railway." In the years that followed, the firm expanded its streetcar lines into the suburbs as well as into Salem and Vinton.[46]

Elsewhere in town, entrepreneurs contemplated far grander moneymaking schemes. The most significant of them began in early 1886, when John C. Moomaw, Crozier Furnace manager David Houston, Henry Trout, Peyton Terry, and other native investors organized the Roanoke & Southern Railroad Company. The firm, which had a North Carolina counterpart, planned to construct a 122-mile line from Roanoke to Winston-Salem, North Carolina, that would essentially complete the second half of the route originally proposed for the Clark firm's Shenandoah Valley Railroad. The city's editors applauded the idea, and predicted that the completed railroad would double the size of Roanoke and usher in the same kind of boom that accompanied the arrival of the SVR. Local property owners—the only residents eligible to vote on civic financial issues—had previously rejected several small bonds for infrastructure improvements, but in April 1886, they almost unanimously approved issuing $100,000 in bonds to buy Roanoke & Southern stock.[47]

In the years that followed, however, the railroad struggled to find other investors and construction of the line stalled. In 1889, local business leaders proposed issuing bonds to cover another $100,000 stock subscription. The road, one merchant explained, was crucial for Roanoke since it "would add millions to the wealth of the city" by opening up a southern trade.[48] The press urged freeholders to endorse the subscription, warning that Salem residents would "gladly give all and more than Roanoke is asked to subscribe" and had even come up with a new name for the line: "The Salem & Southern."[49] Roanoke's property owners voted overwhelmingly to authorize the purchase but on the same ballot rejected far smaller bonds for a hospital and police headquarters.[50]

Later in the year, Trout, Terry, and other business leaders provided the final incentive for the line by purchasing its $75,000 right-of-way into the city. Construction ended in early 1892, and shortly after the first Roanoke & Southern train pulled into town, the firm's stockholders voted unanimously to lease the line to the N&W for 999 years. The hastily arranged lease prevented the N&W's main rival, the Chesapeake & Ohio Railroad, from buying the Roanoke & Southern in an attempt to end the N&W's monopoly on rail access to Southwest Virginia. Four years later, the N&W bought the Roanoke & Southern and turned the line into its "Winston-Salem Division." The lease and buyout, while profitable to a handful of Roanoke residents, maintained N&W's monopoly on local freight and passenger service, a circumstance many inhabitants found unsettling, especially since municipal funds had fomented completion of the Roanoke & Southern.[51]

Old South critic and New South booster Hinton Helper, covering Southwest Virginia for the *New York Sun*, witnessed firsthand the booster spirit and business acumen of Roanoke's residents. He compared the city to Atlanta. "The people here do not sit down and await the action of Providence," he observed, "they help themselves." Roanoke, according to Helper, antebellum author of *The Impending Crisis*, represented what had become possible after Virginians shed their addiction to the backward and corrupting institution of slavery.[52] Indeed, he was so impressed that after finishing his work for the *Sun*, Helper moved to Roanoke from Louisville and convinced Trout, Terry and several other business leaders to organize a Commercial Club to "advertise to the outside world the diversified and splendid advantages offered by this city as a place for investment."[53]

The Roanoke Commercial Club recruited eighty other members in the months that followed, and in the fall of 1890, it moved into posh quarters on the second floor of the Exchange Building downtown. The Club appointed Helper, who had established a similar association in Louisville, its secretary and only paid employee. By the next month, he had dozens of inquiries from northern industrialists to pass on to members.[54] Out-of-town businessmen flocked to the Club's quarters and potential investors arrived as well, but after serving only a couple months, Helper cited health problems, resigned, and left town.[55] His abrupt departure stunned members, as did the front-page story that followed a week later that offered a graphic account of his scandalous affair with a New York socialite. Mrs. Helper, stranded in Roanoke with only $5, published letters detailing the tryst and charged her husband with desertion before fleeing to relatives in Savannah. The story, picked up by the national press shortly after it broke, created a "sensation" in town and had a decidedly chilling effect on the Commercial Club.[56] The organization's president resigned and went on an extended tour of Cuba and Mexico, members stopped paying dues, and even with the addition of billiard tables, the group's quarters went largely unused until the Club finally closed.[57]

Before Helper departed, the Club hired a New York publishing firm to produce *The City of Roanoke, Virginia: Containing an Outline of its Environment, Resources, Development, Prospects and Substantial Inducements to Capital in the Year 1890*. The pamphlet touted the town's "evidence of progressive conditions" to northern and European investors by highlighting the "vast repositories of ores and coals" available nearby and by providing an array of business statistics and illustrations that detailed the city's central connection to the "Industrial Invasion" taking place. Ignoring Big Lick's status as an established and thriving tobacco hub, the brochure hyped Roanoke's magical emergence from "cow-pastures" and "vacant lots" to claim the title of "Standard Bearer of Virginia Progress." Moreover, its rapid rise had just begun; investors still had an opportunity to get aboard: "There is much yet to do. Every hotel is full of inquirers with money to invest; with people who want to learn how and where to locate and become a part of this wide-awake population." Existing industries and businesses paid $5,000,000 a year to workers, and although new enterprises were flocking to town, land for factories was available at reasonable prices. Even apparent drawbacks became, in the pamphlet, selling points: the "natural drainage" via "rapid streamlets" was "one of the city's most advantageous attributes" because it removed "the dangers of pollution which lurk in so many populous places"; streets "yet to be perfected" and numerous "vacant spaces" afforded opportunity to mold the town to an investor's liking.[58]

Early the following year, a local real estate firm followed up with *A Synopsis of Roanoke and Her Wonderful Prosperity*, a similar but occasionally more fanciful account of opportunity that awaited Yankee financiers. The city, the guide pointed out, was located "in the center of the finest coal, iron, timber and agricultural region of the world" and offered cheap access to these resources as well as inexpensive labor, abundant land, and extensive rail power. The New South, the pamphlet observed, was "a new land, progressive and cosmopolitan" and welcomed northern investment to unlock "the vastness of her minerals, sleeping in her valleys or glistening on her mountain tops." The booklet likewise pointed to Roanoke's allegedly pastoral origins and brisk development as de facto proof that its future would be one of continued progress, warning readers "unacquainted with the marvelous development of Roanoke" that much of the information offered was "startling as fiction." Indeed, only a few pages into the text the reader had to digest this fact: "There has not been a single failure in real estate investments in Roanoke—unparalleled in the history of the world." Noting that the development of the town "reads more like a Utopian myth than the true history it is," the booklet offered statistics showing that in just eight years real estate values had tripled, $10,000,000 had been invested in local businesses, and the city's population had increased 5,000 percent.[59]

Peyton Terry added the similar "*Roanoke, Virginia in 1891. Its investment opportunities. Its manufacturing advantages. Its transportation services. Its trade facilities. Its home attractions*" to the local booster canon later in the year.[60] Other businessmen in town mounted a newspaper campaign to solicit outside capital. Roanoke's phenomenal growth, they boasted in one full-page ad, made it "The Magic City of the New South." No town in the nation, the ad claimed, had risen faster or offered better opportunities to "people desiring to better their material condition; to capital and men of small means and skilled labor; to manufacturers desiring more ground room and superior facilities."[61] Boosters also began publishing *The Iron Belt*, a monthly journal devoted to manufacturing, railroad, and real estate opportunities in Roanoke and Southwest Virginia.[62] Speeches to local booster clubs echoed the bravado and attacked outsiders' skepticism as "slanderous utterances or woeful anticipations of petty men." The Magic City, one booster proclaimed, might be "taunted by some boastful weakling" but was "smiling at her defamers" and heading "steadily forward to take her place among the industrial centers of the earth."[63]

The various industrial developments prompted a building spurt unlike any the city had previously experienced. Warehouses and commercial enterprises filled up vacant lots downtown, hundreds of houses went up in nearby neighborhoods, and, overlooking the town on the summit of Mill Mountain, the Roanoke Gas & Water Company built an observatory and tourist resort known as the Rockledge Inn. On the Commerce Street lot where the Trout House once stood, investors constructed the Ponce de Leon, a six-story, 120-room hotel named in recognition of the fresh-water spring bubbling up in its basement. It was the tallest building in town until 1892, when work ended on the Terry Building, a seven-story Italianesque office complex. Peyton Terry financed the stone and pressed-brick structure and it housed his Roanoke Trust, Loan & Safe Deposit Company, Henry Trout's First National Bank, and offices for lawyers and land companies.

Local businessmen, like the emerging business leaders in new towns elsewhere in the South, linked further progress for the town to the maintenance of its business-friendly ethos and booster spirit. They pushed for municipal incentives like tax breaks and land bonuses, advocated modernization of their hometown, and sought ways to generate a Victorian social order that would both attract additional investors and knock the rawness off Roanoke's overwhelmingly rural population. Eventually they also followed other emerging southern business leaders and boosters in constructing a self-conscious class: they built Queen Anne mansions on the outskirts of town, joined elite fraternal orders, patronized the Opera House, and formed exclusive business, social, or civic organizations.[64] Henry Trout and Peyton Terry, while the most prominent, were only two of the hundreds of native boosters who courted outside investments, founded businesses, amassed fortunes, and turned Roanoke into the Magic City.

■■■

The same native businessmen who triggered industrial development in the 1880s were also in the vanguard of local real estate speculation. Indeed, Roanoke's land booms were essentially a concomitant of the city's manufacturing developments. The original burst of real estate speculation in the early 1880s died out during the 1883 depression, but by the middle of the decade, a second

1892 Terry Building, corner of Campbell Avenue and Jefferson Street. Norfolk & Western Historical Photograph Collection (NS5805), Digital Library and Archives, University Libraries, Virginia Tech.

"mini boom" was on. The Roanoke Land & Improvement Company was primarily responsible for the recovery. It encouraged speculation in city lots, suggesting that the "rapid development of the town" rendered it a "particularly desirable point" for investment.[65] The firm placed hundreds of residential and commercial tracts on the market, and since it had purchased the land at bargain rates, its mark-up in almost every case exceeded the original price by at least ten times.[66]

To induce sales, the Company sold alternate lots at bargain prices as long as the buyer agreed to build on the property immediately and thus increase the value of plots nearby.[67] Elsewhere in town, the price of real estate skyrocketed. In 1885, for example, one resident sold a tract for $11,000 that he had purchased four years earlier for only $150.[68] Around 1886, however, land values went into a temporary downward spiral, leaving residents with heavy property investments once again in financial ruin. "In no place," the Reverend William Campbell moralized, "is the transitoriness of earthly things better exemplified." The boom had brought some residents wealth, he observed, but to others, "by stimulating their desire for speculation, it has brought disaster."[69]

The real estate bust lasted only until 1888, when the largest speculation frenzy in Roanoke's history began. The city's first historian recalled twenty years later that the era "marked the beginning of a condition of affairs when land companies were organized almost daily, large tracts laid off into town lots, store-houses and dwellings erected in all parts of the city, with speculation in real estate the dominant feature of all business transactions."[70] Real estate companies "sprang up during the boom like mushrooms," according to Henry Trout, and although most of them were simply "get rich quick schemes," investors lined up to pour money into them. "The spirit of speculation was rampant," Trout recalled, "and frenzied finance became the order of the day." Indeed, once the "frenzy" began, many residents even sold their businesses to invest solely in Roanoke real estate.[71] They had reason to, a correspondent from *The New York Times* reported, citing the example of native real estate agent James Simmons, "who, though scarcely 25 years of age yet, has made a fortune out of land in Roanoke within a year or two."[72] "Rawrenoke" was the Indian word for valuable shells, the *Manufacturers' Record* explained, noting "It has certainly developed into 'precious money,' and its industries, its situation, its railroad facilities, all tend to make it a veritable goldmine to the fortunate property holder."[73]

Land booms hit other towns in Southwest Virginia and Appalachia as well, and northern investors flocked to the area to pour millions of dollars into artificially inflated and often ultimately worthless property.[74] In the nearby Town of Salem, land boosters teamed up with Clarence Clark and other northern investors to organize the Salem Improvement Company. The firm dubbed Salem "The Switzerland of the South," advertised the town as "An Ideal Location for a Large City," promised manufacturers free land, and in late 1889, sold 245 lots to speculators for $105,000.[75] Pulaski, Ivanhoe, Richlands, Wytheville, Lexington, and other towns along the N&W also advertised themselves widely as future industrial cities. According to one speculator, even the aged James River Canal town of Buchanan "decided to wake up and proclaim its existence" as an ideal spot for a metropolis. When a train was due in town, he wryly observed, real estate agents crowded the depot and "had their surveys waiting to receive the suckers and sell them town lots."[76]

Elsewhere along the tracks, land companies sold speculators property in villages with no manufacturing infrastructure or in wholly imaginary "paper cities" that never developed. On thirteen thousand acres bordering the hamlet of Buena Vista, for example, the Buena Vista Company, owned partially by E. W. Clark & Company President Clarence Clark, built a hotel, strung up thousands of light bulbs over fields plotted out as neighborhoods, and sold lots on the empty promise that the "city" was destined to become a manufacturing mecca.[77] It was the only place in Virginia, one visitor recalled, "where you could hunt bull frogs by electric light."[78] The most over-hyped and flagrantly under-realized promotion, however, occurred in Rockbridge County, where former Governor Fitzhugh Lee headed a land company that convinced hundreds of investors—including the Duke and Duchess of Marlborough—that a tiny settlement called Glasgow was fated to be the most important industrial town in Virginia.[79]

Real estate booms, a New South editor in Kentucky complained, were comprised primarily of "brandy, printers ink and midnight, and are as fatal to the community to which they are applied as a dynamite shell."[80] Roanoke residents uniformly discounted such warnings, according to one citizen, who suggested that by 1890 so many inhabitants had an "interest" in a land company that "every man is more or less on the order of a land agent."[81] He hardly exaggerated; between 1888 and 1890, 132 land companies opened for business in Roanoke and offered stock to investors.[82] In 1890, after voters approved bonds for the Roanoke & Southern Railway, the frenzy shifted into overdrive with real estate agencies all over town listing hundreds of lots and tracts for sale in local, regional, and national newspapers.[83] "As a field for investment," one local land company boasted, "you can not find a better place in the South or North."[84] Indeed, a rival firm even suggested that "Every investor in Roanoke real estate has made money," while other agencies guaranteed a "handsome fortune" and "invariable large profits" for money ventured on land in the "Great Industrial and Commercial Center of the New South."[85] Those "who would dare dispute the statement that Roanoke is the best field for investment in the South or anywhere else," another company argued, should be "Lynched!"[86]

Most speculators in Roanoke land simply held their property and waited for it to increase in value. As a result, natives profited heavily from sales but saw little actual growth. All the companies bought land fairly cheaply, plotted it into neighborhoods, "reserved" free tracts for industries, erected one or two substantial buildings, marked the property up 50 to 100 percent, and used promotional propaganda to convince speculators that manufacturing establishments and workers were on the horizon. The companies worked hand-in-glove with the local press, which published "puffs" in special real-estate issues that embellished the city's progress, overestimated its population, and inflated future prospects in order to generate buzz for an impending land auction.[87]

Some of the land schemes were outright swindles; others were simply creative in their sales tactics and overly optimistic. The one common denominator, however, was that native businessmen and town boosters were in almost every case the main force behind the ventures. For example, former Big Lick tobacco manufacturer Samuel W. Jamison created the Belmont Land Company; S. S. Brooke of *The Roanoke Leader* organized The Magic City Land Company; furniture store owner E. H. Stewart started the Oak Ridge Land Company; local lawyer Robert H. Woodrum headed the Mountain View Land Company; and several of Roanoke's Jewish businessmen organized the Phoenix Land Company. Other residents put together the Melrose, Hyde Park, Fairview, River View, Virginia, Jefferson, and Creston Land Companies.[88]

Peyton Terry, Henry Trout, local real estate speculator S. W. Jamison, and Crozier Furnace president David F. Houston organized one of Roanoke's largest real estate firms in the summer of 1888. They purchased a tract fifteen blocks west of downtown and formed the West End Land Company to market the property. The company advertised its development as an elite suburb and zoned it exclusively for "good, handsome dwellings." Lots sold briskly, and by 1890, several "tasteful and expensive" Italianesque and Queen Anne mansions, "all embodying those agreeable details of outer shape and interior finish which are now the delight of the modern-home architect," had gone up.[89] Terry, Trout and other "leading citizens" were also responsible for the Crystal Spring Land Company. That firm purchased nearly a thousand acres below Mill Mountain, laid out lots, constructed streets, and built a bridge over the river for extensions of Jefferson Street and the streetcar line. The development, one paper commented, offered further proof that the town was "stretching out in every direction." In the years ahead, it predicted, "South Roanoke will show a remarkable transformation."[90] The firm sold hundreds of lots, but little actual building occurred.

The same thing happened in the southeast area, after longtime Big Lick businessman Mortimer M. Rogers and former Shenandoah Valley Railroad executive James S. Simmons organized the Buena Vista Land Company. They set aside two hundred acres for "manufacturing and business purposes" and laid out the rest of the property for the future homes of workers. The company brochure and map guaranteed those who purchased stock in the venture that they were "virtually investing in the future of the Magic City of the South."[91] Tracts sold briskly, but no industries moved in and few houses went up.

Passage of bonds to fund the Roanoke & Southern Railroad also boosted land sales throughout town, according to the *Roanoke Daily Times*, which reported in February 1890 that "purchasers are coming in from all parts of the country." Locals were offering "bargains" in the papers, on handbills, and in person, and "once it is known that a visitor is here for the purpose of prospecting," the paper observed, "he is certain to receive every attention at the hands of gentlemen in the real estate business."[92] There were still hundreds of speculators wandering around town looking to broker deals the following month, when a *Times* correspondent described Roanoke as "filled with strangers." "The hotels," he reported, "are crowded to their utmost capacity and hundreds of thousands of dollars are changing hands daily."[93]

The Roanoke Land & Improvement Company promised its stockholders in 1882 that they would see a handsome return on their investment. The company summarily used the boom to divest itself of much of its property and residential holdings. In the summer and fall of 1890, it sold twenty-nine rental homes in the Northeast part of town to a speculator from Maryland, a block of lots one street away to investors from Massachusetts, most of its residential property on Railroad Avenue to local businessmen, and eighty-four acres in the southwest to the Pleasant Valley Land Company.[94] Although the Improvement Company had given its "Woodland Park" on a hill in the southeast to the municipal government in the early 1880s, the firm put that tract on the market in the summer of 1890 as well when the city failed to fence the property as it had agreed to do. Former Big Lick tobacco manufacturer Samuel W. Jamison bought the property soon after, and his newly organized Woodland Park Land Company erected a fifteen-foot-tall granite column on the summit of the tract to advertise the development. Named the "Kimball Tower," in honor of N&W president Frederick Kimball, the monument was essentially a glorified "for sale" sign. In addition to installing the tower, Jamison advertised the tract in several northern papers as 150 prime lots "only three and a half blocks from the business center of Roanoke, the great industrial and commercial center of Southwest Virginia." When the park went up for auction, chartered trains from Baltimore, Norfolk, Hagerstown, and Washington, DC brought in hundreds of investors and Jamison more than tripled his initial $60,000 outlay.[95]

The failure of city officials to retain Woodland Park infuriated working-class residents, most of whom had formerly used it as a spot for outdoor recreation, dances, and picnics. They assumed correctly that the municipality, which had no other public parks, was more interested in industrial development than the health and welfare of its residents. "It was reserved for a park," the editor of *The Roanoke Herald* fumed, "and offered free to the City Council, who, for motives of mistaken economy, regarding the expense of development as too great, refused the offer of a property which is today worth a prince's ransom."[96] In the years that followed, however, no actual development of the property occurred. When one lot owner attempted in 1901 to put the first house in the tract, Roanoke's City Engineer rejected his building permit on the basis that the municipality still owned the property. "About the only tangible object, as it now appears," a reporter sardonically observed, "is the lonely monument erected on the summit of Woodland Park."[97]

The land boom reached its height during the Woodland sale but hundreds of properties continued to change hands every week until late December 1890, when an unusually powerful snowstorm halted sales for several days. The three feet of snow that the storm dumped destroyed the Machine Works' blacksmith shop as well as scores of other buildings in town. Hundreds of roofs collapsed, and those that caved in onto woodstoves ignited fires that burned several houses down. The melting snow flooded streets and cellars and according to most reports, when it finally disappeared, the city looked as though it had been shelled and sacked by an invading army. According to several residents, the storm's psychological impact led to widespread reassessment of property values and investments. In the weeks that followed, Henry Trout observed, "our people seemed to have awakened to the fact that the days of inflated values such as they had been going through had passed."[98] The Virginia real estate convention, scheduled long before the snow, opened in Roanoke the following month, and although there may have been signs of disillusionment from native investors, hundreds of out-of-town agents were still

First wagon to reach Roanoke after December 1890 snowstorm. Passengers in back of wagon were visiting from New York City. History Museum and Historical Society of Western Virginia, Roanoke.

eager to get in on the action. "Everywhere within this thriving city are monuments to your energy and wisdom," the president of the convention informed local delegates, "and throughout the commonwealth your brethren glorying in your achievements, wonder at the magic of the magicians who built so wisely and so well this magic city."[99]

The spell they cast, however, was largely an illusion. For while land sales in 1890 topped all previous years, with over $17,000,000 worth of real estate changing hands, sales the next year leveled off, and in 1892 began a free fall that lasted throughout the decade. The Roanoke Land & Improvement Company, which had used a hundred pages of its sales book to log transactions in 1889 and 1890, needed only twenty-five additional pages to list sales from

1891 to 1901. Property assessments, which had risen over 300 percent from 1889 to 1890, also lost ground in the ensuing years. Indeed, by 1900, real estate appraisals had fallen below what they had been in 1890.[100]

Although many residents got out of the market after the big snow, others lost heavily when the boom fizzled in 1892. By then, Henry Trout observed, grass and weeds had covered up the streets that the land companies had laid out and those with stock in the ventures were "left only with a 'certificate' which would not make good wall paper."[101] News of the boom's collapse in Roanoke chilled investments elsewhere in Southwest Virginia, and by the time the 1893 national depression hit, land values in the region had already bottomed out.[102]

The experience of those who invested in the Janette Land Company of Roanoke was typical. Many of them bought Janette stock soon after a Richmond businessman and W. P. Dupuy, a local speculator, organized the firm in the spring of 1890. The company made a down payment on a tract in southwest Roanoke shortly thereafter and then promptly sold over $100,000 worth of the property. Those who owned stock in the venture, its president boasted, would soon see "handsome profits upon their investments."[103] Business in 1891 did not go as planned, however, and the following year the firm notified stockholders that the company was over $50,000 in debt. "The effects of the many 'Land Booms' and their disastrous consequences has been felt in Roanoke city," the company president explained, noting that the market for land was so abysmal that the firm did not deem it worthwhile to foreclose on $70,000 in delinquent mortgages. Stockholders, he forecast, "may have to wait some time before they can realize on their investment, yet the chances are that they will eventually secure all of their input with a handsome profit." Over the next few years, however, the market continued to deteriorate. In 1899, W. P. Dupuy, secretary-treasurer of the firm, called in another 10 percent of stockholders' subscriptions, explaining that the company also owed over $7,000 in unpaid taxes and loan interest. The city was preparing to foreclose on its holdings, Dupuy reported, and mortgage payments "are practically uncollectible at this time."[104]

Richmond businessman Alfred J. Morrison bought two shares of Janette stock in 1890, and over the next thirteen years, he willingly paid 60 percent on his subscription without receiving a single dividend. By 1904, Morrison had had enough and sought legal advice about recouping his investment. The Roanoke lawyer he contacted, however, advised him that a lawsuit would have no merit since the firm "was just one of those cases where the company did not pan out as expected" and the land in question had "decreased in value owing to the collapse of the boom."[105] Secretary Dupuy died later that year, and the executive who replaced him found the firm's records in utter disarray. "The company's receipts," he informed Morrison and other stockholders, "have not been preserved with any ordinary degree of care." Bills going back to 1893 were unpaid, and land books, deeds, and corporate papers were missing. The company, he explained, had determined from court records that it still owned some property and was resolved to sell it, clear its debts, and offer whatever remained as the first return to stockholders.[106]

■■■

Throughout the 1880s and early 1890s, Roanoke's industries thrived and expanded, natives welcomed and solicited additional enterprises, new manufacturing concerns opened for business, and dozens of homegrown industries started operations. While outside investors funded much of the industrial development, natives' booster ethos and entrepreneurial acumen were equally responsible for the growth. Locals drafted the city's business-friendly tax code and compelled the municipality to purchase hundreds of thousands of dollars of stock in local enterprises. Residents owned most of Roanoke's real estate agencies and convinced outside speculators to invest millions of dollars in property in and around town. Although most of the land deals did not result in much actual development, natives reaped huge profits by marketing lots to eager Yankee capitalists. Moreover, almost all of the land purchased did eventually become industrial sites or neighborhoods in the early twentieth century.

Roanoke's emergence as the Magic City brought accolades from the New South press, which cited the town, along with Atlanta and Birmingham, as an example of modernization taking place in the region. Northern journalists continually compared Roanoke, with its heavy industries and distinctly working-class neighborhoods, to a New England mill town, out of place amongst the mountain hamlets and solitary farms dotting the Highland landscape. By 1890, Roanoke was the fourth fastest growing city in the nation and had grown into a town unlike any other in Virginia. It had little in common with Richmond, Lynchburg, Petersburg, or Danville, all of which primarily processed or distributed tobacco or cotton, or with Norfolk and Newport News, where indigenous laborers built ships or worked in the port trade. In Roanoke, skilled northern workers staffed much of the city's railroad, manufacturing, iron, and machine shop industries, and the output of industrial labor was the main source of income. Most other southern cities, by contrast, continued to rely on agricultural processing as their principal business. Virginia's top two commercial commodities up until 1900, for example, were tobacco and gristmill products. Richmond had a small locomotive factory—the only other in operation in the South—but the Roanoke Machine Works was almost solely responsible for railroad-related manufacturing, becoming the fifth most profitable industry in the state by the turn of the century.[107]

The industrialization of Roanoke, which by 1890 had catapulted the town into the forefront of New South cities, would not have been possible

1893 Lineback Studios photograph of Roanoke bankers on steps of Terry Building. Henry S. Trout, first row, second from left. Peyton L. Terry, first row, fourth from left with hound. Tipton T. Fishburn, first row, fifth from left. S. W. Jamison, second row, third from left. J. B. Fishburn, second row, fifth from left. Norfolk & Western Historical Photograph Collection (NW3569), Digital Library and Archives, University Libraries, Virginia Tech.

without the guidance of insiders like Henry Trout and Peyton Terry. Northern capital, while essential to the city's industrial growth, would likely have gone elsewhere had Roanoke's businessmen not skillfully courted it. Indeed, it took a combination of inside business skill and outside capital to create the Magic City. Had either element been absent, Roanoke would likely never have existed or it would have quickly faded away. In 1893, nearly three years after native real estate speculator S. W. Jamison erected the "Kimball Tower" to advertise his Woodland Park land scheme, he had the stark, largely abandoned granite column misleadingly inscribed as "An Industrial Monument to Mark the Progress of the City of Roanoke." In clear recognition that natives and newcomers had made such "progress" possible, Jamison listed himself, Big Lick entrepreneur Peyton Terry, and the N&W's Fredrick Kimball and Joseph Sands as the men responsible for the city's rapid development.

Chapter 4

Life, Work, Culture, and Community

Many Roanoke residents, despite their differing geographical backgrounds and political affiliations, came together in the first decade of the city's existence to advertise their home in ways that attracted new industries and brought accolades from regional boosters. The community as a whole, however, remained deeply fragmented by race and class. New residents arriving in the 1880s added to these divisions and further fomented the development of a city with several clearly demarcated communities and cultures. The Roanoke community was subdivided between white working classes and poor, white upper classes, and African Americans. Gender, of course, informed each of these groups and added yet another dimension to all three. None of these communities and cultures operated in a vacuum; each interacted with the other in positive or negative ways and contributed to the overall ethos of the town. Moreover, specific events or celebrations often led these disparate communities to coalesce. Class and racial divisions did not simply dissolve during these brief mergers, but they did at least temporarily fade enough to generate a sense of municipal identity among most citizens.

■■■

Roanoke's white working classes comprised by far its largest community. By 1890, about nine thousand white newcomers had arrived in Roanoke, and of the city's roughly sixteen thousand total residents, 70 percent were white. Many came to find work as skilled or semi-skilled laborers. There were at least four thousand white males in town of employable age, and by 1891, local industries employed nearly three thousand of them. Sixteen hundred worked for the Roanoke Machine Works; steel and iron furnaces employed about five hundred; rolling mills, bridge works and a carriage factory provided positions for around seven hundred; and at least five hundred labored for the railroad. Another six hundred white males held skilled construction positions as carpenters, painters, or bricklayers. The city's skilled and trade-oriented workers stood atop the local labor pay scale. Machinists in the shops, for example, earned between $2.50 and $6 per day, construction workers earned from $2 to $4 for the same day's work, and railroad workers made about $2 a day. Common or unskilled laborers, by contrast, could, at the very best, hope to earn only about a $1 for a day's toil.[1]

The lack of an indigenous trained labor force meant that most of the city's skilled laborers and their families came from northern factory towns or overseas. Most southern residents, like William Campbell, pastor of the First Presbyterian Church, found the demographic complexity of their home striking. "Roanoke," he explained to a magazine editor in 1886, "is a strange place. Its rapid growth has made it one of the most cosmopolitan of cities. People have floated in from every direction."[2] Nearly ten years later, the situation remained much the same according to railroad executive Malcolm W. Bryan, who told a business associate that Roanoke was "more of a Yankee town than any other in the state."[3]

Most of the city's northern-born industrial workers and their families rented identical, two-story, prefabricated frame cottages that had been shipped in by the Roanoke Land & Improvement Company (RL&IC) and lined up on streets in the Northwest. By 1890, the company had put up at least a thousand dwellings around the machine shops, furnaces, and rail yard. It also opened at least one general store in the working-class neighborhood behind the Hotel Roanoke. Many of the northern transplants joined Saint Andrews, the town's only Catholic Church. In the early 1890s, its congregation replaced their original brick sanctuary with a four-hundred-seat wooden tabernacle. The church added a private school in 1889 and an orphanage in early 1893.[4]

Thousands of other white laborers arrived from nearby rural areas. Most of them found homes or rooms in the western section of the city and filled semi-skilled or non-skilled trades before getting the training needed to join the skilled labor force. Hundreds, for example, moved into housing built by the Roanoke Development Company around the Norwich Lock Works. Julia Via, a widow from Albemarle County, moved her family there in early 1893. One of her sons immediately landed a job at the lock factory. By April, Via had purchased a house nearby and taken in six boarders to help pay the $17 per month mortgage. To further bolster the family income, her youngest son planned to join his brother at the lock works once the school year ended. The contrast between the family farm and Roanoke stunned Via. "You can see more heare in one day," she explained to her sister back in Albemarle County, "than you can thare in a yeare." The city's electric streetcar line, which passed in front of their home, fascinated her: "Thay are cram and packed full and thay go a fliing thru for the big Factory in rite of our house."[5]

While Roanoke had many advantages over the surrounding counties and country towns, not all rural residents who relocated to the city were impressed. One newcomer complained in an anonymous letter to his pastor that although he had left his farm, moved his family to Roanoke, and attempted to make

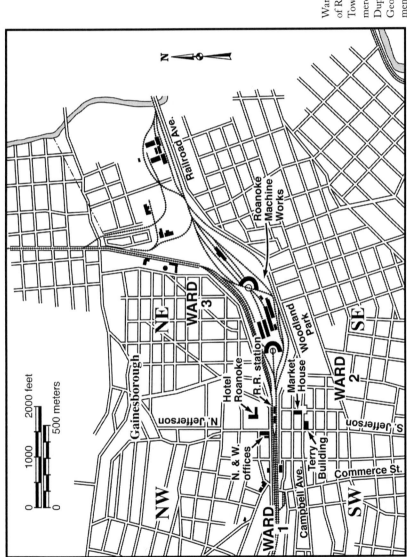

Wards and Sections of Central Area of Roanoke City, early 1890s. Former Town of Big Lick was west of Commerce Street SW. Map by Clifford Duplechin Jr., Cartographic Section, Geography & Anthropology Department, LSU.

an "honest living," he had found it impossible because of "the narrow hearted people of this place." The experience, he explained, had left him entirely disillusioned: "I must say with all candor that the people of Roanoke City are the most narrow minded selfish meanest people that it has been my lot to be cast with. As soon as they get the last cent out of your pocket they think they will ever get then they are ready to let them go to the Devil or any where. But for the suffering of women & children the author of this note would like to see the City of Roanoke burned to the ground the land ploughed up & planted in corn."[6]

Most of the men employed in local industries, skilled or not, frequented the town's numerous saloons when their shifts ended. To them, barrooms were a sanctuary from both their daily industrial environment and their homes—spaces unencumbered by bosses or families, devoted exclusively to male camaraderie, reciprocity, and festivity. Like late-nineteenth-century laborers throughout the nation, they used saloons as an escapist culture rather than an oppositional one, such as a labor union or political party. Roanoke's barroom quarter, like most saloon districts, was an exclusively male territory where cursing, smoking and chewing tobacco, drunkenness, fighting, and general rowdiness were the norm, and into which no "respectable" Victorian female would dare venture. Each barroom in the district had a cadre of loyal regulars, who, based on employment, ethic background, or neighborhood, frequented a particular saloon on an almost daily basis. Indeed, to most patrons, their bar was something akin to a fraternal order or private club, where they could talk with comrades, play cards or billiards, read newspapers, borrow money, cash paychecks, or listen to a pianist or violinist. Along with saloons, the district was also home to male rooming houses, tobacco shops, barbers, bathhouses, and low-cost clothiers.[7]

Barrooms were the quarter's main attraction. By the early 1890s, there were at least fifty-six saloons open for business in downtown Roanoke. Most were crudely constructed wooden shotgun shacks with two-story false fronts, crowded together on or near Railroad Avenue.[8] While a few of the more upscale resorts had tin ceilings, velvet wallpaper, and gas lighting, the majority had stark wooden interiors illuminated by kerosene lamps. Almost all of them had swinging shutter doors, windows cluttered with signs and decorative bottles, counters with foot-rails underneath that ran nearly the length of the front room, and floors covered in sawdust. Several large mirrors, posters, and chromo reproductions of partially clad or nude women often lined the walls behind the bar, along with an assortment of shelves containing various bottles of alcohol. Beer and whiskey were the staples, usually accompanied by assorted bar fare on the house. Most saloons in the quarter, like the White Elephant on Nelson Street, catered to laboring men by providing tobacco, assorted ales on tap for "five cents a schooner," and cold cuts, cheeses, bread,

Railroad Avenue, 1907. From John Nolen, *Remodeling Roanoke: Report to the Committee on Civic Improvement* (Roanoke: Stone Printing & Mfg. Co., 1907).

pickled eggs, potatoes, meat stew, and other complimentary saloon food. Other barrooms offered recreation, novelties, curios, and other attractions. The Rustic, for example, provided billiard tables, while Poteet's & Company on First Avenue had a bowling alley. The Arcadia Saloon on Railroad Avenue had two large owls suspended in a cage from its entrance.[9]

Dozens of saloons in the district offered access to prostitutes who plied their trade upstairs. Indeed, some barrooms, like the Capital Saloon, openly advertised the women with a conspicuous sign denoting "Oysters Upstairs," a well-known euphemism for an upper-floor bordello. Roanoke police, as was the custom, typically only shut down such operations when they became a nuisance. Clandestine gambling dens in the back rooms or upper floors of some of the bars did brisk business as well. Access to the rooms, according to a reporter given a tour of the city's most popular poker establishments, required an elaborate hand "countersign" by patrons. The operators protected the dens so well, he explained, that "any effort on the part of the police to dislodge them has so far proven futile."[10] Although most of the community tolerated orderly gaming houses, a visit by revivalist Sam Jones in 1892 prompted a temporary crusade against illicit gaming. Roanoke was "infested with gamblers," one Evangelical observed, noting that churchgoers "would be surprised at the number of dens in operation here." With Sam Jones's backing, he continued, the time had finally come to stamp out "these gambling hells." Local authorities, however, were far less enthusiastic and did little to stop the operations.[11]

For the most part, the town's upper-class males shunned saloons, preferring to drink in their homes or in private social clubs instead. They tolerated Roanoke's barroom culture as a necessary outlet for workers even though it stood in opposition to the sober, thrifty, family-centered values of the Victorian world they championed. To the city's Evangelicals, however, the saloon quarter represented a dire threat to Roanoke's women, children, and moral purity. Like Evangelicals elsewhere in the nation and especially in the South, they began a successful crusade in the early twentieth century to enact prohibition and end prostitution. By the 1910s, the campaign had closed down the

The Capitol Saloon on Salem Avenue, c. 1906. "Oysters Upstairs" sign in background designates an upper floor brothel. History Museum and Historical Society of Western Virginia, Roanoke.

saloon district and forced the city's working-class men back to their homes and families.[12]

Laboring families had a variety of other inexpensive forms of entertainment available as well. Before it sold Woodland Park, the Roanoke Land & Improvement Company built a pavilion there and organized popular Monday, Wednesday, and Saturday night dances. The Roanoke Machine Works Band, organized in 1883 by Canadians who were employed by the shops, provided the melodies.[13] The RL&IC supervised each dance and promised would-be patrons that "good order will be kept."[14] The sale of the park in 1890, according to *The* (Roanoke) *Daily Bee*, created a "great misfortune" for the town's working classes since it left them with no suitable outdoor recreation space. Parks, much like saloons, served as an outlet for defusing social tensions, and the city's lack of such areas was a concern to business leaders in town. Although *The Daily Bee* pointed this out and begged city officials to fund a new park to "afford some pleasure to the thousands of tied-down men and women," municipal officials allocated no money for the project.[15] As a result, residents looking for outdoor activities mainly walked along the river, strolled around the water company's reservoir at Crystal Springs, or took hikes to the summit of Mill Mountain.

Norfolk & Western employees picnicking in Carr's Woods, early 1890s. Norfolk & Western Historical Photograph Collection (NW3576), Digital Library and Archives, University Libraries, Virginia Tech.

Elsewhere in town, workers and their families found other ways to amuse themselves. A roller skating rink opened downtown in late 1885 and immediately began drawing hundreds of patrons in each night.[16] Strolling along Salem Avenue and Jefferson Street on weekend evenings also emerged as a common pastime. On a summer night in 1890, according to one reporter, six hundred persons passed him in five minutes. "Saturday night," he explained, "is not loafing time for people who work all week. The crowds on the streets do not loiter along, but move with a speed that would make dizzy the visitors from slower going communities."[17] On weekends, according to another correspondent, grifters and quack medicine salesmen operating in vacant lots along Salem Avenue did a brisk trade: "here has congregated a collection of traveling museums, fakers, merry-go rounds and other schemes to beguile the pennies from the pockets of the man who does not know any better." For a nickel, he explained, passersby could even place bets on a mechanical horse race.[18] While most of the games of chance were rigged and almost all the sideshows were faked, these sorts of "lowbrow" entertainment were hugely popular with working classes in Roanoke and throughout the South.[19]

At least some of those who migrated to Roanoke found no work and resorted to begging for survival. The city's position as the junction of two major railroads made it easily accessible not only for those riding in passenger coaches, but also for hundreds of unemployed homeless men and their families who stole rides into town inside boxcars or empty coal hoppers. The practice was not only illegal, it was also dangerous. Accounts of stowaways slipping from hiding spots to be crushed under the wheels of locomotives appeared frequently, and most local reporters showed little sympathy for the unlucky. In one typical story, a writer for the *Roanoke Times* explained that a "negro tramp" who had been run over and killed after he lost his grip on a coal hopper, had died "by his own folly by beating his way on the train."[20]

Other segments of the city's itinerant population arrived on foot or horseback from the surrounding countryside. Whether drawn to Roanoke by the prospect of employment or attracted by its potential as a spot for begging or hustling, most of the town's homeless lived together in camps on the outskirts of the city. In the spring of 1890, for instance, police discovered an encampment of twenty men, women, and children, living in the meadow beside Crozier Furnace. This was not unusual, according to the *Roanoke Daily Times*, which explained that "For a long time the grove opposite the furnace has been the camping place for all the wandering tribes of gypsies that pass this way, and there is a band of nomads nearly always there."[21] Residents showed little sympathy for vagrants in their midst. The following summer dozens of passersby left a gravely ill black drifter lying incapacitated alongside the road for several days before police finally carted him off to the Alms House.[22]

Most "tramps" passing through town were little more than a harmless nuisance. Some, however, resorted to aggressive tactics to solicit money or food. In the fall of 1890, for example, residents reported that a large "gang of toughs" living in the woods around east Roanoke had been stopping carriages by grabbing horses by their bridles. The "toughs" would then beg for money.[23] Police eventually drove that group away, but others quickly took their place. A few months later, residents living near the Roanoke Stockyards complained that dozens of "tramps" had been so "boisterous" and making such "violent threats" when denied charity that the entire neighborhood was afraid to go out after dark. The vagrants, according to one reporter, had a camp nearby and on cold nights slept among the livestock inside the stables. Moreover, he explained, "They utilize the cow heads thrown from slaughter houses near

Tinker Creek by roasting them for food."[24] Other transients escaped the cold by sleeping near piles of warm slag beside furnaces. The warmth, however, was also potentially hazardous since dozing vagrants occasionally were subject to red-hot slag dumped on them.[25]

■■■

A much smaller portion of Roanoke's white residents formed its upper classes. The city's elite whites came from two distinct groups. One was composed of longtime, indigenous families like the Trouts or Terrys and the other consisted of northern newcomers connected to the Clark Company or other industries. In spite of political and religious differences, native and newcomer elites meshed easily into a single, unified class. The only real difference between them was that each lived in a different section of the city. Native upper classes tended to reside in the southwest or in the West End, while Yankee executives and professionals typically had Queen Anne mansions in the southeast or on Orchard Hill. Most of the newcomers arrived from Philadelphia or other northeastern cities, and all of them transplanted a sophisticated, urbane culture to what must have seemed to them like a primitive industrial outpost. Indeed, their presence left a distinct imprint on the city's elite society by prompting it to move more quickly into long-established northeastern forms of bourgeois culture.

Early on, many of the northern transplants lived at the Hotel Roanoke before deciding to build permanent homes in the city. Malcolm W. Bryan, a Shenandoah Valley Railroad executive and superintendent of its real estate and development subsidiary, moved to the hotel from Philadelphia in the spring of 1883. Bryan lived there for the next two years, and after he married his Philadelphia fiancée, Ann DeHaven, the couple moved into a two-room suite. Before DeHaven arrived, Bryan attempted to prepare his privileged bride-to-be for their lodgings, complaining in one missive that the carpets were "abominable" and the ceiling was in such wretched condition that he had demanded the hotel replace it.[26] Life at the hotel, he cautioned, was extremely public and fraught with potential for discomfiture: "Remember love, we mustn't do any billing or cooing before people. Hotels are gossip shops." On the positive side, Bryan explained, Roanoke, even in its primitive stages, was much safer than most of Philadelphia. He never bothered to lock his door, he told DeHaven, because "in this part of the world there are no thieves, housebreakers or tramps."[27] Once the couple moved in, they resided in the hotel until workers finished their Queen Anne mansion "Oak Hurst" near Orchard Hill in the southwest.

Although the children of Roanoke's working classes and blacks had limited educational options, wealthy parents could choose from a variety of private educational institutions in the city. Mrs. Gilmer's Finishing School for Young Ladies, which began classes in the fall of 1886, had over seventy students by the early 1890s.[28] That same year, the National Business College opened, as did the Alleghany Institute, a private boys' school operated by the Valley Baptist Association. The Institute used the former Rorer Park Hotel and its six acres of grounds on upper Campbell Avenue as its campus.[29] Roanoke College, in Salem, and Hollins Institute, a women's college in Roanoke County, also offered higher education facilities nearby. Moreover, in early 1893 the president of the Wesleyan Female Institute in Staunton, Virginia, picked Roanoke as the location for the Virginia College for Young Ladies. The institution, which purchased ten acres in South Roanoke for its campus, was, according to *The Roanoke Times,* the "crowning ornament" for the city as well as a facility that would make the town "a far more desirable place of residence."

By summer, the college had finished a four-floor pavilion of classrooms, chapel, and forty-five dorm rooms. It had also hired twenty-five faculty members.[30] The school recruited over a hundred boarding students as well as numerous day scholars and, according to its president, planned to offer a "progressive" educational experience so that each student would get "a course of study best fitted to her natural tendencies and future vocation."[31] As a result, that fall its academic offerings included Reading, Geography, English, History, Astronomy, Chemistry, Greek, Latin, and French, as well as "finishing" courses like Speech Elocution, Moral Philosophy, Harmony, Guitar, and Calisthenics.[32] The college's inaugural 1893–94 session, according to a local railroad official, was "a most phenomenal success." The school, he reported, was "full to its utmost capacity" and had a student body that included "the nicest girls in Roanoke," all of whom "go out in the electric car every morning."[33]

The city's elite classes found a variety of ways to entertain themselves while simultaneously delineating their status. They ignored working-class forms of entertainment such as saloons, bowling allies, street fairs, and skating rinks, preferring instead to confine themselves to a select group of exclusive events, societies, and organizations. Although upper classes held private social functions in their homes, it was not until the summer of 1883 that the town's "most prominent and best known citizens" staged what *The Roanoke Leader* described as "the first social entertainment ever given in Roanoke"—a dance at the Rorer Park Hotel with music provided by the Red Sulfur Springs Quadrille.[34] Another "hop," "gotten up by a committee of gentlemen," followed two weeks later with music by the newly formed Roanoke Machine Works Band. The waltzing, one attendee boasted, "was kept up in a lively manner until nearly 1 o'clock A.M."[35]

Until later in the decade, the town's single males outnumbered its females. For upper-class white men, most of whom arrived from Philadelphia or other northern cities to work for the Clark Company, an acute lack of eligible elite females compounded the overall gender imbalance. In December 1883, fifteen men attempted to remedy the problem by creating the Roanoke German Club, a dancing society that "imported" single, upper-class females from other cities. The bachelors supplied their dates' railroad tickets and rooms at the Hotel Roanoke and held their elaborate dinners and formal dances in the hotel's ballroom. The first affair, according to *The Leader,* was the "most brilliant and 'recherché' society event that has yet occurred in our city." The dance was chaperoned by the wives of three railroad officials and featured melodies supplied by the Roanoke Machine Works "Orchestra," which, the paper observed, "we are glad to say, has improved very much in their dance music."[36]

The club's membership expanded throughout the decade, and its monthly gatherings at the Hotel Roanoke always received prominent and extensive coverage from the local press. In a typical example from the fall of 1889, the *Roanoke Daily Times* put its account on the front page under the headline: "A Gay and Gallant Assemblage; Beautiful and Elaborate Costumes; Music and Feasting Contribute to Pleasures of Occasion." The paper praised the genteel residents who were responsible for such a sophisticated affair and described in detail the guests, decorations, menu, dances, and toasts.[37]

As the balls grew ever more decorous, they began to feature orchestras from Richmond, "favors" from New York, and refreshments from Philadelphia. Dinners were often served at tables decorated with pyramids of fruit and consisted of multiple courses featuring oysters, iced bouillon, fried smelt, tongue galantine, diamondback Maryland terrapin, quail, lobster, and champagne. The society required each participant to arrange dance partners in advance using a special card printed for the affair, and it limited dancing to polkas, gavottes, and waltzes. The spectrum of women who attended the gatherings grew more cosmopolitan as well, and by the late 1880s, it was common for several of the females to have arrived from New York or Philadelphia. They were often accompanied by their own chaperones, and before departing the following afternoon, they were treated to a "morning German" and elegant luncheon.[38]

"Active" membership in the club was limited to sixty-five bachelors, strictly circumscribed to genteel, young professionals or white-collar workers "of good moral and social standing," and open only to those whom the association approved via a unanimous vote. The club's rules prohibited invitations to non-member males and stipulated that even members had to present their special invitation to get in. Their doorman barred latecomers and those not in "full dress attire." The society banned bachelors from frequenting the second floor of the hotel, preventing even the hint of impropriety with their dates' upstairs lodging. A "floor manager" supervised dance cards and prevented members from "stealing in" (i.e., cutting in) by stopping the music until the offender returned to his seat. The association made "stags" sit out half the dances, and it fined or expelled anyone guilty of violating the rules. In 1891, forty-six of the club's sixty-three active members had listings in the city directory. These included twelve railroad clerks, eight lawyers, six bank clerks or cashiers, four real estate agents, four druggists, two contractors, two managers, two drafts-men, a railroad executive, an architect, an engineer, an insurance agent, and a banker. Twenty-eight of the bachelors lived in the southwest, eight in the Hotel Roanoke, three in other hotels, six in the southeast, and one in the West End. None resided in the Northeast, the city's working-class district. The sixty "contributing" (i.e., married) members were among the city's most successful businessmen, and included Peyton Terry, Henry Trout, S. S. Brooke, Lucian Cocke, and several Norfolk & Western executives.[39]

Although the German Club's members and their dates or wives were among the city's most elite, proper, and respectable residents, in early 1893 William Campbell and other ministers invited concerned citizens to a debate about the morality of the group. In the deliberations that followed, one pas-tor testified that the German Club "originated in the slums of the bawdy houses of France" while another claimed it was "the origin of degeneracy." Afterwards, those in attendance unanimously approved having their minis-ters draft a proclamation calling for the disbandment of the club. Published in local papers the following day, Roanoke's clergy explained that, "Whereas the dance known as the german cultivates immodesty and tends to produce immorality, therefore it be resolved that as ministers of the gospel we will do all in our power to induce the people under our instruction to desist from this hurtful amusement."[40] The appeal, however, had no apparent affect on the German Club, which only four days later held its monthly dance. The affair, according to one paper, was "The Event of the Season" where "Mirth and music reigned supreme." Roanoke's "society circles" turned out in droves and, the paper explained, "beautiful women and their gallant knights entered into the spirit of the occasion and enjoyed themselves to the utmost."[41]

William C. Noland, chairman of the German Club's executive commit-tee, was a typical "active" member. He grew up in Hanover County, Virginia, earned an architecture degree, and worked for firms in New York City and Philadelphia before relocating to Roanoke to begin his own architecture prac-tice.[42] When Noland arrived in early 1891, the city's real estate market and businesses were booming. This, coupled with a shortage of architects, made the town the perfect place to launch his career. Having secured long-term lodging at the Hotel Roanoke, Noland rented a room downtown for his busi-ness and placed ads for his services in local papers. His office in the Commer-cial Bank Building, he told his mother, was "right in the middle of things," and staying at the hotel made good business sense, he explained, because it was "the headquarters for the northern fellows with money."[43]

Within a week, Noland had used his Philadelphia connections to arrange a visit with Clark Company executive Frederick Kimball, who gave him a letter of recommendation to present to Joseph Sands, the general manager of the Norfolk & Western. Roanoke's land boom was in full swing, Noland told his mother, and he was attempting to "gradually learn which way the town is likely to build" before soliciting real estate firms for business.[44] The contact with Kimball paid off a few days later when W. W. Coe, an N&W executive, hired the young architect to design and supervise a small addition to his home on Orchard Hill. The job and the city's boom ethos were enough to make the decision to relocate look fantastic. "Oh!" he exclaimed in his next letter home, "This is a great town."[45] Noland was already convinced that there were "lots of chances for making 3 or 4 dollars for one" in real estate and was trying desperately to come up with sufficient funds for a substantial investment in a land company.[46]

During the next month, however, Noland landed no new clients. He nevertheless hired a "muddy-footed white boy" to sweep his office and maintain its coal-fired stove.[47] There were some good prospects on the horizon, he informed his mother, and a few of them would assuredly "be ripe before long."[48] In the meantime, Noland continued to make contacts around town. One new acquaintance invited him to a "very good" supper party at the hotel that included "wild duck, done to a turn & terrapin etc. & washed down with 2 quarts of Mum's extra dry." He also helped found "a club of engineers and architects."[49] Although over the following month he again failed to find any clients and had to let his office boy go, Noland entered a design for the new Roanoke Hospital and felt good about his chances for getting the contract. In the meantime, he told his mother, he was running out of money, had yet to receive payment for work on the Coe house, and needed a loan.[50]

Noland formulated his entry for the hospital job from seventeen pages of notes taken during extensive interviews with local doctors. The plans he drew up included their suggestions about hallways, laundry rooms, "water closets," heating, and even storage for patients' clothing. The hospital, one physician told him, was only going to have patients "that get well or die in a reasonably short period of time" and would therefore not need a separate dining room for each ward. It would need to have, however, a segregated "colored dining room" as well as an isolated ward for all black patients. Noland's research paid off when the committee of doctors and businessmen behind the Roanoke Hospital Association met. They were so impressed with his design that they decided to take a chance on the untested architect.[51] A few days later, Noland won the superintendent job on a new Episcopal church and the Roanoke Development Company hired him to draw plans for the Norwich Lock Works factory.[52]

Socially, things looked to be picking up for Noland as well. He helped build a tennis court behind the Hotel Roanoke using chicken wire for the net, and he and a group of other lodgers had begun playing there regularly. Even more importantly, he informed his mother, "some regular society girls" had checked in: "Two Misses Pechins of Cleveland who have been nearly everywhere. So there are enough to make a crowd."[53] A month later, however, Noland sadly confessed that he had been far more socially active in Philadelphia and had "hardly any friends here to write about." "Roanoke," he explained, "is unsatisfactory to me socially, so far, but I hope to become better informed as to the lay of the social land and then find congenial spots here and there." On the other hand, single women in his new home had very few elite bachelors from which to choose, creating a dramatic contrast between "the social advantages of a place like this and an old wealthy town like Philadelphia." Noland, too conceited to appreciate the two most recent gatherings he had attended, told his mother that he felt nothing but disdain for his fellow guests and hosts:

> I found the ladies surrounded by many young men who don't suit my taste. The ladies are, I dare say, as smart and so forth naturally as any; but the conversations, which were naturally general were not interesting and the assemblages were so cosmopolitan that I felt not at all honored in being invited. I hope I am not a snob; but I have been knocking about and met enough people to know that I prefer those who have inherited enough good blood and been brought up among enough well bred and highly honorable ladies and gentlemen to make them exclusive in their acquaintances and certainly in their intimate friends.[54]

By summer, the collapse of Roanoke's real estate boom had diminished Noland's economic outlook and led some clients, including the Norwich Lock Works, not to pay him "with the promptness" he expected. The one prospect at hand, he told his mother, was the "colored pastor of the negro church" who had inquired about a design for a new sanctuary. The job would bring in some needed funds, he explained, especially since he required African American clients "to be more prompt in paying me than the whites."[55] In addition, the Federal Government planned to build a new post office in Roanoke, and Noland, who had passed the Civil Service architecture exam a few years earlier and worked as chief assistant on the Philadelphia City Hall project, believed his chances for the job were excellent. The only problem, he explained, was that there was another young architect in town who was a staunch Republican, and with patronage in the hands of the Harrison administration, party affiliation could make a difference.[56]

By then, the summer social season was in full swing, and Noland, like most other privileged residents, frequented springs in the area to escape the heat and dust of the city.[57] Indeed, after a visit to Blue Ridge Springs, he told his mother that most of the society crowd "stay there in the summer and come to Roanoke every day."[58] Earlier that year, Noland moved to a boarding house and quickly become friends with John Payne, a fellow boarder and bachelor. The two young men traveled the circuit of local springs, often renting rooms at each one for several days. That August both were invited to a "morning German" at Alleghany Springs, but only Payne accepted. The idea of "dancing in the high noon of an August day," Noland informed his mother, was far too decadent and unseemly for him.[59] Noland instead arrived at the springs a few days later to visit the Howards, family friends from Richmond. Their daughter Annie, he explained, was flirtatious and beautiful, and had been his date at several Germans there. Annie was among dozens of eligible women staying at the springs for the summer. Indeed, there were so many that Noland asked his mother to send his younger brother for a visit so he could "look the field over and we can see what can be done."[60]

In the fall, Noland and Payne entered a tennis tournament in Salem, and, he reported, they were going to a "big German" the night before. Noland, who wanted to leave early and get some rest, had not intended to take a date but had asked "a Miss Harrison of New York" if she had an engagement, "supposing, of course, that she had," and found himself with "a very sweet partner and perhaps a good dancer; but I'll feel worse on Tuesday than I should like at the tournament."[61] The German lasted until four in the morning, and Noland left for Salem only a few hours later. "We arrived," he told his mother, "just in time for me to change my clothes and get a good licking at tennis."[62]

Although most local businesses had suffered from the collapse of the land boom, according to Noland there had still been "great additions and improvements in the town" since he had arrived ten months earlier. He nevertheless was having trouble finding a steady stream of clients and had to admit to his family that "I am only managing to make buckle and tongue meet; but that is something."[63] He contacted local Democrats concerning the post office commission, and although they and Senator Edward Daniel wrote letters in his favor, the contract went to his Republican competitor. On the bright side, the Roanoke Development Company gave him a job that December to draw plans for a combination company store and boarding house near the Norwich Lock Works "to be built of wood & be as cheap as possible."[64] Moreover, early the following year after Noland partnered with Horace de Saussure to create Noland & de Saussure Architects, the backers of the city's new Academy of Music hired the men to design their venue.[65] Despite these successes, however, Noland eventually decided to relocate to Richmond and become a partner in another firm. During his Richmond career, he went on to design numerous prestigious projects, including the Jefferson Davis Memorial on Monument Avenue, the

Crystal Springs reservoir in south Roanoke, 1898. Charlotte Gale
Dryden Photograph Album (CWGALE0022), Digital Library and
Archives, University Libraries, Virginia Tech.

Eastern State Mental Hospital, Mary Baldwin College's McClung Hall, and
Richmond's St. James Episcopal Church.[66]

As Noland's example illustrates, Roanoke's elite residents socialized in
a variety of ways, but always within the circumscribed limits of Victorian
decorum and usually entirely within the relatively small cadre of local upper
classes. Like successful businessmen and their families in places such as
Atlanta or Nashville, the city's upper classes created or patronized institutions
that certified and advertised their status. Participation in the New South's
"social circles" required more than money; it was essential to live in the right
neighborhood, belong to the correct clubs, associations, and charity organizations, fraternize only with fellow elites, and attend only the most refined
entertainments. Roanoke's upper classes, although from two geographically
distinct backgrounds, were no different, and in the 1880s and 1890s, they sub-
tly created their own exclusive world away from the city's working classes and
blacks. They lived in Queen Anne or Italianesque mansions in specific neighborhoods, formed select social organizations, belonged to professional societ-

ies, attended only private educational institutions, established or belonged to numerous charities, and patronized only "highbrow" culture.[67]

One of the most obvious ways that the city's elites separated themselves and celebrated their class was by staging elaborate and exclusive parties at their mansions. The city's press, always on the lookout for ways to prove that Roanoke was not a raw and unsophisticated "hick town," gave the affairs prominent and detailed coverage. *The Roanoke Leader*, for example, put an account on its front page of "an early English tea" hosted by Mrs. and Miss Terry at their Elmwood estate. Candles illuminated the grounds, its reporter observed, a choir provided melodies, and the one hundred guests, "all attired in handsome party costumes," experienced "an evening of rare enjoyment, and one never to be forgotten by anyone present."[68]

At another society event—a "drive whilst" party held in a "spacious mansion" on Mountain Avenue—a correspondent from the *Roanoke Daily Times* reported that an Italian band stationed on the landing of the stairway greeted the dozens of couples who attended. "Among the numerous handsome entertainments given in our social circles during the season just closing," he explained, "this one will be remembered always."[69] Other members of the upper class staged fêtes that were even more creative. Ferdinand Rorer, for instance, held a "boating party" on the Roanoke River. Rorer had six boats built for the occasion and hired the Machine Works Band to play on the banks of the stream. The multi-colored boats, according to *The Leader*, "glided over the bright, clear waters, freighted with happy couples, whose joyous laugh mingled with the notes of music, presenting a scene that was indeed fairy tale like."[70] Another group of wealthy locals held a jousting tournament and ball. "Knights" taking part in the affair paraded down Salem Avenue to the baseball grounds where M. C. Thomas, "Knight of Roanoke," won the competition. Afterwards the "knights" and their "ladies," decked out in medieval costumes, dined on a midnight feast at the Hotel Roanoke and danced until two in the morning.[71]

Many of Roanoke's elites made expeditions to McAfee's Knob, an outcropping of boulders at the summit of a nearby mountain. The spot, unlike Mill Mountain above the city, was far enough away to prevent easy access by the less wealthy, which made it the ideal location for elaborate picnics and camping trips. The journey to the top, even on horseback, was sometimes too much for the city's "delicate" ladies to endure. On one Fourth of July outing, for example, nine of the fourteen women on the excursion dropped out and missed the "scene of beauty and grandeur" that the others witnessed "spread out beneath them."[72]

Although access to Mill Mountain was open to all in town, in 1891 the Roanoke Gas & Water Company, which had acquired the property from the RL&IC, moved to turn it into the exclusive domain of elites. That summer,

Strollers on the path to the summit of Mill Mountain. From Mill Mountain Incline Company, "Views about Mill Mountain and the Incline Railway" (Roanoke: Stone Printing & Mfg. Co. 1910).

it hired a contractor to build a $10,000 hotel and $2,000 observatory on the summit of the peak, nine hundred feet above the city.[73] When completed, the Rockledge Inn featured broad verandas, stone fireplaces, a rustic dinning area, tennis and croquet courts, a four-story observation tower, and a private coach that ran from the depot to the top of Mill Mountain. At the formal opening in the spring of 1892, guests included Clark Company executives Frederick Kimball and Clarence Clark as well as local luminaries Henry Trout, Peyton Terry, Lucian Cocke, and Doctor Joseph Gale. The Inn was impressive, and local papers were quick to predict that during the upcoming summer "the city will flee to the mountain for relief."[74] The hotel, with its "magnificent view and delicious cool breezes" did indeed quickly became a popular "dinner and dancing resort," albeit one with an exclusively elite clientele.[75]

Although the city's privileged classes could choose from a variety of traveling entertainers who performed at venues around town until the early 1890s, Roanoke's theaters lacked the highbrow performances and ornate aesthetic that clearly set them apart as elite space until a group of local businessmen funded the Academy of Music. Initially, Rorer Hall—Roanoke's first seat of government—served as the town's only entertainment venue and featured acts like Signor Bosco the "famous wizard," or "Night in Wonderland," a traveling stereopticon exhibition. General admission for each show was only thirty-five cents, and even "reserved seats" cost just fifty cents, which allowed a wide spectrum of

Roanoke Machine Works Band at Rockledge Inn on summit of Mill Mountain. Norfolk &
Western Historical Photograph Collection (NW4157), Digital Library and Archives, University Libraries, Virginia Tech.

residents to attend.[76] In the spring of 1886, the city rented out the upper floor of its new Market House to a theater manager who named it the "Opera House." The venue rarely offered entertainment befitting its pompous title. More often than not, it was the site for shows such as "Sun's New Phantasma and Refined Novelty Company," which featured the "black arts" along with a "miniature carnival."[77] The first floor of the Opera House was a farmers' market and butcher shop, and by day, the square around it was crowded with venders hawking produce. The venue itself was relatively unadorned and indecorous with undifferentiated seating that placed different classes and races in close proximity.

While the city's upper classes patronized the Opera House, they eventually sought ways to create a more refined and segregated performance space. In late 1890, a group that one paper called "the most prominent men in Roanoke" organized a joint stock company to fund construction of a $95,000 Academy of Music on Salem Avenue, several blocks away from the congested and filthy Market Square.[78] The Academy, while built to create an upper class venue, also advertised Roanoke's lofty cultural ambitions and civic spirit to potential investors.[79] When completed, it had seats for fifteen hundred patrons, electric lighting, marble floors, an interior designed by Monsieur Horace de Saussure—"a French artist of celebrity"—and a dome that rose eighty feet above the street. Along with eight "private boxes" for the city's most well-to-do citizens, the Academy also had a small upper "second gallery" for blacks with a separate rear doorway and no access to any other part of the building. Performances typically consisted of opera, classical music, and sophisticated dramas, but it also served as the venue for dozens of noted speakers, including Thomas Nelson Page, whose spring 1892 reading from *Marse Chan* and interpretation of "the old-time Virginia plantation negro" delighted a packed house of the "leading people of Roanoke."[80] Patrons who chose not to use their own carriages to get to the Academy had complete access to the city's electric streetcar system, which reserved all its cars exclusively for the Academy on performance nights.[81]

The original Opera House, taken entirely out of the market for sophisticated entertainment, turned exclusively to vaudeville and burlesque acts. At one such event in the fall of 1892, a newspaper correspondent reported that scantly clad dancers had performed to a sold out house: "Miss Mattie Lockette the young and talented soubrette, made a great hit with her electric dance, as did Miss Lidia Payne in her tambourine dance. Miss Virgie Arnold in the whirlwind dance also won much applause."[82] Burlesque, while wildly popular with the city's working classes, drew a torrent of criticism from ministers and Evangelicals, who castigated the performances as indecent, immoral, and debased. Municipal authorities, however, did little to restrain or end the shows.[83]

Upper-class residents also distanced themselves from other inhabitants by forming exclusive societies and organizations. By the early 1890s, most of them belonged to at least one club or fraternal order, and many were members of several. Although Roanoke, *The Times* observed, was a "humming, hustling city" with an exceedingly busy population, "the incessant business tensions can not be forever kept up." As a result, the paper explained, "there are to be found in Roanoke many social and intellectual organizations whose aims and purposes are to engage in short hours of pleasure and profit which does not detract from the business qualifications of their members, but only enables them to work better when returning to their routine duties."[84] The city had a Confederate Veterans Association as well as a chapter of the Grand Army of the Republic, four Masonic Lodges, a Knights of Honor, Pythias, and Mystic Chain, a Royal Arcanum Society, a chapter of the Patriotic Sons of America, and several other fraternal orders and secret societies. By the mid-1890s, nineteen such clubs with roughly fifteen-hundred members operated in the city.[85] Other organizations, like the West End Social Club, served solely as dinner party vehicles, while still others, like the Shakespearean Literary Society, the Rorer Park Literary Society, St. Andrews Society, and Clover Club offered outlets for what one paper described as "the most literary, intellectual and accomplished people in Roanoke."[86] The Caecilian Musical Society, a two-hundred-member chorus, performed regularly at the Academy of Music to a packed house, and eventually even sought to enlighten the city's uncouth rural neighbors by offering reduced admission for "friends in the country."[87]

In the spring of 1892, dozens of elite young men in town organized the Roanoke Athletic Club.[88] The group constructed a gymnasium for its members, and in the fall, it fielded a football team, albeit with players who averaged only a hundred and forty-five pounds and were mostly over thirty years old. That Thanksgiving, the Athletic Club played a team from Bluefield in front of a crowd of five hundred that included numerous society ladies. "In the matter of sports," one paper observed, "Roanoke is not behind other progressive cities and celebrated Thanksgiving after the most approved fashion." The game ended in a zero to zero tie, and both teams celebrated at an elaborate

The Rambler Bicycle Club of Roanoke, early 1890s. Norfolk & Western Historical Photograph Collection (NW4205), Digital Library and Archives, University Libraries, Virginia Tech.

dinner and ball at the Hotel Roanoke.[89] Later that fall, the club introduced "Basket Ball," a game it believed "resembles football."[90]

Other elite residents organized professional associations that offered social benefits as well as certification of credentials. A move toward professionalism swept the nation around the turn of the century, and Roanoke proved no exception. In 1889, for instance, physicians there organized the Roanoke Medical Society. The organization allowed only "ethical" doctors to join and blacklisted "physicians" it deemed improperly trained or incompetent.[91] In an effort to standardize prices, the group also established minimum rates for all medical services. The move, however, enraged the city's working classes. The day after doctors published the new pay scale, hundreds of laborers attended a mass meeting to protest fees that they considered "exorbitant and beyond the reach of the average workingman." They also all agreed to patronize only physicians who were not members of the Medical Society, which meant that many of them turned exclusively to Dr. H. A. Sims, a "Master Workman" in the local chapter of the Knights of Labor.[92] Although the controversy eventually led to the downfall of the organization, most of its former members established the Roanoke Valley Medical Association in the spring of 1891.[93] The group evaluated the "character" of all local doctors and barred members from any contact with those it deemed "irregular" or "not in good professional standing."[94] It again established standard minimum fees for services, setting, for example, a $5 minimum charge for amputation of fingers and toes and a $10 minimum on hands and feet.[95]

In addition to literary or recreation clubs, Roanoke's privileged women mirrored elite females around the nation with an interest in forming church-related charity organizations. Most denominations in the city had a "Ladies Aid Society" that was in charge of fundraising activities or a female "Missionary Society" responsible for soliciting donations for religious fieldwork.[96] In the midst of the 1883 national depression, however, the town's Evangelical women organized a "Ladies Union Benevolent Society" (LUBS) so that they could "aid the afflicted poor of our community."[97] The women held several "lawn parties" to raise the money, and eventually donated clothing and provisions to families it deemed to be "worthy persons in our midst."[98] Ongoing assistance from the Benevolent Society and various other female aid groups inevitably brought members into close contact with the city's working classes and African Americans, and while generally all three groups mediated these exchanges without difficulty, the contact sometimes brought class tensions to the surface, especially when those requesting aid did not measure up to elite notions of the "deserving poor."

That was certainly the case during an extended cold spell in early 1893, when members of the LUBS teamed with the "Circle of Charity of the King's Daughters" (CCKD) to distribute aid to "the suffering poor."[99] *The Roanoke Times*, which reported that the frigid conditions had "suspended all outside work and hundreds are out of work who depend on mild weather for a living," donated its building as the group's drop-off point for food and fuel. The aid, the women told the paper, was intended exclusively for the "worthy poor," meaning only those who were out of work due to cold weather.[100] Although most of the candidates for assistance resided in east Roanoke's working-class neighborhoods, finding the correct destitute families, according to the ladies, was difficult because the "worthy poor are cautious even in their indigence." Indeed, according to Miss Josephine Woltz of the CCKD, while there were scores of hard-working families living in "absolute destitution" and not requesting aid, there had been numerous calls for assistance made by "mothers who are burdened by indolent husbands." A representative of the LUBS concurred, but conceded that "When there are cases of old age and little children to be provided for, we cannot refuse our aid, even if the head of the family is unworthy."[101]

Many of those rejected for aid turned to illegal means for survival. Some raided N&W coal hoppers for fuel, while others resorted to tearing up wooden boardwalks or fencing.[102] Donations flooded into *The Roanoke Times*, and within a few days, ministers convinced Mayor Henry Trout to use the city's resources to systematize distribution of the aid. Trout appointed Josephine Woltz, who had "been at the front of all charitable efforts in Roanoke for ten years," to head that effort. While municipal officials thereafter put businessmen in charge of soliciting future donations, they left the LUBS and CCKD responsible for investigating all requests for assistance. According to reporters, there were numerous "charity fakirs" to contend with, including two "warmly clad and buxom" black females who allegedly tried to fake a claim of illness as well as another woman, known widely as "a premium fakir," who had "worked three separate half ton orders of coal within thirty-six hours."[103]

By the end of the month, the LUBS and CCKD claimed to have done all they could to distribute aid and alleviate the "sufferings of the poverty stricken." The ladies, according to *The Times,* had done fine work but had been grossly imposed upon by local blacks: "Many able bodied negroes have applied for help, and through sick tales obtained provisions, clothing and fuel. Some of this class are very hard to please, and desire such delicacies as cheese, canned goods and tea, saying that they can't eat common rations." Whites too, the paper went on, were not above faking hardship and many, it explained, "seem to think that the gates of an inexhaustible bounty have been opened up and they are free to take to their heart's content."[104] The abuse by "unworthy people," according to Woltz, had turned the campaign into such a "farce" and "perfect nuisance" that the ladies had decided to end their involvement.[105] The extreme weather and deluge of requests, she explained, had prevented the women from investigating all the applicants, and in her estimation, only about half of the 156 white families and 129 African American households who received aid actually deserved it.[106]

■■■

Blacks living in Roanoke made up the city's second largest community. By 1890, over four thousand African Americans had migrated to Roanoke. As a result, the city's population was about 30 percent black. Most of the town's African Americans lived on the outskirts of the city, to the north of RL&IC's

neighborhoods, either in what had been the Town of Gainesborough (later shortened to Gainesboro), or in the northwest along Rutherford and Harrison Avenues, or around Tenth Avenue in a neighborhood known as "Peach and Honey." Others resided in the northeast to the north of Madison Avenue, in a neighborhood called "Possum Trot." Some black housing also existed south of the RL&IC neighborhood in the northwest along sections of Henry Street, High Street, and Centre Avenue. Almost no African Americans lived in the southwest or downtown.

Although the city's blacks lived in no distinct single neighborhood, no matter where they resided, they generally lived in clusters along entire blocks

African American neighborhoods, northwest Roanoke, 1907. From John Nolen, *Remodeling Roanoke: Report to the Committee on Civic Improvement* (Roanoke: Stone Printing & Mfg. Co., 1907).

with no whites housed in between. This phenomenon mirrored patterns of African American housing throughout the urban South, as did the fact that black homes in Roanoke were generally inferior to those of whites. Black neighborhoods were usually the last to receive public services like running water, gas lighting, or paved streets, and black residences were located in areas that whites deemed uninhabitable because of their distance from downtown or because they were in low-lying areas or close to polluted streams. Like their poor white counterparts in the city, most African Americans in town had backyard gardens, raised chickens, and sometimes owned a milk cow.[107]

The vast majority of the town's two thousand black males of employable age held unskilled or day labor positions. Like urban African Americans throughout the South, many of them performed unpleasant or difficult tasks that whites refused to do. Black females in town generally found employment as domestic servants or as "washer women," adding a crucial second source of income to their households. Whatever their employment, however, almost all the city's African Americans lived at or below the subsistence level. Wage labor in a city, even at this level, was nonetheless a vast improvement for blacks throughout the South, many of whom remained trapped in the horrid economic and social world of sharecropping.[108] A few dozen local African Americans were able to start successful, black-oriented enterprises. In 1888, for example, in Gainesborough's business section along Peach Road (between modern-day Madison and Orange Avenues), African Americans operated four grocery and dry goods stores, a butcher shop, and a couple of barbershops. Elsewhere in town, blacks owned four "eating houses" and a saloon.[109] By 1890, two black grocery stores had opened closer to downtown—one on First Street Northwest and the other on Railroad Avenue—and two more African American saloons had begun operations—one on Third Avenue Southeast and the other on Railroad Avenue. By then, blacks also owned two boarding houses, a blacksmith shop, and eleven barbershops. The city's black businesses, like those elsewhere in the urban South, served an almost exclusively African American clientele.[110]

Roanoke's newspapers, like most of the southern press at the time, only felt obliged to give the city's black residents coverage when they were involved in disturbances or charged with crimes. Although it admitted the city needed African American workers for the time being, the *Roanoke Daily Times* echoed the racist sentiments of the white population by suggesting that once a "better class of settlers" arrived to replace them, the city's blacks should return to Africa.[111] That disdain for African American Roanokers grew more and more evident in the 1890s, as *de jure* segregation policies began replacing the *de facto* separation customs that had mediated race relations until then. The move marked the beginning of whites' attempts to exclude blacks from the larger community. In the spring of 1890, after a local paper complained that a "gang of negroes" were making the rail depot a "lounging place" and had "long been a nuisance, as it is almost impossible to make one's way through them, and they never think of stepping aside," the N&W banned non-ticketed residents from the station. Police, of course, selectively enforced the new rule and arrested only African Americans for trespassing there.[112]

Black Roanokers who tried to assert their civil rights faced not only arrest, but also violence from outraged whites. These confrontations over access to public space grew more and more frequent throughout the 1890s, especially when African Americans challenged a longstanding separation policy. In the winter of 1889, a black man named Gus Bolling entered the first-class car of a Shenandoah Valley Railroad train at the Roanoke depot and sat down beside a single white woman. While there was no law against this, the SVR and N&W had as a matter of course segregated passenger cars by allowing African Americans access only to third-class tickets. The fact that Bolling had somehow managed to purchase a first-class ticket mattered little to those in the car. "Some gentlemen standing near," the *Daily Times* reported the next day, "ordered the darkey to get up and leave the car, which he in the most insolent manner refused to do." As a result, the "gentlemen" smashed a bottle over Bolling's head and tossed him onto the tracks.[113] Black resistance to traditional or legal segregation, while rare in Roanoke, was usually met with violence, arrest, and the passage of additional separation ordinances. Indeed, throughout the South in the 1890s, it was African Americans asserting their citizenship rights in public spaces that prompted whites to replace traditional segregation practices with "Jim Crow" laws. New cities like Roanoke, which lacked established patterns of black exclusion, were generally the first to adopt such measures.[114]

Roanoke's press rarely offered accounts of black entertainment or society that did not focus on its supposedly detrimental effects on the city. The reporting was biased, but it did at least document the city's black amusements and entertainments. Like Roanoke's white working classes, the city's African American laborers tended to congregate in barrooms at the end of the day. Charlie Morton's bar and "snack shack" and Murray King's saloon, both located on Railroad Avenue in what police dubbed "hell's half acre," were two of the most popular black bars in town. Police repeatedly raided Morton's place, and according to them, it was little more than a gambling den and bordello.[115] In the fall of 1890, as part of an ongoing crusade to denigrate local African Americans, *The Roanoke Times* sent a correspondent on a tour of the city's "colored dives" in "hell's half acre." It was a journey, *The Times* reporter explained, that had taken him into an area "more unfrequented by the average citizen" than anywhere in town. He had first inspected two "shanties" serving as boarding and "eating houses," and then made his way into Huddleston's saloon, where about fifty black patrons were enjoying drinks at the bar. For ten cents, he found out, customers could enter the improvised dance hall in the back room. The "hall," a ten-by-twenty-foot room, was packed, and those dancing were "drunk or getting so and perspiring freely." "The orchestra," he explained, "consisted of a lone Negro, who thrummed a twine on a dyspeptic banjo." Another black-owned saloon nearby, he discovered, operated inside "a little tent about 6 feet square."[116]

Along with newspaper accounts, police reports also reveal a thriving African American saloon and dance hall district in Gainesborough. The "Red Row" or "Red House," a long, red, frame apartment-like complex on Ninth Avenue Northeast, was apparently the most popular site for dances and drinking in the 1880s and 1890s. Police raided it dozens of times, and according to the department's official history, the Red Row was "for years, the habitation of crooks of the worst stamp."[117] Although residents held hundreds of fêtes there without incident, only the occasional fight or shooting made the local papers. In one typical story, the *Roanoke Daily Times* reported in 1889 that an argument over a woman at a Red Row dance had resulted in gunfire and attempted murder. Three policemen and the mayor arrived at the "low dive" immediately and arrested several patrons before confiscating a concealed dirk from one of the female attendees.[118] "Bob Jeffries Place," a saloon and snack shack on Peach Road in Gainesborough was also a popular spot for dances. According to Roanoke Police, however, it was "one of the worst resorts in the city" where "practically every crime known to man was committed . . . at one time or another."[119]

Although local authorities for the most part ignored white gamblers and gaming houses, they consistently raided African American gambling dens and arrested blacks for betting on cards or dice. In the fall of 1890, police broke up several ongoing games. *The Roanoke Times,* sensing another opportunity to deride the city's black residents, gave the raids prominent coverage. The first arrests, the paper reported, came after authorities stormed a poker game in the Bunker Hill section of Gainesborough. Although many of the players escaped by jumping out windows, police rounded up eleven others and seized dice, cards, and chips.[120] A few days later, another officer broke up "a gang of negro boot-blacks playing dice" in a vacant lot.[121] The following month, the paper reported, police uncovered a craps game and "gallantly arrested the 'bones' used by the darkies and the stakes, amounting to 35 cents."[122] Two days later, they raided an ongoing dice game held inside a stable and captured several members of "the Bunker Hill select crap-shooting socials."[123]

Although whites in town and Roanoke's press rarely acknowledged them, there were dozens of black professionals in the city. Most had occupations that mirrored those of educated blacks elsewhere in the South, working as lawyers, businessmen, doctors, teachers, undertakers, and ministers. Like them, they tended to serve an almost exclusively African American clientele and have central leadership positions within the black community.[124] Andrew Jackson Oliver, the city's first African American attorney, opened a practice in 1890. Oliver, a Methodist minister, was born in Blacksburg, Virginia, and earned a law degree in Ohio before moving to Roanoke in 1889. He and his wife Susan, a graduate of the Hampton Institute and teacher at the Third Ward "colored school," lived on First Street Northwest. Oliver's office, in the white business section of downtown, also housed his real estate and development firm, the Roanoke Building & Land Company.[125]

In 1891, Doctor Robert J. Boland opened the first black medical practice in the city. In addition, Boland published the *Roanoke Weekly Press, Colored,* the town's only African American newspaper. Isaac Burrell, another black physician, started a medical practice in Gainesborough in 1893. In 1897, he opened Roanoke's first African American pharmacy. Burrell's wife Margaret, another graduate of the Hampton Institute, also taught at the Third Ward school.[126] Lucy Addison, a graduate of the Institute for Colored Youth in Philadelphia, moved to town in 1887 to teach at the black school in Gainesborough and later became its assistant principal. Addison, who devoted the following forty years to teaching the city's black children, also served as superintendent of the Fifth Avenue Presbyterian Church Sunday School.[127]

Although the children of working-class residents had few educational options beyond the city's poorly funded public schools, black residents, like African Americans throughout the South, had even fewer choices and far less financial support. During the 1880s, Roanoke built five public schools for whites but only one for blacks.[128] Moreover, there was a huge disparity in teacher salary, with white women earning $1,300 a year and black women only $210.[129] This infuriated the city's African American professionals, and in the summer of 1892 they organized an education committee to petition Roanoke's school board for "more and better school facilities."[130] Whatever the effect of the appeal, by the end of the year, the city had funded completion of a new "colored" school on Gregory Avenue Southeast.[131]

Roanoke's black population coalesced around a variety of indigenous institutions. Their six churches, however, were the nucleus of the community as well as the establishment that girded every African American political and social organization.[132] All of them were in Gainesborough or in the Northeast, and most of them had originally been white sanctuaries before African American congregations purchased them in the early 1880s, after whites moved south and built new places to worship downtown. St. Paul United Methodist, Mt. Zion African Methodist Episcopal, High Street Baptist, Greater Mt. Zion Baptist, and First Baptist all built or purchased sanctuaries in the 1880s. At the time, the city's black Presbyterians held services either in the basement of the all-white First Presbyterian Church or in a black schoolhouse. In 1898, however, under the guidance of its pastor Lylburn Liggins Downing, the congregation raised enough money to build its own sanctuary on Fifth Avenue Northeast. Richard R. Jones, minister of the First Baptist Church, held services in a home in the Northeast until the late 1880s, when his congregation funded the purchase of what had been the all-white St. John's Episcopal Church with funds raised from a series of successful neighborhood festivals.[133]

The city's black residents took part in a wide array of other cultural and community organizations. Few, however, received coverage in the press or notice by white residents. When they did, it was generally because African Americans had successfully mimicked acceptable white institutions. In 1886, for example, *The Roanoke Leader* reported that blacks had organized the Roanoke Brass Band and held a parade through downtown streets. The music was so impressive and the overall display so good that even the normally racist *Leader* informed readers that the group deserved "the encouragement of our citizens."[134]

In early 1891, another paper applauded a group of sixty-five black men who organized a military company and petitioned for inclusion in the state militia. The organization's officers were part of Roanoke's small cadre of elite African Americans, and the company met in Davis Hall, a community center established by John H. Davis, the city's most successful black businessman.[135] Blacks used the hall for neighborhood meetings, dances, concerts, and a variety of other purposes, including political gatherings. In 1892, for instance, the four hundred members of the "Harrison Republican Colored Club" met there weekly throughout the campaign season. The Club, headed by John Davis, helped register six hundred and forty new black voters, and even challenged local Democrats to a debate on the issues for the upcoming election. Democrats, according to a local paper, were shocked and appalled at the "heavy negro registration" and "most positively refused" the debate invitation, "giving as their reason that they would not discuss politics before a colored mass meeting with anyone."[136] Harrison won in the heavily African American Third Ward and came close in the Fifth but lost decisively in the other three wards. *The Roanoke Times*, nevertheless, dismissed the high black turnout as little more than manipulation by corrupt white Republicans. "The negroes," it complained afterwards, "were very thoroughly voted."[137]

The African American community usually participated in citywide celebrations, albeit often in a segregated fashion. Their own festivals rarely received notice from whites, but in early 1893, local papers sent several reporters to cover a valley-wide Emancipation Proclamation anniversary celebration. The Roanoke Emancipation Club joined its Salem counterpart in planning and staging the daylong event. The clubs held a parade in Salem that was nearly a mile in length. It featured the Roanoke Brass Band, dozens of mounted riders and carriages, and hundreds of marchers carrying banners and flags. Daniel B. Williams, professor of elocution and oratory at Virginia Normal and Collegiate Institute in Petersburg, addressed an overflowing crowd at Salem's Town Hall afterwards. His speech, a recitation of themes made popular by Booker T. Washington, won praise from *The Roanoke Times* and other newspapers for telling the audience that "white men of the South are the negroes' best friend" and that the only hope for blacks was to educate themselves, learn a trade, and stay out of trouble. John Davis, "the colored capitalist of Roanoke," and several other businessmen and professionals from the city joined Williams onstage. The entire event, according to *The Times*, "was a credible one to the colored folks, and passed off without disorder." Afterwards, Roanoke's Emancipation Club, under the guidance of lawyer A. J. Oliver, business leader Davis, and other black professionals, helped Williams publish the speech in booklet form.[138]

■■■

Although much of the Roanoke community purposefully divided itself by class or segregated itself by race, numerous occasions brought the community together within a specific event or celebration. Baseball games, for example, drew in crowds composed of working classes and elites, men and women, and whites and blacks, albeit often in class- and gender-specific seating and with blacks limited to standing around the outfield fence. The matches, whether amateur or professional, were not only an outlet from daily toil and a way to defuse tensions, but an important part of an ongoing process that forged a sense of community out of the city's disparate elements. Whether cognizant of it or not, those attending the games came together in a common cause that could later translate into municipal pride and civic identity.[139] In May of 1883, the Roanoke Athletic Association organized the first official game held in the city. The Roanoke players defeated a team from Salem in a field near the Rorer Park Hotel.[140] In April, other local men organized the "Rough and Ready Baseball Club" and claimed to be prepared to "receive challenges from any club in the state."[141]

Local blacks formed their own team in the summer of 1883 as well. The "Roanoke Slippers" used the baseball grounds and drew large crowds, albeit exclusively African American. Racial mores limited black teams throughout the South to African American opponents, preventing teams like the Slippers from challenging local whites to a game. Indeed, according to one scholar, that a white team would compete with a black nine was, at the time, "unthinkable."[142] In a typical match that summer, the Slippers paraded to the grounds with hundreds of fans behind the Roanoke Brass Band to face the "Lonejacks," an all-black team from Lynchburg. Unfortunately, the team's enthusiasm did not translate into victory on the field, and it lost thirty-nine to three.[143]

In the summer of 1883, following the success of the town's amateur teams, prominent businessmen organized the Roanoke Baseball Association to field "The Roanokes," the city's first "professional" team. The organization improved the local diamond across from Rorer Park, built grandstands, and brought in a few paid players to join local men on the team. In a typical game that summer, The Roanokes defeated "The Lexingtons" before a crowd of over six hundred spectators that included "a great many ladies" as well as numerous African Americans lining the fence.[144] The Roanokes, a member of the state circuit of baseball clubs, hosted dozens of teams from surrounding cities and towns. The club, according to *The Roanoke Leader,* maintained the reputation of the city and its fans and was responsible for a dramatic increase in civic pride.[145] The team nevertheless suffered the fate of many other early clubs throughout the nation and faded away due to poor management, haphazard play, and an inconsistent roster of opponents.[146] Other local professional teams followed and played for a season or two before fading away as well.

In the spring of 1890, the city's leading businessmen pooled their money and revived the Roanokes once again. This time, the organization vowed to run the club as a regular business venture and it hired three of the best pros available to team up with local talent.[147] A couple of weeks later, another local group organized the "Virginias," and for a time the city could boast two professional teams. The Virginias, however, had trouble obtaining decent players, and in their second game—in what one paper called a "comedy of errors from beginning to end"—the team lost decidedly to a nine from Roanoke College that scored twenty-five runs.[148] Both clubs played at Riverside Park, which had bleachers for over a thousand fans.[149] When the Roanokes played the Virginias in an early game that spring, hundreds of spectators showed up to check out the prospects for the upcoming season. The Roanokes scored nineteen runs and trounced their opponents, leading one paper to observe its players were "getting in good shape and handled themselves with some of their old time vigor"[150]

Local support for both professional clubs was strong. Indeed, the sport was so popular that the *Daily Times* boasted that there was "as much enthusiasm about baseball in Roanoke as will be found in any city in the land."[151] Moreover, the city's baseball aficionados did not limit themselves to merely watching. They also formed club teams connected to their trade or profession. In the 1880s, for example, Norfolk & Western workers battled Shenandoah Valley Railroad employees, Machine Works blacksmiths played the company's boilermakers, and local lawyers challenged the city's printers to a game. Dozens of residents played in amateur games every weekend during the spring and summer, and fan support for these matches was often just as strong as for the city's pros. Indeed, in June of 1887, Shenandoah Valley Railroad lawyer William Travers arrived to find the entire community "quite excited over a match game of baseball" between "two organizations representing the rival hotels—hotel Roanoke and the City hotel."[152]

Much like baseball, circuses and fairs brought out thousands of residents from the city and the surrounding counties. Entertainment on such a grand scale was a rarity in Southwest Virginia. As the hub for a circuit of such shows, Roanoke quickly became a destination of choice for rural residents looking for distraction. John Robinson's Circus, which arrived for a series of shows in the summer of 1884, was one of the first to test the waters in the city. Robinson drummed up excitement for the event by staging a "grand street pageant" featuring three bands—one of which was entirely female. Other entertainment included "a minstrel troupe of genuine darkies who sang comic songs, handsome vans, band wagons, and cages, a beautiful team of ponies, and many other novel attractions." Residents crowded into the big top for the next few days, and according to the Reverend William Campbell, the "whole countryside emptied itself to come to town and see the show" and arrived "in spring wagons and wagons without springs and in buggies and on horseback and on foot."[153]

One problem, local officials quickly learned, was that the crowds of visitors could prove unruly and often violent. When Barnum & Bailey's "Greatest Show

Clown in the 1898 Forepaugh and Bell Circus Roanoke street parade. Charlotte Gale Dryden Photograph Album (CWGALE0018), Digital Library and Archives, University Libraries, Virginia Tech.

on Earth" came to town, for example, the mayor deputized ten extra policemen to handle the mob that was sure to arrive. Although the *Daily Times* did its part to drum up excitement for the show, it also warned residents that "there will be thousands of strangers here to attend the 'greatest show on earth,' and no doubt whiskey will be imbibed freely and broken noses and bloody countenances will be the order of the day."[154] Moreover, hordes of circus followers also poured into town to take advantage of the crowds. Dozens of con artists, prostitutes, and common street swindlers showed up as well when Forepaugh's Aggregation came to town. Eight thousand patrons packed the tent for the actual show, which featured a re-enactment of Custer's Last Stand, including two Sioux warriors who supposedly participated in the actual massacre. Afterwards, hundreds of those exiting the big top faced a gantlet of grifters who offered games of chance and prostitutes who offered other forms of entertainment.[155]

Visitors to Roanoke from the surrounding countryside, in town for amusement or shopping, encountered trappings of modernity in a city that often baffled them. The town, while hardly representative of a sophisticated metropolis in the 1880s and early 1890s, was nevertheless the closest thing to an urban setting that many Southwest Virginians had ever seen. Residents and the local press, proud of their apparent urbanity, found the confusion of their "country cousins" an endless source of entertainment. Indeed, stories about the mishaps of rural visitors dotted the pages of the city's papers throughout the era. In a typical example, the *Daily Times* reported that a "country man who lives back into the mountains" had gone into a local tobacco shop, purchased a cigar, and attempted to ignite it on an electric light bulb, much to the amusement of clerks and bystanders.[156] In another account, the paper explained that a "hayseed" couple from a "rural district" had ridden downtown in their beat-up wagon only to be stunned by a passing bicyclist and horrified by a test of the fire alarm. Crowds around them burst into laughter, and in much apparent discomfort and confusion, the couple fled the scene.[157]

Those living in counties around Roanoke viewed the city as an oasis of urbanity in a desert of isolated farms, small towns, and country stores. Many families traveled a day or two for a shopping spree or for the opportunity to engage in amusements that were unheard of elsewhere in that part of the state. Anna Brown, living in rural Tazewell County with her new husband, passed through when she was on her way to visit her family in Salem. Roanoke's wide array of shops fascinated her, as did its social scene and nightlife. Tazewell County, she informed her father, had no stores carrying fancy goods and little opportunity for social interaction. When she did finally host a dinner party, Brown told her family, she had resorted to cups and saucers purchased locally that were "not pretty at all" and explained that she wished she "had have gotten them in Roanoke."[158]

Brown hoped to convince her husband to move to the city, and in letters to her father and sister inquired frequently about store goods available there. "When you go to Roanoke," she told them in one dispatch, "go to Davis & see what is the price of them little babe bonnets & tell me and I will send money to get one."[159] Although attracted to the dizzying array of available products, Brown knew the city had a promiscuous element uncommon among the farms and villages of Tazewell County. Indeed, after a friend returned from Roanoke with a fancy watch she obviously could not have purchased herself, Brown told her father that she believed "some of them Roanoke men gave it to her" and that "If she was a nice girl she would not get so many presents."[160] Brown continually sought out information on Roanoke from family friends and visitors, and on one occasion talked for hours to a male acquaintance who planned to open a business in the city. It was an exhilarating chat, she told her family, and one that she "certainly enjoyed."[161]

Looking south on Jefferson Street, early 1900s. History Museum and Historical Society of Western Virginia, Roanoke.

Life, Work, Culture, and Community

In addition to circuses and shopping trips, thousands of rural residents visited Roanoke for its annual fair. The extremely popular event began in early 1883, when Henry Trout, Peyton Terry, and other business leaders teamed with Frederick Kimball to organize the "Roanoke Association for the Exhibition and Sale of Live Stock from Virginia and other States."[162] The organization, which sought to provide information or instruction and "not pander to the public taste for amusement and fun," bought its own fairgrounds, constructed pens, exhibition areas, a half-mile racetrack around an artificial lake, and grandstands. It put up several thousand dollars in prize money for a livestock show and several horse races. At the fair that October, over ten thousand spectators turned out during its three-day run. Many of the attendees came from nearby counties and towns. "Nearly every fellow" at Roanoke College went, according to Donnie Caffery, a freshman there. He had been unable to go, he told his family in Louisiana, because he had no money and as a result "was so lonely I didn't know what to do."[163] The "Roanoke Stakes" and "Kimball Stakes," one-mile horse races that offered $1,000 each in prize money, proved the most popular events, but livestock exhibitions and athletic events also drew large crowds.

"So flattering has been the success attending this splendid exhibition," *The Roanoke Leader* boasted afterwards, that the owners had already added more events for the following fall.[164] A correspondent for the Pennsylvania-based *American Volunteer*, who happened to be in town that October, reported that the exhibition was "the finest we have ever seen" and predicted that it could not fail to prove beneficial to the city.[165] J. B. Austin, President of the Roanoke Land & Improvement Company, wholeheartedly concurred and told stockholders that the fair had been "the most complete and satisfactory of the kind ever seen in the State of Virginia."[166] Unbeknownst to the public or press, however, the spectacular turnout had not been enough to allow the association to break even. Indeed, when its board of directors met later that month, its treasurer reported that the organization was $5,000 in debt.[167]

The association covered the deficit with bank loans and carried on with plans for the 1884 exhibition. However, it did decide to raise admission prices and do away with all complimentary tickets. Moreover, at the urging of Henry Trout, the organization asked city council for a referendum on a $1,500 donation to the group as well as public funding for policing the fair.[168] That fall, after multiple parades through downtown that included a "grand cavalcade of livestock" headed by the Roanoke Machine Works Band, massive crowds again packed the fairgrounds. The event that year, according to the local paper, had surpassed the previous version and had been "the best display of stock ever seen in Virginia."[169] Again, the association lost money. Indeed, after using all the funds from the gate to cover expenses, it still needed close to $2,000 more in order to pay premium guarantees to thirty winning entrants. The winners went unpaid, and, the association's treasurer reported, the organization was now $7,000 in debt. The debacle confounded Kimball, Trout, and Terry as well as the other members of the board, and at a meeting the following spring, they voted to suspend the fair in 1885 in order to reorganize and refinance the association.[170]

In early 1886, after the organization debated continuing the suspension, Roanoke's City Council donated $1,000 in municipal funds and pledged additional civic support for the fair. The vote, however, did not please working-

Parade for Roanoke Fair heading north on Jefferson Street, July 1900. History Museum and Historical Society of Western Virginia, Roanoke.

class residents in the southeast because city officials had repeatedly denied them funds for a pedestrian bridge over the nearby railroad tracks. According to one angry shop worker, the vote risked the lives and limbs "of a class of citizens who are in the employ of a corporation that adds more to the material prosperity of our city than all other industries combined" in order "to encourage that taste for fine stock and fast horses to amuse the people."[171] The resentment, however, did not stop the association who, with the city's help, staged the fair in October. From a participation standpoint, the event was once again a wild success. It lasted four days instead of three and in addition to a continuation of livestock exhibitions and horse races, featured exhibits that showed off the New South's latest mechanical, agricultural, horticultural, and domestic innovations.[172] The fair turned a profit that year, and in the years that followed, it continued to prosper.

Much like the agricultural fair, holiday celebrations offered opportunities for all residents, regardless of class or race, to take part in a festivity that involved the entire community. The Fourth of July was just such an occasion, and throughout the 1880s and 1890s, residents turned out en masse to take part in the celebration. The event grew larger and more elaborate every year, and at each celebration, rowdiness and unruliness increased. Early on, the festivities were relatively calm. In 1883, *The Roanoke Leader* proudly reported that the Machine Works Band had entertained a sedate crowd downtown before a fireworks display. "No disturbance of any kind occurred, and no drinking to excess was indulged in."[173] In the years that followed, all-day picnics, baseball games, greased pig chases, and dancing until midnight accompanied the celebration, but the mostly white crowds continued to be well behaved. By 1890, however, papers reported that widespread drunkenness and fighting were common. According to the *Daily Times,* the Fourth that year was especially chaotic: a stray bottle rocket ignited a two-hundred-pound box of fireworks in the Vigilant Firehouse tower, nearly killing two firemen; intoxicated mobs fired "skyrockets" at one another; "street fakirs" set up games of chance on every corner, local blacks "turned out in such numbers as to threaten a watermelon famine;" and along with the other brawls, a "very impudent negro" fought with a fireman on Railroad Avenue in front of hundreds of screaming bystanders.[174]

The increasing rowdiness of the Fourth and the boisterous behavior by rural visitors concerned city leaders, but did not prevent them from planning the largest celebration in Roanoke's history to mark its ten-year anniversary. Big Lick became Roanoke on February 3, 1882, but that decennial date passed largely without notice. Later that spring, however, members of the town's Commercial Association saw the potential that a ten-year anniversary celebration could have as an advertising gimmick for Roanoke. Former Mayor John Dunstan, a member of the association and advocate of the scheme, told those gathered at a special meeting that such a celebration "would not only tend to foster a spirit of patriotism amongst our citizens but would advertise us and show the world what enterprise and vim has done in ten years." The organization appointed Henry Trout, Peyton Terry, and other civic leaders to a decennial committee charged with securing municipal support.[175] News of the potential anniversary celebration created a stir among the city's businessmen, nearly all of whom assumed the event would be an advertising bonanza for Roanoke. Indeed, local capitalists interviewed by *The Times* predicted that the celebration would more than pay for itself, widen the town's "already national reputation," and "bring to us a most desirable class of people, who seeing our progress, would aid in spreading abroad the history of Roanoke's advancement."[176] *The Iron Belt*, a regional booster journal based in the city, argued that the decennial would "attract the favorable notice of thousands." It was therefore imperative, its editor explained, that residents understand that making the celebration a success was "work in which every citizen is interested; let no one shirk his duty."[177]

Although the city offered its support, the Commercial Association assumed sole responsibility for planning the celebration. The group picked the eighteenth of June, the anniversary of the completion of the Shenandoah Valley Railroad's tracks into town, as the date for the decennial. By early June, most of the planning for the affair was complete, but in an address to several thousand residents, land agent James S. Simmons, chairman of the celebration, explained that the group had only been able to raise $1,000 of the $9,000 it needed to cover expenses. "Our reputation is at stake," Henry Trout told the crowd, and donations were crucial. "Every man, woman and child in Roanoke," *The Times* observed, "ought to feel that he or she has a personal interest in this affair and give something."[178] The association's ads for the event belied its financial difficulties and promised that "the most stupendous celebration of the kind that has ever been held in the state" would take place in the "Magic City of the South."[179] Local merchants hoping to capitalize on the hype offered "decennial souvenir spoons" and "decennial whiskey" that had been distilled in 1882.[180]

In the weeks that followed, residents and business leaders donated more than the needed funds, and on the morning of the eighteenth, the celebration got under way with thousands of spectators lining the streets downtown to watch a two-mile-long parade of floats "portraying the growth and progress of Roanoke." Local businesses sponsored most of the displays. The Cold Storage Company's float featured blocks of ice cooling down a butchered hog, while the Hammond Printing Works showed off a working printing press, Fishburne Brothers Tobacco had black workers packing bags with its "Yellow Leaf" brand, and the Pocahontas Coal Company displayed the largest lump of bituminous coal ever mined.[181] All eleven hundred Roanoke Machine Works employees, "their uniforms being a buff cap and blouse, black belt and pantaloons," followed the floats, as did three hundred bicyclists and representatives from all fifty of the city's lodges and secret societies. A "sham battle" between cadets from the Virginia Military Institute and Virginia Polytechnic Institute followed the parade, as did two professional baseball games. That night, spectators packed downtown streets to watch several thousand pounds of fireworks explode overhead.[182] Although the crowd numbered close to fifteen thousand, according to *The Times*, there had been "little, if any drunkenness or disorderly conduct." Overall, the paper went on, the decennial had been "the greatest affair of its kind ever seen in Virginia." However, it explained, the celebration would not be "complete" until the city landed a permanent industry because of its efforts.[183]

Members of the Commercial Association were thrilled with the turn-out of potential investors. Furniture storeowner E. H. Stewart, for example, believed the event had distinguished the city from other "so-called boom towns in Southwest Virginia" that had collapsed. "That Roanoke is on solid, substantial footing no one who saw our trades display can doubt," he told a reporter, "and the effect of the celebration will be to take it out of the list of towns whose future is doubtful and place it in the front rank of the solid, substantial, progressive cities of the South."[184] Stewart and other members of the association voted to use funds left over from the celebration to publish a commemorative pamphlet to further publicize the city's tremendous potential for investors. Beyond a superficial description of the decennial and reprinted accounts of the event published in outside papers, the brochure mirrored other Roanoke booster guides in its effort to illustrate the fantastic growth of the town with a detailed listing of business statistics. It even included the increase in Western Union telegraphs per year—which rose from two hundred in 1882 to thirty thousand in 1892—as evidence of progress. It also bragged about the entrepreneurial spirit of residents, notifying those unfamiliar with the "Magic City" that it had "been developed by the magic of hard work, untiring energy, business shrewdness, and determination, and that is the only sort of magic that amounts to anything in these latter days." Roanoke's prosperity, the guide explained, had "been laid on solid foundation, and there need be no fear that it will share the fate of some of the boom towns in the South which have sprung up in a night only to disappear as quickly as they arose."[185]

■■■

In the 1880s and 1890s, Roanoke's residents divided themselves by race and class into three distinct communities and cultures. The city's white working classes, the largest of the three, coalesced in a variety of ways. Frequenting saloons and gambling dens generated solidarity, as did living in company housing in the Northeast or in boarding homes in the Southwest. Most labor-ers and their families patronized distinctly working-class forms of entertain-ment, amusing themselves at dances sponsored by the RL&IC, attending lowbrow shows at the Opera House, socializing downtown on Friday or Sat-urday nights, or spending time playing carnival games or watching side-show exhibitions in vacant lots.

Roanoke's elite white residents, like its working classes, emerged from groups with differing geographic origins. Although the two groups also lived in different neighborhoods and often had dissimilar religious and political affiliations, they coalesced around a variety of cultural institutions that turned them into a unified class. Their children attended the same private schools, they joined the same clubs, fraternal orders, secret societies, and professional organizations, they frequented the same parties, visited the same springs and resorts, and they eventually created a venue in which they could patronize exclusively highbrow entertainment. Elite women carved out their own distinct world as well, creating church-related societies and charities that advertised their upper-class and morally "superior" status by placing them in positions in which they judged the "worth" of those seeking assistance.

Roanoke's black residents, while composed of differing classes, comprised a distinct and cohesive community. African Americans in the city lived in clusters along the same streets, the vast majority worked similar unskilled or day labor jobs, and most patronized the same all-black saloons and dance halls. The town's African American business owners and professionals assumed leadership roles within the black community, providing guidance on issues ranging from politics to education. No matter what their status, Roanoke's press continually derided and ridiculed the city's blacks. When the press did not single them out for committing crimes or creating disturbances, it ignored them entirely. Indeed, that a thriving black culture and community existed would have come as a surprise to many white residents. Churches, of course, served as the main community-building institution and backbone for a variety of African American organizations, all of which served to foment solidarity between local blacks. Community festivals and celebrations, while for the most part ignored by whites, likewise helped foster an overall sense of community.

Although residents purposely divided themselves by class and race, they frequently lowered these barriers enough to participate in activities that generated a larger sense of community. Baseball, circuses and fairs, the Fourth of July, and the decennial celebration brought all residents together in activities that created a general sense of community. Although geographic origins and political affiliation had originally divided the white community, by the early 1890s these differences had faded. Participation in community-wide events and celebrations, while not solely responsible, played a major role in the deterioration of these barriers. Black residents, while kept on the margins of baseball games and limited almost entirely to spectator status during city-wide celebrations, nonetheless participated in ways that placed them squarely within the larger community. Overall, in the 1880s and early 1890s, Roanokers not only carved out a variety of distinct cultures, they also created a sense of municipal identity and civic pride that had not been present in the city's early existence.

Chapter 5

Riot and Reform

In the decades surrounding the turn of the twentieth century, Roanoke's white community, which had at first fractured into factions of natives and newcomers, divided itself more overtly by class. The city's workers and their families, along with migrants from the countryside, comprised one distinct class; its business leaders, professionals, and their families another. The cleavage between the two groups grew more severe in the 1890s, as the town's upper classes attempted to impose "reforms" on lower-class whites which they hoped would stabilize Roanoke's unruly and disordered environment. While that quest operated on numerous fronts, it was most apparent in moves designed to end workers' access to alcohol and in stands against lower class whites' attempts to exact frontier-style "justice" on black inhabitants.

Not surprisingly, the attempts to enact prohibition generated much hostility and resentment among the city's working classes, almost all of whom saw it as an illegitimate attack on personal liberty. Since most of them also understood justice in terms of personal vengeance, they likewise reacted with disbelief and rage when municipal authorities repeatedly failed to punish black residents for supposed crimes and then attempted to prevent working classes from extracting extralegal "justice" on them. As lower-class challenges to municipal control of the judicial process mounted, elected officials and business leaders—the men most concerned about the maintenance of Roanoke's progressive image—eventually attempted to enforce law and order. When they did, however, working-class whites reacted by rioting. In the ensuing violence, known afterwards as the "Roanoke Riot of 1893," the city's militia shot and killed eight residents before a mob took control of the city, lynched an African American in police custody, and threatened to hang the mayor.

In the aftermath of the riot, local officials and business leaders mounted a vigorous campaign to rehabilitate the city's tarnished image and prevent any recurrence of challenges to their authority. The violence also prompted Virginia's elected representatives to enact reforms that resulted in a striking decline in lynching statewide. The new measures, however, had only a superficial impact on the fate of black Virginians charged with capital crimes against whites. Designed simply to quash mob rule, the moves aesthetically changed the application of "justice," with show trials and the gallows replacing lynching, while doing nothing to safeguard the rights of those accused.

■■■

The interplay of class, race, and reform in Roanoke in the 1890s and early 1900s had part of its genesis in the dramatic increase in tensions between white and black residents. White antipathy for African Americans, while constant in the 1880s, grew more severe in the 1890s as the city's black population increased, putting whites into more frequent contact with African American strangers, at least some of whom refused to conform to contemporary white notions of appropriate black subservience. As noted earlier, by the early 1890s, African Americans accounted for roughly 30 percent of the city's twenty-three-thousand inhabitants.[1] Many of the newcomers were lone black males looking for a better life than what tenant farming or sharecropping provided. In Roanoke, as elsewhere in the South, the presence of unknown black men wandering about town unsettled white males, most of whom understood African American men "on the loose" as manifestations of their worst fears about blacks as chronic criminals and potential rapists of white women.[2] Moreover, as the city's population grew and its economy boomed, traditional boundaries of decorum and space between the races became more amorphous and occasionally broke down altogether as streets, sidewalks, depots, and other public spaces turned increasingly into contested terrain.[3]

As tensions between the races mounted, clashes over appropriate public etiquette intensified. In the summer of 1893, the *Roanoke Daily Record* reported that a black male named Royal Moore had "attempted to monopolize more of the sidewalk than belongs, by custom or good breeding, to any one man" and bumped into a white pedestrian "who resented the encounter by drawing a gun upon the aforesaid Senegambian." C. W. Allen did not shoot Moore, the paper explained, "and many people think he ought to have been imprisoned for neglecting to perform his bounded duty."[4] Such sidewalk confrontations were generally the result of African Americans asserting their humanity in the face of an emerging racially hierarchical society, which sought to define blacks as sub-human and unfit for equal access to public space.[5]

In an effort to keep black males "in check," local authorities arrested them far more often than whites for the supposed crimes of "disorderly conduct," "vagrancy," "suspicion," or "trespassing on N&W property." They also typically imposed a more severe penalty than on whites, which meant that most ended up working off their time on the Roanoke chain gang. While African American men comprised only about a quarter of the city's male population, in 1893 they accounted for slightly over half of all arrests.[6] The emergence of supposedly disease-ridden and corrupt "negro dives" along Railroad Avenue in the 1880s added to white anxiety and fear, as did the constant barrage of local newspaper stories that warned readers about dissipated and depraved African Americans descending into "barbarism" and "savagery." Republican efforts on the national level to protect black voting rights in the South with the 1890 "Lodge Bill" further angered whites. In addition, some whites resented the handful of black residents who had emulated Victorian ideals and managed to establish successful businesses. Others, mainly rural white newcomers, chafed at competing for day labor jobs against African Americans.[7]

One symptom of the growing fear and racism was an increase in incidents for which white residents demanded extralegal "justice." Lynching, after all, served not simply as an attack on one person, but as an assault on all black residents, marking them as outsiders in the community, beyond the bounds of due process and basic rights of citizenship.[8] In the early 1880s, when African American males stood accused of murdering Lizzie Wilson, and again in the late 1880s, when police charged black men with killing Thomas Massie, whites in the community banded together in vigilante gangs to seek extralegal retribution. In both cases, mobs bent on lynching the men arrested gathered around the jail, and each time authorities thwarted riots only by removing the accused to nearby cities. Demands for "lynch justice" appeared again after hung juries or insufficient evidence led to acquittals in both cases. In the aftermath, Roanoke's white community lost nearly all faith in their government's ability to mete out justice, making the potential for vigilantism not just possible but highly likely.

In such an atmosphere, any black-on-white violence had the potential to unleash furious demands by white males for swift retaliation and the potential to put outnumbered authorities attempting to maintain law and order on the defensive. That fact that many Roanoke whites were recent rural migrants whose traditional ideas about justice rested on notions of honor and personal vengeance only made the situation even more likely to escalate into such confrontations.[9] Such was the case in late 1891, when Jeff Dooley, an African American resident of Bunker Hill, accidentally killed a white policeman who was trying to arrest him. Police captured Dooley shortly thereafter and put him in the city jail, where a menacing crowd of several hundred white men had already gathered to demand "lynch law." Falling back on their standard response to such a threat, authorities quickly snuck Dooley out the back door and onto a train bound for Lynchburg.[10] The move, of course, infuriated those who wanted immediate retribution and served only to ratchet up their already high resentment and suspicion of local officials.

Early the following year, after a black man supposedly attempted to rape a twelve-year-old white girl, the town's white residents were again united in their calls for swift extralegal justice. "Little Alice Perry" and Jinnie Critzer,

The Roanoke Times reported, had just crossed the Jefferson Street Bridge when a black man walking in front of them turned around, threw Alice to the ground, stuffed clothing in her mouth, and "attempted to outrage her." Jinnie alerted the girl's relatives, and before the "burly black assailant could accomplish his purpose," the sounds of their approach frightened him away. Alice provided a detailed description of the man, but according to the *Times*, "the police did not seem to appreciate the gravity of the situation and made no effort to investigate the matter." For the paper's editors, the conduct of city police was not surprising, since it was their opinion that the force was "so badly handled and organized" that it was "incapable of properly guarding the lives and property of citizens, or of following up criminals." Relatives of the girls, outraged by police disinterest, armed themselves with shotguns and searched in vain for the man Alice described as medium in height, very dark, who was wearing a gray suit and rubber boots. Perry's mother, a widowed English immigrant, operated a boarding house near the Adams Brothers & Payne brickyard, located along the southern bank of the Roanoke River, just outside the city limits. That the assault happened nearby was hardly shocking, the *Times* reported, since the area was filled with "dirty negro shanties," "crowded with a mean-looking set of negroes," and was an especially "dangerous place to raise up children."[11]

As news of the attempted assault and lax reaction by police spread, other vigilante groups joined in the hunt for Perry's assailant. The chief of police, furious that officers had not directly informed him of the attack, promised residents that the department would do all it could to capture the man responsible. Local papers, while claiming that all black males wearing rubber boots were being "shadowed," reported that authorities were positive that Allen Stevens was the man they were looking for. The evidence included rumors about Stevens's "unsavory reputation" and he had supposedly stolen a pair of rubber boots earlier in the week.[12]

As hysteria mounted and the search expanded, the *Times-Register* in nearby Salem attempted to comfort readers with the news that Roanoke's white men were hot on Stevens's trail and certain to capture the latest "devil at large."[13] Over the next three days, however, city police and local posses failed to locate Stevens. By then, a neighbor of the Perrys had encountered a man wearing rubber boots who matched the description. He immediately hired the man to chop wood while he himself went for help. William Lavender, an unemployed bootblack, was hard at work on a pile of wood when Alice Perry's relatives arrived and forced him at gunpoint to her mother's boarding house. There, Alice and Jinnie identified him as the man who attacked her. Why Lavender would return to the scene of his supposed crime in the midst of a frantic manhunt is unclear, as is the sudden replacement of Allen Stevens as the prime suspect. Lavender was, however, an easy target for white fury. He had moved to town in 1887 and spent close to two years on the chain gang for offenses ranging from vagrancy and disorderly conduct to theft and assault on the chief of police. Lavender had been ordered to leave town on several occasions, but remained in the city, lodging in saloons or eating houses along Railroad Avenue.[14]

After the girls identified Lavender, police placed him in the city jail, where a large and boisterous mob had already gathered to demand his immediate lynching. The mob's outrage was legitimate, according to a "professional man" in the crowd, since "justice in Roanoke could hardly be trusted" and "had failed in too many instances to apprehend and punish crime." Though the legacy of the Wilson and Massie murders forced authorities to worry about their ability to protect Lavender, Roanoke's Chief of Police insisted that they keep him in the city, lest it reflect poorly on the municipality's capability to maintain law and order. Later that evening, however, after the crowd grew larger and more unruly, the chief grew concerned enough to secretly move Lavender to a house that belonged to one of his officers. News of the move quickly leaked, and by midnight members of the mob had located Lavender, easily overpowered the three policemen guarding him, and forcibly taken him to the north bank of the Roanoke River. They placed a noose around his neck and demanded a confession. Though Lavender initially denied everything, after being pulled up by the neck a few times, he admitted to being drunk and accidentally knocking Alice Perry down. With his fate now sealed, Lavender begged for a final prayer from a man in the crowd whom he recognized. After consenting to a quick blessing, several of the men pulled him up again and this time left him twisting and kicking in the air until he died. The men dispersed shortly thereafter, according to a *Times* reporter who had accompanied them, and could testify with evident approval that "there was not a drunken or boisterous man in the party."[15]

The *Times*'s editors endorsed the lynching, proclaiming in oversized type on their front page: "Judge Lynch! Little Alice Perry Has Been Avenged." In an editorial condoning "lynch law," they explained that "when the people come to believe that the machinery which they have erected for carrying out of justice has lost its power to right wrongs, they erect new machinery."[16] Equally important, the actions of the mob fit most whites' definition of a "good" lynching: there had been only a brief and non-violent confrontation between whites, Lavender had admitted his "guilt," and his sober and responsible killers had successfully hanged him and then dispersed. By early the following day, thousands of residents had turned out on a bitter cold February morning to view the "weird, strange scene" of Lavender dangling "frozen stiff and stark" on a rope below a massive oak tree. Indeed, so many spectators cut off pieces of the rope for souvenirs that by mid-morning his body had fallen down. Later, at the funeral home where Lavender was taken, a local photographer "secured a likeness of the man as he lay on the board with the big hangman's knot encircling his neck" to be sold as a memento of the event. The general feeling in town, the *Times* boasted, was "that a good thing had been done" and the "dignity of the people maintained."[17] A subsequent grand jury investigation failed to indict anyone after the only people who admitted being present—two newspaper reporters—claimed handkerchiefs had concealed the identities of others at the scene. Overall, the jury complained, "they never found a lot of witnesses who knew less."[18]

In the aftermath of the Lavender lynching and the failure to hold anyone accountable for the crime, the city's press and white residents called for "lynch justice" even more frequently. Only days after Lavender's extralegal hanging, Jeff Dooley returned to town to stand trial for the murder of a Roanoke policeman. Crowds again gathered outside the jail and demanded he be summarily executed. The mayor, however, called out extra police in addition to the Roanoke Light Infantry in order to protect the prisoner. The trial lasted only two days, and after the jury returned a verdict of murder in the first degree, the judge sentenced Dooley to be hanged in Roanoke in early April. Local papers praised the decision, but noted that the recent lynching had stirred up citizens to the point that they would have settled for nothing less. Indeed, the editors of the *Times* boasted that "lynching has its place" and claimed that citizens would hereafter swiftly administer "justice" any time local officials failed to.[19] Dooley, however, disappointed those excited about his impending hanging by dying in jail before his execution date.[20]

Only weeks after Dooley's sentence, papers notified the public of another "candidate for the rope"—an African American teenager accused of raping a black child. Since the victim was African American, the press reported that few white residents believed it was their duty to get involved. Instead, papers encouraged "respectable" blacks in the community to act responsibly and lynch the "lecherous scoundrel." Before they could, however, authorities removed the young man to Lynchburg.[21] A week later, the *Times* reported that there was "another candidate for Judge Lynch"—Richard Fraling, a white man arrested after he was accused of molesting a four-year-old white girl. Although the mayor again called out the militia to protect the prisoner, several dozen men stormed the jail before it arrived and dragged Fraling out into the street. After some heated debate, the crowd decided against lynching a white man and turned Fraling back over to the police. Authorities then immediately shipped him off to Lynchburg to await trial.[22]

Roanoke's papers not only endorsed local lynchings, they also fanned the flames of race hatred by printing dozens of gruesome and sensationalized accounts of lynchings elsewhere in Virginia alongside editorials forecasting an impending "race war." In early 1893, for example, after a mob in the coalfields of Richlands, Virginia, lynched five black men, the *Times* deemed those responsible "orderly and brave" and noted with satisfaction that "no disturbance of any kind occurred" because the crowd "worked quietly and with determination, giving each of the negroes time to confess."[23] The "orderly" Richlands hangings, like Lavender's murder, could be cast as a "good" lynching, a distinction that made the tidy variety of extralegal killing acceptable to the South's upper classes but marked those marred by violence between whites, where guilt was in question, where the mob was boisterous or drunken, or where the killers botched a hanging, as totally unacceptable. Later in the spring of 1893, a mob in Marion, Virginia, lynched a black "brute" who was accused of committing "a fiendish outrage" on the local sheriff's wife. Men involved in the hanging journeyed to Roanoke and presented the *Times*'s editors with a piece of the rope.[24] The only means of stopping "Judge Lynch," the paper argued afterwards, would be the passage of laws that allowed for the immediate trial and execution of such "beasts."[25] After yet another lynching in the region that summer, the editors of the *Times* noted that "when a certain class of crimes are inevitably visited by speedy death at the hands of the community without waiting for the tardy and uncertain wheels of justice, sure it is that the law is at fault and not the people."[26]

■■■

At the same time racial antipathies and predilections for lynching were reaching new heights in Roanoke, a catastrophic economic depression was sweeping the nation. The 1893 Depression struck Roanoke especially hard, throwing the Norfolk & Western Railroad into a reorganization receivership, driving the Norwich Lock Works out of business, forcing layoffs at the Roanoke Machine Works, and causing four of the town's seven banks to fail.[27] In one sign of how dire the economic downturn had become, one bank even repossessed a local Episcopal Church and sold it at auction under order of the sheriff to satisfy its delinquent mortgage payments.[28] By the fall of 1893, the depression had grown so severe that newly elected Mayor Henry Trout ordered a special session of the council to get permission to suspend all municipal improvements. Few residents had been able to pay their property taxes, he reported, and as a result, the city treasury was empty.[29] The railroad and machine shops cut wages and hours and laid off hundreds of employees. Many of the idle shop and railroad workers packed up their families and left town; those who stayed struggled to make ends meet. Unskilled laborers from the countryside faced even worse economic circumstances, and those who did not leave subsisted on odd jobs, charity, and occasionally begging. Although up until 1893 Roanoke faced a severe housing shortage, once the depression set in, over five hundred homes stood vacant.[30]

In industrialized parts of Appalachia like Roanoke, the depression increased tensions between workers and new professional and upper classes, who managed local businesses and took the blame for the shocking and mysterious economic collapse.[31] To make matters worse, in the fall of 1893, residents became embroiled in a heated "local option" election to decide whether the town would ban the sale of alcohol. While the vote did not break down entirely along racial or class lines, a significant segment of the city's registered African Americans joined local authorities and middle- and upper-class whites in support of prohibition, while the town's white working classes were generally opposed to any restrictions on the sale of alcohol. The debate began in the spring of 1892, in the wake of a weeklong crusade by the renowned revivalist Sam Jones. Roanoke's reputation for debauchery was widespread by the time Jones arrived, which led papers in the region to predict that Jones, who was "never so happy as when fighting the devil," would "find enough of his Satanic Majesty in the Magic City to make the contest interesting."[32] Five thousand residents turned out for Jones's first sermon—a lengthy diatribe against the town's sixty-five saloons, which he believed represented over $300,000 in capital "invested for the damnation of young men."[33] The following day Jones toured the city, and that night told an overflow crowd that from what he had seen of Railroad Avenue "its name ought to be changed to the drunkard's highway to hell."[34] He blasted local authorities for not doing more to suppress gambling dens, whorehouses, and public drunkenness and held them primarily responsible for "ruining the best boys of your town."[35] In his last sermon, Jones read a letter from the wife of a Roanoke Machine Shop worker who testified that saloon keepers in town "rob the wives and children of the necessities of life" by doing all in their power to "get the workingmen's money." If it were up to him, Jones declared, he would use a cowhide whip on the neglectful husbands and run the barkeepers out of town.[36]

In the aftermath of Jones's visit, Evangelical women in the city organized five chapters of the Woman's Christian Temperance Union (WCTU) and over two hundred of their husbands and sons joined a local Prohibition Club.[37] William Campbell, pastor of the First Presbyterian Church and "an active leader in every moral reform," assumed a leadership position in the effort and used his Presbyterian newspaper *Words and Works* to advocate prohibition.[38] In a typical "temperance column," Campbell recounted the pathetic fate of two drunken Machine Shop workers. The first came into town on payday to buy bread and meat for his family but "got into a saloon on Salem avenue, and soon got so full he could scarcely walk." He spent all his pay on beer and returned home to his hungry family empty-handed. The other drank a bottle of whiskey, passed out in a mud puddle, and drowned. Neither tragedy, Campbell noted, "has materially lessened the number of saloons."[39] In early

1893, Campbell got even more involved, leading a successful campaign by the WCTU and Prohibition Club to prevent the licensing of a bar in one of the city's working-class neighborhoods.[40] In the spring, he and the prohibition organizations established "Temperance Clubs" throughout the city to circulate petitions for a "local option" vote on banning alcohol. By summer, the clubs had enough signatures, and a city judge scheduled the election for early September 1893. In an obvious sign that there would be a fierce battle over the issue, only twenty-one of the over eleven hundred names on the clubs' petitions came from residents of the Northeast, the city's main working-class neighborhood.[41]

The fight began in earnest in August, a month before the vote, when organizations representing each side of the issue started staging rallies and marches to attract supporters. Although the issue crossed the boundaries of class and race, it was generally the city's white workers who lined up against prohibition. To them, patronizing saloons among fellow workingmen was a cherished liberty and integral part of their social lives. While many businessmen and politicians refused to support prohibition, most of the town's middle and upper classes viewed saloons as a threat to law and order, production, and family life. Prohibition, in their view, would recast working-class recreation in ways that conformed to a modern, bourgeois, value system.[42]

Since the town's whites were almost evenly divided over the issue, organizers from both groups focused at least some of their efforts on African Americans. At an anti-prohibition rally in Gainesborough's Davis Hall, business leaders and politicians spoke out against local option, reminding their black audience that they had supported funding for a new schoolhouse for African Americans.[43] At a counter rally for blacks held in the Opera House, William Campbell joined African American minister Richard R. Jones and black school principal Daniel W. Harth to encourage those in attendance to save their race from dissipation and extinction by casting votes in favor of prohibition. The local WCTU, like the national organization, reached out to black residents as well, arguing much like Campbell, Jones, and Harth that prohibition would better the African American community as well as safeguard black families. On election eve, the "wets" held a final rally at the Academy of Music that featured some of the city's most successful business leaders, most of whom argued that a ban on alcohol would further destroy the local economy by discouraging workers from settling in Roanoke. The question, Judge William G. Robertson asserted, was "not whether we are to be intemperate or not, but shall the majority say to the minority, you shall not drink liquor." He urged the audience "to be men and not be influenced by the pulpit against your own interests." "Never," the *Times* summed up the campaign, "has a conflict been more vigorously waged."[44]

The next day, the "wets" won decisively in the city's working-class wards. Although they also carried the mostly black Third Ward, it was by the slimmest margin possible, with only 51 percent of voters casting ballots against prohibition. The "drys" won easily in the predominantly middle- and upper-class First Ward, and in the end, they also carried the entire election by 139 votes. Hostility over the outcome was palpable, according to the *Times*, which reported that the vote had engendered "a large amount of enmity and strife" that showed no signs of dissipating.[45] In the days after the contest, anti-prohibitionists accused the prohibitionists of fraud, hired a team of lawyers, and filed a suit contesting the election.[46] The lawsuit, according to William Campbell and other local option supporters, was a bald attempt to "defy the will of the majority."[47]

■■■

The city's working classes were despondent over the outcome of the election, and though there were many obvious targets for their fury—the WCTU, clergy, reform-minded middle and upper classes, government officials—the fact that blacks had played a major role in removing their right to drink was perhaps most galling of all. In the aftermath of the vote, workers' and poor whites' mistrust of local authorities and intolerance for African Americans reached their zeniths in Roanoke, creating an atmosphere so poisoned with suspicion and disgust that any spark might ignite class warfare or a racial pogrom. Only two weeks after the vote, when rumors spread that a black man had robbed and killed a farmer's wife on the City Market, the flame had clearly been lit.

Sallie A. Bishop, a middle-aged white woman, and her twelve-year-old son had come to town Wednesday morning, September 20, 1893, from neighboring Botetourt County to sell produce on Market Square. Not long after arriving, Bishop stumbled into a nearby grocery store in a daze. She was bleeding from several large gashes on her head. About thirty minutes earlier, she explained to the throng of men who quickly surrounded her, a black man had offered her sixty cents for some grapes on the condition that she go with him to deliver the fruit to a "Miss Hicks" on Salem Avenue, which was not far from Market Square. Bishop followed the man into the basement of the building given as the address, where he drew a straight razor and demanded money. After she handed over $2 or $3, he beat her unconscious with a brick and fled the scene. The man, she told those gathered around her, was in his early twenties, "tolerably black," and wearing a faded gray frock coat, gray pants, and a "large, black slouch hat." Word of the assault spread quickly, as did rumors that a black "brute" had murdered or raped Bishop. Within minutes, patrons poured out of saloons and local businesses to look for the culprit, and dozens of farmers at the Market unhitched their teams and rode bareback through the city searching for him.[48]

Market Square in the early 1900s. Norfolk & Western Historical Photograph Collection (NS5780), Digital Library and Archives, University Libraries, Virginia Tech.

William Edwards, a black teenager who had joined the hunt, witnessed someone matching Bishop's description jump aboard an outbound train under the Randolph Street Bridge which was a couple of blocks from the Market. Edwards hopped aboard as well and pulled the man off. As the suspect fled toward woods in the southeast near Belmont Boulevard and Tazewell Avenue, a posse nearby joined the chase. William G. Baldwin, chief detective of the Norfolk & Western Railroad, rode into the lead and first overtook the man. Baldwin drew his revolver, ordered him onto the back of his horse, and proceeded back to town through dozens of men throwing rocks and demanding that the suspect be immediately turned over to them. Baldwin took the suspect to Conway's Saloon, where doctors were treating Bishop, and forced his way through the enraged men gathered outside. Over shouts of "lynch him" or "hang him," Bishop tentatively explained that the man resembled her attacker and asked to see his hat, which she identified as the one worn by the person who robbed her. The detective, gun drawn, rushed the suspect back to his horse and headed for the jail. An immense and hysterical mob followed close behind.[49]

Baldwin beat the crowd to the jail and turned the man over to authorities, who lodged him in a cell on the second floor. Within minutes, according to a reporter at the scene, the municipal building was "surrounded by over a thousand men clamoring for revenge and blood." The mob was almost entirely composed of lower- and working-class white men, almost all of whom interpreted the attack on Mrs. Bishop as yet another assault on the white community. Mayor Henry Trout and the city's Commonwealth Attorney addressed the increasingly boisterous crowd and promised swift justice. Trout, a Big Lick native, former state legislator, well-known bank president, and member of the N&W's board of trustees, was widely admired by residents, and his speech at least temporarily mollified the mob. In a clear sign of the crowd's mistrust of local authorities, however, its members entirely surrounded the jail to make certain officials did not attempt to remove the prisoner. Others in the mob headed off for Botetourt County to gather Bishop's kin and neighbors. The man in custody, Thomas Smith, was married, and an unemployed former Crozier Iron Furnace worker from nearby Vinton. He denied any knowledge of the attack. Beyond the identification of his slouch hat, there was no actual evidence against him. Moreover, why a black male, witnessed by dozens of farmers leading Bishop away from the Market, would rob her, beat her, and then remain nearby for the next half-hour defied logic. Although Smith was probably innocent, the city's press assured readers that he was the culprit. *The Roanoke Times* even falsely claimed that Bishop "immediately knew her assailant and said so."[50]

Protecting Smith from the lynch mob was made far more precarious in Roanoke because the police force charged with safeguarding him was under-

1887 Roanoke Municipal Building and Jail, at the corner of Commerce Street and Campbell Avenue, early 1900s. Norfolk & Western Historical Photograph Collection (NS5798), Digital Library and Archives, University Libraries, Virginia Tech.

Riot and Reform

staffed and inept. The last mayor had removed the department's former chief after he had embezzled over $2,000, and numerous officers had been dismissed for fighting, drunkenness, or sleeping on duty. Some were caught consorting with prostitutes while on duty.[51] The city's 1892 charter put the mayor back in charge of the force, and when Henry Trout assumed office that year, he quickly reorganized the entire department. "I desire to have a police force," the newly elected mayor told the department, "that will be a credit to the city, and I expect to have it." Trout praised the new chief, John F. Terry, a Civil War veteran and former N&W Yardmaster, for restoring order to the department. Trout left him and Sergeant Alexander H. Griffin, a Pennsylvanian and former Machine Shops worker, in their leadership positions. Neither man, however, had any formal police training, nor had either been on the force more than a year.[52] The sixteen other officers in the department lacked formal training as well, and most of them were wholly unprepared for the danger and mayhem they encountered on Roanoke's streets. They came and went as quickly as they could, according to Sergeant Griffin, who observed that many "started out very bravely as patrolmen in the morning but could hardly lay aside their badge fast enough at night."[53]

Throughout the remainder of the day, the crowd outside the jail grew in size and became more belligerent. Bottles of whiskey passed freely between its members all afternoon, and as the men become more and more intoxicated, their demands for "lynch justice" steadily increased in volume. Unlike other municipal officials in Virginia, who generally acquiesced to the demands of lynch mobs, Henry Trout vowed to protect Smith, knowing full well that he risked social ostracism and retribution. Given state authorities' silence on the issue and hesitance to protect potential lynching victims, his stand was all the more remarkable.[54] It did not take Trout long to realize that his police force would be no match for the mob and that he could not remove the prisoner, so rather than risk Smith's safety, Trout called up the Roanoke Light Infantry, the city's component of the Virginia Militia. According to Jack W. Hancock, a member of the infantry, when he and seventeen other militia members marched to the municipal building, Trout again came outside and pleaded with the crowd to disperse before ordering the squad to clear the street in front of the jail. The mob, Hancock reported, laughed at the men and "made fun of us saying we were afraid to shoot." The militia, although armed with bayonets and rifles, was hardly threatening. A social organization as much as an infantry, its crisply uniformed members, most of them young clerks for the railroad or other businesses, had no experience with actual combat. Although outnumbered by at least twenty to one, the infantry was able to clear the street in front of the municipal building, giving police an opportunity to arrest two of the most vocal men in the crowd when they refused to back up.[55]

Roanoke Light Infantry clearing Campbell Avenue side of Municipal Building and Jail, September 20, 1893. History Museum and Historical Society of Western Virginia, Roanoke.

After driving the crowd back, John Bird, Captain of the Infantry, stationed his men along Campbell Avenue from Commerce to Roanoke Streets, creating a block-wide perimeter around the municipal building. Bird, who had moved to Roanoke from Connecticut a couple of years earlier to help operate the Norwich Lock Works, believed the situation was under control even though hundreds of men remained nearby, milling about Campbell Avenue beside the Ponce de Leon Hotel. In an obvious indication of just how confident Bird was, at 7:30 PM he walked several blocks to Catagonis Restaurant to check on a take-out order for his troops. According to Hancock, Bird had been gone only a few minutes when he frantically telephoned from Catagonis to report that the mob was rushing up Commerce Street and Campbell Avenue. Bird beat the crowd back to the municipal building and had his men take up defensive positions along the front steps and at the windows. Hancock, stationed on the steps with four other soldiers, saw what he believed to be at least a thousand men running up the street and "cheering as they came." Its leaders, according to local papers, were Mrs. Bishop's oldest son and fifty to a hundred other men from Botetourt County who had just arrived in the city. "It seemed," Hancock reported, "that they would attempt to rush over us at every moment."[56]

Thousands of spectators followed the mob to the municipal building and watched the confrontation. E. P. Tompkins, a railroad clerk among them, recalled that he gossiped with friends and never dreamed of danger.[57] William

Campbell, like other ministers, wandered through the crowd, doing what he could to talk its members out of an attempt to lynch the prisoner. Campbell, who like most residents believed the rumor that Mrs. Bishop was dead, left the scene to hold a special prayer meeting at his church a few blocks away. "We have a murderer in our city," he told his congregation, "and I fear we shall have a number of others."[58] While Campbell preached, the mob closed in around the jail. Trout and Bird, who had drawn his sword, pleaded once again for calm, informing those close enough to hear them that the infantry's guns were loaded and would be used to protect Smith. "They replied with curses and abuse," Hancock recalled, "saying that they were not afraid of us, that we were afraid to shoot, and that they would have the negro."[59] With the situation clearly spiraling out of control, Bird wired the governor to warn him that the infantry was surrounded by a mob of five thousand and would be "wiped out shortly."[60]

Around 8:00 PM, according to a reporter at the scene, the shouting and screaming mob made a "wild rush" toward the western side of the jail, battering a door there with logs and shattering every window with rocks and bottles. In the chaos, Bird issued the "ready" command and signaled his men to cock their rifles and take aim at the crowd below.[61] Seconds later, a shot rang out. Who fired it remains unclear. Hancock, stationed out front, swore that it and four or five others that rang out afterwards in rapid succession came from the sidewalk across the street.[62] A correspondent for *The Roanoke Times* concurred, reporting that "in the fever heat of excitement and suspense . . . several imprudent persons in the street opposite the jail, near the Chinese laundry, fired a number of pistol shots."[63] E. P. Tompkins, however, claimed that as soon as the mob started bashing the door there "came a volley of shots from the windows over my head, and men fell right and left in the street."[64] The *Daily Record*'s correspondent at the scene agreed and reported there were thousands of other witnesses who saw the militia open fire on the crowd. Whatever the origins of the first shot, after it rang out, the infantry opened fire. Over the next two minutes, it and the mob exchanged about a hundred and fifty shots.[65]

Many of the bullets hit Greene Memorial Church next door, forcing parishioners to seek shelter under their pews.[66] A couple blocks away, at William Campbell's prayer vigil, he and his congregation heard the "terrific roar of musketry" and rushed outside to see what had happened. Campbell passed several of the wounded as they were dragged away and he saw thousands of men and women "running in every direction to get out of reach of other shots that might come."[67] In the panic, the mob and crowd of spectators fled down Campbell Avenue or tumbled into piles behind the Ponce de Leon Hotel's railing. "The street before the jail," according to E. P. Tompkins, "looked a shambles, blood in forty places, the street car rails slippery with it."[68] In the alley beside the jail, the *Daily Times* reported, the ground was "soaked with blood, stones splattered and walls splashed with the same dreadful dye." The melee killed eight men in the crowd, wounded thirty-one others, and left Mayor Trout, the only casualty inside the courthouse, with a bullet lodged in his foot. According to local papers, most of those struck down or wounded had been spectators standing on the outskirts of the mob. S. A. Vick, proprietor of the St. James Hotel, was among the dead, as were three Norfolk & Western employees, a Roanoke County distiller, and George Settles, a popular member of the Roanoke Athletic Club's baseball team. Charlie Morten, the black saloonkeeper, was wounded, as were two African American women who had been watching the mob from across the street. Most of those hit in the volley were horrifically injured. One man had his leg blown off, another lost his foot, and several others had wounds to the groin, stomach, or head. In the chaos of the assault, the militia and mob both fired haphazardly, and according to doctors who treated the injured, pistol shots from the crowd hit at least three spectators in addition to Mayor Trout.[69]

Within a few minutes of the clash, N&W Detective William Baldwin made his way to the courthouse to warn the militia and city officials that members of the mob were breaking into hardware stores downtown to steal rifles and dynamite. According to a *Times* correspondent in the area, "incendiary speeches were being made by a dozen men," all of whom had vowed to mount another attack on the infantry and to lynch Mayor Trout along with Smith. When Judge John W. Woods and local politician J. Allan Watts attempted to dissuade the crowd, men in the mob shouted them down and fired pistols in the air. According to Jack Hancock, shortly after Baldwin's warning, Trout limped into the Ponce de Leon Hotel and Captain Bird ordered the militia to shed their uniforms, go home, and stay inside. Before leaving, Trout instructed the police force to take Smith into hiding. Once the mayor left, however, Chief Terry suggested that they save themselves by turning him over to the mob. Sergeant Griffin and two other officers ignored him, and along with George Gordon, another black prisoner, they took Smith across the Roanoke River to a hiding spot beyond the southwestern limits of the city.[70] When the mob returned and found the courthouse empty, according to Tompkins, one of its leaders climbed onto a table inside, "swinging a coil of rope with many oaths calling for volunteers to help hang the mayor."[71] William Campbell once again begged the crowd to disperse but found the men so enraged that "they would not listen to reason or anything else."[72]

After a frenzied search of both the courthouse and the Ponce de Leon Hotel failed to turn up the mayor or Smith, the crowd followed Mrs. Bishop's son to Trout's house. The mayor had slipped out the back door of the hotel only minutes earlier, after getting treatment on his wounded foot, and remained

Ponce de Leon Hotel, at the corner of Campbell Avenue and Commerce Street, early 1900s. Norfolk & Western Historical Photograph Collection (NS5768), Digital Library and Archives, University Libraries, Virginia Tech.

in hiding among his friends.[73] Having failed to find the mayor or Smith, the mob then broke up into several ten- to fifteen-man squads to ransack the homes of city officials and guard the railroad tracks to prevent either man from escaping by train.[74] Sometime later that night, George Gordon—the prisoner who helped Smith escape—and Sergeant Griffin returned to the jail. By then, Griffin had had a change of heart and told Chief Terry that Smith was "nothing but a damned negro" who deserved to be lynched. Terry agreed, and at around three that morning he ordered Smith brought back to the jail. He then informed at least one member of the mob about the plan. As a result, twenty-five armed men, their faces hidden behind handkerchiefs, were waiting in a vacant lot halfway between Commerce and Roanoke Streets when Smith and his escorts appeared. Smith spotted the posse first and took off running but made it only a few dozen yards before he was knocked down. The gang ordered Griffin and the other officers to "take a walk." They then headed off into the darkness with Smith.[75]

The men proceeded only a short distance before they stopped beneath an electric light at the corner of Franklin Road and Mountain Avenue. Unlike William Lavender, who in a desperate attempt to save his life admitted he was drunk and accidentally knocked Alice Perry down, Smith refused to confess to assaulting Mrs. Bishop, denying his executioners their final prize and leaving them determined to stigmatize his body. They promptly tossed a rope over a hickory tree, strung Smith up, riddled him with bullets, and desecrated and decorated his body in ways that marked him both physically and socially as one who had transgressed the boundaries of allowed behavior. To them, Smith's supposed assault of a "defenseless" and "respectable" white woman was an attack on their masculine responsibility to protect white women from the black "menace" roaming Roanoke. Moreover, Smith, the former "property" of local officials, was the symbol of middle- and upper-class efforts to impose order on the city's working classes and rural immigrants. His hanging thus served two purposes: it terrorized black residents and rebuked white authorities.

In the morning, the *Times* reported, thousands of residents turned out to view the tree's "ghastly fruit." Signs pinned to Smith's back proclaimed him "Mayor Trout's Friend" and warned "Do Not Cut Him Down—By Order of Judge Lynch." Hundreds of those who came to view Smith took bark from the tree, slices of the rope, or pieces of his clothing as souvenirs.[76] A photo of the scene, sold as a keepsake by Lineback Photography Studio, reveals throngs of smiling men and women as well as several black residents in the immense crowd around Thomas Smith, who hangs, much like a prize buck or bear, as a trophy to be admired. Smith, dressed in a shabby suit and wearing pants with patches over the knees, dangles only a few feet off the ground, his white socks hanging off his feet, his eyes and tongue protruding out of his badly swollen head, and his ears bleeding from spots where hunks had been cut off as souvenirs.[77] That residents felt not only comfortable but also enthusiastic about posing for cameras next to Smith says a great deal about their self-righteousness and evident pride in his violent demise. The carnival-like atmosphere that followed Smith's extralegal hanging was common in lynchings throughout the South, and much like participants in other "lynch festivals," Roanoke residents sought to prolong their "victory" by further desecrating Smith's body.[78] The difference, however, was that they wanted to do so in a way that further solidified their disdain for city authorities as well. Indeed, when members of a coroner's jury arrived and had Smith cut down to be taken to the city morgue, the enormous crowd refused to release him and insisted that they were going to lay Smith in state on the mayor's dining room table before burying him in Trout's front yard.[79]

William Campbell learned of the plan to further demean Mayor Trout from Robert Moorman, an elder in his church, and insisted that Moorman rush him to the scene so that he could prevent it. When Moorman and Campbell arrived, several men had just begun to drag Smith down the street, and there were at least a thousand people cheering them on. Campbell pleaded with them to stop. Their reply, according to him, consisted of "angry words" and fists waved in his face. Several men pushed Moorman down and started dragging Smith away again before Campbell grabbed the rope and told them "they should not drag the body through the streets; that we had already suffered enough." His stand convinced at least a few men in the group to back him up, and with their added pleas, the mob eventually decided to burn Smith on the banks of the Roanoke River instead. A crowd of hundreds then followed the wagon that bore Smith's body down Mountain Avenue, cheering and tearing down fences along the way. When they reached a spot near the narrow gauge railroad bridge, several men gathered brush and tree limbs to build a pyre, doused Smith with coal oil, and set him afire. "The flames roared and cracked, leaping high in the air," according to a reporter at the scene, "while all around stood 4,000 people, men, women, boys and children on foot, in buggies and on horseback, and numbers of them shouting over the pitiful scene." Hundreds of onlookers fed the flames by tossing braches and twigs into the fire, and by noon, according to another correspondent, all that remained of Smith "was a few ashes and here and there a bone."[80]

After the fire burned out, the mob turned its fury back to the militia and mayor. Trout, who was still hiding in town, decided to leave after the torrent of threats against him showed no signs of abating. The following evening, accompanied by railroad detective Baldwin, he boarded a special Norfolk & Western coach east of the Machine Works and rode to Lynchburg. When a reporter visited Trout later that evening, he found the mayor in a "highly nervous and overwrought condition and laboring under much mental perturbation." In a sign of just how troubled Trout was, his thirty-eight-caliber pistol was on the hotel room table.[81] Back in Roanoke, R. A. Buckner, president of the city council, had taken over as mayor. In an attempt to restore order, he and a citizens' committee headed by Joseph H. Sands, vice-president of the N&W, issued a broadside. "It is most desirable," the flyer proclaimed, "that all excitement should be allayed, exciting speeches or conversation discouraged, and the majesty of the law shall be respected as being competent to deal fully and justly with all persons who may be suspected of sharing illegally in the events of last night." The committee advised all citizens to go home or back to work and summoned a grand jury to investigate the lynching and riot. Buckner suspended Police Chief Terry and several other officers and appointed dozens of special policemen "whose duty is to urge upon citizens to preserve order and disperse to their homes." He and the committee also convinced saloonkeepers to close their businesses.[82]

Later that day, Joseph Sands addressed all N&W and Machine Works employees and asked them to abide by the law and help restore order. Although the workers voted to follow Sands's advice, they also passed a resolution declaring the militia's actions unprovoked and demanded a full investigation of the mayor, police force, and infantry. The city's Masons and Odd Fellows pledged to assist municipal authorities, as did the William Watts Camp of Confederate Veterans and the local post of the Grand Army of the Republic. The Blue and Gray veterans issued a joint statement that backed the citizens' committee and condemned the "lawless persons" responsible for tarnishing the reputation of the Magic City.[83]

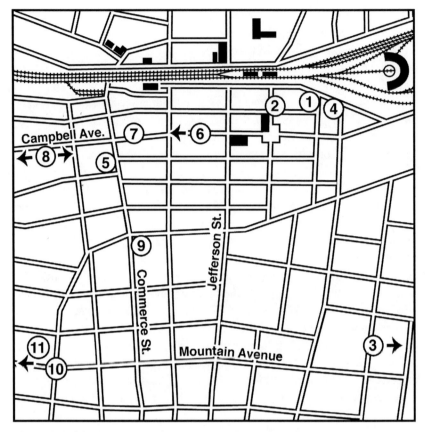

Roanoke Riot of 1893. LEGEND: (1.) At the request of an African American male who claimed he had been sent by " Miss Hicks" to arrange the purchase of grapes, Sallie Bishop left her produce stand on Market Square and followed him into the cellar of a vacant building at 134 Salem Avenue, where she was subsequently robbed and beaten. (2.) Dazed from a blow to the head, Bishop made her way out of the cellar and stumbled into nearby Akers Grocery, where she gave an account of the attack to dozens of bystanders. (3.) Thomas Smith, who fit Bishop's vague description, was captured entering a wooded area in lower Southeast Roanoke, about a mile from Market Square. (4.) Bishop, having been removed to Conway's Saloon on Railroad Avenue, tentatively identified Smith based on his "slouch hat" as the man who assaulted her. (5.) After Smith was lodged in the city jail, a mob gathered outside to demand he be immediately lynched. Authorities called out the Roanoke Light Infantry to clear the Campbell Avenue side of the jail. (6.) Around 8PM, a mob led by Bishop's son charged up Campbell Avenue and surrounded the jail. Spectators lined the streets behind the mob. Shots of an unknown origin were eventually fired, prompting the infantry to open fire. Eight residents—primarily spectators—were killed in the exchange. In the chaotic aftermath, Smith was secreted out of jail to a hiding spot across the Roanoke River. (7.) The mob, having turned its fury against local authorities, rampaged through the Hotel Ponce de Leon in an unsuccessful attempt to capture Mayor Henry Trout. (8.) Hundreds of men from the mob marched up Campbell Avenue to search Trout's home while scores of others headed downtown to gather guns and block his possible escape routes. (9.) After Police Chief Terry ordered Smith returned to the jail, a heavily armed posse overtook Smith and his police escort on Commerce Street at Franklin Road. (10.) The

The mob, nevertheless, continued to roam the streets in search of city authorities and militia members. Although most infantrymen stayed in hiding, Jack Hancock, a bank clerk, reported to work the morning of the lynching and stayed there until friends convinced him to leave. Like all members of the militia, Hancock later received a death threat from the "Headquarters of the Vigilant Committee." "Sir," the note read, "prepare yourself to meet your creator—one day longer in Roanoke you will sleep the sleep of the brave. We want your blood—you shot our friends. Yours to administer death, 163 Citizens." After getting the threat, Hancock recalled, "Nearly all the boys left town or stayed off the streets Thursday, Friday, Saturday and Sunday." He did not leave but did decide to lodge with heavily armed comrades at a boarding house rather than go home.[84] Other infantrymen and city officials hid in Salem, which according to the *Richmond Dispatch,* had become a "city of refuge for many of those who have incurred the wrath of the mob."[85] According to E. P. Tompkins, an N&W clerk, all of his co-workers in the militia stayed away from the office until the following week, when one by one, they slowly began appearing at their desks again.[86]

The coroner's jury that was charged with investigating the shooting and lynching called its first witnesses on September 22, the day after Smith's hanging. The men who testified failed to concur on who fired the first shot but agreed that Mrs. Bishop's son and Walter Davis, a seventeen-year-old Roanoke resident, led the assault on the jail and that the most violent and determined members of the mob were fifty to one hundred of Bishop's neighbors from Botetourt County. Captain Bird of the infantry admitted that he gave the order to fire on the crowd, but swore that he did so only after men in the mob fired several shots at him. Several witnesses claimed that Chief Terry attempted to turn Smith over to the mob after the shooting but that Mayor Trout had insisted that the police force continue to protect him. At the conclusion of testimony, the jury found that all the men killed except Smith died as a result of Bird's order, and it forwarded the case to a grand jury to determine the legality of the shooting.[87]

Mayor Trout, who had gone to Richmond the day after he arrived in Lynchburg, refused all requests for interviews but told reporters that he hoped to return to Roanoke as soon as possible. Trout's wife, who had been at the

Continued from previous page

posse removed Smith down Franklin Road to the corner of Mountain Avenue, where it lynched him from a hickory tree, riddled his body with bullets, and decorated him with signs indicating that he was "Mayor Trout's Friend." (11.) The next day, thousands of residents turned out to view Smith and gather souvenirs of his lynching. After being dissuaded from burying Smith's body in Mayor Trout's yard, the crowd carted the body down Mountain Avenue to the bank of the Roanoke River and burned it. Map by Clifford Duplechin Jr., Cartographic Section, Geography & Anthropology Department, LSU.

144

World's Fair in Chicago during the riot, joined him in Richmond shortly after he arrived there.[88] Back in Roanoke, the Citizens' Committee issued a statement to the Southern Press Association urging the mayor to return. "It is our purpose," they claimed, "to demonstrate to the world that the charge we are under mob rule and the course of law cannot be pursued on account of intimidation and threats is false."[89] Virginia Governor Philip W. McKinney, who had previously been hesitant to use the power of the state to suppress lynching, changed course after the mayhem in Roanoke. The riot, he told the state senate, was a "terrible lesson" that should make all Virginians realize the need to "respect the authorities and obey the law." Henceforth, he warned, the state would maintain order "and the consequences must rest upon the heads of those who make it necessary."[90]

Reaction to the lynching and riot appeared in newspapers around the nation and as far away as London.[91] The New York Herald, like most papers, praised the "heroic example of Mayor Trout" and called the ensuing riot and lynching an outbreak of barbarism that had disgraced Roanoke.[92] The New York Evening Post likewise condemned the mob as "savages" and claimed "the volley of the Roanoke militia must carry some comfort in the heart of every civilized man in the country." In Philadelphia, the Telegraph applauded Trout but noted that he would "be a fortunate creature if he does not hereafter walk the earth a marked and hunted man."[93] Most editors cited damage done to the city's reputation as a progressive and booming business center as the most lamentable outcome of the violence. "Roanoke," the New York World observed, "is at the parting of ways. It is for her people to determine whether the officers of the law or the ring leaders of a mob shall be municipal rulers."[94]

Most Virginia newspapers expressed similar opinions. The conservative Richmond Dispatch claimed that there could "be no doubt of the Mayor's courage" in attempting to maintain law and order, and while the black-owned Richmond Planet commended Trout too, it also called Smith's murder yet another example of "southern depravity."[95] The Lynchburg News backed the mayor as well and observed that the sooner residents acknowledged their debt to him for warning them "against the wretchedness they brought upon themselves, the sooner the town will deserve the respect of enlightened people's opinion everywhere."[96] The Petersburg Index-Appeal, though also complimentary of Trout, argued that he and other officials did not go far enough in protecting Smith. "No more glorious opportunity to die with credit in the performance of duty," the paper explained, "will ever be afforded Mayor Trout."[97] The Norfolk Landmark blamed the mob for the "disgrace and humiliation of an entire community" and called the lynching a "brutal and cowardly" act that must not only be condemned but also accounted for in a court of law.[98] Editors at the Richmond Evening Star, by contrast, praised the community for exterminat-

Riot and Reform

ing a "fiend" and argued that the actions of city officials and the infantry were "nothing more or less than murder."[99]

Coverage of the riot in out-of-town newspapers shattered the progressive image of the Magic City that local boosters had cultivated, directly threatening continued economic investment. The press accounts justifiably horrified Roanoke's business leaders, who reacted to the riot with strong support for municipal authorities and loud demands for law and order. Roanoke's papers, longtime supporters of "lynch justice," did an abrupt about-face and called for speedy punishment of the men responsible for the riot. The *Times* extolled Trout's leadership and acknowledged that the infantry had no choice but to fire upon the mob. The *Daily Record* likewise informed readers that unless they were "ready to see their hopes of building a metropolis turned to despair, her streets turned to pastures, and her houses the roosting places of birds of night, they will with one accord, sustain the constituted authorities in the maintenance of law and order."[100] In a special edition of *Words & Works*, William Campbell called for "calm counsels" and "earnest prayer" with the hope that men "aroused to fever heat" by the shooting would commit no further bloodshed. Lynch law, he declared, is "the expression and developer of lawless spirit" and so horrid that "no man is safe where it prevails."[101] The papers also did all they could to shift the blame for the riot onto "country people" from Botetourt County.

City editors' stance against "lawlessness" did do much to quell tensions and bolster public acceptance of the stand against the mob, and when Trout returned a week after fleeing for his life, a crowd of three hundred residents cheered his arrival at the depot.[102] According to the *Times*, by then, "the great mass of the people" had begun to sympathize with authorities and finally "recognized the fact that the laws of the land are supreme and must be enforced."[103] Mrs. Bishop, who had been recovering in Roanoke since the attack, left for her home in Cloverdale the same day Trout returned. Although a week earlier she had only been able to tentatively identify Smith based on his "slouch hat," when questioned leaving town, Bishop reported that she was absolutely certain the man who had beaten her had "met his just deserts."[104]

Roanoke's papers, while admonishing lawlessness, simultaneously damned Smith as a monstrous brute who deserved to die for his crime. They entirely ignored the lack of any real proof against him. They not only embellished the meager evidence against him, but also spun the assault on Bishop into an attempted rape. Although it is impossible to prove, it seems likely that Smith was innocent. In the immediate aftermath of his murder, anti-lynching activist Ida B. Wells claimed to have learned that Smith was not guilty and that this fact was "well known in the city before he was killed."[105] The Cleveland *Gazette*, like other northern papers, reported only weeks after the riot that the "poor Afro-American lynched, and whose body was riddled with bullets, then burned, is now generally acknowledged to have been innocent of the offense charged."[106]

Although Wells and the northern press offered no evidence to support their contentions, more credible accounts of Smith's innocence appeared in the years that followed. According to former infantryman Jack Hancock, a subsequent chief of Roanoke's Police Department informed him that detectives had eventually uncovered evidence that "the man lynched was not the one guilty of the crime for which he was taken up as a suspect." Hancock, unfortunately, did not reveal what the new details were, nor did he name the informant. One intriguing possible source for the information is former police sergeant Alexander H. Griffin—one of the officers who turned Thomas Smith over to the mob—who advanced to Chief of Police in 1912. In the end, however, it is perhaps best to keep in mind that Hancock had a personal stake in proving Smith's innocence since killing white men to protect him would then be more justifiable.[107] In 1916, the NAACP's journal *Crisis: A Record of the Darker Races,* backed up Hancock's claim, reporting much like he did that a high-ranking Roanoke police officer had "recently revealed the fact that the colored man Smith, who was lynched Sept 21, 1893, for assaulting a woman, was innocent and known to be so by officials a short time afterwards." According to the *Crisis,* by the time Baldwin captured Smith, another suspect had admitted his guilt. Authorities ordered him to leave town immediately.[108] If that was indeed the case, then Trout's stand against the lynch mob makes all the more sense.

With Trout back in town and the tide of public opinion now running against the mob, a semblance of law and order returned to the city. Over a hundred "special policemen" teamed up with what was left of the local force to maintain the peace, and many businesses and fraternal orders pledged to do all they could to assist authorities. By September 30, nine days after the lynching, participants in the riot had even returned twenty-six of the forty-one pistols they had stolen from Evans Hardware.[109] The torrent of bad press worried city fathers, but most assumed a looming grand jury investigation would result in punishments against members of the mob so severe that Roanoke's reputation would be at least somewhat rehabilitated. When the jury met for the first time in early October, Judge John Woods made that point clear by informing its members that the eyes of the state and nation were upon them. The lynching and riot, he went on, had been "a withering, blighting curse" and had done so much damage that in his opinion the time would "never come when the city of Roanoke can wipe away the disgrace it has heaped upon her."[110]

During the subsequent hearing, the jury heard over two hundred witnesses before it handed down nineteen indictments on sixteen men for felonies and misdemeanors. Oddly enough, the jury failed to charge Mrs. Bishop's son, the openly acknowledged leader of the mob. It proclaimed the action of the mayor and militia lawful, declared some of those killed active participants in the riot, and charged Police Chief Terry and Sergeant Griffin as accessories to the lynching. Of the fourteen other men indicted, only four stood accused of felonies, and only three of them were accused of lynching Smith. The other felony indictment was against James G. Richardson, a Botetourt County farmer, who allegedly threatened to hang the mayor and who broke into Nelson & Myers Hardware store to steal guns and dynamite. Most of the misdemeanor charges were for inciting the riot or burning Smith's body.[111]

Trout suspended Terry and Griffin following their indictments. He also created a permanent reserve police force of one hundred and fifty "discreet men" to quell riots.[112] A couple of weeks later, the mayor left for the Columbian Exposition in Chicago to take part in "Mayor's Day" as the guest of Chicago Mayor Carter Harrison. If Trout and his wife expected to relax at the Exposition, however, they were sadly mistaken. Still reeling from events in Roanoke, the couple was no doubt horrified by the news that a disgruntled former police officer had assassinated Mayor Harrison on the eve of the "Mayor's Day" celebration.[113]

The November 1893 trials of those charged by the grand jury ended up doing little to help the city's restoration efforts. Edward Page, who had openly boasted of placing the noose around Smith's neck, found plenty of witnesses willing to provide him an alibi, and his jury cleared him of any responsibility in Smith's death.[114] James Richardson, who testified that he had been drinking all day in a Salem Avenue saloon the day of the riot, claimed that he had been too drunk to recall anything about leading the search for Mayor Trout or breaking into a hardware store. Numerous witnesses, however, placed him at the scene and recalled his threatening language against the mayor. The jury found him guilty and the judge sentenced Richardson to thirty days in jail and also fined him $100. The two other rioters found guilty of misdemeanors, S. W. Fuqua, a carpenter, and D. D. Kennedy, an N&W employee, received one-day prison sentences and one-dollar fines.[115] Such light sentences bewildered the *Times*'s editors, who deemed them "travesties upon justice" and yet "another blow to blacken the eye already badly bruised by those acts of lawlessness."[116] In Petersburg, the *Index-Appeal* went even further, claiming that the "verdict practically licenses lawbreaking" and that the trial was "as palpable a miscarriage of justice as could have been imagined outside the opera bouffe or farce comedy."[117] The Philadelphia *Public-Ledger*, like other northern papers, predicted that the sentences would serve as "an encouragement for the lawless to take it upon themselves the functions of Judge Lynch at the slightest provocation."[118]

To make matters worse, prosecutors found no witnesses willing to testify against Chief Terry or Sergeant Griffin. As a result, their jury did not even leave its seats before proclaiming them not guilty of being accessories to the lynching.[119] Mayor Trout, outraged at the acquittals, not only refused to reinstate the men, but he also had them both charged with conduct unbecoming an officer of the law. "I am further of the opinion," he informed the town council, "that the best interests of the City require reorganization of the police force."[120] At their subsequent hearings in December, Terry and Griffin testified against each other, and this time numerous witnesses claimed that both men had plotted to turn Smith over to the mob. Although they were once again acquitted, Trout fired Terry and demoted Sergeant Griffin to patrolman.[121] Early the following year, a Roanoke jury found four men, including mob leader Walter Davis, guilty of felonies for rioting and burning Smith's body. The judge sentenced all of them to a year in jail and imposed $100 fines. None of the men, however, served any significant time in jail or had to pay their fines. Some of them won subsequent appeals. Others, like Walter Davis, received pardons from the governor.[122] Indeed, even James Richardson's thirty-day jail sentence for threatening to hang Mayor Trout was eventually reduced to just twenty-four hours.[123]

In the aftermath of the trials, Roanoke's business and civic leaders kept up their campaign to restore the city's progressive image. In early 1894, as part of that effort, they mounted a campaign to convince Henry Trout to run for re-election.[124] Tensions from the lynching and riot still simmered, and it was unlikely that Trout would have repeated the easy victory he claimed two years earlier. Having survived both Pickett's Charge at the Battle of Gettysburg and the Roanoke Riot, Trout decided the time was right to withdraw from public life. While most of the community forgave their former mayor for his role in the riot, other officials were not so lucky. Captain John Bird of the Roanoke Light Infantry, for example, found the lingering hostility against him impossible to live with and by mid-January, he had resigned his position and left town.[125] Roanoke's businessmen and politicians, well aware of the public relations damage done by the lynch riot, did what they could in the years that followed to downplay its significance or conceal its occurrence.[126] In mid-January 1894, many of them even attended a lecture by civil rights activist Frederick Douglass at Reverend Richard R. Jones's African Baptist Church. Although Douglass was well known for his belief that lynching was proof that the "enemies of the Negro see that he is making progress and they naturally wish to stop him," according to a *Times* reporter, his lecture "was chiefly a literary one, and only occasionally did the speaker touch on the question of the day."[127]

Many of the city's other white inhabitants, by contrast, attempted to keep memories of the lynch riot alive with scrapbooks, souvenirs, folklore, and photos.[128] "Haunt tales" circulated widely in town after the hickory tree from which Smith was hanged died in mid-October. So many residents saw the tree's death as a sign of God's wrath that the *Times* felt obligated to investigate the matter and inform readers that street grading along Mountain Avenue was the actual culprit. City workers cut it down later that month, but folk legends about the hanging tree persisted as late as 2001, when landscapers removed a huge dead ash tree on Franklin Road that many residents incorrectly believed had been used to hang Smith.[129] A few weeks after the actual tree was removed, a suspicious fire gutted the house directly across the street from where it had stood. The *Times,* aware that "silly, hallucinary stories" about the fire's genesis were rampant, lectured residents again, informing them "that the ghost of the departed black man had nothing to do with the origin of the fire."[130] A more likely suspect was Fred Primity, an African American arrested the following month for using coal oil to set fire to the cellar in which Mrs. Bishop had been assaulted.[131]

At least one white resident even wrote a popular ballad about the lynch riot. Sung to the melody of the well-known British ballad "Barbara Allen," the lyrics of the "Roanoke Riot," also known as the "Roanoke Outrage," are perhaps the best representation of contemporary public sentiment about what happened:

It was the twentieth of September
when the moon shown from on high
in the Magic City of Roanoke
nine innocent men did die.

They were shot down by the militia
that was stationed at the jail.
It was the awfulist outrage
that ever did prevail.

The captain gave his orders to fire
when he heard the people shout
for he had instructions from the mayor—H. L. Trout.
It was the awfulist outrage
that was ever heard about.

And I think it was foolish
to call out the militia
all because of
a dirty low down Negro

Some were shot through the heart
while many were shot through the head.
After the firing was over,
nine innocent men lay dead.

Many people did many cruel things,
yes, things we call hard
for they wanted to bury the Negro
in the Mayor's backyard.

But the preacher pleaded with them,
yes, loudly he did shout,
"have some respect for your neighbors here,
if not for Mayor Trout."

Some suggested they burn him
at the stake
for the awful crime attempted,
Mrs. Bishop's life to take.

So they built the fire upon him
out of oil and pine,
and all looked on him to see him burn
yes, everyone that could.

That it was outrage in our city,
yes, everyone that could be clear.
Let's all be quiet now
and have no lynching here.

For the Negro is dead
and gone to a different world from this,
but all do know that he did not go
to a world of heavenly bliss.[132]

Lynching ballads were generally an accurate depiction of a community's interpretation of the event as well as a way to preserve its social memory and add to the "production" of the extralegal hanging by keeping its messages alive.[133] "The Roanoke Riot" illustrates quite vividly that in the public's opinion, city authorities murdered innocent citizens to protect a subhuman criminal. The ballad adds one to the actual number killed in the melee and incorrectly implies that Mayor Trout gave the militia an order to fire. Because eight white men died, the folk song does not celebrate the lynching of Thomas Smith as much as it mourns the loss of good citizens in the process. It also seeks repentance for the many "cruel things" done by the mob and counsels against future extralegal hangings. Traditional lynching ballads served as a way to enshrine lynchers, prolong a "glorious" event, and remind blacks of their subservient and precarious position in society. "The Roanoke Riot," by contrast, is as critical of white authorities as it is about Thomas Smith, and it is ambivalent about lynch "justice." It celebrates William Campbell's actions, which prevented additional "outrages," but in a final blow against the "low down dirty Negro" responsible for the tragedy, the ballad envisions Smith in hell.

Thomas Smith was one of twelve blacks lynched in Virginia in 1893, and one of one hundred and fifty-three blacks lynched in the South that year. Unlike his fellow Virginia victims, who had all been easily and immediately hanged after accusations of rape, murder, or barn burning, Smith stood accused of a comparatively minor offense and had received what protection city officials were able to muster.[134] Although unsympathetic toward Smith, contemporary writers generally found the Roanoke authorities' stance admirable. Popular Virginia novelist Thomas Nelson Page, for example, derided Smith as nothing but a "negro ravisher and murderer" but praised the "brave and faithful" Mayor Trout for his stand "against that most terrible of all assailants—a determined mob."[135] Anti-lynching activist Ida B. Wells, by contrast, used Smith's murder as further proof that black men in the South were being "lynched for anything or nothing."[136] Smith's "offense," according to Wells, was simply quarreling with Mrs. Bishop about incorrect change from a purchase.[137] While Wells commended the militia's "stubborn stand on behalf of law and order" and called Trout's actions a "splendid endeavor to uphold the law," she observed that "for an offense which would not in any civilized community have brought upon him a punishment greater than a fine of a few dollars, this unfortunate Negro was hung, shot, and burned."[138]

Although Roanoke authorities and businessmen adamantly opposed lynching after the 1893 riot because of its potential for civil unrest and negative publicity, they nonetheless chafed at criticism from activists like Wells and continued to regard blacks as unfit for citizenship. Local Board of Trade member Nathaniel Burwell Johnston, a potential candidate for mayor in 1894, held views on the topic that mirror his fellow native business leaders. Johnston, a devout racist who believed that no African American "had ever emerged from savagery except when brought into contact with its superior," advocated segregation, paternalism, and Christianity as the best means to prevent future racial conflicts.[139] "Miss Wells and her sympathizers," Johnston complained in a letter to the New York City Independent, were stoking racial animosities with their "grossly exaggerated statements," making it all the more difficult for Christian men like him to "do something towards the situation." The "ignorance" of northerners about lynching, he went on, was a major part of the problem. In Roanoke, he claimed, northern-born residents were just as involved in the riot as the "country people" vilified in local papers. "We find those who have least patience with the weaknesses of the Negro," he explained, "to be those who came from Northern homes, with all their preconceived ideas altogether in favor of their dark brother, but who when they have fully understood and comprehended his nature, are prepared to, and do go much further in their distrust of him than their former masters."[140]

Virginia Governor Charles T. O'Ferrall, elected only six weeks after the Roanoke Riot, alluded to the chaos there in his inaugural address and vowed to do all he could to prevent any repetition of mob rule, "let it cost what it will in blood or money."[141] Such anti-lynching rhetoric, however, had little to do with sympathy for African Americans but was instead part of a conservative quest to maintain an orderly society in which the power of elected officials did not come into question. Indeed, by the time O'Ferrall assumed office, the 1893 Depression, the rise of the Populist Party, and the Roanoke Riot had combined to make politicians and business leaders alike believe that an under-class revolt could plunge the Old Dominion into anarchy.[142] To counter this threat, O'Ferrall called out the state militia on dozens of occasions to protect potential African American lynching victims. He also demanded thorough investigations of extralegal violence and ordered local officials to do whatever necessary to safeguard prisoners who were held in their jurisdictions. As a result, lynchings in the state declined from twelve in 1893 to one in 1894, zero in 1895 and 1896, and two in 1897.[143]

In Roanoke, the stand made by Henry Trout against "lynch law" set a precedent to which subsequent mayors adhered. The city's 150 reserve police-men stood ready to quell potential disorder, as did its citizen militias, which increased in number after the riot. Before he left office, Trout reorganized the police force once again, bringing in a far more seasoned chief who demanded professionalism from the squad. The death of eight residents, torrent of bad press, and city fathers' embarrassment combined to subdue white residents' predilection for extralegal "justice," and during the remainder of the 1890s, few, if any, called for "lynch law." The main causes of the lynch riot also sub-sided. The depression ended, the city's courts did a better job of imposing the type of "justice" residents expected, and saloons stayed open in the wake of anti-prohibitionists' successful appeal of the local option vote. White antipa-thy toward African American residents, however, remained constant.[144]

■■■

In the eleven years after the riot of 1893, Roanoke experienced no extralegal executions or serious racial disturbances. In early 1904, however, after word spread that a black man had assaulted, robbed and raped a white woman, over a thousand hysterical white men surrounded the city jail and demanded that the "beast" thought to be locked inside be turned over to them. According to a reporter at the scene, "the spirit of riot and misrule threatened to rise upper-most." Mayor Joel Cutchin, in a stand reminiscent of Henry Trout's, climbed to the top of the courthouse steps and told the crowd that police had made no arrests and that they must "keep their heads and not stain the name of the city by a riot." Judge John Woods, who presided over the 1893 riot indictments, pleaded with the men as well before being shouted down and nearly hit with a beer bottle that smashed into the helmet of a nearby policeman. Cutchin and Woods were finally able to convince the mob to send a committee through the jail to see for themselves that no one was in custody.[145]

The attack on Alice Shields, *The Roanoke Times* reported, had occurred in the heart of downtown, in the Henry Street home of her husband George Shields, an employee of E. Wile's clothing store. According to Mr. Shields, he had returned home for lunch to find his three-year-old daughter Mildred unconscious in a pool of blood near the door and his wife locked in a bedroom closet upstairs with her throat cut from ear to ear. Alice Shields, the paper explained, was able with the aid of opiates to recount that a young black male had broken into her home, beaten her and Mildred with a hatchet, raped her, demanded money, dragged her upstairs, stolen two gold watches, and then cut her throat with a straight razor. Though the *Times*'s editors counseled against lynching, they conceded that residents' "frenzied" reaction was a natural response to the news that "a white woman's throat was ripped ear to ear, her person subjugated to infamous ravishment, her infant child fiercely assaulted with a hatchet's edge—all due to the savage nature, uncontrollable brutal lechery, and the strong, merciless black hand of a creature who holds place in American civilization as a fellow citizen of the white man." "The black menace being brought home to them," the paper explained, "many were to be found favoring a lawless remedy, who are in other respects absolutely law-abiding citizens."[146]

In the days that followed, as police searched frantically for a suspect, additional and far more sensationalized accounts of the assault appeared in papers alongside accusations that the rapist would have been caught "save for the reason that the hand of racial sympathy had been extended him." In a later rendition of Alice Shields's attack, the *Times* reported that while her attacker was "engaged in the dastardly act he placed one foot upon the child's throat in order to suppress its cries." After raping Shields again, the story continued, the intruder burned Mildred with a red-hot poker to get her mother to turn over the family's valuables, then dragged her upstairs and raped her once again before slicing her throat. City officials posted a $1,000 reward for information about the assailant but continued to receive scathing criticism for not apprehending the man responsible.[147] About a week after the attack, Alice Shields spoke to the press and corrected some points made in previous stories. Her assailant, she explained, had attempted to rape her, "but did not succeed in accomplishing his purpose." Nor had he burned Mildred. Residents and the press, nonetheless, continued to rely on the earlier, incorrect versions of the attack when recounting the episode. Indeed, shortly after Shields revised the accounts of her assault, several thousand residents signed a petition encouraging the state legislature to pass a law that made protecting rapists punishable by death.[148]

As the search continued, letters damning blacks flooded local papers. Memories of the Lizzie Wilson and Thomas Massie murders and 1893 assault on Sallie Bishop were still strong, according to one female resident, who called for the "entire separation of the races" as the only solution. "Hardly does the death knell sound for one of these ravenous beasts," she observed, "until our hearts are made to bleed at news of another act more atrocious than the one preceding."[149] "Prudence," another female resident, suggested that whites post "No Negroes Allowed" signs on their fences and that women carry derringers and use them "freely" on blacks caught trespassing. She also argued in favor of firing domestic servants because "every negro cook or maid has her male satellites, generally of the most idle, vicious and insolent type."[150] Another writer lamented the replacement of the "old timey negro" with "the 'Text Book' gentry of the present, with their false and fatally dangerous ideas of equality, and their criminal, and devilish attempts for its accomplishment."[151]

Whites held a strong belief that African Americans were harboring Shields's assailant, which intensified white rage and led to widespread threats and violence against local blacks. The first incident occurred only days after the attack, after rumors spread that Reverend Richard R. Jones, pastor of the African Baptist Church, had accused George Shields of beating his wife and making up the assault accusation.[152] Jones, who already had a reputation among white residents as a "trouble maker," had spoken out against Virginia's 1902 disfranchisement of blacks, claiming in a letter to *The Roanoke Times* that God would avenge the wrong done to African Americans.[153] Jones had also waged a battle against the Roanoke School Board to get white principals appointed to manage the town's deteriorating black schools, vowing in correspondence with the board reprinted in local papers that "if something is not don [sic] there will be blood shed in this city before things are settled." In response, the head of the school board dismissed Jones as "ignorant and vicious," and the *Times* branded him "a stuffed prophet and a bigoted and hopelessly benighted ignoramus."[154] Even some of the town's black businessmen distanced themselves from the Reverend, deeming him "a menace to the good order of society."[155]

After Jones's supposed comments about George Shields, over a thousand white men stormed across the Henry Street Bridge into Gainesborough to lynch him. Before they arrived, however, a policeman warned Jones, who fled for his life. The irate mob searched Jones's home and church, cursing black bystanders, tearing down fences, and firing pistols into the air along the way.[156] According to James Hurd Davis, an N&W clerk who spoke with

155

men in the crowd, they believed Jones had "said that no negro did it but that Shields himself did it because of jealousy." If they caught the Reverend, Davis told his fiancée, "what they will do for him will be plenty."[157]

Elsewhere in town, brutality against African Americans flared almost out of control. Henry Wilburn, a black Machine Works employee who supposedly endorsed Jones's comments, was chased from his job and out of the city by an enraged crowd of white men. Tom Hale, a member of Jones's congregation, rumored to have made "similar remarks," was "notified that he had better shake the dust of Roanoke from his feet."[158] Red Acres, alleged to have made "intemperate remarks relative to the Shields case," dodged a hundred-man lynch mob before fleeing the city. In Gainesborough, another mob hunted down a "negress" believed to have made "a very obnoxious remark" about Alice Shields. As they prepared to whip her, however, the frantic woman had a seizure and collapsed in a fit of spasms.[159] On downtown streets, the *Times* reported, throngs of white boys had for several days pummeled black pedestrians with rocks and snowballs.[160]

The climate of hysteria even spread to nearby Salem, where a gang of seventy-five white men used wire cables to flog Taylor Fields—"a negro roustabout"—after he reportedly made "an absurd and dastardly statement in regard to the horrible Shields tragedy." "After the lesson was taught," a correspondent observed, "the negro was warned to keep better control of his tongue, and was then freed."[161] Nearly a week after the attack, Alice Shields had cleared every suspect brought in and police had few promising leads.[162] The unruly mobs terrorizing local blacks had impeded the investigation, according to Mayor Cutchin, who asked white residents "to restrain their wrath and indignation" and "not to force authorities to adopt vigorous measures."[163] In the wake of Cutchin's remarks, several fraternal and labor organizations passed resolutions against assembling in the streets and in favor of refraining from "all angry and unnecessary discussions in order that the criminal may be apprehended."[164] A couple of days after his appeal, Cutchin also published a "Proclamation to Colored People," warning local blacks that "the idea that some of the colored people know the culprit and will not give information has gained strength daily until nearly every white person in the city believes it implicitly." Police, the mayor pointed out, had protected African Americans "as good citizens," but the time had come for black inhabitants to prove their worth by telling authorities everything they knew about the crime.[165]

On February 13, nearly two weeks after the attack, news reached Roanoke that a Baldwin-Felts detective had apprehended Henry Williams, a twenty-four-year-old black male who had reportedly attempted to sell George Shields's gold watches in the coalfields of West Virginia. According to detective Al Baldwin, Williams had been arrested at his mother's home in Gulliam,

West Virginia, where Shields's watches had been discovered buried in the yard. Afterwards, Baldwin told a reporter, Williams freely admitted stealing the watches and attempting to scare Alice Shields by lightly cutting her throat, but he denied attempting to rape her or burn her daughter. His original intention, he explained, had been to simply steal some food. According to Williams, he had lived in Roanoke and worked as a brakeman for the N&W until 1894, when he left for Pittsburgh. He had only been back in town one day when he robbed the Shields. Aware that lynch mobs were already gathering in Roanoke, Baldwin put Williams on a special N&W train that passed through the city at forty miles per hour on its way to Richmond.[166]

The next day, police interrogators at the state prison reported that Williams cheerfully told them he had been in the crowd outside the Shields's home after the robbery and had even mixed in with the mob around the jail later that night. According to Williams, he had grown up in Roanoke, spent two years in a Baltimore insane asylum, spent two years imprisoned in Philadelphia, and worked as a "horse doctor" in rural Pennsylvania before making his way back to the Magic City. A grand jury in Roanoke indicted Williams the day after his arrest. The next day, police brought him to town to stand trial for "attempted criminal assault" (i.e., attempted rape) and "felonious assault and robbery."[167] Virginia Governor Andrew Jackson Montague, determined to have no repetition of the 1893 riot, ordered eight hundred Virginia infantrymen to Roanoke before Williams arrived.[168] Although the *Times* bemoaned the arrival of so many troops, it also reminded readers about the riot and lectured them to refraining from behavior that might give the town similar bad publicity.[169]

Williams's trail the following day lasted barely two hours. His court-appointed lawyers failed to cross-examine any witnesses and presented no defense whatsoever of his not guilty plea. Alice Shields did not testify, and the jury, which included businessman Malcolm W. Bryan and former infantryman Jack Hancock, took only five minutes to reach a guilty verdict. After the proceedings, the presiding judge sentenced Williams to hang until he was "dead, dead, dead," in Roanoke in thirty days—the minimum interval allowed by state law. In the meantime, he was to be held in the Lynchburg jail. According to local papers, all white residents were relieved "that full justice had been meted out to one of the blackest scoundrels who ever polluted the earth with his presence."[170] The death sentence stunned the black-owned *Richmond Planet*, which pointed out correctly that Williams had not raped Mrs. Shields and that the press had grossly exaggerated the details of his attack. Roanoke, the *Planet*'s editor observed, was clearly in the hands of "hot-headed white hoodlums," making it best for African American residents to arm themselves against further terror.[171]

Criticism about the huge show of force for the trial deluged state and local authorities. After learning of the widespread negative reaction, Governor Montague admitted that "the actual number of troops may have been a few too many" but argued that in light of the 1893 riot, he had no choice.[172] Mayor Cutchin complained that he had done all in his power to limit the infantry to 250 men but that Montague had overruled him. "Those who could have done a better job," he lashed out, "are welcome to it."[173] Cutchin and the town council, at the behest of anxious and still somewhat hysterical white residents, ordered the police force to compile a list of "suspicious characters" and implement a "war" on black vagrants.[174] City authorities, the *Times* reported, "are determined to rid the city of trifling, worthless negroes."[175] Over the following weeks, police arrested dozens of unemployed black men for "vagrancy," and local judges sentenced them all to a minimum of six months on the chain gang.[176]

Since Virginia's execution statutes required the construction of the gallows for Williams' hanging in an area shielded from public view, officials built it between the courthouse and jail, behind a hastily constructed wooden fence.[177] Once the scaffold was completed, thousands of curious residents visited it and chipped off bits of wood as souvenirs. The police force, one of its officers reported, had been "besieged" by locals hoping to find a way to witness the execution. Hundreds had also recommended that officials deputize George Shields so that he could spring the trap that would send the "fiend" to his death.[178] Williams arrived in Roanoke on the eve of his execution date along with several hundred members of the state militia. According to a reporter who visited Williams, he was "cheerful and composed" about his impending execution because he believed that he was "going straight to heaven."[179] Williams, who would have been only thirteen at the time, denied widespread rumors that he was the man who assaulted Sallie Bishop in 1893, claiming instead that Will Jeffers, a black man still living in Roanoke, had actually beaten and robbed her. When questioned by reporters, Jeffers, not surprisingly, denied any involvement in the crime.[180]

The following morning, what seemed to reporters to be "the entire population of Roanoke" gathered peacefully in front of the jail to wait for the execution. Hundreds of residents lined rooftops nearby or peered down from telephone poles and trees to get a look at the proceedings. Once Williams had been hanged, authorities opened the fence to let spectators view his body or gather bits of rope and pieces of the black hood over his head.[181] They also allowed Marion F. Landes to photograph the "condemned brute," and afterwards Landes sold hundreds of copies of the image as a souvenir.[182] City officials donated Williams's body to the University of Virginia Medical School, and in one final act of desecration, shipped him there in a potato barrel re-labeled "Potatoes a la Coon." In the judgment of Governor Montague, Roanokers had

Souvenir photograph of the March 1904 execution of Henry
Williams at Roanoke City Jail. History Museum and Historical Society of Western Virginia, Roanoke.

exhibited "exemplary behavior" at the hanging. Their conduct, he told reporters, was "not only highly gratifying to me, but should be an example to the
world."[183]

Reverend Richard R. Jones, who had been living in Washington, D.C.
since he fled Roanoke, sent several letters to Mayor Joel Cutchin, requesting
a formal guarantee of his safety if he returned. In reply, Cutchin claimed to
be unaware of any past or impending threat. "You will have to do as I do," he
explained, "go in and out among the people, trusting to your worth to protect
you from harm."[184] To white authorities in Roanoke, Jones clearly represented
the "wrong" sort of black leader—he was an outspoken activist for his race,
repeatedly questioned elected officials' decisions, and demanded that local
blacks receive their fair share of municipal resources. Even Roanoke's white
pastors feared Jones. They advised him to stay away and claimed that "his use-
fulness as a preacher has ended." The *Washington Post*, however, reported that

Jones had received letters from George Shields and other prominent white residents exonerating him and asking him to return. The preacher, according to the *Post*, had not given a sermon on the day in question, had been one of the first residents to sign the petition making harboring rapists punishable by death, and had condemned Williams in the strongest terms possible.[185]

A few days after Williams's execution, a rumor spread that Jones had returned and several dozen masked men burst into his house and ordered his wife to leave town. After Mrs. Jones fled, the black-owned *Richmond Planet* advised her husband to return to Roanoke, make funeral arrangements for himself, purchase a shotgun, and kill a few of the "white hoodlums" who were sure to show up at his house.[186] In nearby Salem, one paper reported that black residents had taken the *Planet*'s advice to heart and purchased forty Winchester rifles and sixteen pistols to protect Jones if he returned.[187] In mid-April, after Jones resigned as pastor of the African Baptist Church, a committee from his former congregation told local reporters that they were searching for a "conservative" replacement. Jones, nevertheless, continued his quest to return. In July, at the advice of Governor Montague and United States Senator John Daniels, he wrote Roanoke's City Council to present his case for receiving the protection he would need to come home. Most importantly, he explained, he had not made the remarks for which he had been blamed and he would be glad to meet his accusers face to face to prove it. Jones, who had been born a slave and lived in Roanoke for over thirty years, informed the councilmen that he had been forced to sell his home, give up his pastor's position, leave his friends, and been "made to start life over again" at the age of fifty-five. He listed several dozen prominent white businessmen who would vouch for his integrity and begged city authorities to "heed my cry." Roanoke officials, however, did nothing to assist him.[188] "The consensus opinion," the *Times* observed, "is that Roanoke will manage to get along without Jones and that he is better off in Washington than he would be here."[189]

Almost exactly a year after being attacked, Mildred Shields died from wounds to her head. "The little girl," the *Times* reported, had "suffered torture" from her diseased skull and had never fully recovered from the assault in spite of several operations.[190] The fact that authorities had captured, prosecuted, and executed her supposed killer was no doubt some comfort to those who learned of Mildred's sad fate. For whites, "justice" had been exacted, and even though it had come through channels created to maintain Roanoke's progressive image, most residents were satisfied with the outcome. A few weeks after Mildred Shields's death, Richard Jones filed a $50,000 lawsuit in Federal Court against Roanoke City, Mayor Cutchin, and City Sergeant J. A. Manuel for making no effort to disperse the mob or protect him.[191] Cutchin, in an address to city council, claimed Jones's "intemperate" remarks had provoked unknown persons to "look for the preacher for purposes unknown to the mayor and chief of police."[192] Roanoke's City Solicitor filed a seventeen-point demurrer against Jones's suit, and when the Reverend was unable to pay a bond to bear the cost of the case should he lose, a judge dismissed his suit.[193] Jones moved to Homestead, Pennsylvania shortly thereafter. The following year he wrote Cutchin a final dispatch, informing the mayor that he was doing well and believed "a Divine hand turned him from Roanoke."[194] Jones spent the remainder of his life in exile from his longtime home.

■■■

The Roanoke riot of 1893 had a dramatic impact on both the city and the state of Virginia. In its wake, both city and state implemented reforms to quell the potential for unrest or mob violence and both enacted measures to prevent lynching. Before the riot, Roanoke authorities, business leaders, and newspaper editors granted "respectable," sober, and responsible white men the right to dispatch black transgressors. In the case of William Lavender, the arrangement worked well for those in power. In the case of Thomas Smith, however, drunken and unruly poor whites demanded the same right. When officials resisted, these men protested by attacking those in power, threatening the very core of elites' social, political, and economic status. As a result, Smith's execution took on the trappings of a true "carnival"—rioters turned the world upside down and disrupted the orderly hierarchy that had taken control of him. In its wake, Roanoke authorities created a reserve police force, reorganized and strengthened the city force, and vowed publicly to do whatever was necessary to protect prisoners from "lawless" residents. The city's newspapers instigated an editorial campaign against lynching, and its business leaders condemned extralegal violence in the strongest terms possible.

On the state level, Virginia's governors, who had previously done nothing to prevent lynching, began calling out the state militia to protect prisoners from lynch mobs. They also began holding local authorities accountable for extralegal violence in their jurisdictions. Combined, these efforts reversed the growing wave of lynching sweeping the state. It is not surprising that the replacement of lynchings with state-sanctioned executions occurred at precisely the time Virginians began to fully embrace modern capitalism. Having partially recovered from the economic disaster of the Civil War, Virginia was "open for business" in the 1880s and 1890s. As a result, northern capital and industry flocked to the region, encouraging cities like Roanoke to appear seemingly out of nowhere. In the process, however, lynching, urban rioting, and mob violence also emerged, to distract workers, halt production, threaten property, and worry investors. The state responded with measures designed to prevent future disruptions to its economic and political systems:

order replaced disorder; state, municipal, and corporate hegemony replaced underclass challenges to the power structure. Authorities in Virginia cloaked this new arrangement as "progressive" and "humane" reform, selling it to disgruntled whites as part of modernity and to potential northern investors as proof of Virginia's capitalist transformation.

As the fate of Henry Williams illustrates, however, for African Americans accused of capital offenses against whites the results were hardly any different. Williams faced a sham trial without real legal representation in front of an all-white jury composed of infuriated and biased Roanoke residents before he was quickly executed under circumstances so carnivalesque that they almost mimicked a lynching. Residents collected souvenirs and photos of the event in much the same fashion they had after the lynching of Thomas Smith, and while Williams's body was not burned in front of a cheering crowd, it was shoved into a potato barrel and shipped away for "scientific" dissection. In many ways, the contrasting fates of William Lavender, Thomas Smith, and Henry Williams parallel what scholars have described as the move by authorities to suppress the threat of lower-class disorder at executions by moving such punishments inside the confines of prisons and thus outside the view and grasp of unruly mobs.[195] The fissure, while of little real difference to African Americans charged with capital crimes against whites, marks the end of previously sanctioned lynching rights for Virginia's white men.

Chapter 6

Depression and Recovery

Roanoke's business boosters, editors, and elected officials were the first to recognize the dangers that lynching and underclass revolt represented to the city. In the aftermath of the cataclysmic 1893 riot, they rushed to mitigate the damage it caused to the city's progressive reputation with calls for swift prosecution of lawbreakers and a public relations campaign that touted Roanoke's upstanding population and business-friendly ethos. Moreover, they successfully sorted out white inhabitants' class roles in administering "justice" to African Americans who were accused of capital crimes, thus locking in place mechanisms that forestalled the potential for underclass disorder. During the remainder of the 1890s, the city's businessmen and promoters faced an even more daunting challenge when the national depression that began in 1893 showed no signs of abating. Dozens of local firms went bankrupt, scores of residents lost their jobs and left town, and the city itself teetered on the edge of ruin. In an 1893 Christmas sermon to Roanoke's Junior Order of United Mechanics, William Campbell, longtime pastor of the Presbyterian Church, described the mood around town as "dark and ominous" because workers were desperate and looking for any means to improve their economic plight. Campbell cautioned the mechanics against strikes or violence, arguing instead to turn to reasonable solutions "without overturning the social order."[1]

Roanoke's business leaders could not have agreed with Campbell more. Most did all they could to ease the effects of the depression and forestall any "overturning" of the city's social order. Some pushed for another railroad, others courted new industries, and hundreds toughed it out until prosperity returned. Although several domestic enterprises never recovered, many of those that survived were poised to rise to the pinnacle of the local economy. A couple of those businesses—The Virginia Brewing Company and The Stone Printing & Manufacturing Company—not only endured, but grew into two of Roanoke's most important indigenous enterprises. In addition, once the depression ended, the city's boosters successfully promoted their town to outside investors using its cheap land, docile labor force, and generous corporate welfare system as incentives. By 1910, their campaign had lured dozens of new manufacturers and fomented a complete recovery from the disastrous economic collapse of the 1890s.

■■■

In a clear sign of just how dire that collapse became, in late 1893, plummeting tax revenue forced Roanoke's municipal government to close local schools, end infrastructure work, and lay off non-essential employees. At the Roanoke Machine Works, orders for new railroad cars and locomotives dropped off almost completely and the firm cut its remaining workers' hours to four per day. Hundreds of others who were laid off by the Works packed up their families and left town.[2] Dozens of other local businesses failed or remained shuttered. Some, like the Roanoke Iron Company, proposed reopening if employees would work for reduced wages. The iron puddlers' union rejected the offer because its members were already deep in debt to the company's commissary.[3]

The Norwich Lock Works laid off dozens of employees, cut wages, reduced hours, and still failed to turn a profit. By the fall of 1895, according to Malcolm W. Bryan, a company trustee, the firm's numerous creditors were threatening to foreclose. Bryan, appointed to shepherd the business through the difficulty, complained not long after taking charge that its affairs were "simply abominable."[4] The Lock Work's Connecticut owners, who had already invested $125,000 in the company and were ready to cut their losses, instructed him to find a buyer. Although advertisements for the plant ran in several trade journals, Bryan reported that there had been "no results—in fact, no inquires." Even worse, the firm's stock was nearly worthless. It had neither capital nor credit, and if it closed, he explained, "I couldn't get 10,000 for it."[5] Bryan's efforts failed but his prediction turned out to be prescient: the company closed and stood dormant until 1898, when local businessmen purchased the plant for $6,500 with the aim of turning it into the Roanoke Hardware Company.[6]

The city's population, which had increased by over seven thousand residents from 1890 to 1892, declined by over three thousand from 1893 to 1895, to drop to around twenty thousand inhabitants. Vacant houses dotted the city's landscape, and in some African American sections of the Northeast, entire neighborhoods stood empty.[7] Many of the city's unemployed workers and their families turned to charity organizations to make ends meet. Some relied on the Roanoke Machine Works Relief Association, which distributed coal, clothing, and food to laid-off machinists. Others looked to the Ladies Union Benevolent Society, which operated a commissary on Salem Avenue where the "worthy poor" could sign up for street work in exchange for their fifty cents per day of rations.[8] Elite residents, by contrast, sought ways to sustain their social and cultural organizations in the midst of the economic downturn. The Roanoke Athletic Club, for example, staged a benefit performance of the opera *H. M. S. Pinafore* in order to "raise a sufficient sum of money to liquidate the indebtedness of the club and thus enable it to establish on firm foundation, a credible Base Ball Team for the coming season."[9]

The depression, chance for possible work or charity in Roanoke, and easy access to the city via a stolen ride in an N&W boxcar served as a magnet for hundreds of unemployed and homeless men and their families from the surrounding countryside. By 1895, local papers reported that the town was flooded with "tramps" and "gypsies." Some of the homeless families lived on the banks of the Roanoke River in makeshift shanties, others invaded abandoned homes or businesses, and some lived in mothballed railcars. Many of the men drank crude bootleg whiskey known locally as "Roanoke stagger juice." According to a pair of "tramps" found sleeping in an N&W boxcar, they "landed in Roanoke because they had nowhere else to go."[10]

Other men, like Charlie Burgess, a laid-off machinist from Baltimore, arrived in Roanoke looking for skilled work. Burgess, who came to town in the fall of 1895, hunted an entire day before finding one dim prospect as a pump operator in a blast furnace. The job would require a seven-day workweek, he complained to his wife, but since it paid $75 a month, he took it. Roanoke, he lamented, was "not so good a city" as others he had visited in the South. "The sidewalks are board," he grumbled, "and only 2 or 3 streets are paved." The only bright spot was steady work and cheap rent.[11] When Burgess arrived at work the following morning, however, he found his new position already occupied. "They had changed their mind," he wrote his wife, "and was going to promote one of the old men instead of hiring a new man—they payed only $65 per month, 7 days in the week and perhaps 24 hours in the day." Burgess left town disgusted but admitted he "didn't care much" because the job was awful and the city a mess.[12]

The town's business leaders sought outside investment as the best possible remedy for Roanoke's economic decline. Negative publicity from the 1893 lynch riot, however, made that task arduous. In October 1893, a month after the riot, Edward L. Stone, president of Stone Printing & Manufacturing Company and later one of the town's most significant civic boosters, instigated an ad campaign in regional and national papers to rehabilitate Roanoke's business-friendly reputation. His full-page advertisements, which cited the usual booster statistics about the city's spectacular population growth and phenomenal economic expansion, claimed that Roanoke was the "gateway" to the iron and coalfields of the southwest and a "marvelous city" with a moral and upstanding population.[13]

Stone and other boosters also pushed hard to bring in a new trunk rail line to improve Roanoke's economic prospects. The move paralleled solutions employed by western railroad towns, which having also experienced a general economic downturn after an initial period of hyper-development also sought another rail connection to boost their economic outlook.[14] After the Chesapeake & Ohio Railroad showed interest in making a move to Roanoke to compete with the Norfolk & Western, which maintained a monopoly on rail access in town, natives' campaign for a new line moved into high gear. The town's businessmen, most of whom thought a new railroad would reduce freight and passenger rates and bring an increase in investments by manufacturers, as well as boost the local economy, pushed elected officials to offer the C&O at least $100,000 in municipal stock subscriptions. Members of Roanoke's Board of Trade lined up behind the scheme, and though they acknowledged their "obligations" to the N&W, they told a local reporter that it was high time for the city to leave the "cradle" and "walk alone."[15]

Norfolk & Western president Fredrick J. Kimball, in an interview shortly afterwards, not only lambasted the plan but issued a warning that his railroad would reconsider any additional investments in the town if it offered the C&O $100,000. "If Roanoke can raise $100,000," he complained, "it had better spend it in making the city attractive rather than building a railroad."[16] Kimball's remarks, not surprisingly, elicited a torrent of local criticism. According to the editor of the *Daily Record*, the time had passed in the history of Roanoke "when the opinions of her citizens and their freedom of action can be dominated by any corporation or body of men, and the sooner Mr. Kimball realizes that fact, and either disclaims the authenticity of the implied threats imputed to him to intimidate our citizens, . . . the sooner the indignation aroused by his reported comments will be lessened."[17] Another railroad booster summed up the opinion of most businessmen in *The* (Roanoke) *Evening World* when he proclaimed that "Roanoke does not belong to the Norfolk & Western railroad." No citizen, he argued, should submit "to monopolies dictating what we shall do." The editors of the *Evening World* concurred and complained that the $200,000 the city had contributed to complete the Roanoke & Southern Railroad had been largely wasted since the line had been immediately absorbed by the N&W to forestall any competition.[18] The N&W, while crucial to Roanoke's development, had by 1893 ceased being a critical component of native boosters' business schemes. Indeed, by then, the N&W's monopoly had become an anathema to them.

Kimball's criticism did nothing to halt the campaign for a new line. In November 1893, city boosters chartered the Roanoke Railway Construction Company and proposed raising $50,000 to build a link to the Baltimore & Ohio or Chesapeake & Ohio railroads at Buchanan, in neighboring Botetourt County. The firm assured potential investors that they would not have to pay for their stock until the rail link was completed and guaranteed that any deal to connect with the new railroads would contain clauses that precluded the N&W from buying the line.[19] City papers and business leaders encouraged residents incessantly to invest before a golden opportunity to mitigate the effects of the depression dissipated.[20] Not funding a new rail link, the *Daily*

Record warned, would mean "the delay of the material progress and prosperity another trunk line of railway will surely bring."[21] Investment, by contrast, would reduce coal prices and freight rates, increase property values, and "awaken at every step, new hopes and new energy, until our beautiful valley is once more aglow in the sunshine of prosperity and our people again made happy by their own efforts."[22] In an appeal aimed at property owners, editors for the *Record* also promised that the new road would "give employment to a large number of our laboring classes, who are now out of employment, and thereby enable them to meet their rents, which they are now unable to do."[23]

Board of Trade member and prominent business booster Nathaniel B. Johnston was one of the driving forces behind the new line. "An additional railroad," he told a local reporter, "is an absolute essential, not only to the progress of this community, but to maintaining the position to which it has attained, and without wishing to be understood as prophesying a boom, I believe that upon the day on which the work is commenced . . . there will be a new spirit of life taken on by every enterprise and business in Roanoke."[24] Johnston, a partner in Brown & Johnston Hardware on Jefferson Street, wrote dozens of letters on behalf of the Board of Trade to regional officials to drum up additional support for the line.[25]

The N&W's opposition to the deal and simultaneous failure to fully staff its machine shops infuriated members of the Board of Trade. Like other members, Johnston turned to local contacts to voice his disgust. In a letter to Peyton L. Terry—a director on Roanoke Machine Works' board—he pleaded for pressure on the N&W to create more jobs in town. Kimball and the N&W, Johnston observed, had ignored their plight too long and could blame only themselves for the recent crusade for an additional railroad. "While the men formerly employed by the Machine Works were idle," he fumed, "and the interests of many whom all was dependent upon their employment were frustrated, the Norfolk & Western RR Co had built at other points as many as 3,000 freight and coal cars, . . . which had they been built here would have added immeasurably to the prosperity of every interest." Although he acknowledged that without the N&W and Roanoke Machine Works the city would not exist, Johnston told Terry that he and the other men behind the new railway felt that Roanoke "now occupies very much the position of a plant which having been raised to a certain point by the fertilization and irrigation suddenly has those assurances of its growth withdrawn and is left to fend for itself."[26]

In the months that followed, as the depression grew more severe and most railroads halted all expansion projects, the deal to forge a new rail connection collapsed. Even worse, by then the N&W had fallen onto precarious financial footing and cut employee wages from 5 to 15 percent. Vice-President Joseph

Sands, in a circular to workers, explained that while the N&W's management appreciated the "fidelity and zeal" of their employees, the firm had been "forced by circumstances over which it has no control to make the reductions."[27] Between 1893 and 1895, passengers had fallen 11 percent, tons of coal hauled decreased 16 percent, and gross earnings were down by over $500,000. The line had been unable to pay rental fees on its railcars or interest on its loans in both 1893 and 1894, prompting Fredrick Kimball to go to Europe in an effort to re-finance the firm's mortgages. His attempts failed, and by early 1895, the N&W was over $1,000,000 in debt. That February, with few other options available, the company chose to enter a temporary reorganization receivership under the guidance of Kimball and longtime N&W executive Henry Fink. The reorganization effort, however, faced grave difficulties shortly thereafter, when miners at the Pocahontas coalfields went on strike and coal shipments declined even further. In a portent of even worse times to come, in early 1896, the N&W's decorous Queen Anne office building in Roanoke burned entirely to the ground. Not long after, creditors forced a foreclosure sale of the Norfolk & Western Railroad's assets. Before the auction, Kimball, Fink, and other N&W executives created the Norfolk & Western Railway Company, and at the sale, they purchased E. W. Clark & Company's N&W Railroad. The new railway named Fink president and appointed Kimball chairman of the board.[28]

The effect of the depression on the city's land and development companies was equally devastating. Although many Roanoke real estate firms had gone bust when the town's biggest boom collapsed in the early 1890s, others held on and dozens of new ventures began operations. Indeed, in early 1894, Malcolm Bryan told a business associate that from his office in the Terry Building, "I see in every direction and as far as the eye can reach, land companies."[29] Bryan, who was on the board of directors of thirty-seven real estate firms, had saved enough money to weather the storm. Several of his associates, however, were not so fortunate. W. Lawrie Reid, an architect who helped design the massive Terry Building, suffered through twelve months of unemployment and was, according to Bryan, completely broke. Bryan, who tried desperately to find a position for Reid in Philadelphia, told a friend living there that the architect had a wife, three children, and parents to support and was in such financial ruin that "I do not know upon what he has existed."[30] By 1895, even the city's most heralded land companies were so deep in debt that Bryan warned a fellow real estate investor that he had "no faith in the ultimate realization by any stockholder of anything like our 'intrinsic valuations.'" His stock in the Buena Vista Land Company was by then "worthless." According to Bryan, the firm was over $65,000 in the red and had resorted to selling its $46,000 glass plant for $3,500 and its $192,000 furnace for $11,000. Peyton Terry's Roanoke Development Company, of which Bryan was vice-president, was in even worse shape, with a debt of at least $175,000 and assets consisting mainly of lands "mortgaged far in excess of their value." Both companies, according to Bryan, "went into *everything* in 1889 and 1890" and were "reaping the whirlwind now."[31]

In the summer of 1895, the Roanoke Machine Works re-hired some of its former employees and the Crozier Iron Company put its "number two" furnace back into blast. Although only a few hundred men had gone back to work, it was enough to make the *Daily Times* boast that "Roanoke has stemmed the tide of depression and is now on the high road to a successful future."[32] The financial disaster, however, was far from over. Rumors were rampant that the new N&W Railway planned to relocate its headquarters rather than rebuild its offices in town. Several competing cities made moves to acquire the N&W, but in the end, the line decided to build a new six-story office building on the lot of its former headquarters.

Having dodged one potential economic catastrophe, residents immediately faced another. On June 14, 1896, Peyton Terry's Roanoke Trust, Loan & Safe Deposit Company failed to open for business. The bank had grossly overextended itself in real estate loans. It repossessed much of the land for delinquent mortgages but found itself holding property worth only a fraction of its original cost, that would not sell even at rock-bottom prices. Terry and his son-in-law, S. W. Jamison, secretary-treasurer of the company, declared the firm bankrupt, leaving depositors no choice but to sue the bank to recoup at least a portion of their money. Terry and Jamison lost their personal fortunes in the fiasco, but a grand jury declared them negligent rather than liable for the loss of close to $1,000,000 in deposits. Terry forfeited his ornate Italianesque office building in the immediate aftermath, and two years later, the man who, along with his brother-in-law, Henry Trout, was responsible for the rise of Roanoke City, died of pernicious anemia, broke, humiliated, and distraught.[33]

■■■

Although some of Roanoke's businesses and businessmen did not survive the depression, others found a way through the hard times and thrived later. In addition, once the economic outlook brightened, dozens of new manufacturers established plants in town. Many of the firms received free land from the municipality; all of them benefited from Roanoke's fifteen-year tax exemption for new manufacturers. Most also arrived knowing full well that the city's labor unions, while strong in membership, rarely resorted to strikes or walkouts. The city's businessmen and capitalists, like their counterparts elsewhere in the South, fully appreciated the benefits a docile and tractable labor force offered potential investors; in their promotional literature, they never failed to mention the advantages of hiring Roanoke workers.[34]

While efforts of the city's laboring population to become a stronger force gained momentum in the 1890s and early 1900s, their crusade never seriously challenged the power of local corporations. From its founding, the City of Roanoke's "open for business" outlook and corporate welfare policies made union agitation unappealing to municipal and commercial leaders. Most enterprises allowed organized labor to exist but used a variety of methods to ensure that workers remained submissive. The near absence of labor disruptions, especially when compared to the almost constant drumbeat of strikes against northern corporations during the same period, had numerous sources. Primarily, it was the result of an ardently pro-business government structure, a lack of viable employment nearby, comparatively high wages, and corporate or governmental paternalism and welfare. An abundant pool of available labor, high turnover of residents, and lingering differences between native and newcomer workers were lesser factors, but added to the problems local unions faced.[35]

Unlike most other southern towns and cities where unions struggled to gain footholds in mills or mines, Roanoke had a vibrant organized labor component. The Knights of Labor (KOL) were the first significant local union, and by the mid-1880s, hundreds of men from the town's industries had become members. Although elsewhere in the country the KOL was active in demanding better wages and hours and in organizing strikes and walkouts, in Roanoke the union served more as a social organization than an agitation tool. In addition, most of the town's industries worked hand-in-glove with the two local KOL assemblies. In the spring of 1886, for example, the Roanoke Machine Works gave its employees an advance in pay and a day off to attend an elaborate KOL picnic at Coyner Springs in Botetourt County. Its sister company, the Norfolk & Western, provided free passage to the affair for workers and their families. At the springs, the union's members and their guests danced, played baseball and croquet, and held foot races and long-jump contests. KOL leaders later wrote the superintendent of the machine shops to thank him for his "kind consideration" and to let him know that his actions "will ever be held in grateful remembrance by this assembly."[36]

In early 1890, skilled workers in the city organized the Roanoke Federation of Labor (RFL), an umbrella organization for all local trade unions as well as a subsidiary of the American Federation of Labor. In the fall, after over four thousand printers, painters, plasterers, iron moulders, mechanics, boiler makers, amalgamated steel and iron workers, carpenters, bricklayers, stone masons, joiners, blacksmiths, and brewers had signed on as members, *The Roanoke Times* began publishing a special column for the city's "laboring people."[37] By then, the paper observed, the city had become a "working people's town" with laborers "largely the majority" of the population.[38] By the end of the year, almost all the city's skilled unions had joined the RFL. According to the *Times*, the success of the union was largely the result of "a very determined effort on the part of laboring men of Roanoke" as well as a sign that "the growth of labor organizations during 1890 kept pace with everything else in the Magic City."[39]

The RFL allowed only skilled workers to join and excluded women and blacks entirely. Like skilled laborers in Birmingham—the southern city that most closely resembled Roanoke—the town's trained workingmen guarded access to skilled positions by maintaining the color line in their trade unions.[40] The RFL built an assembly hall downtown on Commonwealth Avenue, and though the union originally vowed to stay out of politics, its leaders soon began pushing members to cast votes in ways that benefited workingmen. A leader in the carpenters' union, for example, encouraged members before the fall 1890 elections to take "political action" that would place the municipal government in the hands of labor. At the same meeting, according to a reporter, the president of the iron moulders union "dwelt upon the political force workingmen possessed" and pushed RFL members to vote to abolish Virginia's convict labor and apprenticeship systems.[41] According to the *Times* labor column, RFL members had also begun discussing unlimited silver coinage as one solution to national currency shortage. At another meeting, the paper explained, an RFL leader told those gathered that "the recent movements of the laboring men and farmers indicated a political upheaval, and that the people were getting ready to rule the United States."[42]

Although the RFL encouraged members to stay informed on national issues and to become politically involved, it found few reasons locally to justify calling for strikes. When it did, however, the city's corporations paid close attention. In early 1891, for instance, after Blair Construction fired union carpenters, the RFL organized a boycott of Blair building sites as well as all businesses and homes built by the firm.[43] More often than not, however, the city's manufacturers did little to antagonize workers. Indeed, in 1891 local writer Thomas Bruce claimed that Roanoke's industries had "treated the mechanical and laboring part of the population well, and in return the latter has been peaceful and quiet, making good, faithful, and efficient citizens." According to Bruce, relatively high wages and company homes, where workmen lived "in comparative ease, enjoying their own firesides and many of the comforts, and not a few of the luxuries, of life," were the main reasons that "disturbances and agitation have been almost unknown on the part of the laboring population."[44]

Company paternalism, in the form of housing, baseball teams, beautification contests, decent pay, and prompt recognition of workers' requests, did much to foster the sense of harmony Bruce alluded to. Other factors, however, also contributed to the lack of antagonism. Unlike other small factory-towns, where outside industrialists frequently clashed with native politicians and needed privately funded militias to protect their interests, in Roanoke, most elected officials were stridently pro-business. Those who were not—the two or three Republicans elected by workers—could not seriously challenge the majority. Moreover, because the city's charter granted only freeholders the right to cast ballots on spending issues, workers living in rental housing had no say in municipal funding for industry, city subscriptions to corporate stock, or spending on civic improvements. The city's native elite, although in the minority, held most governmental power and dictated the city's pro-business attitude. Like local industrialists, shopkeepers, and grocers, however, they understood workers' potential power in the form of boycotts or walkouts and therefore, at least publicly, accorded them a great deal of respect.[45]

The RFL organized the city's first Labor Day celebration in the summer of 1890. Like working-class barrooms and company neighborhoods, Labor Day built solidarity among the city's workers by strengthening their sense of community.[46] Almost all local industries halted production to allow all their employees to attend.[47] During the celebration, thousands of working-men paraded through downtown carrying flags and banners representing their trades. After the parade, they and their families held a massive picnic in Carr's Woods, the meadows and woodlands south of the city. Various union leaders addressed the crowd, and according to one, the day had demonstrated "to every man the power of labor in this city." Baseball, a greased pig chase, and three-legged races followed, as did racial turmoil. The city's unions, like labor organizations throughout the South, excluded black workers, and during the celebration, participants even refused to allow African American spectators. Indeed, chasing away blacks who were "hanging around the edges of the crowd" eventually became part of the entertainment. "This was fine fun," the *Daily Times* explained, "and the boys continued it for a while." Most African Americans fled the scene, the paper observed, and although one returned and "stood bravely" for a few minutes, "the flying rinds from the hands of nearly 100 boys caused him again to beat a hasty retreat."[48]

Since Roanoke's population was overwhelmingly working-class, and most of its residents were either in a union or relatives of a union member, strikes had the potential to erupt into economic and class warfare, with all workers and their families on one side, and most businesses and businessmen on the other. Any union member boycott against a local firm could cause significant economic damage. For this reason, when strikes did occur, most businessmen responded immediately to demands or at least reacted in a way that defused tensions until they brokered an agreement. In April 1900, for example, when boilermakers employed by the Roanoke Machine Works threatened to strike for increased wages, their superintendent gave them the afternoon off to contemplate pay-scale documents that revealed that their wages were already six cents more an hour than Baltimore & Ohio Railroad boilermakers. The following day, the workers rescinded their threat and returned to the job.[49] Such capitulations were the rule rather than the exception in Roanoke. One local paper boasted a couple years later that disputes between capital and labor, so common elsewhere in the country, were "foreign" in the city because the "greatest harmony and understanding exists between employer and employee in every branch of business."[50]

In the early 1900s, in a sign of workers' growing desire for collective bargaining power, the Roanoke Central Trades and Labor Council (RCT&LC) replaced the RFL as the umbrella organization for all local unions. Unlike the Federation of Labor, which had been solely an alliance of the city's skilled, male, trade unions, the RCT&LC represented male and female skilled and unskilled workers. The RCT&LC published its own paper, *The Labor Unionist,* and in the spring of 1902, in an indication of the organization's growing significance, it hosted the annual convention of the Virginia State Federation of Labor. By then, members had elected Roanoke resident M. B. Thompson president of the state organization and appointed five other residents to various leadership positions.[51] The RCT&LC held the event in its "Labor Home" above the Stag Saloon on Commerce Street, and in examples of the sort of corporate welfare that was common among Roanoke businesses, the N&W provided reduced fare to all labor leaders in attendance. In addition, the city's Virginia Brewing Company donated several kegs of beer.[52]

The RCT&LC took charge of the city's annual Labor Day celebration and parade, an event attended by thousands of workers and their families. Roanoke's mayor and local dignitaries customarily addressed the crowd and praised the various union men in attendance, albeit in a paternalistic and condescending fashion. In September 1901, for example, Mayor J. Randolph Bryan Jr. told the thousands of workers gathered below his platform that local unions could get what they wanted as long as they went about it in "the right way" and refrained from striking. Judge William Gordon Robertson, who spoke after Bryan, gave a lecture on the common goals of capital and labor, going so far as to suggest that any discord between the classes had disappeared with the dawning of the twentieth century. Both men received hearty applause and commendations by the labor leaders who spoke after them.[53]

■■■

Throughout Roanoke's early existence, the city was known primarily for its railroad-related industries. Its other indigenous enterprises, many of which survived the catastrophic 1893 depression in better shape than the N&W, rarely received much outside acclaim or notice. They were, however, as vitally important to the town's economic recovery as the rehabilitation of the N&W and Roanoke Machine Works. Chief among them was The Virginia Brewing

Company (VBC). Six native entrepreneurs, well aware that the only other brewery in the state was located in Alexandria, some two hundred miles away, chartered the corporation in the fall of 1889. Subscriptions to the brewery's stock went well, and by December, the company had raised $30,000 in capital. The VBC hired twenty-five-year-old Baltimore brewmeister Louis A. Scholz that same month, after Scholz assured the firm that water from Roanoke's Crystal Spring was perfect for brewing beer.[54]

Scholz, a master brewer trained in his native Freiburg, Germany, arrived in early 1890. A local correspondent spoke to him at the brewery's construction site and reported later that Scholz "expressed himself as very much pleased with the Magic City and said that there were all the requisites here for building up a first-class city."[55] The wooden brew house stood just south of the Machine Works on Railroad and Wise Avenues between Twelfth and Fourteenth Streets. It was an impressive, three-story, frame structure that sloped to one story in the back. The firm constructed a rail connection across its property to the nearby tracks of the N&W and built stables, an ice plant, an office complex, a home for Louis Scholz, and the Wayside Inn, a beer garden that Scholz's brother Henry would manage.[56] Although its first batch of ale did not go on sale until later in the summer of 1890, that spring the brewery's baseball team brought a sample keg to its match with "The Roanokes" and offered any player who made it to third base a glass of VBC pilsner.[57]

Employees, beer wagons, and first brewery building, Virginia Brewing Company, c. 1890–92. Norfolk & Western Historical Photograph Collection (NS5770), Digital Library and Archives, University Libraries, Virginia Tech.

In mid-August, 1890, the company's pilsner lager beer went on sale. By three that afternoon, the city's saloons had purchased the brewery's entire stock of two hundred and fifty kegs. In a sign of the growing alliance between the VBC and local bars, all Roanoke saloons immediately allowed the company to affix its trademark sign of a winged Virginia Brewing Company globe of "Southern Progress" on their front doors. The VBC's first print ad boasted: "Virginia Brewing Company's Pure Lager Beer, On Draught From Today On. Brewed From Pure Malt and Hops. Try It!"[58] Three months later, when a correspondent from *The Roanoke Times* visited the brewery, Louis Scholz reported that the firm was shipping over six thousand bottles of its "Export Beer" out of town each week and supplying city saloons with twenty kegs of "Munich Brew" pilsner lager per day. "The company," the *Times* explained, "has two beer wagons and one ice wagon constantly going, and employs thirty-five men in the brewery."[59]

Over the course of the following year, the young brewery opened branch distributorships in Lynchburg, Shenandoah, and Pocahontas, Virginia; and Henderson, North Carolina.[60] By then, demand for the VBC's beers was so overwhelming that the brewery could not fulfill all the orders coming in. Although the success of the VBC had much to do with the fine quality of its beer, it also benefited from a lack of competition and from the ability to sell its products for less than other breweries. The VBC's chief competitor, Robert Portner's Alexandria-based brewery, had to ship its product to Roanoke via boxcar and thus sell at a higher price. The Anheuser-Busch Brewing Company of St. Louis also distributed its beer in town at a higher price. In the summer of 1891, however, not long after the Virginia Brewing Company cornered the local market and eroded the regional sales of its outside competitors, Busch's St. Louis executives instructed their Roanoke distributors to drop the price of its kegs from $9 a barrel to $4, a price well below the actual cost of production. The move, conducted explicitly to drive the VBC out of business, made Anheuser-Busch by far the cheapest beer in town. Local editors, infuriated by the scheme, rushed to the VBC's defense. The brewery, the *Times* declared, was a crucial "home enterprise" with a payroll of $8,000 per month that deserved every residents' patronage, even if that meant paying a few cents more for a mug of beer. Anheuser-Busch, according to the paper, was a "foreign enterprise" that could rely on "many millions of capital to destroy the Virginia Brewing Company, an infant industry, built up and owned in great part by Roanoke people."[61] Roanoke's beer drinkers, either out of loyalty to their hometown brew or because the VBC's pilsner tasted better than Budweiser, stood by the company. The "Beer War," as it was called by locals, lasted eleven months before Anheuser-Busch, aware that patronage of the VBC had not been adversely affected, surrendered and put its kegs back on the market at $9 a barrel.[62]

Not long after winning the battle with Anheuser-Busch, the VBC's brew house burned to the ground. The company, Louis Scholz informed customers, had enough reserve kegs on hand to last until it could build a new brewery. Insurance covered the firm's losses, and in the end, the fire gave the enterprise the opportunity to construct a much larger brewery.[63] By the spring of 1892, a new brick brew house, capable of turning out twenty-five-thousand kegs per year, was in operation, and the firm had built a larger ice plant, installed an electric generator, opened a bottling works, and constructed dozens of company homes to rent to its employees.[64] Once the new brewery began operations, its workers, most of whom had watched helplessly when the old brew house burned down, organized the "Alert Fire Company," the VBC's private fire brigade.[65] Shortly after reopening, the brewery introduced its "Famous Bock," its "1892 Roanoke Decennial Lager," and its "Wuerzburger Ale," a Bavarian-style beer that complemented the VBC's popular Bohemian-style pilsner lager. The company advertised its "Wuerzburger" as "highly recommended by physicians for its nutritious qualities" and as an excellent "tonic for nursing mothers or convalescents."[66]

The firm's directors elected Louis Scholz president of the company in the mid-1890s, and under his guidance, the VBC continued to expand its facilities and enlarge its distribution territory. By 1898, the brewery complex had grown to include five buildings "fitted up with the best and most modern machinery known to the brewery trade." The company also had begun production of its "Kola Nerva" along with several other soft drinks.[67] In the early 1900s, the VBC vertically integrated its operations, opening its own saloons in underserved parts of Southwest Virginia in 1901. It also purchased and consolidated all of Roanoke's other ice plants into the "Consumers' Ice Company" in 1904.[68] The following year, the company added a "crowning machine" that was capable of sealing eighty to a hundred bottles a minute and up to eighteen thousand bottles per day. Sales in 1905 topped the three million bottle mark, up from one hundred and fifty thousand bottles only nine years earlier.[69]

Roanoke's periodic "local option" campaigns, however, unnerved Scholz and the VBC's directors. To counterbalance the prohibition crusades, the firm advertised its brews as "tonics," low in alcohol content and even as suitable for mothers and children. In 1902, the VBC received a much-sought endorsement from the United States Health Bulletin of New York, which deemed its beer a disease preventative, digestion aid, and elixir that promoted mental and physical activity. Thereafter the company advertised its pilsner as "endorsed by the highest medical authorities" and "pre-eminently a family beverage" that "promotes the cause of true temperance" and "guards the safety of health and home." The firm's motto, its ads boasted, was "not how cheap we can brew beer, but how good."[70]

In subsequent ads, the company claimed that its "absolutely pure" pilsner was not only "healthful" and responsible for "stamina," but also a likely cure for tuberculosis.[71] To ensure that its message reached the city's upper classes, the VBC ran a constant stream of ads on programs for the city's Academy of Music. On one opera program, for example, the brewery informed patrons that "Pure Beer is Pure Food" and argued that "the two most powerful and cultivated nations of Europe, the German and English, are beer drinking nations."[72] In keeping with its claims of being the most pure and wholesome beer on the market, and to counter claims by the Anti–Saloon League that all beer contained "poisons" and "impurities," the VBC advertised a $1,000 reward for anyone who could prove it used corn grits or glucose in its brewery. "Can our competitors make the same statement?" The implication infuriated other beer distributors in town. Robert Portner Brewing Company, which operated a bottling works for its Alexandria brewed "Hofbrau" on Shenandoah Avenue, countered with an ad offering $5,000 to anyone who could prove its beers contained adjuncts. Moreover, Portner complained that such "unwarranted inferences" gave "aid and comfort to the enemies of the liquor business."[73]

In 1905, the VBC increased its capital stock to $250,000 and in 1906, it distributed its beers throughout Virginia, North Carolina, West Virginia, Kentucky, South Carolina, Tennessee, Maryland, and Ohio. Sales increased that spring and summer to nearly two million bottles, and by August the firm had run entirely out of its yearly stock of beer bottles.[74] In 1907, the VBC beat dozens of other entrants in the Jamestown Tercentennial Exposition's beer competition, taking home the gold medal award for "its perfect brew and purity."[75] The firm immediately thereafter added a Jamestown gold medal to its bottle trademarks and advertising. The accolades and endorsements further boosted sales, and equally important, quieted some of the criticism heaped on beer by temperance groups. "There would be far less talk of prohibition," one local paper contended, "if all breweries conducted their business on the lines followed by the Virginia Brewing Company."[76] By 1912, after the VBC's directors made Henry Scholz the firm's secretary-treasurer, the Scholz brothers were in total control of the company. They employed over one hundred men and women in the brewery, supplied the entire city with ice, produced fifty thousand barrels of beer per year, sold nearly five million bottles of beer each year, and managed saloons and distribution warehouses throughout the region. Beer sales had increased over 100 percent since 1904, when the firm sold twenty-five-thousand kegs.[77]

The German-born Scholz brothers, whose entrepreneurship quickly garnered the respect and admiration of local business boosters, were active participants in the city's Chamber of Commerce as well as officers and partial owners of the Roanoke Glass Company and the Roanoke Fair Association.

Their commitment to quality and their zeal to expand their brewery business while fostering economic growth in Roanoke was emblematic of the sort of capitalist success city residents respected. The company's beers, sold with the VBC trademark label of "Southern Progress—Brewed in Roanoke, Virginia," did much to advertise their home as a progressive and up-and-coming New South city to beer drinkers throughout the southeastern United States. Indeed, the VBC logo was New South propaganda and Roanoke boosterism melded into one. The city's promotional organizations and press, not surprisingly, did all they could to feature the VBC in their literature. The company, they boasted, had been organized by native investors and had, through determined effort, business acumen, and excellence of product, become one of the most successful regional breweries in the South.[78] Although the Scholz brothers' accomplishment in the brewing business in an area traditionally underserved by breweries was indeed the sort of "southern progress" that prophets of a New South longed for, after Virginians voted in favor of statewide prohibition in 1916, their product was outlawed. With little hope for a reversal of the new law, the Virginia Brewing Company closed down, sold its brewery equipment as scrap metal, and boarded up its brew house. Though no longer brewing, the Scholz brothers continued their ice, bottling, and glass plant operations, and remained active in the Roanoke Fair Association.[79]

The Virginia Brewing Company was not alone in its rise as an important domestic enterprise. The Stone Printing & Manufacturing Company, originally organized in 1883 as a branch office of the Bell Printing Company of Lynchburg, would grow by 1912 to employ over two hundred workers to be the largest and most modern printing establishment in the South. The firm's owner, Edward Lee Stone, was the archetypal New South businessman, having adopted the most progressive and enlightened methods on his path to success. He rose from humble origins through sheer determination and a keen sense of business acumen. Stone, who had only an elementary school education, was by the early 1900s one of Roanoke's most well-respected and admired business leaders, an important civic booster, a progressive reformer, a steadfast investor in native enterprises, and a principal and generous patron of the city's high-brow culture, clubs, and organizations. His "first love," The Stone Printing & Manufacturing Company, was by then only one of his numerous corporations, but it was a model for the type of business that local boosters hoped to emulate throughout their city.

Nineteen-year-old Edward L. Stone arrived in Roanoke in 1883, one of the three employees of Lynchburg printer J. P. Bell's branch office in the town. Stone worked as a compositor for Bell, having learned the printing trade beginning at age twelve, when he went to work as a "printer's devil" for the Bedford *Sentinel* in his hometown of Liberty, Virginia. By 1882, Stone had worked his way up to printer of the Buchanan, Virginia, *Democrat,* and in early 1883, he briefly held the same position for the Lynchburg *News* before joining Bell's company later in the year. The Roanoke shop, located on Commerce Street, printed its first order of five hundred postcards for local entrepreneur Ferdinand Rorer in July 1883. The following month, it completed its initial run of tickets and schedules for the Norfolk &Western and Shenandoah Valley Railroads, its principal commercial clients for the following seventy-five years. Despite some early successes and several lucrative railroad contracts, the Roanoke branch of the Bell Company lost money over the next couple of years. Even worse, in 1885, the branch manager died. Rather than close the shop and cut his losses, however, Bell appointed the twenty-one-year-old Stone the new manager.[80]

Under Stone's guidance, the branch began to eke out a profit, and in 1887, Stone convinced Bell to purchase a modern steam-powered press to replace the hand-powered antiquated one. The new equipment facilitated even more business, but in 1889, fire destroyed the Commerce Street shop. Stone used the fire as an opportunity to talk Bell into enlarging the Roanoke branch by purchasing an even more elaborate and modern press system. As a result, by early 1890, the company and its new press had moved into rented rooms on the second and third floors of the Gale Building downtown, and within months it was up again and thriving. By then, the company was printing tickets, schedules, letterhead, and booklets for the N&W, which had formerly sent the majority of its print work to Philadelphia. The company also produced a wide array of blank business ledgers and print work for local businesses and residents. Stone, never satisfied with the status quo, was not content with the space in the Gale Building, and in late 1890, he encouraged Bell to build a new printing shop and invest in even more modern presses. The success of the firm and its young manager's persistence convinced Bell to make the investment, and in 1891, shortly before he retired, Bell funded a three-story brick shop on north Jefferson Street beside the N&W office complex and across the street from the Hotel Roanoke.[81]

After Bell retired, Stone immediately tried to find a way to purchase Bell's Roanoke printing branch. Almost a year earlier, Stone had married Minnie Tinsley Fishburn, daughter of longtime Big Lick and Roanoke tobacco manufacturer and merchant James Addison Fishburn. When the print shop became available, Stone convinced his new brother-in-law, local banker Junius Blair Fishburn, and Albert Stone, his brother, to join him in purchasing the company. The three agreed later that Edward Stone would be president of the firm, Fishburn the vice-president, and Albert Stone the secretary-treasurer. In the fall of 1892, the business changed its name to The Stone Printing & Manufacturing Company (SP&MC), and by the following summer, the firm claimed it was "the best equipped printing establishment in the state, none excepted," as well as "the best general job print shop south of Philadelphia." The business, Stone boasted, had "all conveniences for the annihilation of time" at its disposal. Indeed, the company's policy of keeping up with any and all advancements in printing technology had by then made it the most efficient, modern, creative, and cost-effective printer in the state. The SP&MC began producing college and university yearbooks in the mid-1890s, and by the early 1900s, it had contracts for annuals with dozens of schools throughout the South. It had done well enough by then to purchase Bell's Jefferson Street building, and in 1905, the company had it torn down to make way for a fifty-thousand-square-foot replacement. One hundred and thirty employees worked in the new plant when it opened in 1907, and by 1912, the business had over two hundred workers on its payroll.[82] The company's success made it one of the most important homegrown industries in the city, and made its president, Edward Stone, the envy of local capitalists and boosters. "The rise of the Stone Printing Company," one paper lectured, "furnishes an object lesson that every ambitious young man should note." The firm, it claimed, had perhaps done "more than any single establishment to spread the name and fame of Roanoke."[83]

Stone managed his company as a strict paternalist, rewarding employees by merit rather than seniority and paying them wages far above average for print shop workers. Starting in early 1893, the firm began hosting seasonal banquets for its employees. That year it rented a downtown restaurant and treated workers to oysters, veal, ice cream, cake, fruit, milk, and cocoa.[84] The banquets grew more elaborate in the years that followed, but in 1896, Stone replaced them with annual "outings" to nearby springs or resorts. In August of that year, for example, the company transported workers by train to Elliston, Virginia, where they participated in singing, running, wrestling, and pie-eating contests. They could also fish, play croquet, and dine on a catered luncheon while listening to the SP&MC band.[85]

Stone was zealously opposed to organized labor but ran his printing company as an "open shop," allowing union and non-union members to work but refusing to broker any deal or respond to any demand from union representatives. In the mid-1890s, about fifteen of the firm's fifty employees belonged to the national typographical union. Stone, who paid nearly all his workers above the union scale and awarded promotions or raises based on merit alone, claimed that organized labor had no right to instruct him how to run his business. Although his paternalism and the company's high wages did much to prevent labor disturbances or walkouts at his shop, Stone's strident refusal to acknowledge organized labor's right to collective bargaining earned him numerous enemies among union organizers. In 1904, for example, Roanoke's Central Trades and Labor Council, in a move directed specifically against

Stone, instructed all union men in the city to make a stand against "organized greed" by refraining from reading any material that did not contain the typographical union label.[86]

In the fall of 1905, when the national typographical union ordered members not working an eight-hour day to strike, Stone informed his employees that the company would stick by its fifty-four-hour work week and notified any worker wanting to work less to find employment elsewhere.[87] When the walkout commenced, only six of the SP&MC's 130 employees went on strike. The firm's eleven other union members stayed on the job, and Stone immediately replaced the six who left. When questioned by local papers, Stone claimed to believe the majority of his employees were "well satisfied with the conditions that exist in our establishment, and that there is a mutual feeling of confidence and esteem between employee and employer."[88] Soon after, the Roanoke Typographical Union expelled the men in Stone's shop who refused to strike. Overall, however, the union proved no match for Stone, who held steadfast to a fifty-four-hour work week.[89] In the aftermath, Stone published a pamphlet that claimed business at his shop had increased after the walkout because Roanoke's capitalists admired his strong stance. The booklet infuriated the leaders of the Central Trades and Labor Council, all of whom blasted Stone and called on good union men to read nothing without the typographical union seal.[90] Stone's anti-union stance, which was unique in Roanoke, was only possible because he could depend on steady sales to the Norfolk & Western and other outside corporations that made boycotts of his printing work by local laborers of little significance.

In the fall of 1907, pressroom workers organized another strike for an eight-hour day. It ended in the same fashion: thirty-six men walked out, Stone fired them, and then quickly hired replacements. The strikers manned a picket line for several weeks, but were unable to get the company to speak with them. Stone, a reporter observed, "absolutely refuses to offer them any proposition whatsoever."[91] In a letter to Roanoke's mayor in which he explained the firm's position, Stone claimed that he and the shop's directors "have never been opposed to the union, but we have objected to having them run our business, unless they acquired it by ownership."[92] Although his stance might seem coldhearted, Stone, a progressive paternalist, always made his non-arbitration position known. He sympathized with his union workers, but never to the point of cutting deals with any of them. If they chose to work for SP&MC, he believed, then their strongest loyalty should be to the firm, not to any labor organization. When the strikers gave up and asked for their jobs back, Stone immediately rehired them. His firm, he told a London friend after the strike, treated its employees fairly and equally. If its workers walked out, it was not because they were not paid decent wages or because they were subjected to

Stone Printing and Mfg. Co., Jefferson Street, early 1900s. Norfolk & Western Historical Photograph Collection (RRE0041), Digital Library and Archives, University Libraries, Virginia Tech.

dangerous or harsh working conditions. Their "dissatisfaction," he explained, had been caused "by the agitators and organizers who are shrewd enough to keep themselves in position, and in order to hold their position must make a show for money received, which is generally more per diem than they earn at their trade."[93]

By 1910, Stone's printing shop dominated the regional market and was one of the largest and best equipped in the South. Its profits, which came primarily from work for the N&W, rose steadily, along with its customer base, which by then included universities and colleges across the nation. In addition to railroad work and college annuals, the company developed a broad niche market in the production of high quality, short-run publications for private clients and well-established publishers. Indeed, Edward Stone's obsession with book collecting and printing techniques led his shop to develop production artistry, excellence, and attention to detail that was unmatched throughout much of the nation.

Stone's reputation as an impeccably honest, pragmatic, and gifted capitalist put him in select company and made his political and business opinions well respected and much sought after. In 1896, a group of prominent local Democrats, "believing that the interests of the City of Roanoke demand that the Executive office be filled by a business man," published a petition encouraging Stone to run for mayor. Stone considered it but declined after he learned that a local ordinance forbade municipal business contracts with firms owned by elected officials.[94] Six years later, after voters in the second ward pushed Stone to run for city council and he again declined because of the contract law, he complained in local papers that "under the present Ordinance, the more interest a businessman takes in the welfare of the city by investing his money in enterprises that contribute to the upbuilding of the city, the less chance there is for him to have any voice in the enactment of laws that affect the welfare of the whole city."[95] Local officials, however, declined to amend the ordinance, and as a result, Stone refused to make a bid for public office.

Although Stone never held any municipal position, he was throughout his life a gifted and tireless civic and business booster. He invested heavily in dozens of homegrown Roanoke enterprises and constantly fielded entrepreneurs' requests who sought his financial backing or advice. He usually put civic betterment above monetary gain and called most of his investments more "patriotic" than practical.[96] In 1902, Stone published *Picturesque Roanoke,* a compilation of booster photographs illustrating the city's vast industries, mansions, public buildings, and places of leisure.[97] The booklet, not surprisingly, offered no images of the city's African Americans, substandard working-class housing, dirt streets, polluted streams, filthy Market House, saloons, child laborers, or dilapidated schools.

In the late 1890s, Stone, his brother-in-law J. B. Fishburn, and William Cowell Stephenson, a Roanoke-based coal baron, pooled their substantial resources and business acumen to form a venture capital firm called the "Young Men's Investment Company" (YMIC) with Stone as its president. In one of its first investments, the YMIC bought Peyton L. Terry's "Terry Building" for about $70,000, or around a fourth of what it had actually cost to build.[98] In 1900, Stone and Fishburn established the Century Banking and Safe Deposit Company with Stone as the bank's president and Fishburn as a director. When Fishburn later assumed control of his uncle's National Exchange Bank, he absorbed Century Banking.[99] By the early 1900s, Stone, who was already president of Stone Printing and Manufacturing Company, had been elected chairman of Fishburn's National Exchange Bank, president of the Virginia Bridge & Iron Works, vice-president of the Walker Foundry and Machine Company, and a director of the Southwest Virginia Trust Company and *The Roanoke Times.*[100]

In 1904, Stone, backed in part by the Young Men's Investment Company, purchased the Borderland Coal Company of Mingo County, West Virginia, and Pike County, Kentucky. He was Borderland's chief stockholder, its president, and eventually its chairman of the board. Soon after the takeover, he expanded the company's land holdings from 1,000 to 3,000 acres and raised its

Edward Lee Stone. Norfolk & Western Historical Photograph Collection (NW3156), Digital Library and Archives, University Libraries, Virginia Tech.

output, which increased from 246 railcars of coal in 1904 to 3,781 only six years later. The company's town—Borderland, West Virginia—included miners' housing, several commissaries, a church, and a school. Although in Roanoke Stone operated his printing firm and an open shop, he and Borderland's directors vehemently opposed organized labor in their mine. The firm refused to employ union members, fired and evicted miners who responded to overtures from organized labor, and hired dozens of spies to keep management abreast of unionization efforts.[101]

Stone and J. B. Fishburn amassed personal fortunes that permitted a lifestyle totally unlike Roanoke's predominately working-class residents. Beyond compiling a personal library recognized upon his death in 1938 as the largest and most valuable private collection in Virginia, Stone's other diversions included membership in dozens of civic, professional, and cultural organizations, including the Roanoke Board of Trade, Roanoke Chamber of Commerce, American Institute of Graphic Arts, United Typothetae of America, Virginia Historical Society, Roanoke German Club, Roanoke Gun Club, and Roanoke Country Club.[102] In the early 1900s, he and Fishburn took a six-month journey to Hawaii, Siberia, Japan, China, India, Egypt, and Europe. The duo made the voyage, according to Stone, because doctors had informed them that their "systems" had been "very much run down as a result of too close application to business matters." The tour, family physicians had assured the men, would restore their "former robust health."[103]

Stone's phenomenal financial, cultural, and societal ascent, made all the more stunning by his modest background, made him the archetypal "new man" of the New South. It was a rise only possible in a city like Roanoke, with no past to encumber entrepreneurs and no solid caste system to prevent their success. Reflecting back some fifty years after arriving in the Town of

Roanoke as a nineteen-year-old assistant with Bell Printing, Stone acknowledged that he and his associates were indeed lucky to have been "citizens of a wonderful community in a marvelous age."[104]

■■■

Native business leaders like Edward Stone and J. B. Fishburn coalesced around a variety of businessmen's clubs and societies, forming a counterculture to the town's predominately working-class ethos. Unlike the city's first generation of business boosters, exemplified by men like Henry S. Trout or Peyton L. Terry, who served on the board of directors for the N&W and the Roanoke Machine Works and were tied overtly to the interests of Frederick Kimball and the E. W. Clark Company, the town's second generation of promoters operated far more independently. Many of them saw the N&W's monopoly on rail access as an impediment to progress and worked hard to secure a connection to a rival line. In the Roanoke German Club, Roanoke Country Club, Shenandoah Club, and the Century Club, the city's elite networked and fraternized in ways that encouraged local investment as well as further solidified their hegemony over workers. They also eventually organized themselves into businessmen's leagues in ways similar to how local workers organized themselves into unions. The Roanoke Commercial Club (1890–91), Roanoke Board of Trade (1892–1904), and Roanoke Chamber of Commerce (1904–2000s) were hardly unions but they were vehicles through which boosters could amalgamate their power, pool their financial resources, and entice outside investment. The groups helped pull Roanoke out of its economic doldrums in the 1890s and fostered subsequent industrialization that pushed the city to the forefront of Virginia and New South municipalities.

Most of the city's successful businessmen were invited to join elite fraternal orders or exclusive social clubs once they reached a certain plateau of economic worth and social standing. Membership in organizations such as the Roanoke German Club and Shenandoah Club were the barometer of personal cachet in the 1890s, and in the early 1900s, local patricians augmented associations to those organizations with memberships in the Roanoke Country Club or in the more restrictive Roanoke Century Club. The Country Club, organized in 1899 when Roanoke's tennis and golf clubs merged, was built originally in South Roanoke with two tennis courts, a shooting range, a bowling alley, a clubhouse in what had been a residence, and a primitive golf course laid out on property rented from the Crystal Springs Land Company. The club, according to *The Roanoke Times,* had nevertheless "supplied a long felt want" by offering a place "where friends may always be found and a pleasant hour or two spent as the fancy dictates."[105] The following year, when the board of governors of the Country Club sought ways to address their organization's deficiencies, they invited Edward L. Stone to a private board meeting "in order that this subject, which is closely related to the social welfare of our City, may have the benefit of the widest experience available in relation to a matter of the kind." After the meeting, Stone purchased memberships for his family and bought several hundred dollars worth of Country Club stock.[106]

Other prominent businessmen and their wives also joined, and in 1905, the Country Club purchased fifty-one acres in Roanoke County, about two miles from the city, to use as its new grounds. Three years later, after constructing a clubhouse, golf links, and tennis courts, the organization moved to the new site.[107] In the meantime, members elected Edward Stone to the Club's board of governors and its Bowling Committee. The Club also formalized its rules, noting in its brochure for the 1906–7 season that no uninvited visitors, guests from Roanoke County, or men under the age of eighteen were allowed, that no cards or other games could be played in the Club House on Sundays, that all donated furniture had to be approved by the Furnishing Committee, "so that harmony may be preserved therein," and that "furniture belonging to the Reception and Dining-room must not be removed to the porches, nor porch furniture to the grove." Although male members governed the Club and all its sports and membership committees, several of their wives and daughters staffed the Club House Committee and were responsible for supervising house servants along with all receptions, meetings, and entertainments.[108]

In 1905, Edward Stone, J. B. Fishburn, and the nine other former officers and directors of the Century Banking and Safe Deposit Company formed the Century Club, an association of Roanoke's most elite businessmen, dedicated to "social, intellectual, and other pleasures."[109] Stone served as president throughout most of the Century Club's existence. The original coterie was a who's who of local luminaries and included Lucian H. Cocke, Roanoke's first mayor and general counsel for the Norfolk & Western Railway; Lucius E. Johnson, president of the N&W; James C. Cassell, former general superintendent of the N&W; William H. Lewis, superintendent of motive power for the N&W; Thompson W. Goodwin, president of the Southwest Virginia Trust Company; and Francis A. Hill, president of the Red Jacket and Hull Coal Companies. In the years that followed, the Century Club tapped five new members, each of whom the association deemed essential in "converting the village of Big Lick into the City of Roanoke." The new members included Joseph A. Gale, chief surgeon of the N&W; Arthur Needles, general manager of the N&W; Nicholas D. Maher, vice-president of the N&W; and John B. Newton, general manager and vice-president of the Virginia & Southern Railway and the Virginia Iron, Coal, and Coke Company.[110]

The Century Club's annual dinners usually received front-page coverage in local papers. In 1912, for instance, *The* (Roanoke) *Evening World* reported that after dining on an eleven-course meal in the main dining room of the Hotel Roanoke, which had been decorated with hundreds of American Beauty Roses, members received gold lapel pins before being surprised by the arrival of their wives, who had arranged cello and piano music for dancing.[111] In addition to hosting ornate fêtes, the Club made numerous outings in private N&W railcars to promote Roanoke. After one such trip—a journey to Cincinnati and Memphis—the club's members reported that the organization had "resolved itself into a Roanoke Boosting Club as well as a pleasure seeking Century Club and was entertained royally at every stop."[112]

Almost all the members of the city's elite clubs and fraternal organizations also belonged to the town's various booster organizations. Although prominent N&W executives joined most of the groups, native businessmen were the main force behind the commercial and civic clubs. Most had originally enlisted in the Roanoke Board of Trade after it began operations in 1892. The Board, which emerged not long after the collapse of Hinton Helper's short-lived Commercial Club, quickly became a vital cog in Roanoke's widespread civic promotion efforts. The association, a "harmonious, organized and united effort" of businessmen, used a variety of means to publicize the advantages Roanoke offered to outside industries.[113] In early 1893, for example, the Board brokered a deal with a South Carolina cloth manufacturer to bring a ten-thousand-spindle cotton mill to town. "It will not only add greatly to the population of the city," one of the men behind the project explained, "but will give employment to a class of people who have not heretofore found suitable work."[114] After the mill's executives chartered the corporation, members subscribed $50,000 in stock.[115] Not long after, however, the 1893 depression set in and the deal fell apart.

In the midst of the depression, Board members pooled the funds necessary to publish *Roanoke, Virginia 1894: Pluck, Push and Progress Illustrated,* an elaborate guide to the city's phenomenal rise and abundant business opportunities. Edward Stone's print shop designed and published the booklet, and he and a committee from the Board compiled the text and dozens of photographs accompanying it. *Pluck, Push and Progress,* while acknowledging that a large number of skilled workers had recently been thrown out of employment and left town, explained that the city was so young that most local enterprises "have run for the most part in grooves given by the forces that started its growth; hence departments of industry are still undeveloped, though facilities for successful operations are abundant." The guide guaranteed free land to any manufacturing enterprise that located in Roanoke and suggested that a paper mill, tannery, tin can factory, barrel factory, and wool mill were the ventures most likely to succeed there. As a further inducement, it bragged that Roanoke had never been "afflicted with strikes and boycotts" because local labor was "abundant, cheap and contented." "When the whole North and West were in the throes of labor troubles," it explained, "we were quiet and serene." The pamphlet, written for a northern and possibly immigrant or Catholic population, assured its readers that while other parts of the former Confederacy might be prejudiced against them, "Roanoke is the most cosmopolitan city in the South; so that any man or family who should be attracted hither can come with the assurance of a hearty welcome, and with the certainty of finding on arrival enough people of their nationality, or section, to form a coterie of friends."[116]

In 1898, the efforts of the city's boosters attracted the attention of *Headlight*, a Chicago-based investment and tourism journal, which devoted a special edition to the "Magic City, Roanoke, Va., and Scenes along the Norfolk & Western Railroad." According to the journal's correspondent, promoters there were more vehement than any he had encountered elsewhere. The town, he explained to the magazine's largely northern audience, "is noted beyond all southern cities for the hustling, aggressive character of her business men." According to the correspondent, Roanoke offered so many investment advantages—including a submissive pool of labor from which to select workers—that "She is in very deed the belle of the New South, extending with jewel-bedecked hand, to the some-seeker and the business man in search of wealth and happiness, the richest gems and the most tempting opportunities offered by the lovely southland."[117]

In 1901, local wholesalers organized the Roanoke Merchants' and Manufacturers' Association. It co-existed with the Board of Trade until 1904, when the groups merged into the Roanoke Chamber of Commerce. The new organization, its founders explained, sought ways "to advance by every means the development and growth of the city," "remove impediments to progress," and "induce cordiality and friendship among business men." The Chamber of Commerce (RCOC) elected Edward Stone as a director, and not long afterwards, he oversaw production of its first promotional pamphlet, *Roanoke: The Magic City of Virginia* (1904). The booklet, much like its 1894 predecessor, suggested that Roanoke's business friendly ethos, docile labor force, and low cost of living made it an ideal location for manufacturers. "There is no reason," the RCOC argued, "why certain goods could not be made here as well or as cheaply as in the North." The organization, which boasted a membership of the city's most influential businessmen and politicians, claimed it was ready to offer potential investors "every assistance which is in our power."[118] The RCOC also advertised the advantages of the city in various national trade magazines, including the *Manufacturers' Record* of Baltimore, and in the spring of 1906, the *Record* ran a feature on the wonderful investment advantages available in Roanoke.[119]

In 1907, the 250 members of the RCOC raised $100,000 to back the Roanoke Industrial Securities Company, a firm designed to assist the establishment of new industries by offering capital to needy corporations at 5 percent interest. That same year, the RCOC elected a committee to present displays of Roanoke's industries at the 1907 Jamestown Tercentennial Exposition in Norfolk. Committee members, including Edward Stone and the Virginia Brewing Company's Henry Scholz, distributed forty thousand copies of a special RCOC promotional pamphlet.[120] *Roanoke, Virginia: Its Location, Climate and Water Supply, Its Manufacturing, Commercial and Educational Advantages and General Desirability as a Place of Residence* (1907), contained typically abundant economic and cultural data for the potential northern investors along with a lengthy and misleading sermon on the emergence of a New South. Local and regional businessmen in the post–Civil War South, the booklet (mis)informed readers, had easily adjusted to the "new conditions" wrought by the conflict, and using "an intense devotion to the exalted ideals of the past" as their guide, had "reared an empire of civic and industrial grandeur upon the ruins that covered her desolate battle-scared soil." According to the guide, Roanoke City was foremost among the copious examples of splendor that dotted the landscape of the former Confederacy.[121]

The RCOC kept up a constant campaign to lure additional manufacturers and issued yet another booster guide in 1910. *Busy Facts for the Busy Man about the Busy "Magic City," Roanoke, Va., U. S. A.,* inaugurated the organization's new creed of "Acorn to Oak, Watch Roanoke," which incorporated an elaborately drawn tree to illustrate the city's fantastic growth from what misleadingly was claimed had been 400 residents in 1882 to 35,000 residents in 1910.[122] By then, the RCOC's campaign had reaped substantial economic rewards: between 1900 and 1909, twenty-eight new manufacturers began operations; industrial employment increased 46 percent, expanding to seven thousand workers; the value of city-made products increased 34 percent; and real estate assessments grew by $13,000,000, an increase of 117 percent.[123] The city's population growth, which had declined during the mid-1890s, rebounded in the early 1900s; from 1890 to 1910, Roanoke moved from Virginia's fifth largest city to its third, behind only Richmond and Norfolk.[124] In its 1910 brochure, the RCOC bragged that such phenomenal growth was only possible in Roanoke, a city with abundant and inexpensive factory sites, easy access to inexhaustible raw materials, excellent rail service, low corporate taxes, and "ample cheap labor."[125]

Much of the city's industrial expansion was the result of a booster-driven successful campaign to lure the Virginian Railroad to Roanoke. The Virginian, a branch line of the Tidewater Railroad Company, was by far the largest of the numerous new enterprises. From 1905 to 1908, it built a rail connection, a depot, and railroad shops in Roanoke and in 1909, when the line opened for business, it ended the monopoly on local rail access held by the Norfolk & Western since 1882.[126] By 1910, dozens of other new manufacturers had begun operations as well. The five-thousand-spindle Roanoke Cotton Mill, established in 1901 through a combination of native investors and a New York City financier, employed several hundred women, girls, and boys. The company, which took over the former Norwich Lock Works facility, primarily produced yarn for carpets. It took control of cottages constructed by the Norwich Company and built additional company housing near the plant, along the banks of the Roanoke River. Edward Stone and J. B. Fishburn helped organize the firm and contributed a substantial amount of capital to the project. Stone, Fishburn, and the other owners of the mill claimed that the plant was a philanthropic investment, organized for the benefit of poor women and impoverished families with children old enough to work. Fishburn served on the mill's board of directors and Stone served as its secretary-treasurer until 1907, when the plant closed briefly before it changed ownership.[127]

In 1906, three of Lynchburg's leading industrialists opened the Adams, Payne & Gleaves Brick Factory in Roanoke. Four years later the company was producing forty thousand bricks per day. The Roanoke Bridge Company, incorporated in 1906 by several southern businessmen, employed 350 workers and built over 600 bridges from 1906 to 1912. The Virginia Lumber Company began operations in 1906 with fifty men on its payroll. The Griggs Packing Company, opened in 1906 by Big Lick native Robert B. Griggs, employed fifty men and was by 1910 capable of slaughtering and dressing 100 hogs an hour. In 1907, a group of Richmond businessmen established the Virginia Metal and Culvert Company; in 1908, another group of investors founded the Roanoke Marble and Granite Works; and in 1911, native businessmen incorporated the Dominion Metal Products and hired several hundred skilled iron and steel workers.[128]

Industries already in existence expanded throughout the 1890s and early 1900s. By 1910, for example, the Virginia Bridge and Iron Company, which assumed control of the American Bridge Company in 1895, had grown from 75 employees to over 600 and was producing 45,000 tons of manufactured products per year. Edward Stone and J. B. Fishburn assisted in the bridge company's 1895 reorganization and later served on its board of directors.[129] The growth of established firms and the arrival of dozens of new manufacturers did not displace the N&W and its Machine Works as the largest and most significant employer in town. Indeed, by 1910, the number of residents employed by the railroad increased to over three thousand. The rise of other industries, however, did do much to diversify the city's business infrastructure and usher in a period of significant economic growth. Native businessmen and boosters were the main forces responsible for the growth, and it was hardly coincidental that they profited the most from the continuing industrialization.

For most of Roanoke's workers, however, the industrial progress brought few rewards. Boys and girls working in the Roanoke Cotton Mill, the Reverend William Campbell observed in 1905, not only labored in dangerous and difficult conditions, they also had no time to attend public school. Campbell, who sought ways to fund an evening school for children, found thirty-three prospective students working in the mill, including one fifteen-year-old girl who told him, "I would love to go. I have no mother, and have had very little opportunity to get any schooling."[130] In Roanoke's working-class neighborhoods in the Northeast and Southeast, families crowded into company housing built in the 1880s. Most workers' homes lacked plumbing and electricity and existed in neighborhoods blighted by soot and pollution from nearby industries. "Brick Row," a block of identical, cheap, tenement buildings in the southeast, for example, was not only aesthetically offensive and shoddily constructed, it was also filthy and crime-ridden. The housing project, built in 1883, was home to scores of impoverished white families. By the time the property changed hands in 1898 and the new landlord evicted scores of tenants who had been unable to pay rent, residents in other parts of the city referred to Brick Row as "Poverty Flats."[131] The overall disparity in living conditions between workers and businessmen is vividly apparent in municipal property assessments, which show that from 1895 to 1905 homes owned by middle- and upper-class whites in the southwest and West End accounted for about 80 percent of the total value of all white residences. Black housing, which accounted for about 30 percent of all homes in town, comprised just slightly over 2 percent of their total value.[132]

Roanoke's business boosters, always on the lookout for ways to promote or enhance their city, decided in 1909 to form a corporation to construct and operate an incline railroad on the one-thousand-foot face of Mill Mountain. The peak, which remained in Roanoke County until annexed along with "South Roanoke" in 1915, had been considered a valuable civic asset since the founding of the city, and various schemes to build an incline railway up its face had been put forward since at least 1901.[133] The Rockledge Inn and Mill Mountain Observatory, opened by the Roanoke Gas & Water Company on the summit in 1892, had initially done well but closed in the late 1890s after patronage dropped off because it was difficult to access. Walking to the top of Mill Mountain along a precarious zigzag path took over two hours, and the hotel company's horse-drawn carriage was even slower. The inn and observatory both fell into disrepair after shutting down. Indeed, when a party of Virginia College students hiked to the top in the fall of 1902 they found "an old negro woman" living in the hotel and using its former dining room to cure tobacco leaf that she had grown in what had once been the inn's picnic grounds.[134]

Edward Stone, J. B. Fishburn, and other members of the Century Club were heavily involved in the incline proposal from the beginning. In the fall of 1909, the twenty-five investors in Mill Mountain Incline Incorporated met to work out the financial details of the project. Stone put up $5,000 of the $15,000 first mortgage, and like most of the other investors, which included the Virginia Brewing Company's Scholz brothers, purchased $1,000 in stock.[135] In a letter to Lucius E. Johnson, president of the N&W, Stone explained the boosters' rationale. "Those most interested," he wrote, "think that the proposition will yield at least a fair return on the investment, besides being a splendid advertisement for Roanoke, and quite an attraction for visitors to our city; people who attend conventions, coming on excursions, or anything of the sort."[136] Stone convinced Johnson to invest as well, but not before warning him that he had gotten involved "more from a patriotic standpoint than anything else," completely aware that his investment "may not pay very handsome dividends."[137]

Albin B. Hammond, of Hammond Printing, put up the other $10,000 of the first mortgage and served as the Incline's president. Stone, who was on the committee charged with finalizing plans for the railroad, recommended the firm that had installed the cableway at his Borderland Coal Company, "so that we would have the greatest possible feeling of security in its safety design and construction."[138] The estimated cost of the incline and property for its tracks turned out to be about $25,000 more than initially expected, and as a result, in early 1910 the corporation increased its bonded indebtedness from $15,000 to $40,000.[139] Construction began shortly thereafter. By summer, workers had installed rails produced by the Roanoke Iron Company up the face of Mill Mountain and the J. G. Brill Company of Philadelphia had built the incline's electric pulley system and cars. Each of the two identical carriages, which simultaneously ascended and descended on parallel tracks, had a sixty-person capacity and took only four minutes to climb up or down the mountain. The cars, according to the incline company, had "every appliance for safety known to mechanical and electrical engineers."[140]

In the summer of 1910, only weeks before the incline was scheduled to open for business, Edward Stone informed all the railway's investors that he either wanted to own enough of the company to make it worth his while or sell the bonds and stocks that he already owned. In a letter sent to all stockholders, Stone warned the investors that "I do not see much chance for immediate returns on this speculation" and reiterated the fact that his interest in the business came only "from a patriotic standpoint." He was willing, therefore, to purchase the stock at its par value.[141] John Hartman Marsteller, a local marble yard owner who had invested $500 in the incline, informed Stone that he "went into it like a good many others did to help get it started regardless of whether it paid anything or not." Although Marsteller believed that in a couple years the railway could "be made a paying investment," he sold Stone all his stock. The Virginia Brewing Company's Scholz brothers, who had invested $1,000, sold their stock as well.[142] A dozen or so other stockholders sold out to Stone too.[143]

When the incline opened on August 14, 1910, enormous crowds of curious onlookers turned out and over fifteen-hundred patrons paid the railway's twenty-five-cent fare. The steep ascent straight up the face of Mill Mountain, according to local papers, impressed and fascinated riders. Not everyone, however, felt safe. Norfolk & Western clerk Frank G. Payne, for example, took the incline to the top on August 23 and noted that night in his diary that "it is a nice piece of work but I do not like to ride on it."[144] Although the incline initially did a brisk business, its customers were mainly residents of Roanoke or nearby locales. To sustain profits and promote the city, the incline's owners

Mill Mountain Incline, c. 1910. Norfolk & Western Historical Photograph Collection (NS5827), Digital Library and Archives, University Libraries, Virginia Tech.

understood that they needed to also draw tourist and visitor trade. As a result, not long after opening, they published a promotional brochure to advertise the incline to outsiders. Roanoke, the booklet bragged, was "a progressive and prosperous city" and its mountainside railway was but the latest of the "many successful enterprises" it could boast. Roanoke residents owned the Mill Mountain Incline, the brochure explained, and all of them "went into the enterprise because they hoped it would prove a big advertisement for the City, and contribute to the development of a modern municipality."[145]

The incline company rented and refurbished the dilapidated Rockledge Inn and its overgrown grounds and built a new, much taller observatory to replace the one constructed in 1892.[146] The hotel, which had capacity for only a dozen or so guests, was far too small and primitive to make Mill Mountain the sort of resort that the incline's investors hoped for. As a result, only months after opening, they sought ways to purchase the entire, one-hundred-acre summit of Mill Mountain from the Roanoke Gas & Water Company so they could construct a larger and more modern lodge. Edward Stone, the main advocate of the plan, informed fellow stockholders only a week after the incline began operations of his belief that "to make a success of the proposition a good deal more money has got to be put up in order to put the top of the mountain in attractive shape and to secure or build attractions up there that will make people feel that it is worth while to spend their money to get to the top of the mountain."[147] In October 1910, Stone advised Albin B. Hammond, the incline company's president, that the firm needed to move quickly because Roanoke's mayor had already suggested that the city purchase the summit for a municipal park. Even then, Stone informed Hammond, the company could make a tidy profit by immediately buying the land and selling it to the city "at some figure above the purchase price."[148] Fostering civic betterment, at least to Stone, was even more worthwhile if the process yielded a substantial return on investment. In the years that followed, however, neither the incline company nor the city purchased the summit.[149]

Seasonal changes strictly dictated the incline's business; its peak months were always from the late spring to early fall. Ridership during the winter was nearly nonexistent. From August through October 1910, for example, the incline sold almost nineteen thousand fares, while in December, it sold only about two hundred. Business did not pick up again until May the following year, when slightly over 4,000 patrons paid for a lift up and down the mountain.[150] By then, the incline company had installed new walkways, benches, and swings on the summit, and had mounted a telescope and massive electric "searchlight" in its observatory that could "light up the country for miles around." It opened a souvenir store on the observatory's first floor that sold postcards manufactured by Stone's print shop along with other incline and Mill Mountain

Mill Mountain Observatory, 1910. From Mill Mountain Incline Company, "Views about Mill Mountain and the Incline Railway." Roanoke: Stone Printing & Mfg. Co. 1910.

memorabilia.[151] With a larger hotel, one local paper observed, the mountaintop, with its cool air that "invigorates mind and body," could easily draw in tourists in the summer months who would otherwise spend their vacations at nearby mineral springs. Moreover, the paper's editor explained, the view, which "presented to the man of business the prettiest prospect for a great industrial community," would facilitate manufacturing investments by at least some of the thousands of out-of-town businessmen who made a visit.[152] The panorama from the top offered a view of the entire Roanoke Valley and was indeed astounding. Eleanor Armistead, a nurse from Richmond who was working temporarily in the city's Lewis-Gale Hospital, came to the conclusion of most visitors after she rode the incline to the summit in the fall of 1911, informing her fiancé afterwards that the vista was "the most surprisingly beautiful view I have ever seen."[153]

Ridership on the incline, despite the company's advertising efforts, declined sharply from 1910 to 1912, dropping from 4,433 fares per month in 1910, to 2,605 in 1911, to 1,801 in 1912. The plummet, which continued in the following years, vividly reveals that the much sought tourist trade never arrived, and that local patrons, after riding the railway once or twice, lost interest. The Rockledge Inn, which was open only from May to October, cost much more to operate than it made in business. Paid admissions to the observatory, which had to be rebuilt after a violent thunderstorm knocked it down in the summer of 1911, declined over 160 percent from 1910 to 1912.[154]

After paying operating expenses and interest on its mortgages, Mill Mountain Incline Incorporated lost $875 in 1911.[155] Early the following year, the company's treasurer notified its stockholders that although it had been "impossible, through lack of funds, to meet the interest on the second mortgage bonds," the firm "hoped that the revenues derived from the operation of the property during the coming summer" would make up for it.[156] Despite slashing operating expenses by over 50 percent, in December 1912, the incline's treasurer reported that the company had lost another $540 and would be unable to pay bondholders their full interest.[157]

After Albin B. Hammond, the incline's president and principal financier, died in the spring of 1912, stockholders elected Jack W. Hancock their president. Shortly thereafter, a few of the incline's directors proposed placing a giant, electric booster-slogan sign on top of Mill Mountain to advertise the city and railway. The Roanoke Chamber of Commerce, once informed of the plan, notified the Roanoke Gas & Water Company that its members had "instantly and unanimously expressed their deep regret at this possible despoliation of one of Roanoke's very best civic assets." The company concurred, and in its response explained its belief that Frederick Kimball and Peyton Terry would have been appalled at the idea, and that Hammond, "who had more to do with building the Incline than any other man," would never have approved such a request being made. "The Incline," the company observed, "was not built for commercial profit" and as such, needed no gaudy advertising to make money.[158]

Edward Stone, who had been appointed to the incline's board of directors in early 1912, received notice from Hancock that fall that a local organization had requested hundreds of free passes from the railway to entertain visitors at its convention.[159] To Stone, who always paid the fare of his printing shop customers and rarely even used his stockholder pass, the appeal, which had been couched in the language of civic advertising, was baffling. In his reply, Stone told Hancock that "to ask the Mill Mountain Incline (which is hardly paying expenses) to bear the brunt of this special advertising, is, in my opinion, asking a little too much." Investors, he complained, put their money into the project "more from a patriotic standpoint than anything else, and when they have done this, I think they have gone quite far enough, at least until the proposition begins to show up as a money making one."[160] It never made money, and in 1919, Stone and the incline's other investors voted to sell their $40,000 railway for $7,000. In the years that followed, the incline continued to struggle. In 1929, a few years after workers carved a zigzag road for automobiles up the mountain's face, it closed. The following year the incline company had the system dismantled and sold as scrap.[161]

■■■

Although boosters' dreams of creating a tourist attraction on the summit of Mill Mountain never materialized, their campaign to bring new businesses to town was an astounding success. When the city's fortunes plummeted during the 1893 depression, the town's business leaders did what they could to mitigate the economic turmoil. Some pushed for a new railroad, others funded promotions by the Board of Trade, and hundreds dug in and weathered the storm. Having not only survived but thrived in the aftermath, many boosters moved to capitalize further by widely advertising Roanoke's cheap land, inexpensive labor, weak unions, and low corporate taxes. Their campaign, instigated through the Board of Trade or Chamber of Commerce, lured dozens of manufacturers to town and placed Roanoke in the forefront of Virginia's industrialized cities. In addition, domestic enterprises like the Virginia Brewing Company and Stone Printing & Manufacturing Company, rose to prominence, giving the city an industrial cachet not built entirely by reliance on the Norfolk & Western Railway. To the Magic City's promoters, the promise of a New South, while largely fictional elsewhere in the region, was real.

Not everyone, however, benefited from Roanoke's "open for business" ethos. White workers, who were the vast majority of all residents, held little collective bargaining power and received only a portion of the wages and benefits they could have gained from successful strikes. Unlike their brethren in the North, Roanoke's laborers remained docile in the 1890s and early 1900s. They could hardly afford not to, since the city's government was entirely in the hands of business-friendly officials. Moreover, they were isolated in the mountains of Southwest Virginia and blinded with paternalism, modest pay, and token concessions doled out by local corporations. Indeed, the entire social, cultural, and economic structure of Roanoke induced apathy among the working classes, who, upon sensing some injustice chose to walk out, were immediately dealt a largely worthless but symbolically rewarding remedy. Clergy, elected officials, and barons of commerce all walked softly amidst the city's thousands of laborers, promising them "justice" and "reform," but only when it was requested in the correct way and bore no threat of overturning the Magic City's social order.

For the city's non-white laborers, the situation was worse. They had no access to unions, worked on the lowest and most difficult level of labor, and made even lower wages than whites. The coming of new industries, while providing employment, did so mainly in the form of jobs that whites deemed too arduous or filthy to hold. The benefits to working-class women were little better. The Roanoke Cotton Mill, which opened specifically to fill a niche for female employment, offered an alternative to domestic labor, but did so at the cost of long hours, low pay, and child labor. Indeed, when Lewis Hine toured the South in 1911 to photograph boys and girls working in its fabled industries, he stopped in Roanoke long enough to take a picture of a young girl, decked out in a dress and bonnet, working amongst the spindles of the city's cotton factory. For her, boosters' quest to open the town for business meant difficult and mind-numbing labor, no formal education, and lungs filled with cotton dust. If Roanoke was emblematic of the New South, then for much of its working-class or African American population, it was hardly new, hardly spectacular, and hardly rewarding. Boosters' rhetoric was no match for the cold, hard reality of life in the city for the vast majority of its laboring residents, who continued to barely get by, often did without adequate public services, and on whose labor Roanoke moved forward into the forefront of industrialized southern cities.

Chapter 7

Reordering Roanoke

Roanoke's business boosters—the men who successfully promoted the city to outside investors and industries—had an almost blind faith in economic development as a panacea for all the town's problems. Their faith, however, failed to shape the city in the fashion they expected. As a result, by the turn of the century, the town still seemed more Big Lick than Roanoke. It was a city with numerous dirt streets, hundreds of free-ranging cattle, a polluted farmer's market, few enforced health regulations, a rowdy saloon and brothel district, overcrowded and dingy schools, and no public parks or library. In addition, racial conflict over politics or public space continued to generate anxiety among most whites.

Three core groups of "progressive reformers" eventually stepped forward to attempt to remedy these and other issues. Local business leaders, alarmed that Roanoke's primitive conditions and "disordered" environment might threaten additional economic investment, moved to disfranchise and segregate black residents as well as ban cows from city streets. The town's Evangelicals, appalled by the city's unruly saloons and thriving bordellos, moved to enact prohibition and close down local brothels. The wives and daughters of business leaders, outraged by impure milk, shoddy schools, and decrepit playgrounds, moved to protect their children and families by creating a healthy, regulated public environment. Those being "reformed"—African Americans, white migrants from the countryside, farmers, workers—opposed almost all these efforts in one way or another but proved no match for the forces of progress.

While Roanoke's reformers generally had the same overall goals, much like progressive reformers elsewhere in the nation, they did not always act in concert or agree with one another. Some of the hardest fought battles on the reform front were between factions of civic improvement advocates with different aims. Roanoke's reformers were, however, predominantly white, educated members of the town's middle and upper classes, businessmen, professionals or their wives, and above all, they were willing to devote considerable energy to modifying their city in ways that recast it as a progressive metropolis. They shared a great deal in common with urban reformers throughout the nation—mainly because these paternalistic Roanokers sought to impose their version of order on the chaos they perceived all around them. The city's reformers also mirrored their progressive counterparts elsewhere in the South, who like them privileged economic growth, order, planning, and efficiency over all social justice issues.[1]

■■■

As a first step in the process of reordering the city, its executives and elected officials eagerly endorsed disfranchising black and poor white residents—the main groups opposed to livestock and health restrictions. They also supported segregation as the best means of ending white and black conflicts over public space. Up until the early twentieth century, local African American voters, almost all of whom favored Republicans, held about 25 percent of potential ballots. On their own, of course, they had little real chance of gaining political power. In Roanoke, however, black voters joined immigrant workers from northern cities who also tended to vote for the GOP. Both groups generally resided in the Third and Fifth Wards, albeit in deeply segregated neighborhoods. As a result, black and white voters in those wards continually elected Republicans to the city council and gave state and national representatives of the GOP decided victories inside the districts.

As an example, roughly 60 percent of the vote for governor and state delegate in the Third and Fifth Wards went to the Republican candidates in November 1901. In the First, Second, and Fourth Wards, by contrast, Democrats received upward of 70 percent of ballots cast.[2] Since Democrats comprised about 60 percent of all the city's voters, the party usually won citywide elections or contests for state or national offices. The balloting, however, was sometimes much closer than the party would have liked, and on rare occasions, Republicans even won. Moreover, because of a viable GOP opposition, Democrats had to wage extensive campaigns in both primaries and general elections, whereas elsewhere in the South the Democratic primary victor usually ran unopposed in the subsequent election. In 1898, for instance, James P. Woods, the Democratic candidate for mayor, waged an aggressive and expensive campaign but still barely managed to beat his Republican opponent by twenty-seven votes. According to Woods, "it was a nip-and-tuck race," but only because "the negroes were voting and voting the Republican ticket."[3] The situation, the editors of *The Roanoke Times* later complained, created "animosities that would not otherwise exist" and aided "in destroying that feeling of fellowship and co-operation so necessary to the advancement and progress of our city."[4]

A chance to eliminate Roanoke's black Republican vote emerged in early 1900, when the state debated modifying its Reconstruction-era constitution in ways that would disfranchise most African Americans and some poor whites. Democrats in Roanoke, not surprisingly, did all they could to get the new constitution in place. The editors of the *Times,* like most local Democrats, believed that all progress in Roanoke had occurred as the result of Democratic rule. Republican opposition, they agreed, was simply a hindrance to "further advances." Moreover, the paper argued, allowing local blacks to vote had actually retarded business growth because northern investors were weary of establishing industries in a place where their fate would be "in the keeping of an illiterate element that knows not how to discharge the rights of suffrage."[5] In the balloting that spring, 79 percent of local voters endorsed holding a constitutional convention. Residents of the city's Third Ward, who elected two Republican councilmen in the same election, cast 60 percent of their ballots against staging the convention. Citywide, however, around 450 (white) Republicans sided with Democrats and endorsed drafting a new constitution. Statewide, 56 percent of voters favored holding a convention.[6]

In the vote to elect a delegate to the constitutional conference, Roanoke Republicans ran no candidate, and as a result, the Democrats' nominee claimed nearly all the ballots cast.[7] At the convention, delegates drafted a new constitution that restricted suffrage to males who served in the Confederate or United States armies or navies during a time of war, to their sons, to men who had paid at least $1 in property taxes, to men who could read and explain any portion of the new constitution, and to men unable to read who could explain any portion of the constitution read to them. All those who registered, except former Civil War soldiers, had to pay their poll taxes for the three previous years. These registration options, however, existed only in October 1902 and 1903. In 1904, those who tried to register had to meet all the above criteria plus prepay their poll taxes for the next three years and make a written application to vote, without assistance, in the presence of a registrar.[8] Rather than risk a statewide vote on the new constitution, Democrats in control of Virginia's government simply imposed it in 1902, effectively killing the state's Republican Party.[9]

In October 1902, one Roanoke reporter estimated that the new constitution had disfranchised 80 percent of local black voters along with a few hundred poor whites. Overall, he explained, 2,546 whites had successfully registered while only 127 blacks had managed to pass the new qualifications. As a result, the percentage of black voters in the city fell from around 25 percent to roughly 5 percent.[10] White Republicans clung to power in Third Ward, but in the state elections that followed, the Democratic candidate for Congress received 92 percent of ballots cast in Roanoke.[11] Once the 1904 regulations took effect, the city's 111 registered African Americans comprised barely 4 percent of the total electorate.[12] In 1905, GOP leaders believed they had more to gain by making their party all white than by courting the roughly one hundred black votes still available and they began excluding the city's handful of registered blacks from annual conventions.[13] Although residents of the Third Ward continued to elect Republican or Socialist-Labor representatives to the city council, nominees from all-white Democratic primaries easily won city-wide ballots and state elections by the end of the decade. Former mayor James Woods, who had barely defeated his Republican challenger in 1898, welcomed the sea change. The new constitution, according to him, was "a very good thing—it gives us a better electorate."[14]

"Reforming" Roanoke's electorate by disfranchising its black voters, however, was but the opening salvo in a war to marginalize, denigrate, and further segregate the city's African Americans. Starting in the summer of 1900, after Virginia's "Separate Coach" law went into effect, making different train cars for whites and blacks mandatory, residents and their representatives approved municipal and state "Jim Crow" legislation with increasing frequency.[15] From what they had seen of it on Norfolk & Western trains, local reporters observed, the "Separate Coach" law was a "success and has proved to be a good measure." The only problem, they complained, was that white men who wanted to smoke were limited to very cramped accommodations.[16] Some white Roanokers did object to similar legislation for city streetcars, but their state representatives joined other elected officials in passing a statewide "Jim Crow Streetcar Bill" in 1906. The editors of the *Times*, who believed wholeheartedly that "the negro should remain where he belongs," rejected the law as "far fetched," "radical," and "carrying it too far." Once the streetcar rules went into effect, however, the paper revised its opinion and admitted that they were a good thing. Local blacks, it reported, offered no complaints, "accepted the order and are obeying it." Indeed, the only difficulty came from white riders who would not stay in their designated portion of the car.[17]

Elsewhere in town, most of the city's entertainment venues adopted "Jim Crow" segregation polices as well. The Roanoke Academy of Music, which had been built with a special side entrance and balcony for black patrons, continued to host shows for mixed-race audiences. The folly of such separation, however, was frequently evident, especially when black-oriented performers played the Academy to a packed balcony and empty floor seats. In 1903, for instance, humorist Robert A. Kelly—"the original coon"—performed in front of hundreds of African Americans jammed into the upper gallery while nearly all the seats below them stood vacant.[18] Venues less formally equipped moved to entirely exclude African American patrons. Most, like the Electric Parlor, a downtown movie theater, openly advertised themselves as "for white people only." Mountain Park, a commercial recreation area at the foot of Mill Mountain, excluded African Americans as well. The Park on rare occasions did offer "colored days" for black inhabitants, but in a sign of how deeply racist some residents had become, its management guaranteed white patrons that everything would be done "to see that the colored people conduct themselves properly."[19] The Academy of Music eventually turned to similar measures when offering black-oriented fare. When the "Original Dandy Dixie Minstrels" played there in the fall of 1911, for example, the theater explained in its ads that its "entire house" was "reserved for colored people."[20]

Negative newspaper coverage of local blacks, which had been constant in Roanoke since its founding, grew more severe, more elaborate, and more frequent in the early 1900s. By then, most papers were running special columns specifically dedicated to the derision of African American residents. The *Times,* which ran a society column that heaped praise on white residents for their cultural sophistication, limited coverage of blacks to its court section, which it titled variously as "African Day in Police Court," "The Reconstruction," or "At the Misery Mill." In that column, reporters brutally satirized, criticized, and lampooned African Americans and their culture. Those "hauled in," for example, were frequently described as "dusky," "sable," "ebony hued," "pickaniny," "coal black," "very colored," "congomen," "negro troublemakers," or "sambos." Most stood accused of petty crimes such as trespassing, vagrancy, disorderly conduct, or drunkenness, and almost all blacks arrested who were not sent immediately to jail ended up there anyway when they were unable to pay the fines imposed. The vast majority had to work off their time or fines on the chain gang. In a typical daily report, the *Times* described those on trial as "big black men from the coal fields, little brown picininnies from railroad avenue, and colored damsels from any old place." Most on trial in the report had been arrested for being "disorderly," "drunk," "misbehaving," or "trespassing on N&W property." "Well here is Kate," a reporter recounted, "known to the police as a champion profanity user. Tall, brown and slender, she has doubtless put the charm on many colored youths. But occasionally she goes on a spree and there is trouble." In another column, he detailed the fate of Burrell Woods, "a little black, drowsy-orbed pickaniny" who had been arrested for "monkeying with something he hadn't fallen heir to."[21]

Residential segregation, while always in place to some extent in Roanoke, became more formal in the early 1900s. "Reforming" neighborhoods drove blacks out or had authorities crack down on African American saloons or dance halls that were near white residential districts. Such campaigns became commonplace. The city's black population, confined to what had originally been the Town of Gainesborough and to neighborhoods in the northwest, eventually began to move south, closer to the downtown district.[22] White residents in the northwest who had long complained about "disorder" emanating from African American neighborhoods nearby, eventually demanded that Davis Hall, a black community center serving as a dance hall, be condemned because it was a place of debauchery where "crowds of colored people were wont to congregate." When an arsonist burned it to the ground in the summer of 1900, one white neighbor expressed relief and told a reporter that most whites believed the fire was "the work of the Lord."[23] Blacks in the northwest elicited an even more furious response when they began "encroaching" on white neighborhoods. In the spring of 1905, for instance, several hundred white homeowners, "who were all eager to do anything that could possibly be done to rid that section of undesirable tenants," drafted a petition to city officials that declared that African Americans who had moved into nearby homes had lowered property values, increased immorality, and taken residences that should belong to "good white people." The *Times,* noting that whites in the area "quite naturally and inevitably . . . don't want negroes as neighbors," called on the city council to "unite in holding that beautiful section of our city as 'white man's territory.'"[24]

In the southwest, a traditionally all-white neighborhood, residents reacted even more ruthlessly when African Americans settled nearby. In early 1905, for example, after a few dozen black families moved into "shacks" on the edge of the district, whites posted a sign reading "Notice—All Colored people living on this block are notified to Vacate as Soon as Possible." When questioned by reporters, blacks complained that their homes were constantly pelted with rocks.[25] A few days later, one paper observed, most had fled the neighborhood and found "new nests to lay their troubled noggins." Few could afford not to, according to another correspondent, who learned that they had been told "if they didn't get a move on, somebody was going to set the block on fire."[26] The few who refused to leave, the reporter explained, had their homes pelted with "a shower of brick-bats and nigger-head rocks and clods of dirt and other missiles." After whites again threatened to burn down the homes of any blacks in their neighborhood, all but one elderly African American woman packed up their belongings and left.[27]

In Roanoke, reordering race in ways that removed blacks paralleled similar "reforms" throughout Virginia and the rest of the South. It galvanized white residents in a crusade that limited black access to the ballot and segregated black entertainment, public services, and housing. Having lived with the political threat of a combination of white and black Readjusters or Republicans in the 1880s and 1890s, white Democrats jumped at the chance in the early 1900s to eliminate the city's African American vote. To the men who imposed the city's race-based progressive reforms, the segregation and marginalization that followed disfranchisement lessened the potential for conflict between whites and blacks and thus forestalled any chance of a repeat of the city's catastrophic 1893 riot. Local blacks, outnumbered at least two to one by whites, faced an onslaught from the entire white community that left them little choice but to conform or leave town. While lynching was no longer a real

205

threat, angry white mobs, unsympathetic police, racist editors, unfair courts, and uncaring politicians were. The physical and psychic toll of institutionalized racism left local blacks virtually powerless and entirely on the margins of the community, a "reform" that was precisely what the larger white community demanded. Having "purified" the electorate and removed a potentially dissenting voice from the ballot box, the city's businessmen quickly set their sights on other "reforms."[28]

Although race "reforms" pitted all whites against all blacks, Roanoke's white community was deeply fractured over other issues, especially over what to do about hundreds of free-ranging cattle that roamed city streets. Middle- and upper-class residents, almost all of whom favored banning cows completely, had worked steadily to prescribe the behavior of newcomers from the countryside or African American inhabitants, passing ordinance after ordinance to make these citizens conform to living in an urban setting. Having first banned bathing in streams, damaging trees, putting up barbed wire fencing, and dumping "slops" into the streets, they later outlawed owning hogs and then passed an ordinance prohibiting cattle from wandering unattended. After the ordinance passed, police occasionally impounded cows found loose and fined their owners $1 to get the animals back. Most cattle owners, nevertheless, continued to let the animals roam freely. As a result, middle- and upper-class residents carped incessantly to elected officials about ridding the town of what to them seemed an appalling nuisance.

In the fall of 1894, for instance, land agent Malcolm W. Bryan notified city authorities that he had returned from church and found a dead cow on the sidewalk in front of his Queen Anne mansion on Orchard Hill. "It being Sunday and warm, and several buzzards in sight," he explained, "I sent for a team and some men and had the cow removed beyond City limits and buried." Bryan paid for the removal but issued officials a bill for $3.[29] In the spring and summer of 1895, white residents in the southwest notified authorities that "marauding cows" had eaten shrubs and flowers in their front yards, "attacked" a child, littered the neighborhood with manure, and made sleep impossible by the constant clanging of their bells during the night. In the aftermath, the city's police, understaffed and busy enough with human lawbreakers, waged a futile month-long campaign against wandering cows in the district.[30] Other short-lived crusades against unattended cattle also had little effect, since it was legal for cows to be driven up and down city streets as long as their owners or shepherds were in attendance.[31]

By the turn of the twentieth century, hundreds of cows, owned mostly by working-class whites in First, Fourth, and Fifth Wards or by African Americans in the Third Ward, still wandered local streets and yards.[32] By then, one paper was running a daily tally of cattle captured by a special unit of the police force it jokingly referred to as the "Bovine United Order for the Protection of Private Grass and Shrubs."[33] In the fall of 1902, middle- and upper-class whites living in the southwest or even more elite West End demanded that Blair Antrim, their city council representative, get an ordinance passed that would prohibit cows in the Second Ward. Antrim, a thirty-three-year-old University of Virginia–trained lawyer, petitioned for the law, which would also limit cow ownership elsewhere in the city to two per household. Since he suspected, correctly, that those opposed to the ordinance would criticize it as class-based, Antrim argued in a letter to local papers that his request was not "class legislation," but based entirely on the desire of his constituents. "Certain it is," he argued, "that the cow should be excluded from the business section of the city, and certain it is that any district or ward of a town has the right to ask for the vote of council against a nuisance which is being imposed upon them by other sections of the city." In addition, Antrim pointed out that "one of the officials of the N&W railway company has been reported as saying that as long as Roanoke is so provincial as to allow cows to run at large, the present depot is sufficient for all needs."[34]

Local editors wholeheartedly endorsed the anti-cow legislation and claimed that no other city the size of Roanoke permitted "a lot of stray cows to roam around at will, endowed with liberties which, if exercised by a citizen of the town, would result in confinement in the city jail." They additionally claimed that the town's free-ranging cattle were holding up construction of a more modern N&W depot and that ninety-seven local cases of typhoid were the result of persons "engaged in the dairy business in this city with a whole host of cows running through the town, half starved, eating from piles of manure and anything else that can be found, and the milk of the cows sold to our citizens."[35] In another series of letters to local papers, Antrim maintained that the existing ordinance favored only the small fraction of Roanoke property holders who owned cows.[36] The situation, the *Times* observed, was "ridiculous." "With all our boasted pride, our prosperity, our invitation to capital—with the record of being the third city in importance in the state," its editors griped, "it can be said to our mortification that the cow runs at large and is often seen on the principal business thoroughfares of our city."[37]

With the strong endorsement of local papers, Antrim withdrew his original district-specific legislation and proposed a bill that would ban wandering cattle citywide. Anyone opposed to the legislation, one southwest resident argued, should "move on and not get in the way of the wheels of progress."[38] Citizens opposed to the measure, however, quickly organized a counter movement in support of the cow. After Antrim introduced his new bill, close to three hundred pro-cow men staged a rally in support of the city's "working people" and their cattle. A petition from the group, sent to the city council the following day, claimed that banning cows would "make it practically impossible" for working men to supply their families with milk and butter. The *Times,* like other local papers, issued a scathing rebuttal: "We fail to understand this disposition on the part of this class of our citizens, for there is no reason except the most gross inconsideration for the rights of others who own no cow and for the health and good name of our beautiful city, which these people seek to humiliate by putting it on a level with the smelliest country village."[39]

In a demonstration against pro-cow forces, several hundred business leaders held a rally to explain their opposition to wandering cattle. Lucius Johnson, general manager of the N&W, pledged that the city would "never have a new depot by his sanction as long as they allowed the town cows to commit depredations on all public property." Edward Stone, president of Stone Printing & Manufacturing Company, claimed that he had driven cattle as a boy "and would continue until he had driven them out of the city." Doctor B. C. Keister, a local physician, certified that dozens of recent cases of typhoid among residents had come from "drinking impure milk from cows that run at large through the city and drink sewage water along the streets and eat garbage." All the men at the demonstration endorsed a resolution that backed the Antrim bill. "We believe," they explained, "that in a city of nearly thirty thousand people, village customs and village nuisances should be abated, and that the growth of the city should not be retarded by nuisances and filthy streets."[40]

As debate over the cattle issue continued to heat up, residents flooded papers with letters to express their opinions on the bill. One cow owner, for example, complained that on his $50 a month factory salary, a family cow was the only means of providing milk and butter for his eleven children. "It might be a good thing," another reader responded, "to restrict the number of children a man with $50 per month . . . should maintain." Moreover, the writer argued, any man who needed a "scavenger cow's milk" to survive ought to move back to the country. "Don't try to hold the city back because you can't go forward. This is a day of improvement and progress, and the cow must go back to the pastures and keep off the streets of the city."[41] A "number of lady subscribers" agreed, griping in a subsequent letter that "The eleven children recently alluded to in your columns would be better without any milk than with the milk of a cow fed in so unsanitary a manner."[42]

Instead of voting on the bill and possibly incurring the wrath of constituents, in October 1902 members of the city council's ordinance committee put the measure on that November's election ballot.[43] Shortly after that, anti-cow business leaders staged another rally at which they insisted the measure was in no way an attack on "poor people."[44] Pro-cow forces responded promptly with a counter rally at which speaker after speaker blasted the ordinance as a blatant attack on the liberty of Roanoke's working classes.[45] At another demonstration sponsored by the "Fourth Ward Cow Club," Gustavus W. Crumpecker, a Fifth Ward councilman, railed against Antrim and his supporters, suggesting that Roanoke was "not a rich man's town" and certainly "not a town for people who wished to plant flower beds, to sit and watch them grow, with poodle dogs in their laps." The question, he asserted, was whether it was a city "for the poor people or the corporations, such as the Norfolk and Western and others?"[46]

In the days before the vote, business leaders pitched in "a considerable sum" to fund anti-cattle clubs, which offered free carriage rides to the polls, issued campaign literature, and paid for "general election expenses."[47] The "Friends of the Cow" responded with yet another rally at the courthouse. It was widely suspected, their spokesman claimed, "that the anti-cow element would try unfair tactics at the polls to carry the ordinance."[48] On Election Day, editors at the *Times* maintained that the "cow people" had lost support and that passage of the ordinance was certain. Victory, the paper observed, would mean "clean streets, beautiful shrubbery, the removal of unsightly fences, and generally the taking off of our swaddling village garb."[49]

In the balloting that followed, however, those opposed to the anti-cow ordinance won by a single vote. Sixty-six percent of voters in the city's predominately white, middle- and upper-class First and Second Wards cast ballots in favor of the bill; 63 percent of voters in the mostly working-class Third, Fourth, and Fifth Wards cast ballots against it. Disfranchising most of the city's black residents and a few hundred of its poor whites, most of whom would have likely voted against the bill, reduced the size of the pro-cow victory by at least several hundred ballots.[50] In the aftermath, the Magic City's cow debacle received widespread coverage statewide. In Richmond, for instance, one paper reported that the "cow came under the string a winner in a canter and last night lowed victorious notes and chewed her cud with tranquil happiness; secure in the knowledge that for another year at least she will dominate the Roanoke landscape."[51] In Newport News, another paper joked that Roanoke "grew up so fast around the cow lot that it has never had the time to drive out its livestock."[52]

At the city council meeting that followed the vote, Blair Antrim demanded a recount and offered proof that three men living just outside the city limits had cast ballots in opposition to the ordinance, meaning his bill had actually passed by two votes. Fifth Ward councilman Gustavus Crumpecker immediately objected, insisted that "the people were sick and tired of hearing the cow discussed," and convinced all but Antrim and two other council members to vote in favor of tabling the recount motion.[53] Although the cow issue appeared settled, nine months later, in August 1903, Antrim reintroduced the bill and secured a majority of the council's votes in favor of making the ordinance a law on January 1, 1904. The nine members who approved the legislation were primarily from the First and Second Wards; the six who voted against it were mainly from the Fourth and Fifth. The five councilmen absent that night were mainly from the Third, Fourth, and Fifth.[54] The new bill, not surprisingly, outraged cow owners. A cattle owner in the Fourth Ward, like others upset by the overturning of the vote, claimed that the nine councilmen who approved the ordinance "with shameless hands have struck a blow at the rights and liberties of the citizens of this city."[55] Nearly a thousand pro-cow men rallied downtown to protest the measure. Fifth Ward councilman Crumpecker, according to a reporter on the scene, told the crowd that "the expressed opinion of the people of Roanoke had been trampled upon." Those gathered unanimously endorsed a resolution condemning the "action of council in the most positive and emphatic terms, and do proclaim that such action is in violation of faith; that it is undemocratic and strikes at the very tap root of civic principles and would, if persisted in, destroy the foundation of all civil government."[56]

The following day, Roanoke's newly elected mayor, Joel H. Cutchin, vetoed the anti-cow ordinance and proposed holding another municipal election to settle the matter. "I am unwilling," he explained, "to sit in judgment as an arbitrator in this matter."[57] Blair Antrim, foiled once more in getting the ordinance, blasted the notion of putting the measure to another popular vote. The first vote, he reminded Cutchin, had made the city "the butt of ridicule and the subject of satyre by the press all over the country."[58] The day after Cutchin's veto, over a thousand pro-cow residents gathered on Market Square to demand that Antrim and the other eight councilmen who backed him immediately resign. According to a correspondent in the crowd, Reverend D. P. Chockley of the Third Ward drew thunderous applause for stating that "It was in his opinion a poor people's fight, the issue not being a cow issue but the deeper question of equal rights for all."[59]

At the next meeting of the city council, Antrim openly accused Cutchin of vetoing the measure to position himself for a re-election in 1904. "Judas Iscariot when he betrayed the Lord," he lashed out, "had enough self respect to go off and hang himself, whereas the mayor of this city when he vetoed the cow ordinance just went off to Washington." A subsequent attempt by Antrim to override Cutchin's veto lost ten votes to six. Three of the nine councilmen who initially approved the measure were absent, one who voted against it was also absent, and the five who missed the initial vote on the ordinance all lined up behind Cutchin.[60] Although the issue finally appeared to be settled, the city's pro-cow forces organized the "Independent Order of Freemen" as a political association that would "endeavor to elect men to council who favor the cows running at large in the city streets."[61]

The city's voters, as stipulated in Virginia's 1902 constitution, elected an entirely new, bicameral council in the spring of 1904. They also re-elected

Joel Cutchin, who defeated pro-cow councilman Gustavus Crumpecker in the Democratic primary. The old city council remained in control until September. That summer, however, Blair Antrim again introduced an anti-cow ordinance. By then, the N&W had formally announced that if Roanoke banned cows it would immediately construct a modern, $100,000 depot to replace the one built in 1882. As a result, the measure passed twelve votes to eight, and would go into effect January 1, 1905. Two of the bill's former opponents, including one who had just lost his seat in the spring elections, endorsed the ordinance this time. Gustavus Crumpecker, frustrated about losing the mayoral primary, skipped the vote.[62] Although Cutchin strenuously objected to the council's actions again, he conceded that in September the new council would pass the bill, use the same date of effect, and likely override his veto. Rather than leave cow owners in "a continual state of uncertainty as to what will be done," Cutchin let the ordinance stand in order to give cattle owners the maximum time possible to decide the fate of their cows. "I am anxious," he explained to a reporter, "that our people should suffer as little from changed conditions as possible."[63]

Buoyed by the victory, Blair Antrim and his supporters passed "An Ordinance to Create the Office of Inspector of Milk and Food Supplies" the following month. The bill outlawed the sale of milk and foodstuffs without a permit, granted by a newly appointed dairy and food inspector. It also made the sale of milk products from cows fed "swill" or "any other substance of an unwholesome nature," illegal and gave authorities the right to impound and destroy "unwholesome" dairy products, meat, fruit, and vegetables and fine any person attempting to sell such products.[64] Mayor Cutchin, citing the complexity of the ordinance and the "great hardship" it would impose on residents, promptly vetoed the law. "Once more," the editors of the *Times* griped, "the mayor has seen fit to use his official weapon and for the time being he has struck down one of the most wholesome and beneficial measures exacted by council in years."[65] After Antrim gave a lecture on the "fallacy" of Cutchin's statements at the next council meeting, the body promptly overrode the mayor's veto. The milk and food ordinance went into effect sixty days later.[66]

Work on the new N&W depot began soon after the cow ordinance passed. By the time it went into effect in January 1905, the new station, located on the north side of the tracks below the Hotel Roanoke, was already partially completed. Demolition of the original Queen Anne style depot, which was situated precariously between numerous sets of railroad tracks, was under way. The new station, colonial in design with four massive, limestone columns supporting its portico, ended up costing $125,000 to complete by the time it opened in June 1905.[67] On the surface, the fight over cows was a struggle for the aesthetic direction of Roanoke—would the town permit cattle to run at large and look like a "country village," or would it ban them and embrace the appearance of a modern municipality? Since they had put up with the "humiliation" of living with wandering cattle since the city's inception, business leaders and progressive politicians chose the latter. Cow owners, most of whom were far less worried about how Roanoke looked, understood the issue solely in class terms. The city's poor whites, however, were simply no match for the undemocratic forces of modernity and its agents—N&W president Johnson, Edward Stone, and hundreds of white businessmen—and as a result, the cow, which had roamed the city's streets since 1882, was relegated to pastures outside the city.

■■■

Roanoke's Evangelicals were much more interested in enacting prohibition than disfranchising blacks or banning cattle, and as a result, they stood largely on the sidelines during those "reforms." To them, Roanoke's longstanding reputation as a debauched, "wide-open" town, where saloons and brothels outnumbered churches and schools, was the more appalling problem. Like their counterparts elsewhere in the South, local Evangelicals viewed the masculine and uninhibited culture of the saloon district as a dire threat to women, children, home, and family.[68] Ministers, members of the Woman's Christian Temperance Union, and devout Christians were in the vanguard of the city's prohibition crusade, but they had widespread support from the wives and daughters of working-class men. The city's business leaders, most responsible for disenfranchising African Americans and banning cows, were for the most part overwhelmingly opposed to prohibition. Black voters, some of whom helped push local option to a short-lived victory in 1893, had almost entirely lost their right to vote in the wake of Virginia's new constitution, and thus played hardly any role in subsequent prohibition debates.

William Campbell, longtime pastor of the city's First Presbyterian Church and a veteran of previous prohibition battles, led the early twentieth-century fight to protect residents from "the baneful influence of the saloon."[69] In early 1902, after pastors from ten local churches organized an affiliate of the Virginia Anti–Saloon League, they quickly appointed Campbell chairman. The Roanoke Anti–Saloon League (RASL), according to Campbell, was part of a burgeoning statewide effort to enact prohibition throughout Virginia. "The temperance forces hereto operating independently," he argued, "are now crystallizing into one great organization."[70] At the time, however, no Virginia cities had enacted prohibition and only fifteen of the state's one hundred counties had voted themselves "dry" through local option ballots.[71] *The Roanoke Times,* longtime arbiter of "progressive reforms," did not herald the emergence of the RASL, nor did it endorse prohibition. Instead, its editors encouraged "self-control" and "self-possession" as the best means of curbing alcohol abuse.[72]

Membership in the RASL, nevertheless, grew over the following months, and in the spring of 1903, the group scored its first victory by convincing the city council to ban women from local saloons.[73] At a Pentecostal revival the following month, hundreds of residents turned out to hear a sermon on "The Saloon as God Sees It." "We have declared war against the liquor traffic in the city of Roanoke," one pastor promised, "and will fight to the bitter end."[74]

In the fall of 1903, members of the RASL elected local evangelist and public school superintendent Tipton Tinsley Fishburn chairman of the organization. Fishburn, president of Roanoke's National Exchange Bank and uncle of local business booster J. B. Fishburn, called immediately for a local option campaign.[75] By November, the RASL had gathered enough signatures to force a vote on the issue that December. "It is understood that from now on," the *Times* reported, that "a most aggressive campaign will be waged by the drys in the ways of mass meetings in various sections of the city, and from the pulpits."[76] In an address to voters published a few days later, the RASL encouraged them to consider the "the lives and souls of men and the blood and tears of helpless women and children whom the saloon robs of all that enters into life to make it desirable."[77]

Those opposed to local prohibition met for the first time only weeks before the vote. According to a reporter at their rally, the group was composed mainly of business leaders, which demonstrated quite vividly "how thoroughly the business sentiment has been aroused by the proposed measure." Moreover, the reporter observed, the Anti–Local Option supporters came from a wide spectrum of political and civic affiliations, including "cow men and anti-cow men" as well as "citizens who were divided on other questions of more or less importance touching on the city's welfare." Those present elected J. Randolph Bryan, the city's mayor from 1900 to 1902 and its current police justice, president of the Citizens' Anti–Local Option Club, and appointed dozens of prominent businessmen and politicians, including several city council members, to other leadership posts. Former state senator and current chief counsel of the N&W J. Allen Watts, argued in an address to the Club that prohibition would be "inimical to the best interests of Roanoke's growth and prosperity" as well as a disaster for its workers, who would have to "slink into obscure alleyways and live like a hunted being" in order to enjoy a beer after a hard day's toil.[78]

At a RASL meeting that same night, William Campbell led a sparsely attended rally in favor of prohibition. The featured speaker, Theodore Low, an N&W real estate agent, told those gathered to "go to the brothels or the gilded saloon and you will find men, young and old, going to hell." Money wasted by workingmen on whores and whiskey, he fumed, had practically starved their wives and children. Local minister C. M. Hawkins, who spoke after Low, suggested that anyone who cast a ballot in favor of the saloon was endorsing insanity, suicide, prostitution, pauperism, widows, and orphans. Before concluding, several pastors in attendance from dry counties in the region rose and volunteered to do what they could to aid the RASL cause. Although the small turnout disappointed William Campbell, he promised those who had shown up that before the campaign ended, no building in Roanoke would be large enough to host their meetings.[79]

A week before the vote, the Citizens' Anti–Local Option Club published its charter and principles in all local papers. The Club, its secretary and local business booster Edward Boyle Jacobs explained, was "wholly composed of business men and citizens of Roanoke who are not directly or indirectly interested in or connected to the Liquor traffic." The question, the group argued, was not one of morality on one side and immorality on the other, but one of pragmatism and temperance. Prohibition, according to the Club, would turn Roanoke's "unusually temperate, industrious, law-abiding people" into criminals, forced to fulfill their desire to drink in "unlicensed secret dives" that promoted "disorder" and intemperance. The law, the organization further argued, was simply unenforceable and would drain municipal revenue because taxes on alcohol and saloon licenses would disappear. "We believe," members concluded, "the business interests of the city would be injured by a Prohibitory law, and no compensating good accomplished."[80]

RASL president Tipton Fishburn, in a rejoinder to the Citizens' Anti–Local Option Club statement, demanded proof and facts to support its "outrageous" arguments. "We covet," he told a reporter, "this opportunity to turn all the light possible on the question."[81] In a written response that was published in the pro-prohibition (Roanoke) *Evening News,* the RASL disputed every issue raised by the Anti–Local Option Club. "If we should not have local option because the law is now and then violated," the League asked, "then why have any law that is in some places now and then violated?" By this logic, the RASL argued, citizens should rescind the ban on Sunday alcohol sales since residents occasionally violated it. "Any one with a grain of intelligence," it contended, "knows that this law, though broken, prevents saloon men from turning Sunday into our worst day of drunkenness and disorder as many men while idle would spend the day in debauchery." Finally, the League asserted, profits from local bars did little at all to supplement municipal income, especially when weighed against the cost of policing drunkards. Instead, profits added to the ill-gotten gains of saloonkeepers, brewers, and distillers. In an ironic twist of fate (or by hand of a cynical typesetter), an ad for "pure apple brandy at $2 per gallon" accompanied the RASL rebuttal.[82]

Thousands of residents turned out for the final rallies held by the Anti–Local Option Club and the RASL. At the "wets'" last convention, which was held at the prestigious Academy of Music, local judges, business leaders, and politicians exhorted the hundreds of men present to spend Election Day encouraging their fellow citizens to defeat prohibition. The "drys" packed the assembly hall of the municipal building to hear an address by the president of the Virginia Anti–Saloon League, who claimed that "the home, the church, and the school" were "powerful moral forces arrayed against the traffic, and will in the end compass its overthrow."[83] On Election Day, women and children affiliated with the RASL paraded in front of polling places with banners reading: "Vote As God Would Have You"; "Vote In The Interest of Women"; "The Saloon Can Not Be Run Without Boys"; and "The Women Stood By the Men For Four Long Years During The War—Will You Stand By Us For Just One Day?" Their efforts and the campaign by the RASL, however, resulted in the worst defeat of prohibition in the city's history. Only 31 percent of the ballots cast favored a ban on the sale of alcohol.[84]

The power of local businessmen, saloon owners, brewers and distillers, along with the absence of any significant black vote, doomed the prohibition campaign but did not end the fight. The resounding defeat, however, did quiet prohibitionists for the following four years. In the meantime, the RASL brought in regional and national Anti–Saloon League leaders and sought tangential measures to restrain bar business in the city.[85] Elsewhere in the state, the Virginia Anti–Saloon League won a series of local option victories. Indeed, by 1908, "drys" had triumphed in 66 of the state's 100 counties, 141 of its 162 towns, 9 of its 19 cities, and had eliminated 1,016 of Virginia's 1,718 saloons as well as 573 of its 641 distilleries. Roanoke County and four of the six counties that bordered Roanoke City had all enacted prohibition, as had all towns and cities in Southwest Virginia except Bristol.[86]

In the summer of 1908, buoyed by prohibition victories elsewhere, the RASL gathered enough signatures to get another local option vote scheduled for the end of December. That fall, in a sign of just how important Roanoke was becoming in the prohibition battle, Virginia Anti–Saloon League members elected William Campbell vice-president.[87] In Roanoke, the RASL enlisted thousands of women in its crusade with guidance from the state League. Before the vote, 2,489 female residents signed a petition that begged their brothers, sons, husbands, and fathers to cast ballots in favor of prohibition. The petition, published in pamphlet form by the League under the title *We Have No Protectors But You*, let local males know that the women who signed it believed that a ballot cast in favor of saloons was "a vote against our homes and the future of our boys." "Now that the warfare is on against the Saloon," the women complained, "our hearts are stirred, but our hands are tied. We can not vote; we can not protect ourselves." Illustrations accompanying the text and lists of names showed "drinkers" pouring $1,200,000 into their "appetite" for "the liquor traffic" of which "Mrs. Roanoke" received $36,000 in taxes while a scruffy bartender pulled away a barrel containing $1,164,000. Elsewhere in the booklet, text beside a photo of two young lads proclaimed: "Pay Your Taxes With Money And Not With Boys." Like prohibitionists on the national level, the RASL sought to portray local drinkers not as morally backward but as corrupted by their "appetite" for sensual pleasures. It likewise cast saloonkeepers as unrestrained in their "avarice" for profits from whiskey. Local women were portrayed as the morally superior victims of alcohol, who bemoaned the fate of "our boys" as the price paid for debauchery.[88]

Roanoke's saloon owners, sensing the danger that prohibition might pass, responded by brokering a deal with the city's Business Men's League—an unofficial branch of the Chamber of Commerce—that placed new restrictions on local bars. According to the executives involved, "prohibitive laws will prove to be impractical and abortive as well as detrimental to the moral and material interests of our city." Edward L. Stone, a brandy and "moonshine" aficionado and a leader of the Business Men's League, assisted the liquor dealers in composing the agreement. Stone, like the other businessmen in the group, believed that enacting prohibition would spell economic ruin for Roanoke because it would drive local saloons, distilleries and the Virginia Brewing Company out of business and also consume tax dollars to pay for enforcement, which might alienate potential residents. He, too, sensed real potential for a "dry" victory, and complained to a Kentucky distillery that it looked to him like "the 'drought' might extend to this section."[89] The contract that Stone and the other businessmen negotiated with saloon owners, they argued, was proof that bar owners understood that "the Retail liquor business should be conducted upon the highest plane of respectability and strict obedience to law and good morals." As a result, the agreement stipulated that all saloons would pay a $1,000 annual fee, close at 10:00 PM, prohibit treating, ban credit, have no secret entrances, eliminate "dives and objectionable places," weed out "unfit and objectionable" barkeepers, and prohibit gambling. Having brokered the deal, the businessmen pledged to do all in their power to defeat the local option.[90]

In the election, however, the prohibitionists won a stunning 56 percent of the vote, setting Roanoke on a course to become a "dry" city in ninety days. The "wets," who lost 43 percent of their 1903 votes, immediately filed an injunction against the election results. Before a court ruled on the case, Mayor Joel Cutchin, who had made his anti-prohibition views well known before the election, petulantly responded to "drys'" complaints about lax enforcement of all local ordinances by ordering the police to immediately do so. As a result, the force issued hundreds of citations for breaking sidewalk regulations, awning and sign rules, Sunday closing laws, and anti-prostitution codes. "Mayor Cutchin," N&W clerk Frank G. Payne noted in his diary that January, "has put on the lid and closed the shoe shines, cigar stores &c. for Sunday and will drive out the bad women." On the eve of prohibition going into effect, a local judge ruled that the election had not been properly advertised, that there was substantial evidence of voting irregularities, and that as a result, the election was void.[91]

In 1908 and 1909, other counties and towns near Roanoke enacted prohibition, causing dozens of displaced bar owners and distillers to relocate to the city. The Roanoke Anti–Saloon League, furious about an apparent victory overturned, petitioned successfully to schedule yet another local option vote for September 1909. Before the election, local anti-prohibitionists redoubled their efforts to get out the vote. On Election Day, they managed to increase their ballot total by 57 percent from ten months earlier. The "drys," by contrast, picked up only a handful of new votes and went down in defeat once again.[92] After the disappointing loss, the RASL joined the Virginia Anti–Saloon League in focusing solely on enacting statewide prohibition as the ultimate means of "drying up" Roanoke. In 1910, 1911, and 1912, the RASL brought in scores of League spokesmen to address residents, and the ardently prohibitionist (Roanoke) *Evening World* usually carried their speeches on its front page. In the fall of 1911, for example, the paper cited statistics from an address by the president of the League in which he claimed that 85 percent of criminals in Virginia were "saloon made," that 47 percent of the state's paupers were "saloon made," and that 35 percent of the Old Dominion's mentally ill population "were made insane by the saloon."[93]

In 1912, the Virginia House of Delegates passed an "Enabling Bill" to put statewide prohibition to a vote. Back in Roanoke, *The Evening World*, already furious that the city's delegate voted against that bill, argued that its state senator John Hart, who represented the city along with Roanoke and Montgomery Counties, had no choice but to endorse the legislation since both counties were "dry" and close to 1,600 Roanoke City residents had voted in favor of prohibition in 1909.[94] Hart, nevertheless, voted against the bill along with twenty-two of the senate's other thirty-eight members. Defeat of the "Enabling Act," the editor of the *World* argued, had only been possible because Hart and his fellow senators had been elected "directly or indirectly by the liquor dealers" and had followed the "dictates of their masters."[95] The forces behind prohibition lost that battle, but they won the war in early 1914, when Virginians overwhelmingly endorsed a statewide ban on alcohol. As a result, Roanoke, a persistent thorn in the side of the Anti–Saloon League, went "dry" along with the rest of the state on November 2, 1916.[96]

Prohibition, like the cow issue, fractured the white community. This time, however, poor whites, working classes, and businessmen coalesced against local option while ministers, Evangelicals, and lower-class women stood in favor of it. Unlike most "progressive reformers" and New South boosters (who generally supported prohibition), Roanoke's business leaders were more concerned about the ways in which an alcohol ban might impede economic development than they were about instilling social controls on residents.[97] As a result, the same pro-cow men who had previously accused the city's business leaders of engaging in class warfare against them greeted them as allies in the battle to protect the saloon. Indeed, without the support of executives, it is extremely likely that the anti-prohibition movement would have suffered a quick and fatal defeat. And though some working-class women joined the prohibitionists in their fight, they not only lacked the vote, their lack of social prestige severely limited their political impact on the issue.

■■■

Middle- and upper-class women—the wives of the businessmen against prohibition—were largely silent on the issue. They more than likely resented working-class saloons, but their lack of actual exposure to the "problem" and their husbands' stance against prohibition severely circumscribed their attitudes. As a result, to these women the saloon debate seemed far less imperative than "protecting" families and regulating the "home." Like progressive women nationwide, they deemed domestic issues as wholly within the female sphere of influence, and they used a definition of "home" that encompassed a wide array of public and private spaces. They believed mainly that women possessed unique moral powers that made them especially suited for "civic housekeeping." In addition, as respectable "southern ladies," Roanoke's reform-minded women mirrored their regional counterparts by prefacing any task with a firm commitment to the maintenance of a feminine ideal that precluded any strategy other than polite suggestions to public officials. While these women sought to adjust the city in ways that eased problems associated with its chaotic origins, they, like their husbands, were not interested in altering the town's social or racial order or in questioning the economic benefits promised by the New South creed. They believed that cleaning, sanitizing, and beautifying the city, and protecting and educating its children, were as vitally as important to economic modernization as investments from outsiders.[98]

Most local women became involved in the reform campaign because they were concerned about Roanoke's abysmal appearance, lack of adequate infrastructure, and widespread reputation as disease-ridden. Throughout the city's early existence, upper-class residents and newspaper editors had complained loudly about the poor appearance of the town and the various illnesses caused by its improper sanitation. Many of them placed the blame squarely on rural migrants or African Americans who refused to conform to "proper" urban hygienic measures. Roanoke, they believed, had been blessed with natural beauty in the form of elevation, drainage, mountain air, and fresh water springs, but had, through the neglect of some inhabitants, been rendered unattractive and unhealthy. As a result, one paper suggested, the city had lost investors along with new residents: "It 'pays' to keep a city neat and clean and beautiful—not only from the standpoint of general health but because thereby a most seductive and wholesome advertisement is made to the world of its attractions and advantages."[99] The situation embarrassed well-to-do residents, who, while blaming less sophisticated citizens for much of the mess, also condemned city officials for neglecting to remedy infrastructure difficulties. Most of the town's streets were either dirt or poorly macadamized, its 1892 sewer system was inadequate, and many of its wooden sidewalks were rotten or dilapidated. Concerned citizens, according to the *Times,* had even placed a sign in front of a fetid "swamp" on Campbell Avenue in the heart of downtown that warned travelers to "Prepare to meet thy God." The paper demanded something be done to at least "screen it from the view of visitors."[100]

In the summer of 1903, Mayor Joel Cutchin, facing a non-stop tide of complaints, called for the formation of a female-led "Civic Improvement League" to "tidy up" the city. "Nearly every progressive city," he told the council, "has one or more civic improvement societies in which the ladies are interested. The object being to beautify their respective cities."[101] Cutchin had high hopes that such a group would supervise a spectrum of reforms he characterized as important to municipal cleanliness, the creation of parks, and the planting of shade trees. Besides being "an agent of beautifying the city," he claimed that such an organization would also "be an important factor for the increase of healthfulness and decrease of sickness and death among the people."[102]

Cutchin, Roanoke's mayor from 1902 until 1912, was an unlikely municipal reformer. Indeed, except for a brief stint in the Confederate Army, his only professional experience until he was in his mid-thirties had been helping manage his father's farm in rural Nansemond County, Virginia. With a wife and four daughters to support, Cutchin relocated to Norfolk in 1880 and opened a peanut business. By 1885, however, the company faltered, and by 1889, Cutchin had made his way to Roanoke where he worked as a land agent until the town's real estate boom collapsed. Then, nearing fifty, he entered law school in Richmond. After completing his degree in 1894, Cutchin returned to Roanoke and opened a successful commercial law practice. Four years later, he won a seat on the city council, and in 1902, residents elected him mayor for the first of four consecutive terms. Once in office, Cutchin became a student of the national civic improvement movement as well as a tireless advocate for municipal reform. His initial call for female assistance in that campaign, however, went unanswered.[103]

Two years later, after pleading again for women to take charge of the issue by forming a "Municipal Betterment League," Cutchin asked freeholders to approve $400,000 in bonds to improve sewers, streets, and sidewalks. An overwhelming endorsement, he told voters, would "show all the world that Roanoke as a municipality is waking up and putting on city methods." In the subsequent election, all three issues received hearty approval.[104] Early the next year, when a female-led civic improvement club failed to materialize, several dozen businessmen and professionals met and formed the Civic Betterment League of Roanoke. Its goals, the club explained, were to give "patriotic" citizens a means to aid city authorities in "execution of the city's laws and ordinances," "to support the forces of good against the forces of evil," to ensure that municipal funds were spent "wisely," and "to further the growth of wealth." It invited white males over twenty-one who endorsed its platform to enlist. Most of its members, however, were middle-aged businessmen. Although the organization united many of the city's prohibition and anti-prohibition leaders, with men such as Theodore Low, William Campbell, and Edward L. Stone all joining, few, if any, pro-cow men supported the group.[105]

In a series of letters written under the pseudonym "CIVIC," an anonymous spokesman for the Civic Betterment League claimed that Roanoke's mayor and councilmen were too "interested" in political gain or graft to improve the town. He also argued that the League needed an auxiliary of "progressive women" to enlighten the city authorities, all of whom were "cold, practical men without a thought of taste or beauty in their make up." Indeed, "CIVIC" suggested that because Roanoke lacked an excess of men of wealth and leisure "to look after such things," its beautification crusade had to be led by women.[106] At the League's second meeting, several members lambasted elected officials for their failure to carry out infrastructure improvements or to properly enforce ordinances and laws. Mayor Cutchin, listening in the audience, was outraged. If the Civic Betterment League was out to get him, he shouted at those gathered, then it should tender its charges in the courts. He was not an idiot, he yelled, and understood that the "hidden purpose" of the association was to impeach him. Roanoke's residents, he fumed, "would understand the object of the whole movement" and promptly rebuke it. Cutchin's harangue, according to a reporter present, "had about the same effect as a bombshell thrown into the midst of the meeting."[107]

In the aftermath of the mayor's accusations, the Civic Betterment League lost much of its public support and faded away. When it did, however, middle- and upper-class women, especially those who had worked to fund a public hospital or staffed charitable organizations, took up its cause. They did so at first only in response to child welfare issues, staying clearly inside the spectrum of what they and other "progressive women" considered the female sphere of expertise. In the spring of 1906, for instance, dozens of "public spirited women" interested in the welfare of schoolchildren organized an Educational League.

That same month, most of them also insisted that Roanoke officials hire a milk inspector to enforce its 1904 milk and pure food ordinance.[108] Almost all of the women who called for these reforms had attended a lecture a couple weeks earlier on the "Physical, Mental, and Moral Hygiene of the School" given by local physician Leigh Buckner. Roanoke's severely overcrowded public schools, which had a student to teacher ratio of fifty-eight to one, were little more than tuberculosis and typhoid fever incubators, according to Buckner. They lacked proper ventilation, provided water out of a common bucket, endured poor lighting, and had "mud holes" for playgrounds. The results, Buckner argued, were children with "a lowered vitality, a weakened constitution, a system ready to furnish an excellent culture medium for the myriads of noxious germs that swarm in these unsanitary conditions."[109]

Women in the Education League inspected local schools, found a litany of sanitary problems, and circulated a petition to "earnestly demand" that the city council double its $25,000 school improvement appropriation. Before turning in their petition, Mrs. Sarah Johnson Cocke, president of the Educational League and wife of local lawyer Lucian Cocke, advised members to "lay siege to the husbands, brothers and fathers and urge them to use their influence with members of council."[110] At the League's next meeting, members warned elected officials—most of whom were up for re-election in a couple weeks—that any resistance to proper school funding would not be in their best interests.[111] At the next city council meeting, Lucian Cocke presented the League's petition and argued that no infrastructure improvements, no matter how pressing, were more important than providing adequate educational facilities for Roanoke's children.[112] In the weeks that followed, Sarah Cocke and the League's other officers met privately with city councilmembers to lobby for the money, and barely a month later, the council endorsed an additional $7,000 appropriation to address problems at the city's most overcrowded white school.[113]

Many of the women involved in getting school spending increased were also in the vanguard of the city's pure milk and food crusade. At that group's first meeting, Sarah Cocke, also president of that movement, called for a city bacteriologist, an effective board of health, and proper removal of garbage to limit the number of flies in the city. All present endorsed Cocke's recommendations and agreed to circulate petitions as part of an official complaint to the council about "filth" in the local milk supply. "Our province," Cocke explained afterwards, "is not in municipal authority, but when you come to the province of the home, the health of our husbands and children, we rise up and claim that it is time to talk matters over." Once authorities remedied their concerns, she promised, the women would "disband our mothers' meetings and retire contentedly to our darning and mending again."[114] A local physician turned in the group's sanitary petitions at a subsequent council meeting and told officials that the town's inordinately high death rate from typhoid fever, which was four times the national average, was proof enough that "there is something radically wrong in the sanitary condition of your city."[115]

The women had a staunch ally in Mayor Joel Cutchin, who at the next council meeting loudly endorsed the pure milk and food petitions. A week later he proclaimed "A General Clean-Up Day" with prizes for the neatest residences in town.[116] The following month, at Cutchin's insistence, the city council approved the hiring of a sanitary policeman to inspect milk, foodstuffs, privies, yards, and homes.[117] In the fall, while on a visit to Boston, the mayor wrote a series of letters to local papers advocating the sort of "progressive" sanitary and infrastructure reforms he had seen there. Roanoke, he observed, needed parks for its boys in order to keep them from seeking "forbidden pleasures in paths that lead downward." Moreover, it had to do what it could to join in the "City Beautiful" movement, from paving its dirt streets, to creating public squares, to planting trees, to—in a southern twist on City Beautiful—removing "loafing, swearing, worthless and dangerous negroes."[118]

When he returned from Boston, Cutchin condemned several local springs that his sanitary policemen designated "contaminated." He also ordered that all local dairies pass inspection before they could sell their products in the city. Cutchin's reforms, nevertheless, drew numerous critics who felt he had not gone far enough. One "civic interested" resident, for example, complained in a letter to the *Times* that many of the cows that passed muster were fed a diet of germ-laden "malt slops" from the Virginia Brewing Company. "Our mayor," he fumed, "is as conversant with the above facts as he is with the continued flourishing of negro dives on Railroad avenue between Jefferson and Henry streets, where licentiousness, bestiality and public indecency run riot."[119] The criticism did little to slow Cutchin's crusade. In an address to the Chamber of Commerce, he critiqued local boosters for not taking more interest in civic affairs. "More civic pride must prevail," he argued, along with "more desire to see Roanoke the most beautiful, most cleanly, most healthy, best governed and best paved city in the land."[120]

Local businessmen, most of whom were otherwise too occupied to devote much time to civic improvement, did little to heed the mayor's advice. Their wives, however, were eager to become more involved. In the fall of 1906, Sarah Cocke and the women behind the school funding and pure milk movements met to discuss forming an umbrella organization to address all "matters pertaining to the good of the children of the city, the condition of the city as to health, and the precautions that are taken to secure immunity from disease."[121] At the group's first official meeting, those present endorsed calling their organization the Woman's Civic Betterment Club of Roanoke (WCBC).[122] The goals of the Club, its members explained, were "to gain the co-operation of all loyal and progressive citizens in making the Magic City a city beautiful, to promote health and cleanliness, to advance present conditions, and to point to higher ideals." The seventy-five initial members elected Sarah Cocke president, and in her subsequent acceptance speech, she advised them to advocate for reforms by being "suggestive rather than active" and to use "the wisdom of womanly women."[123] Membership in the Club was open only to women nominated by the original cadre of members, and then only to women approved by the executive committee, and finally, only to those who received a favorable vote from members. Non-attendance and failure to pay yearly dues were grounds for dismissal.[124]

Although papers claimed that women in WCBC came "from every ward and section of the city," in reality almost all of them resided mostly in two all white, middle- and upper-class neighborhoods. The group's 1910 roster lists southwest or downtown addresses for 140 of its 152 members. Of the remaining twelve, six lived in the southeast, four in the mostly black northwest, and three in the predominately working-class Northeast. All but twelve of the members were married; of those who were not, four were the daughters of members. The vast majority were Roanoke natives or had at least lived in the city for several years after arriving with their husbands from cities such as Philadelphia, Baltimore, Chicago or New York. Several members had husbands in the Chamber of Commerce, a few were married to city councilmen, five had spouses in the elite Century Club, and dozens belonged to the Roanoke Country Club. Most members also belonged to the same churches along with various other local women's clubs such as the Daughters of the Confederacy, the Daughters of the American Revolution (DAR), the Ladies Union Benevolent Society, the Circle of Charity of the King's Daughters, or the Women's Christian Temperance Union. Like tens of thousands of elite women throughout the nation who joined female organizations in the 1890s and early 1900s, Roanoke's clubwomen used their voluntary associations to exert political power in ways that were not open to them at the ballot box or otherwise.[125]

Like most members, the officers of WCBC resided in the southwest and were all the wives of prominent business leaders or professionals. President Cocke's husband was general counsel for the N&W, vice-president Willie W. Caldwell was married to a lawyer, vice-president Mrs. B. C. Keister was married to a physician, vice-president Mrs. C. Markley was married to a construction company owner; secretary Mrs. Denny E. Spangler was married to the general superintendent of transportation for the N&W; and secretary Mrs. Fleming R. Hurt was married to the vice-president of Stone Printing & Manufacturing Company. Other members included Mrs. Anne Bryan, the wife of a prominent land agent; Mrs. Lucius E. Johnson, the wife of the president of the N&W; Mrs. Minnie Stone, the wife of Edward L. Stone and daughter of Big

Lick merchant James Fishburn; and Mrs. Martha Goodwin, the daughter of Peyton Terry, who had been the city's most successful native businessman.[126]

Sarah Johnson Cocke, the group's first president, had moved to Roanoke from Atlanta in 1903 shortly after she married N&W lawyer Lucian Cocke, who was the town's first mayor and the son of the founder of Hollins Institute, the first women's college in Virginia. Johnson, who was born on the eve of the Civil War, grew up in Atlanta, the privileged daughter of a successful physician. Her mother was the sister of Howell Cobb—the former governor of Georgia, a presiding officer in the Confederate Congress, and a senior advisor to Jefferson Davis. Varina Davis, former first lady of the Confederacy, was one of her mother's best friends. New South aficionado Henry Grady, another close family friend, was a frequent dinner guest as well as an inspirational figure to the youthful Miss Johnson. After attending Waverly Seminary in Washington, D.C., Johnson married New York City physician Hugh Hagan. The couple moved back to Atlanta while she was still in her early twenties. In addition to raising the couple's two boys, the young Mrs. Hagan became a charter member of the Daughters of the American Revolution, a Colonial Dame, a Daughter of the Empire, chairman of the Ways and Means Committee of the Woman's Board for the 1895 Cotton States and International Exposition in Atlanta, and the first treasurer of the Atlanta Woman's Club. After her husband unexpectedly died, Hagan turned to writing and eventually published numerous "local-color" stories in *Century Magazine* and the *Saturday Evening Post*. Reviewers compared her early "Mammy Phyliss" yarns to those of Joel Chandler Harris and Thomas Nelson Page, and the work attracted enough notice to merit several extensive speaking tours.[127]

After marrying Lucian Cocke in the fall of 1903, Sarah Johnson Cocke moved into her husband's Queen Anne mansion, "Cockspur," in southwest Roanoke, where her two sons joined Cocke's two daughters and two sons from a previous marriage. Her initial impression of the city, she later recalled, was of being "surprised to find such a progressive city, and one so cosmopolitan tucked away in the Valley of Virginia." "Roanoke," she observed, "was like the younger sister of Atlanta, or an infant of New York posterity, save that neither Atlanta or New York could boast its setting in the Shenandoah Valley." Its numerous infrastructure problems, however, were also readily apparent. "The city," she recalled, "had grown so rapidly that its busy citizens had, to a great extent, overlooked the inadequacies of village conditions to cope with the requirements of city necessities." Not long after settling in, she joined the local DAR and organized a Roanoke branch of the Colonial Dames, which she chaired. She and her husband, a Democratic Party activist, entertained numerous political luminaries at Cockspur, including U.S. Senator John Daniels, former U.S. House of Delegates representative Henry St. George Tucker, former

Virginia Governor James H. Tyler, and perpetual presidential candidate William
Jennings Bryan, whose daughter Grace was a student at Hollins Institute.[128]

Willie Walker Caldwell, the WCBC's first vice-president and eventual
long-term president, was, like Sarah Cocke, a recent émigré to Roanoke. She,
however, arrived from the rural countryside. She had lived in the town of
Wytheville with her husband, lawyer Manley Morrison Caldwell, until early
1906. Manley Caldwell, who like Lucian Cocke had graduated from the University of Virginia's law school, had been a partner in his father-in-law's firm
in Wytheville before deciding to try his practice in the Magic City. Willie
Caldwell, born Willie Walker only months before the Civil War began, was
the daughter of Confederate General James A. Walker, last commander of the
"Stonewall Brigade" in the Army of Northern Virginia who became a Republican politician after the war. She graduated from Mary Baldwin Seminary
before marrying Manley Caldwell in 1887 and the couple had three children.
Only a month after settling in on King George Avenue in southwest Roanoke,
Willie Caldwell joined dozens of other concerned mothers to discuss the city's
inadequate school facilities, explaining later to a reporter that part of the reason her family had relocated "was that her children might have more advanced
school opportunities than the town of Wytheville could afford but that if conditions were as bad as they were painted she was going back to the mountains
where her children could at least have air and health." While Manley Caldwell
got involved with the local Republican Party, his wife joined the Roanoke
chapter of the DAR and became fast friends with Sarah Cocke.[129]

Once the WCBC published its aims, local politicians, editors, and physicians lined up behind the group and advised all Roanokers to do likewise.
Mayor Joel Cutchin, who had for years been advocating for the formation of
such an organization, heralded the Club and quickly became one of its most
dedicated and powerful supporters.[130] The goals of the Club, the *Times* proclaimed in a lengthy editorial endorsing it, "belong exclusively to the sphere of
femininity" and were "the fundamental principles upon which the true home
is constructed."[131] Local physician Lewis G. Pedigo, in a series of letters to the
paper on "Roanoke's Sanitary Condition," congratulated the women on their
initiative and reminded readers that the city, home to 35,000 residents, had
no public library, no public parks, backed-up sewers, and a largely ceremonial
board of health. "Altogether," Pedigo pointed out, "it must be confessed that we
are still an overgrown country village, not a well developed city."[132] In another
move to show its support, the editors of the *Times* gave the WCBC a column in
early 1907 to publicize its goals, announce its achievements, print letters from
residents, and offer civic improvement news from around the nation.[133]

Although the Club had dozens of goals and departments devoted to sanitation, pure milk, pure food, education, art, and music, its library committee

was initially the most active. In late January 1907, it held a fundraising gala at the town's skating rink, which committee members decorated with American flags and Japanese lanterns. The women, according to one reporter, "served a very inviting and delicious menu of substantials in the daintiest manner" and raised "a nice sum."[134] In another move, the WCBC inspected the Randolph Market, a newly constructed thirty-two-stall market facility about two blocks east of the dilapidated Market House and polluted Market Square. Club members were so "favorably impressed" with what they saw that they endorsed the facility as a "grand institution for the improvement of market conditions."[135] In addition, the Club's pure food committee distributed circulars to farmers on Market Square that outlined "simple practices for cleanliness," including instructions on how to keep their wagons and stalls "clean and tidy," suggestions to cover their butter, sausages, and scrapple in oil paper, and to use attendants who were "clean and tidy." Other suggestions included keeping dogs away and not "expectorating about the city market in compliance with the city laws prohibiting this vile practice in public places."[136]

The timing of the WCBC's market campaign, not coincidentally, paralleled a fierce debate over municipal funding for either improving the aging Market House or purchasing the Randolph Street Market.[137] While the city council debated the issue, the owners of Randolph Market placed ads that claimed their facility had "the endorsement of our established sanitary rules by the Women's [sic] Civic Betterment Club." The WCBC, despite being an "earnest advocate of a market with cleanly and sanitary surroundings, whether provided by municipal or private enterprise," promptly disavowed the endorsement since the market matter was a "public policy" issue for city officials to decide.[138] After months of political wrangling and public outcry against abandoning Market Square, the council passed an appropriation to refurbish and expand the old Market House. Nearby property owners, however, filed an injunction against expansion. The legal battle that ensued lasted another dozen years. In the meantime, the aging Market House continued to deteriorate and Market Square, much to the dismay of the WCBC, continued to serve as the symbolic heart of the city—a place where farmers and city folk both white and black mingled amidst covered wagons, pull carts, and shanties filled with butchered hogs and cows or freshly picked fruit and vegetables, where horse manure, spoiled produce and rotting meat littered the landscape, and where patent medicine vendors and traveling salesmen plied their wares. Indeed, residents' devotion to the public market doomed the far more modern Randolph Street facility, which saw business decline so severely that it closed only a few years later.[139]

In keeping with its mantra of offering suggestions to city officials only after it had thoroughly investigated a problem, the Club organized dozens of lectures by sanitary and planning experts. At each of the presentations, business leaders and elected officials introduced the speakers and sat on the stage with the men while WCBC members sat in the audience unacknowledged, entirely in keeping with their goal of working quietly behind the scenes. In early 1907, for instance, the Club arranged a talk by J. Horace McFarland, president of the American Civic Improvement Association. Mayor Cutchin, who was up for re-election in the fall, welcomed McFarland to the stage and apologized for the fact that Roanoke had not "grown in beauty with her industrial growth." Lucius Johnson, N&W president, introduced the speaker and tried to comfort the audience, explaining that there was "no reason Roanokers should be ashamed of their city in consideration of the fact that Roanoke has sprung up in a night." McFarland, who toured the city that day, suggested the ways in which Roanoke could be transformed into a beautiful city, despite abundant existing problems. After the lecture and during a more candid interview, McFarland singled out black-owned shanties near the rail depot as particularly offensive and told reporters that "he would like to see this unsightly lot of houses burn down." "He further stated," according to one correspondent, "that Roanoke is dirty. Her streets are filthy and she is in sore need of parks."[140] The following moth, the Club funded a visit by a Richmond bacteriologist who critiqued the town's predilection for typhoid, tuberculosis, and polluted milk as well as its impotent board of health.[141]

Public opinion about the WCBC, measured by the tone of letters sent to its newspaper column, varied from admiration to outright disdain. Some writers, as a way of "poking fun or even possibly jeering at the pretensions of this most humble band of women," provided long lists of civic nuisances for them to tackle. Others, having reportedly "heard so much for and in opposition" of the Club, wrote to question its motives and goals. Advice streamed in as well, including a warning not to "get radical or extreme." Others suggested that the WCBC get involved in issues clearly outside the realm of the Victorian-era sphere of female responsibility, asking it, for instance, to do something about "negro loafers" and "bad boys." Such requests, the WCBC responded, were "entirely foreign to the club's aims and desires," which it claimed were non-partisan, discrete, and limited entirely to the suggestive realm. To bolster their claims, the Club devoted most of its resources that spring to bringing in expert lecturers, supporting its "Woman's Exchange" by donating cakes and cookies to sell, facilitating the formation of a "Mothers and Teachers" organization, staging a citywide cleaning day, and publishing numerous columns on pure milk, proper playgrounds, and civic beautification.[142]

In the spring of 1907, after running the WCBC's column for several months, the *Times* ran a large front-page story titled "What Will Make Greater Roanoke?" It solicited dozens of the city's most influential businessmen for opinions, including bank president J. B. Fishburn, former mayor Henry Trout, Virginia Brewing Company president Louis Scholz, and E. B. Jacobs, secretary of the Chamber of Commerce. Although their recommendations varied to some degree, nearly all the men who were interviewed suggested that attracting additional manufacturing concerns would be the best panacea for the city's troubles. None dwelled on cityscape aesthetics, sanitary problems, adequate schools, or the absence of a public library or public parks, which were the chief concerns of the WCBC.[143]

Nonetheless, a couple weeks later, the WCBC asked five of the men interviewed to serve on its male advisory board. Edward L. Stone, whose wife Minnie was a Club member, received an invitation from vice-president Willie Caldwell, who asked him to join what she described as "a committee of businessmen to consult and assist us in our work." Although Stone initially declined, citing his "love for Roanoke" as what drove him to get involved in so many civic associations that many were under the "impression that I really did not have much else to do," acquiesced after some additional prodding and joined the board. The four others invited—the Virginia Brewing Company's Louis Scholz; Lucius Johnson; J. Taylor Gleaves, vice-president of the Adams, Payne and Gleaves brick factory; Robert H. Angell, owner of the Central Manufacturing Company and former Republican state delegate—also agreed to serve. Gleaves, whose wife was a WCBC member, headed the board but he apparently never learned the official name of the Club, since he referred to it in correspondence over the following year as the "Woman's Civic Betterment League."[144]

The men on the advisory board met about once a month to discuss the Club's projects and tender their advice. They also served as the male emissaries of the organization, handling contracts, soliciting donations, and working out the details of services provided by experts. According to Edward Stone, however, he and his fellow board members knew very little about civic betterment and even less about playgrounds, schools, parks, and sanitation. As a result, his first advice to the WCBC was to "have some experts in one of two lines tell us really what we do need and how we should go about securing it."[145] Nevertheless, much like other female reform groups in the South, the WCBC benefited enormously from the backing of these local business leaders. With male guidance, the women not only mitigated the risks of public condemnation but in many ways recreated the "home" by installing symbolic "fathers" as the protectors and benefactors of their organization.[146] Sarah Cocke, reminiscing years later in an address to the Virginia Federation of Women's Clubs, clearly understood the importance of the advisory board and pointed to the "strength of the business men . . . behind us" as a key element in the WCBC's achievements.[147]

In keeping with Stone's advice, the WCBC funded a lecture in the spring of 1907 by John Nolen, an urban planner from Cambridge, Massachusetts who had recently designed a public park in Charlotte, North Carolina. He had also redesigned the nearby campus of Hollins Institute.[148] Although invited by the woman's Club, Nolen met primarily with its male advisory board to discuss the bold changes he envisioned for Roanoke.[149] Not long after his lecture, the board funded preliminary studies by Nolen and two sanitary engineers to get some idea of the overall improvements needed.[150] After their initial reports arrived, the WCBC requested a civic improvement appropriation from the council to fund completion of the two studies along with some of its other work. When the council voted against the measure, according to Sarah Cocke, the Club decided "it was no more expensive to build a beautiful city than it was to permit an ugly one" and voted to stage a "Great Southwestern Virginia Fall Festival" to raise the money.[151] The women chose "All for Roanoke" as the event's theme. They scheduled it for November, and promised "every cent made will be spent for Roanoke's betterment."[152] After appealing for "patriotic contributions" to supply the festival's booths, the Club hired a local business-man as festival manager and appointed fifty other executives to co-staff the various planning committees.[153] The project, according to the *Times*, was a "great opportunity" for Roanoke, and along with other local papers, it did all it could to publicize the upcoming festival on its front pages.[154]

After donations for the festival failed to appear in the quantities expected, the WCBC created a "Business Men's Opportunity Committee" to solicit support. "The ladies," one paper explained, "do not want to appear that they are begging expeditions, but want it to be known that they are engaged in a work in which every man, woman and child is interested—and that every dollar's worth of goods contributed will bring returns many times in excess of the actual value of the articles given." Those who aided the group, the Club assured readers, would garner "extensive publicity" for their generosity with ample acknowledgement in *Festival Facts and Fancies,* the event's in-house newspaper.[155] On orders from N&W president Lucius Johnson, the railroad provided free transportation for all goods donated by firms outside the city.[156] In the weeks leading up to the festival, the Club denied rumors that it was paying local newspapers for publicity and rebutted accusations from the Meth-odist Ministers Conference that it planned to include "dancing, vaudeville, or other theatrical performances" at the event.[157] In a last-minute effort to include the city's working classes, several of the businessmen involved convinced the Central Trades and Labor Council to encourage union members to attend.[158]

On opening night, over a thousand patrons paid twenty-five cents to get into the downtown skating rink where the WCBC held the festival. Dur-ing the opening concert, however, adversity struck. Just as the WCBC choir began singing the opening verses of "Onward Christian Soldiers," a fuse blew, the lights went out, and the thousands of visitors nearly panicked before electricity was restored. Receipts from opening night totaled over $500. In an editorial congratulating the Club for getting its festival under way, the *Times* claimed that "what they have done and will accomplish under all the discouragements and vicissitudes, the 'knocks' from sources from which they had a reasonable right to expect assistance and encouragement, is by far greater than any similar accomplishment from a like body of the sterner sex."[159]

The festival's "Floral Parade," led by newly re-elected mayor Cutchin, rolled through the streets a few days later. The fair itself attracted scores of patrons over its two-week run. The entrance fee, however, priced it out of reach for most working-class residents, and although the WCBC published no segregation policy, the women and men staffing the event almost assuredly restricted patronage to whites only. Those who did pay to get in could patronize dozens of elaborately decorated booths that offered postcards, foodstuffs, souvenirs, and exotica for sale. Hundreds of visitors stood in line each night to get inside the "Dixie" stall, which featured WCBC members dressed in hoopskirts baking biscuits in a "thoroughly equipped electric kitchen" that was decorated with dozens of Confederate flags. Other booths featured "pure food" demonstrations, advice from the Women's Christian Temperance Union, or displays of historical memorabilia from Asia and Europe.[160] The

Woman's Civic Betterment Club floral parade for November 1907 Fall Festival. Sarah Johnson Cocke in carriage, back left. Willie Walker Caldwell in carriage, back right. History Museum and Historical Society of Western Virginia, Roanoke.

Club also raised funds from sales of its *Roanoke Cook Book,* a collection of WCBC recipes compiled by Edward Stone's sister-in-law and printed by his firm. "Purchasers," the Club promised readers, "may congratulate themselves on acquiring so much kitchen lore in clear and condensed form."[161]

In its daily editions of *Festival Facts and Fancies,* the WCBC published dozens of articles on civic improvement written by members, elected officials, ministers, and business leaders. The paper's masthead featured a giant toddler dubbed "Roanoke" positioned alongside the Blue Ridge Mountains with the caption: "A lusty infant, lying amid inexhaustible resources. What should be done for it?" In each edition, a different local luminary answered. Mayor Cutchin advised residents to elect councilmen who could "see beyond their own particular property holdings, with a due regard for the health, cleanliness, and improvement of the city."[162] Others offered a broad range of suggestions: Doctor L. G. Pedigo recommended intensifying the campaign against "dirty milk" to defeat the "supine indifference" of most residents; members of the Women's Christian Temperance Union advocated prohibition as the best means of ending access to "brain poison" and Edward Stone called for the systematic re-planning of the entire city in addition to a move to a commission form of municipal government. The Virginia Brewing Company's Louis Scholz favored forming a federation between the WCBC, Chamber of Commerce, and Central Trades and Labor Council to press for municipal improvements while Reverend William Campbell cautioned against neglecting the moral climate of the city in favor of beautification, warning that such a course would lead to "impending evil" and a "fateful harvest."[163]

The festival, according to Sarah Cocke, netted about $5,000, almost half of which went immediately toward paying for a comprehensive city plan by John Nolen and a sanitary study by two Baltimore-based hygienic engineers.[164] The Club enlisted its male advisory board to supervise the funding and compilation of both studies. Later it had Edward Stone's printing shop publish Nolen's *Remodeling Roanoke* and the health engineers' *Sanitary Roanoke.* Each elaborately illustrated and lavishly printed book carried a notice denoting that they had been "Presented to the City of Roanoke by The Woman's Civic Better Club."[165] Nolen's plan came with a price tag of at least a million dollars. It called for turning downtown's principal avenues into tree-divided boulevards, developing a more rational arrangement of streets and street names, and creating a system of radial greenways and parks that extended from downtown to the Roanoke River and Mill Mountain. The most radical facet of the plan, however, was its call for a complete transformation of Market Square. Once rid of all its current structures and lined with trees, the former Square could become the location for an array of municipal buildings. The plan, which was one of only six comprehensive city designs completed in the United States

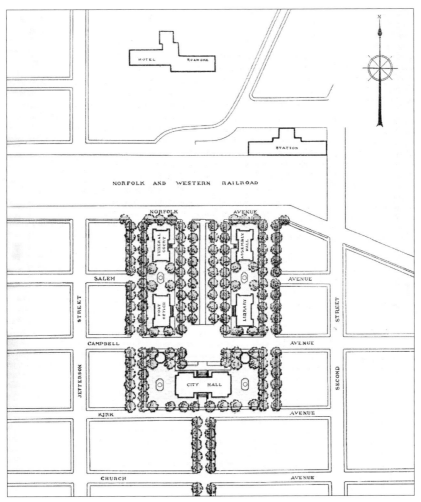

John Nolen's plan for reconfiguring Roanoke's municipal buildings at Market Square. From John Nolen, *Remodeling Roanoke: Report to the Committee on Civic Improvement* (Roanoke: Stone Printing & Mfg. Co., 1907).

up until then, meshed civic beautification with functionality in ways that Nolen believed would correct Roanoke's jumbled and makeshift boomtown origins.[166] *Sanitary Roanoke* offered chapters on overall sanitation problems, street cleaning, garbage collection, sewerage difficulties, paving needs, fire protection requirements, and the development of a more powerful board of health staffed by "Health Wardens."[167]

By publishing the reports and donating them to the city, the WCBC strongly reinforced and coupled its own wants to those of supposedly disinterested national experts. It also mirrored clubwomen throughout the South, who in the early twentieth century funded urban planning efforts in nearly every major southern city.[168] Nolen's study completely adhered to the City Beautiful movement, an idiom premised on a belief that urban splendor and systematic planning would serve as an effective social control apparatus by inducing public order, civic loyalty, tranquility, and decorum. To achieve these goals, the movement emphasized aesthetic improvements to cityscapes through the creation of public squares, proper arrangement of municipal buildings, and an integration of natural environment in the form of tree-lined boulevards, parks, and greenways.[169]

According to Nolen, who quickly became one of America's most renowned urban planners, Roanoke had been blessed with abundant "natural advantages" but had developed so rapidly and in such chaotic fashion that it had simply gone from a village of 500 to a village of 35,000, or in his words, "from Big Lick to Bigger Lick." As a result, he noted, the Roanoke of 1907 was "plain, commonplace and in some localities, distinctly unsightly." It had "no public gardens, parks, parkways, no playgrounds, no attractive school yards, no monuments, no public library, no open plazas or public squares, no wide avenues with well grown trees, no segregated fine residence sections, free from objectionable features, and no public buildings of distinction." Although Nolen admitted that remedying these myriad civic embarrassments would be costly, he argued that the city's small size and lack of distinctive buildings made his plan more economically feasible sooner rather than in the future, since structures standing in the way were not worth preserving and would "never be so cheap as today."[170]

Nolen returned to Roanoke after the WCBC published his study, and in an address to its leaders and male advisory board, he suggested that they implement a "thorough and systematic campaign of education" in order to arouse widespread public support for his plan. The changes called for in *Remodeling Roanoke*, he vowed, would transform the town into the "most attractive city in the state if not the entire country."[171] Nolen's plan, which was later widely recognized as one of the first comprehensive efforts to mesh City Beautiful with city planning, received accolades from the American Civic Association and from architects and engineers from London to San Francisco.[172] Not long after publishing Nolen's plan, the WCBC's male advisory board presented it to Mayor Cutchin and the city council. Cutchin, a longtime advocate of City Beautiful improvements, pushed immediately for $800,000 in bonds to begin implementing parts of the plan. "Never in the history of Roanoke," he told the city's councilors, "has the future held out to her the same bright prospects of stability and importance as today. Everything urges and beckons us on to greater achievements municipally. No excuses can be given for timidity or lagging."[173]

The city's bicameral council, however, debated the issue for another year before finally agreeing to put $530,000 worth of bonds—earmarked specifically for school, street, and sewer improvements—up for a vote by property owners. Nolen's plan, which called for a total reordering of the cityscape, was not included on the ballot. Although the WCBC was disappointed, its members held tightly to a platform that precluded "political" involvement. Indeed, as the council debated the plan, Sarah Cocke, in a speech to the Civic Betterment Club of Virginia, told hundreds of progressive-minded women from around the state that they should "have no hand in politics." "Hue strictly to the Civic lines of health, beauty and education," she advised, and "stand on the high ground of home, where motherhood, wifehood, womanhood, shines brightest."[174] After voters approved the bonds, Joel Cutchin called again on the city council to put an even larger bond issue up for a vote in order to carry out Nolen's plan. "I believe," he informed them, "the time is now ripe for a consideration of these plans, which have been generously donated to the city by that noble band of women."[175] Over the next few years, however, the council failed to act. As a result, according to Sarah Cocke, Nolen's study was "graciously received and safely deposited in the city's archives."[176]

The WCBC, while discouraged by the failure of elected officials to endorse *Remodeling Roanoke*, kept up its "quiet" campaign for parks and libraries. In the immediate aftermath, however, it redirected its work toward ameliorating conditions for impoverished residents during the 1908 national depression by collecting donations for orphans, hiring unemployed artisans to construct a "model schoolyard" based on John Nolen's plans, and holding citywide yard beautification contests. After that, the WCBC all but disappeared from public view. According to Sarah Cocke, the lull stemmed mainly from demands by members' husbands that they "rest."[177] The Club remained active, albeit in a more benign way. It continued to meet regularly and to encourage municipal authorities to invest in civic improvements. By the spring of 1910, its work behind the scenes contributed to the city's reorganization of its board of health, the hiring of a Health Officer, and the funding of a sanitary laboratory.[178] The Club also influenced the city council to pass a pure milk, meat and food ordinance in early 1911 that required local vendors to undergo inspection by the Health Department.[179] In addition, municipal authorities fulfilled a longstanding WCBC aim when they purchased Peyton Terry's seven-acre Elmwood estate and turned it into the city's first public park. In a clear move to acknowledge the Club's work, the city let the WCBC use several rooms in Elmwood mansion as its headquarters after the park was created.

By the time the Club moved into Elmwood in the spring of 1911, Joel Cutchin, one of its most ardent and longtime champions, had been indicted by a grand jury for gross neglect of duty for failing to close down the city's segregated red light district.[180] WCBC members were mortified, not only because of their close association with the mayor, but also because they had invited him to deliver the keynote address to the Virginia Federation of Woman's Clubs convention they were hosting that May. Not long after Cutchin's indictment, the Club informed him that "in view of existing circumstances" it had unanimously voted to "release" him from his promised address. The mayor, no doubt stung by offer, promptly canceled the city's pre-convention "clean-up day" and informed the WCBC that he was "convinced that one may work and work, make themselves unpopular in certain directions to their own detriment in trying to do something for the future, and with the first blast of ill wind comes obliteration of the work of years." With the city a mess and progressive women from around the state scheduled to arrive, the WCBC turned to its allies in the Chamber of Commerce who pressured the city council to order a citywide cleaning. At the subsequent Virginia Federation of Woman's Clubs convention, Judge John W. Woods, one of Cutchin's Democratic rivals, delivered the keynote address, and Willie Caldwell, who by then had become president of the WCBC, was elected first vice-president of the state association.[181]

When Cutchin went on trial a few weeks later, WCBC members and most of the mayor's former allies did all they could to distance themselves from him. Like almost every resident of Roanoke, however, they were aware that upon assuming office in 1902 Cutchin had adopted the policy of his predecessors in continuing a longstanding practice of allowing brothels to exist in a segregated district in the northwest part of town. Indeed, since the early 1890s, it had been the unofficial policy of municipal executives to confine houses of prostitution to a four-block section of High Street and to a single block of Railroad Avenue across the railroad tracks. In creating this sanctioned and supervised red light district as an answer to an unregulated and sprawling brothel trade, Roanoke's mayors were following the exact response of city authorities throughout the nation, who like them, arrested streetwalkers and shut down bordellos outside the district as the best means of shielding citizens from vice and maintaining order where it was allowed to exist.[182] In 1905, when questioned by local ministers about the legality of such a policy, Cutchin had informed them that his police force had the district under constant supervision, even going so far as to take a quarterly census of each house operating there. The answer, however, did nothing to mollify Roanoke's clergy, who, led by Reverend Campbell, promptly organized a "Ministers' Conference" to campaign against the policy.[183] After Cutchin defended the practice at a meeting of the League of Virginia Municipalities in Richmond, members of the "Ministers' Conference" had their congregations sign petitions demanding that he enforce state laws and close the district.[184] Although Cutchin resisted the campaign and was subsequently re-elected, he did so at the cost of completely alienating William Campbell and the local forces of morality. Cutchin's overall civic reform efforts, however, earned him nothing but accolades from mayors throughout the Old Dominion, and in 1906, they elected him president of the League of Virginia Municipalities.[185]

By the time a grand jury indicted Cutchin, progressive reformers across the nation and especially in the South had joined Evangelicals in the anti-vice crusade. Alarmed by hysterical reports of girls being sold into "white slavery" as prostitutes, by the threat of rampant venereal disease, and by the apparent need for passage of the Mann Act, which made it a Federal offense to transport women across state lines for "immoral purposes," progressives began pushing for red light abatement laws in hundreds of cities.[186] In Roanoke, after business leaders and Evangelicals joined forces in a campaign against vice, prosecutors called a grand jury to investigate the issue, which resulted in Cutchin's indictment. Made aware of the secret proceedings only days before its judgment, Cutchin did what he could to save himself by calling for the formation of fifty-man advisory board to decide if the brothel district should be shut down.[187] Before that board could assemble, however, the grand jury handed down its ruling. While likely not the result that businessmen had intended, once the indictment became public, they had no choice but to line up against the mayor. To Cutchin, who believed wholeheartedly that segregating and regulating prostitution was a crucial component of civic improvement, the charges must have seemed particularly exasperating.

During Cutchin's trial that spring, a parade of bordello operators and prostitutes testified about *quid pro quo* arrangements with the mayor in which they exchanged sexual favors for municipal protection. In some of the most damning testimony, Vici Isom, a well-known brothel madam, claimed that the mayor bought two houses in the red light district for her to operate. In exchange, prosecutors charged, Isom had given Cutchin a diamond ring and expensive rugs and furniture for his law office. To make matters worse, a former police officer testified about encountering a visibly intoxicated Cutchin dancing with prostitutes at one of Isom's bordellos.[188] These and other accusations astounded most Roanoke residents. According to a local paper, their mayor's two-week trial was "the most sensational and nauseating investigation ever known in Virginia."[189] After the jury returned a unanimous guilty verdict, Cutchin, to the dismay of most residents, proclaimed his innocence, appealed the ruling, and remained in office.[190]

In the immediate aftermath of the verdict, the city council ordered Roanoke police to shut down the town's brothel district. In the weeks that followed, authorities reported that almost all bordello occupants had vacated the area.[191] While Cutchin awaited a ruling from the Virginia Supreme Court, business leaders, ministers, and WCBC members convinced Judge John Woods to seek the Democratic nomination for mayor. At a subsequent rally for Woods, Lucius Johnson introduced the candidate and William Campbell gave the closing prayer. Woods, speaker after speaker promised, represented the "cleanest and strongest Virginia manhood" and would correct the widespread notion that Roanokers were dissolute.[192] Not long after, the Virginia Supreme Court turned down Cutchin's appeal and dismissed him from office. Cutchin, undaunted and determined to clear his name, promptly entered the Democratic primary for mayor.[193] All local papers endorsed Woods, and if things did not appear bleak enough for the former mayor, two weeks before the balloting, he suffered a near fatal stomach hemorrhage that kept him off the campaign trail. Cutchin lost the primary, garnering only about 37 percent of the ballots, but he did carry two working-class wards. In a note carried in papers afterwards, he told his followers that their support "in view of the forces arrayed against me was very gratifying and very complimentary."[194] The former mayor, who had a wife and four daughters, blamed his fall from grace on political opponents and misguided clergy. The entire ordeal, he claimed later, had put him and his family through "the torments of hell."[195]

Although the WCBC had steered clear of "morality" issues, in the midst of Cutchin's unsuccessful appeal, the Club drafted a petition asking the city council to maintain a "higher standard of vaudeville and moving pictures."[196] Like clubwomen elsewhere in the South, WCBC members took up the issue as part of their moral responsibility to protect children. Indeed, in a subsequent request, the group demanded outright censorship because the "existing conditions tend to demoralize and weaken the character of our growing youth." "We ask," they explained, "that not only immoral vaudeville and coarse jokes be censored, but also pictures giving needlessly criminal exhibition."[197] When the council failed to act, the Club enlisted the support of Evangelicals and the Chamber of Commerce, and together they convinced theater owners it was in their best interests to abide by recommendations made by a jointly staffed board of censorship. The board, according to representatives from each group, sought to "guard the public against ultra-objectionable phases of the stage and screen" by removing sections of film it deemed "off color."[198] In another move into the morality sphere, the WCBC publicly endorsed the candidate it deemed most morally fit to serve on the city's revived Board of Police Commissioners.[199]

In 1912, members of the State Federation of Women's Clubs, impressed by the accomplishments of the WCBC, elected Willie Caldwell as their president. In a later article in the progressive journal *The American City*, Caldwell detailed the Roanoke Club's work, which included building new school and adding to old ones; providing drinking fountains; creating better sanitary arrangements and libraries; providing photo collections in all schools; encouraging better care and handling of foodstuffs on the city market; organizing an annual municipal cleaning week and a yearly yard beautification contest; creating a board of health with a physician as its chief officer; purchasing land

for public parks; organizing a park commission; providing a proper and supervised playground; developing a yearly art show; and managing a weekly civic
betterment column in local papers.[200] In the years that followed, the WCBC
helped establish a juvenile court, a restroom in the Market House for "country
women and children," and a Parent Teacher Association. The city's department
of health, which conducted thousands of inspections of food, milk and water,
checked the town's typhoid fever death rate, recording that it dropped from
1.2 per 1,000 in 1905 to 0.3 per 1,000 in 1912. After the United States entered
World War I, Roanoke's Chamber of Commerce convinced the WCBC to
become its "Civics Division," responsible for helping instill patriotism in local
children. The Club maintained that role until 1923, when it withdrew from
the Chamber of Commerce and became the Woman's Club of Roanoke, a
vastly less public organization, devoted primarily to "civic art," domestic education, current events classes, gardening, and philanthropy.[201]

■■■

The civic improvement campaigns that swept through Roanoke in the early
twentieth century were hardly unique. On one level, what took place there was
part of a crusade by businessmen nationwide to ensure political, social, and
economic stability following a period of financial uncertainty and social chaos.
The city's business leaders, like their national counterparts, sought undemocratic and bureaucratic ways of guaranteeing continued economic modernization by imposing order on conditions they believed stood in the way. As a
result, their "reforms" meshed completely with the ideology of the New South
creed, which promised a solution to all municipal problems through economic
development, diversification, and scientific methodology.[202]

On another level, progressivism in Roanoke mirrored the regional variant
of the movement: it was paradoxical, hierarchical, undemocratic, racist, paternalistic, and won only through coercion of those being "reformed."[203] It was
also led in part by Evangelicals, who throughout the South tended to be in the
forefront of reform crusades.[204] It likewise fit the conservative and reaction-
ary response throughout Virginia to the anxiety caused by the Old Dominion's post–Civil War business boom, speculation frenzies, racial turmoil, and
underclass revolts, such as the Roanoke Riot of 1893.[205] Unlike other parts of
the region, where the descendants of antebellum elite often stood in the way
of "reforms," in Roanoke—a city with no concrete antebellum past—hardly
any anti-progressives emerged to challenge increased government spending on
civic improvement. Nor did longtime Roanoke natives oppose reforms championed by newcomers, as was the case elsewhere in the region.[206]

When progressives in Roanoke were at odds over a particular issue, it was
difficult to discern a coherent local reform movement. Overall, however, they

had a remarkably similar goal: reorder the town in ways that would ensure continued economic modernization, promote healthiness, and facilitate social stability. The vision of how best to accomplish that, however, ran in three, sometimes oppositional, currents. Businessmen viewed disenfranchising black and poor white residents as the best means to enact civic improvement legislation like restricting cattle. Evangelicals sought prohibition and red light abatement, while clubwomen pushed for sanitary regulations, improved schools, and civic beautification. Although each group sought distinct means to remedy the problems they perceived, their methodology was almost always hierarchical in orientation and their solutions were generally aimed at residents who either cared little about the issue or opposed the change. The city's reformers defined "reform" but those definitions were fluid. Indeed, as the case of Joel Cutchin illustrates, even a champion of civic improvement could eventually be cast as part of the problem when the meaning of "reform" suddenly changed. In spite of their different methods, Roanoke's progressives were uniformly conservative in their outlook—they did not advocate social justice, were not interested in social uplift, and never doubted the absolute suitability of Roanoke's economic and racial order. Indeed, they were not seeking change as much as they were looking to solidify and burnish the society that already existed.

From Magic City to Star City

The history of early Roanoke forms part of the larger story of southern urbanization from 1880 to 1900—a period when the number of areas qualifying as cities mushroomed from 119 to 320. Most of those nearly 200 other new municipalities had a similar past. Their town fathers also peddled the places with booster propaganda, made backroom deals offering tax exemptions, land, and cash bonuses to northern financiers, and promised a pliant, cheap, white labor force waiting for jobs in new factories, mills, or mines. As a result, the citizens of those communities suffered from under-funded municipal governments, poor city infrastructures, inadequate public services, dismal public schools, and lack of proper sanitation, public parks, and libraries. Hundreds of thousands of rural southerners, looking for a way out of the parochialism and misery of the countryside, started their lives over in the region's new cities. Whether white or black, however, they arrived with enough embedded pastoral customs to make the transition difficult not only for them, but also for municipalities where they settled. In the end, these factors and others contributed to a South with scores of cities that by the early twentieth century resembled overgrown country towns. Dirt streets, free-ranging cows or hogs, polluted markets and yards, dilapidated wooden buildings, open sewers, racial turmoil, and vigilante justice were the norm, not the exception, as were the reform efforts that rose to ameliorate these conditions.

While Roanoke had much in common with these places, it also differed from them in several substantial ways. From 1882 to 1900, the percentage of manufacturing workers in the city's population far surpassed the average for other southern municipalities. The commercial developments that gave rise to Roanoke were not unique—they also gave rise to numerous other magic cities such as Birmingham, Chattanooga, Knoxville, Dallas, Houston, and San Antonio. Roanoke's demographic growth of around 2,000 percent from 1882 to 1890, however, far surpassed every other urban area in the South. Birmingham, which grew by 748 percent, Asheville, North Carolina, which grew by 291 percent, and Chattanooga, Tennessee, which grew by 125 percent, were the only places that came anywhere close to matching its expansion. Over the same period, the South's other cities grew at a pace below the national average of 56 percent.

For New South boosters, the region's handful of magic cities were cause for optimism; a sign that the modernization they promised was on the way. As one historian has wryly noted, to the region's "true believers" these places were an indication that "the millennium was at hand." Other magic cities were supposed to follow and blossom into colossal southern metropolises, but few did. Rather, from 1880 to 1900, the typical urban area in the region was an antebellum port or river city dependent on agricultural processing for economic survival. The results of the quest for a New South, especially when measured in terms of gaining economic equality with the North, were by the early twentieth century a colossal failure. Roanoke, which exemplified what

Winter view of downtown Roanoke and Mill Mountain from N&W General Office Building, c. 1900. Terry Building right center. Market Building left center. Mill Mountain Observatory visible in distance. History Museum and Historical Society of Western Virginia, Roanoke.

southern boosters claimed the region needed most, was the prototypical New South city—an extreme version of everything that was supposed to remedy the South's torpid post–Civil War economy. Whether or not it met this promise is ambiguous. More, it is beside the point. For if Roanoke failed to fulfill the overblown accolades and ridiculous predictions heaped upon it, it's largely because the promise of a New South was an empty one.[1]

Over the course of the twentieth century, as America transitioned into a post-industrial economy, the engines of commerce that powered industrial towns like Roanoke diminished in value. The Norfolk & Western Railway continued operations in the city, but the company's massive Roanoke Machine

Works stopped manufacturing steam-powered locomotives in the late 1950s. The move threw thousands of men out of work, and as other production at the shops and neighboring iron furnaces continued to decline, scores of workers and their families left. What had originally been the N&W's company town in the northeastern section of the city deteriorated, and in the 1960s, the municipality used Federal "urban renewal" funding to raze hundreds of cottages and row houses put up in the 1880s and 1890s by the Roanoke Land & Improvement Company. In the early 1980s, after merging with the Southern Railway, the N&W became the Norfolk Southern Railway and relocated its headquarters to Norfolk. Roanoke, along with Atlanta, became one of two regional offices for the line, which, following subsequent mergers, currently operates on over twenty thousand miles of track with over thirty thousand employees. The railroad's tracks, former office complex and hotel, partially mothballed shops, and new general office building still dominate Roanoke's landscape, but the company ceased being the town's largest employer long ago.

One consequence of these changes has been the steady erosion of Roanoke's population, which grew from roughly 1,000 in 1882 to over 50,000 in 1920, but thereafter expanded mainly through the annexation of surrounding lands, which over the course of the following sixty years finally pushed it above the 100,000 mark around 1980. While Roanoke took only eighteen years to become Virginia's third largest municipality in 1900, over the course of the next hundred years, it fell to ninth, and it will likely tumble further still since the town is steadily declining in population while the rest of urban Virginia is increasing. Much of the city's landscape has changed as well. In addition to the removal of workers' housing in the Northeast, in the 1950s, the city also used urban renewal grants to purchase and demolish nearly all of what had been the black neighborhood of Gainesborough. In the decades that followed, an interstate spur, Civic Center, and dozens of commercial developments went up over of both neighborhoods, effectively obliterating any sign of these once thriving communities. The saloon quarter on Railroad Avenue never completely recovered from prohibition, and after rail passenger service to the city ended in the 1970s, the town reoriented itself away from the railroad tracks. What businesses remained on Railroad Avenue closed, and today the street, which is called Norfolk Avenue, supports no commercial enterprises. The 1882 business district and farmers' market around Market Square, by contrast, experienced an astounding cultural renaissance after falling into disrepair, and is now Roanoke's premier downtown destination.

The path cut up the side of Mill Mountain in 1910 by the Incline Company is still visible, but the mountain itself has changed dramatically. In 1949, on the spot where the Incline's observatory once stood, the Roanoke Chamber of Commerce and Merchants' Association erected an eight-story neon star.

Although originally intended as a seasonal Christmas decoration, the star proved so popular that its owners decided to keep its two thousand feet of neon lit year round. Moving to capitalize on the star's publicity, the Chamber of Commerce eventually dubbed Roanoke the "Star City of the South," a moniker that has replaced the town's "Magic City" nickname. In keeping with its post-industrial economy, Roanoke has also turned to railroad-related tourism to fill in gaps left by the transformation of its most important early industry. Although the town still lacks rail passenger service, it has constructed a self-guided rail history walkway from downtown to its railroad-themed Transportation Museum, which houses dozens of long-retired locomotives. It also built an enclosed observation walkway over the Norfolk Southern's tracks from the Market to the refurbished Hotel Roanoke and opened a gallery for Winston O. Link's railroad photographs in the N&W's 1905 passenger depot. One hundred and twenty five years after becoming a railroad town, Roanoke still is—albeit one that looks to its rail past, not its rail future.

Notes

Abbreviations

HMHSWV	History Museum and Historical Society of Western Virginia, Roanoke
LVA	Archives Department, Library of Virginia, Richmond
N&WRA	Norfolk & Western Railway Archives, Special Collections, Virginia Tech, Blacksburg
TMs	Typed manuscript
UVA	Manuscripts Department, Special Collections, University of Virginia, Charlottesville
VHS	Virginia Historical Society, Richmond
VR-RCPL	Virginia Room, Roanoke City Public Library

Newspaper Citations

Location of newspapers cited is specified when newspaper is not available on microfilm or from another location.

Introduction

1. C. Vann Woodward, *The Origins of the New South, 1877–1913* (Baton Rouge: Louisiana State University Press, 1951), 111–41, 152–74, 300–59; Edward Ayers, *The Promise of the New South: Life After Reconstruction* (New York: Oxford University Press, 1992), 56–80, 105–58; Paul Gaston, *New South Creed: A Study in Southern Mythmaking* (Baton Rouge: Louisiana State University Press, 1976), 4–13.

For a sample of urban New South historiography that focuses on the entire region, see Lawrence Larsen, *The Urban South: A History* (Lexington: University Press of Kentucky, 1990); David Goldfield, *From Cotton Fields to Skyscrapers: Southern City and Region, 1607–1980* (Baton Rouge: Louisiana State University Press, 1982); Blaine Brownwell and David Goldfield, eds., *The City in Southern History: The Growth of Urban Civilization in the South* (Port Washington, NY: Kennikat Press, 1977). For a sample of work that focuses on older cities, see Don Doyle, *New Men, New Cities, New South: Atlanta, Nashville, Charleston, Mobile, 1860–1910* (Chapel Hill: University of North Carolina Press, 1990); James M. Russell, *Atlanta, 1847–1890: City*

Building in the Old South and New South (Baton Rouge: Louisiana State University Press, 1988); Don Doyle, *Nashville in the New South, 1880–1930* (Knoxville: University of Tennessee Press, 1985); Vernon Burton and Robert C. McMath Jr., eds., *Towards a New South? Studies in Post–Civil War Southern Communities* (Westport, CT: Greenwood Press, 1982); Joy L. Jackson, *New Orleans in the Gilded Age: Politics and Urban Progress, 1880–1896* (Baton Rouge: Louisiana State University Press, 1969). For a sample of the work on company towns or mill villages, see Douglas Flamming, *Creating the Modern South: Millhands and Managers in Dalton, Georgia, 1884–1984* (Chapel Hill: University of North Carolina Press, 1992); Jacquelyn Dowd Hall, et al., *Like a Family: The Making of a Southern Cotton Mill World* (Chapel Hill: University of North Carolina Press, 1987); David Carlton, *Mill and Town in South Carolina, 1880–1920* (Baton Rouge: Louisiana State University Press, 1982).

2. Gaston, *New South Creed*, 189–245; Woodward, *Origins of the New South*, 185–204; Ayers, *Promise of a New South*, 187–213; Goldfield, *From Cotton Fields to Skyscrapers*, 80–132; Harold Woodman, "How New was the New South?" *Agricultural History* 58, no. 4 (Oct. 1984): 529–45. Scholars have written extensively about the early history of Birmingham. Roanoke, by comparison, has received very little attention. For a sample of the work on Birmingham, see bibliographies in Carl V. Harris, *Political Power in Birmingham, 1871–1921* (Knoxville: University of Tennessee Press, 1977); Henry M. McKiven Jr., *Iron and Steel: Class, Race, and Community in Birmingham, Alabama, 1875–1920* (Chapel Hill: University of North Carolina Press, 1995).

3. For a sample of work done on Appalachia's extractive industries or company towns, see Ronald Eller, *Miners, Millhands, and Mountaineers: Industrialization of the Appalachian South, 1880–1930* (Knoxville: University of Tennessee Press, 1982); Crandall A. Shifflett, *Coal Towns: Life, Work, and Culture in Company Towns of Southern Appalachia, 1880–1960* (Knoxville: University of Tennessee Press, 1991); Ronald Lewis, *Transforming the Appalachian Countryside: Railroads, Deforestation, and Social Change in West Virginia, 1880–1920* (Chapel Hill: University of North Carolina Press, 1998); David Corbin, *Life, Work, and Rebellion in the Coalfields: The Southern West Virginia Miners, 1880–1922* (Urbana: University of Illinois Press, 1981).

When explaining modernization in Appalachia, historians have generally focused their efforts on the region's extractive industries and related developments, ignoring cities on the periphery like Roanoke. Those who have commented on Roanoke's early development have typically done so in ways that seek to disconnect it from the region or downplay industry there. Ronald Eller, for example, portrays Roanoke in the 1880s and 1890s as the booming industrial base of operations for an "assault" on the nearby mountains by northern capitalists (Eller, *Miners, Millhands, and Mountaineers*, 70). That the city was in Appalachia or that natives were responsible for much of its development has generally seemed less important to scholars than the fact that a few wealthy Philadelphians owned the Norfolk & Western Railroad. With regard to Roanoke as part of Appalachia, see Ann DeWitt Watts, "Cities and Their Place in Southern Appalachia," *Appalachian Journal* 8 (Winter 1981): 106–8;

and Gordon B. McKinney, *Southern Mountain Republicans, 1865–1900: Politics and the Appalachian Community* (Chapel Hill: University of North Carolina Press, 1978), xii.

Chapter 1

1. Population figures from Lawrence H. Larsen, *The Rise of the Urban South* (Lexington: University Press of Kentucky, 1985), 155, 157; for a sample of "Magic City" designation, see *The Virginian*, 6 Dec. 1885, in Shenandoah Valley Railroad Scrapbook no. 4, N&WRA (cited hereafter as SVRS4); *Manufacturers' Record*, 22 December 1888; *The Roanoke Times*, 22 Jan. 1891; for Roanoke being commonly known by the appellation, see Thomas Bruce, *Southwest Virginia and Shenandoah Valley* (Richmond: J. L. Hill, 1891), 132. The term "magic city" originally developed as a popular nickname for western railroad towns. See Shelton Stromquist, *A Generation of Boomers: The Pattern of Railroad Labor Conflict in Nineteenth-Century America* (Urbana and Chicago: University of Illinois Press, 1987), 143.

2. Frederick B. Kegley, *Virginia Frontier: The Beginnings of the Southwest, The Roanoke of Colonial Days, 1740–1783* (Roanoke: Southwest Virginia Historical Society, 1938), 179; George S. Jack, *History of Roanoke County* (Roanoke: Stone Printing & Mfg. Co., 1912), 12; Robert D. Stoner, *A Seed-Bed of the Republic: Early Botetourt* (Roanoke: Roanoke Valley Historical Society, 1962), 145, 152. The "Great Road," also known as "Indian Road" and the "Great Wagon Road," follows the roadbed of present day U.S. Route 460. The "Carolina Road," known variously as "Traders Path" or "Neeley's Road," follows the roadbed of present-day U.S. Route 220.

3. Town of Gainesborough, 1834–1874 Map, VR-RCPL; William McCauley, *History of Roanoke County, Salem, and Roanoke City, Va., and Representative Citizens* (Chicago: Biographical Publishing Co., 1902), 149–50; Erin Baratta, "Gainesboro Neighborhood, 1890–1940," *The Journal of the History Museum and Historical Society of Western Virginia* 14, no. 1 (1999): 49; Raymond P. Barnes, *A History of Roanoke* (Radford, VA: Commonwealth Press, 1968), 21–23; Clare White, *Roanoke 1740–1982* (Roanoke: Roanoke Valley Historical Society, 1982), 35.

4. McCauley, *History of Roanoke County, Salem, and Roanoke City*, 151.

5. Deedie Kagey, *When Past is Prologue: A History of Roanoke County, Salem, and Roanoke City* (Roanoke: Roanoke County Sesquicentennial Committee, 1988), 106, 111–12.

6. "The First Train Into Big Lick," TMs (1927), HMHSWV; "Recollections of Henry S. Trout," in *The* (Roanoke) *World News*, 24 Apr. 1913.

7. For agricultural impact of the railroad in the Highlands, see Kenneth W. Noe, *Southwest Virginia's Railroad: Modernization and the Sectional Crisis* (Urbana and Chicago: University of Illinois Press, 1994), chap. 2; for impact on Big Lick Depot, see Bruce, *Southwest Virginia*, 133; McCauley, *History of Roanoke County, Salem, and Roanoke City*, 151–52.

246

8. "Recollections of Henry S. Trout," in *The* (Roanoke) *World News,* 28 Apr. 1913.

9. "Recollections of Callowhill Turner," in E. P. Tompkins, "Medical Annals of Roanoke," 2, TMs (1922), VR-RCPL; "Recollections of Henry S. Trout," in *The* (Roanoke) *World News,* 28 Apr. 1913.

10. Anna Clayton Logan, "Recollections of my Life," TMs (July 1917), VHS.

11. "Recollections of Callowhill Turner," 2–3.

12. Charter of the Town of Big Lick, Approved by Virginia General Assembly, 28 Feb. 1874, rpt. in Barnes, *History of Roanoke,* 71–72.

13. McCauley, *History of Roanoke County, Salem, and Roanoke City,* 152.

14. United States Bureau of the Census, U.S. Census of 1880, Schedule of Population, Town of Big Lick, County of Roanoke, State of Virginia.

15. E. F. Pat Striplin, *The Norfolk & Western: A History* (Forest, VA: Norfolk & Western Historical Society, 1997), 10–30.

16. "Minute Book Shenandoah Valley Railroad, 1870–1881," 1–87, Shenandoah Valley Railroad Records, N&WRA; see also Joseph T. Lambie, *From Mine to Market: The History of Coal Transportation on the Norfolk and Western Railway* (New York: New York University Press, 1954), 9–14; Striplin, *Norfolk & Western,* 32.

17. Born in Philadelphia in Mar. 1844, Kimball worked as a "rodman" in the engineering department of the Pennsylvania Railroad from 1862 to 1866. He then worked for English railroad corporations in the U. K. for the next two years. Returning to the U. S., Kimball worked for various railroads until 1881, when he was appointed president of the SVR and vice-president of the N&W. In June 1883, he was named president of the N&W, and in 1895, he was the court- appointed receiver for the company. From 1896 until 1902, Kimball was chairman of the board for the N&W, and from 1902 until he died in July 1903, Kimball served again as president of that line. Biographical information from Edward B. Jacobs, *History of Roanoke City and History of the Norfolk & Western* (Roanoke: Stone Printing & Mfg. Co., 1912), 142.

18. Lambie, *From Mine to Market,* 12–14; Striplin, *Norfolk & Western,* 32.

19. Quote and route information from *Description of the Shenandoah Valley Railroad* (Philadelphia, 1881), 23, rpt. in Lambie, *From Mine to Market,* 13–14.

20. Information on the purchase and plans are from Jacobs, *History of Roanoke City,* 146; Lambie, *From Mine to Market,* 6–7; "Minute Book Shenandoah Valley Railroad, 1870–1881," 244–94; management, ownership, and spur routes into coalfields is from *The New York Times,* 3 May 1881.

21. For early nineteenth-century up through 1870s exploration of the coalfields, see Robert H. Smith, *General William Mahone, Frederick J. Kimball and Others: A Short History of The Norfolk & Western Railway* (New York: Newcomen Society in North America, 1949), 23; Jacobs, *History of Roanoke City,* 147–48; Lambie, *From Mine to Market,* chap. 2; Eller, *Miners, Millhands, and Mountaineers,* chap. 2; Harold W. Mann, "Economic Development in Southwest Virginia," *Journal of the*

Roanoke Valley Historical Society 11, no. 2 (1982): 75; for quote, see Charles R. Boyd, *Resources of South-West Virginia, Showing the Mineral Deposits of Iron, Coal, Zinc, Copper, and Lead* (New York: John Wiley and Sons, 1881), 1.

22. Lambie, *From Mine to Market,* 27.

23. Smith, *Short History of The Norfolk & Western,* 23; Striplin, *Norfolk & Western,* 43. The twelve-foot-wide Flat Top–Pocahontas seam ran for six miles before dividing into two five-foot seams for the next eight miles, bringing the total "Pocahontas" deposit to around six to ten thousand tons per acre, and making it one of the largest coalfields in the United States. See Jacobs, *History of Roanoke City,* 148.

24. Smith, *Short History of The Norfolk & Western,* 23–24; Striplin, *Norfolk & Western,* 44–46; Lambie, *Mine to Market,* 30–36; Bruce, *Southwest Virginia,* 136–37; Jacobs, *History of Roanoke City,* 146–47.

25. Norwood Middleton, *Salem: A Virginia Chronicle* (Salem: Salem Historical Society, 1986), 124–27.

26. Elizabeth Dabney Coleman, "The Night Ride That Made Roanoke," *Virginia Cavalcade* 4 (Summer 1954): 10.

27. Quote from "Recollections of Henry S. Trout," in *The* (Roanoke) *World News,* 1 May 1913.

28. *Big Lick Weekly News,* 2 Mar. 1881, in Shenandoah Valley Railroad Scrapbook no. 3, N&WRA (cited hereafter as SVRS3).

29. Committee appointment is in Big Lick Town Council Minutes, 23 Feb. 1881, Clerk's Office, Roanoke City Municipal Building; quote is from *Big Lick Weekly News,* 12 Mar. 1881, in SVRS3.

30. Survey team visit recounted in *The Salem Register,* 18 Mar. 1881, in SVRS3; delegate being dispatched from Big Lick Town Council Minutes, 22 Mar. 1881.

31. Coleman, "Night Ride That Made Roanoke," 10; Big Lick resident and future Roanoke City Mayor William K. Andrews remembered that Moomaw was working to secure right-of-ways into Salem. See "Member of First City Council of Roanoke Tells of Early Problems," unidentified newspaper clipping (3 Aug. 1926), vertical files, HMHSWV; for specifics about Moomaw's business operations, see stationery of his 4 and 6 Mar. 1882 letters to Frederick J. Kimball in the Roanoke Land & Improvement Company Records, HMHSWV.

32. W. K. Andrews remembered Moomaw's rebuff in "Member of First City Council of Roanoke Tells of Early Problems."

33. Coleman, "Night Ride That Made Roanoke," 9–10. Unfortunately for Salem, the Valley Railroad only made it to Lexington before the 1883 depression ended future construction.

34. Anna Clayton Logan, "Recollections of My Life," 56, TMs (July 1917), VHS. Local legend continues to corroborate this rebuff. It seems unlikely, however, that Salem's elected officials acted quite so cavalierly knowing that hundreds of

thousands of dollars of development were on the line. For perpetuation of this story, see Writers' Program of the Work Projects Administration in the State of Virginia, *Roanoke: Story of County and City* (Roanoke: Roanoke City School Board, 1942), 139; Kagey, *When Past is Prologue,* 271.

35. For Terry's presence and the resulting actions, see Roanoke Police Pension Fund Association (cited hereafter as PPFA), *History of the Roanoke Police Department* (Roanoke: Union Printing, 1916), 68.

36. Written accounts of why the railroad chose Big Lick vary on sequence, in details, and in what the town pledged. Nevertheless, it is possible to piece together at least a semblance of the event from: "Recollections of Henry S. Trout," in *The* (Roanoke) *World News,* 1 May 1913; Coleman, "Night Ride That Made Roanoke," 9–13; Jacobs, *History of Roanoke City,* 93–94; McCauley, *History of Roanoke County, Salem, and Roanoke City,* 155; PPFA, *History of the Roanoke Police,* 68–69; Striplin, *Norfolk & Western,* 40–41; Lambie, *From Mine to Market,* 15–16; for the entire survey team being relocated to Big Lick, see *Big Lick Weekly News,* 2, 23 Apr. 1881, in SVRS3; for payment of Big Lick's ten thousand dollar donation, see John C. Moomaw, Cloverdale, VA, to Frederick J. Kimball, President Shenandoah Valley Railroad, Philadelphia, PA, 22 Nov. 1881, Roanoke Land & Improvement Company Records, HMHSWV; for Kimball's endorsement of the selection, see "Minute Book Shenandoah Valley Railroad, 1870–1881," 298.

37. Jacobs, *History of Roanoke City,* 94.

38. Town description from William C. Campbell, "Fortieth Anniversary Sermon," in *The* (Roanoke) *World News,* 4 July 1921, clipping in William Creighton Campbell Papers, HMHSWV (cited hereafter as Campbell Papers); William C. Campbell, "Historical Roanoke," TMs, no date, Campbell Papers.

39. For purchase of Trout's land, see *Virginia Free Press,* 11 June 1881, in SVRS4; for quote, see "Recollections of Henry S. Trout," in *The* (Roanoke) *World News,* 1 May 1913.

40. Big Lick Town Council Minutes, 29 June 1881.

41. For similar selection processes by railroads, see Stromquist, *A Generation of Boomers,* 151–53.

42. For name change vote, see Jacobs, *History of Roanoke City,* 94; *Virginia Free Press,* 30 July 1881, in HMHSWV; quote is from J. C. Moomaw, Cloverdale, VA, to Frederick J. Kimball, Philadelphia, PA, 28 June 1881, rpt. in Lambie, *From Mine to Market,* 16.

43. *Big Lick Weekly News,* 9 July 1881, in Shenandoah Valley Railroad Scrapbook no. 4, N&WRA (cited hereafter as SVRS4). According to Kagey, *When Past is Prologue,* 6–7, there is considerable confusion over the meaning and genealogy of the English word "Roanoke." Its origins, however, are likely from the Powhatan world "rawrenoc" or "rawrenoke," meaning polished shell money, or from what was originally called "Roanoak" Island, home of the Lost Colony.

44. *Big Lick Weekly News,* 16 July 1881, in SVRS4.

45. *The Salem Register,* 22 July 1881, in SVRS4.

46. *Virginia Free Press,* 30 July 1881, in HMHSWV.

47. Terry's appointments are available in Roanoke Land & Improvement Company Directors' Report, rpt. in *Roanoke Saturday News,* 25 Mar. 1882, in SVRS4; and "The Roanoke Machine Works–Agreement of Corporation and Certificate of Incorporation," 2, in Roanoke Machine Works Records, printed materials folder, N&WRA; Trout's appointment by Frederick Kimball to the presidency of Roanoke's First National Bank is recounted in Recollections of Henry S. Trout in *The* (Roanoke) *World News,* 1 May 1913.

48. Henry Trout inherited the land from his father John Trout. First 100 acres of sale for $20,000 noted in *Virginia Free Press,* 11 June 1881, in SVRS4; details of the other 399 acres purchased are from First Annual Report of the Roanoke Land & Improvement Company, 6 December 1882, published in *The Roanoke Leader,* 7 Dec. 1882.

49. *Big Lick Weekly News,* 6 Aug.; 24 Sept. 1881, in SVRS4. Streets named for former governors include: Henry, Jefferson, Nelson, Jameson, Harrison, Randolph, Lee, Tazewell, Campbell, Gilmer, Patton, Rutherford, Gregory, Wise, Wells, and Walker.

50. See various 1881 Roanoke Land & Improvement Company Housing Contracts, Roanoke Land & Improvement Company Records, HMHSWV; see also, Roanoke Land & Improvement Company Directors' Report, in *Roanoke Saturday News,* 25 Mar. 1882, in SVRS4.

51. H. L. Moore, Roanoke, VA, to C. D. Armond, Esq., "Sec & Treas RL&Ico," no 37 & 39 S. 3rd Street, Philadelphia, PA, 7 Oct. 1881, Roanoke Land & Improvement Company Records, HMHSWV.

52. Bruce, *Southwest Virginia,* 133; First Annual Report of the Roanoke Land & Improvement Company, 6 December 1882, published in *The Roanoke Leader,* 7 Dec. 1882.

53. See mention of the 1881 Terry sale in *The New York Times,* 27 Aug. 1883.

54. Information and quotes from First Annual Report of the Roanoke Land & Improvement Company, 6 December 1882, published in *The Roanoke Leader,* 7 Dec. 1882.

55. "Proposition and Contract—Julius G. Holmes—To erect 8 houses for colored people," 10 Mar. 1882, Roanoke Land & Improvement Company Records, HMHSWV.

56. *The Roanoke Leader,* 2 Nov. 1882.

57. Barnes, *History of Roanoke,* 120.

58. First Annual Report of the Roanoke Land & Improvement Company, 6 December 1882, published in *The Roanoke Leader,* 7 Dec. 1882.

59. *The Roanoke Leader*, 16 Nov. 1882.

60. Ibid., 7 Dec. 1882.

61. Donlan Piedmont, *Peanut Soup and Spoonbread: An Informal History of Hotel Roanoke* (Roanoke: Virginia Tech Real Estate Foundation, 1994), 16.

62. *The Roanoke Leader*, 26 Oct. 1882; Piedmont, *Peanut Soup*, 16.

63. *The Roanoke Leader*, 2 Nov. 1882.

64. Ibid., 7, 28 Sept. 1882.

65. Donlan Piedmont, "The Railroad Offices," *Journal of the Roanoke Valley Historical Society* 13, no. 2 (1996): 18–22; *The Roanoke Leader*, 27 Sept. 1883.

66. *The Roanoke Leader*, 7 Dec. 1882; 27 Jan. 1883.

67. *The Bulletin of the Bureau of Immigration and Mining Intelligence*, Oct. 1882.

68. *The Roanoke Leader*, 4 Jan. 1883.

69. Second Annual Report of the Roanoke Land & Improvement Company, 5 Dec. 1883, published in *The Roanoke Leader*, 17 Jan. 1884.

70. *The Industrial South*, 10 Sept. 1882.

71. *Richmond State*, qtd. in *The Roanoke Leader*, 23 Nov. 1882.

72. *Richmond Dispatch*, 15 Nov. 1882, in Shenandoah Valley Railroad Scrapbook no. 6, N&WRA (cited hereafter as SVRS6).

73. *The New York Times*, 27 Aug. 1883.

74. Warner's letters to the *Hartford Courant* qtd. in *The Virginias*, July 1883 and rpt. in *The Roanoke Times*, 22 Jan. 1891. Warner, co-author with Mark Twain of *The Gilded Age*, is widely credited with initiating the literary "discovery" of Appalachia in the 1880s and 1890s. See Eller, *Miners, Millhands, and Mountaineers*, 39–43.

75. Earnest Ingersol, *To the Shenandoah and Beyond: A Chronicle of a Leisurely Journey Through the Uplands of Virginia and Tennessee, Sketching their Scenery, Noting their Legends, Portraying Social and Material Progress, and Explaining Routes of Travel* (New York: Leve & Alden Printing Company, 1885), 59–60.

76. *The Roanoke Leader*, 14 Sept. 1882; and additional information on Brooke from McCauley, *History of Roanoke County, Salem, and Roanoke City*, 529. *The Roanoke Leader* began operations in Sept. 1882. In 1886, Brooke left as editor to become clerk of the local Hustings Court, and in 1887 the paper ceased operations. See Lester J. Cappon, *Virginia Newspapers, 1821–1935: A Bibliography with Historical Introduction and Notes*, Guide to Virginia Historical Materials Part I (New York: D. Appleton–Century Co. for the Institute for Research in the Social Sciences at the University of Virginia, 1936), 196–97; I. M. Warren, *History of Newspapers Published in 23 Counties of Southwest Virginia* (Roanoke: Works Progress Administration, 1937), 8.

77. For businesses listed here, see ads in *The Roanoke Leader*, 14 Sept. 1882.

78. Geraldine (I. Stewart), Roanoke, to "Aunt" (Mrs. F. C. Norman), Culpeper County, Virginia, 15 May (1883), Norman-Lewis Family Papers, microfilm, UVA (cited hereafter as Norman-Lewis Family Papers).

79. See ad in *The Roanoke Leader,* 14 June 1883.

80. Geraldine (I. Stewart), Roanoke, to "Aunt," (Mrs. F. C. Norman), Culpeper County, Virginia, 15 May (1883), Norman-Lewis Family Papers. The 1888 city directory lists the couple as living together on the corner of Jefferson Street and Day Avenue and has E. H. Stewart & Co. in business on Salem Avenue. See *Haddock & Baily's Roanoke Va. City Directory 1888* (Richmond: Haddock & Baily, 1888), 113, 138.

81. See ad in *The Roanoke Leader,* 14 Sept. 1882.

82. See ad in *The Roanoke Leader,* 26 Oct. 1882.

83. William Hicks Travers, Diary Number Five, 23, 24, 25, 30 Oct. 1882, William Hicks Travers Papers, VHS; see also notice of sale in *The Roanoke Leader,* 2 Nov. 1882. In addition to the SVR, Travers worked for the Cumberland Valley Railroad and the Luray Cave and Hotel Company. Travers visited Roanoke for the first time in early July 1882. His daughter Sallie and her husband William W. Coe, the railroad's chief construction engineer, along with their seven-year-old son William, had moved to town earlier in the year and were residing temporarily in the Rorer Park Hotel.

84. Information on the 1882–83 land boom is from "Recollections of Henry S. Trout," in *The* (Roanoke) *World Ne*ws, 8 May 1913; see real estate supplement in *The Roanoke Leader,* 31 May 1883.

85. William C. Campbell, "Fortieth Anniversary Sermon," in Roanoke *World News,* 4 July 1921, clipping in Campbell Papers. Campbell moved to Big Lick in July 1881 from Harper's Ferry, West Virginia, where for the previous two years he had held his first position as minister after graduating from Hamden-Sydney College and then Union Theological Seminary. For this and other biographical information, see McCauley, *History of Roanoke County, Salem, and Roanoke City,* 379.

86. Jacobs, *History of Roanoke City,* 96.

87. Second Annual Report of the Roanoke Land & Improvement Company, 5 December 1883, published in *The Roanoke Leader,* 17 Jan. 1884; see also First Annual Report of the Roanoke Land & Improvement Company, 6 Dec. 1882, published in *The Roanoke Leader,* 7 Dec. 1882.

88. Town Council of Roanoke, "Census of the Town of Roanoke, December 1883," vols. 1 and 2, VR-RCPL. Volume 1 contains 1,715 names on 86 pages; volume 2 has 1,074 names on 54 pages.

89. United States Bureau of the Census, U.S. Census of 1880, Schedule of Population, Town of Big Lick, County of Roanoke, State of Virginia; Town Council of Roanoke, "Census of the Town of Roanoke, December 1883," vols. 1 and 2, VR-RCPL. Occupation categories derived in part from Stephen Thernstrom, *Poverty and Progress: Social Mobility in a Nineteenth Century City* (Cambridge: Harvard University Press, 1964), 90–94. Non-manual commercial category includes railroad management as well as railroad and retail clerks. "Black," "Mulatto," and "White" categories listed on 1880 Census. Only "Black" or "White" listed on 1883 Census.

90. Goldfield, *Cotton Fields and Skyscrapers,* 96–98.

91. Roanoke Town Council Minutes, 18 May 1882, Clerk's Office, Roanoke City Municipal Building.

92. Hog ordinance rpt. in *The Roanoke Leader,* 19 Oct. 1882; refuse ordinance in Roanoke Town Council Minutes, 2 Sept. 1882.

93. *The Roanoke Leader,* 4 Jan., 21 May 1883.

94. Roanoke Land & Improvement Company, Premium Announcement of 14 Apr. 1883, Roanoke Land & Improvement Company Records, HMHSWV.

95. *The Roanoke Leader,* 27 Sept. 1883.

96. Information on early Catholics in Roanoke is from Margaret M. Maier, "Father Lynch, Founder," 2–3, 6, TMs (Apr. 1941), in Emma B. Lynch Papers, VHS; notice of Roanoke Land & Improvement Company lot donation is in *The Roanoke Leader,* 2 Nov. 1882.

97. *Roanoke Saturday Review,* 27 Jan. 1883, in SVRS6.

98. Ibid., 24 Feb. 1883, in SVRS6.

99. Statistics derived from data published in *The Roanoke Leader,* 4 Jan. 1883.

100. In boomtowns, saloons were almost always the most abundant and popular retail establishment. See Kelly J. Dixon, *Boomtown Saloons: Archaeology and History in Virginia City* (Reno and Las Vegas: University of Nevada Press, 2005), 25–32.

101. See ads in *The Roanoke Leader,* 26 Oct. 1882, 31 May 1883.

102. *Baltimore Sun,* qtd. in *The Roanoke Leader,* 21 June 1883.

103. *Roanoke Saturday Review,* 16 Dec. 1882.

104. *The Roanoke Leader,* 5 Oct. 1882; 28 Apr. 1883.

105. Ibid., 21 Dec. 1882.

106. Ibid., 11 Oct. 1883.

107. William C. Campbell, Roanoke, VA, to Anna Campbell, Harper's Ferry, WVA, 25 June 1883, Campbell Papers.

108. Warren Moorman, "Roanoke Valley Medicine," *Journal of the Roanoke Valley Historical Society* 9, no. 1 (1973–74): 27; for "Big Lick Fever," Moorman cites Otis F. Vance, M.D., "Sketches of the Endemic Diseases of the Roanoke Valley of Virginia and North Carolina," *Virginia Medical-Surgical Journal,* Jan.1855; see also, "Recollections of J. B. Ruddell," in *The* (Roanoke) *Evening World,* 9 June 1911; for emergence of "Lick Fever" in the 1880s, see letter to editor in *The Roanoke Leader,* 10 May 1883.

109. *The Roanoke Leader,* 18 January 1883.

110. Ibid., 3 May 1883.

111. Tompkins, "Medical Annals of Roanoke," 8–9; for nearby towns banning Roanokers, see WPA, *Roanoke: Story of County and City,* 135.

112. William C. Campbell, Roanoke, VA, to Anna Campbell, Harper's Ferry, WVA, 23 May 1883, Campbell Papers.

113. Ibid., 18 June 1883.

114. *The Roanoke Leader,* 14 June 1883.

115. Tompkins, "Medical Annals of Roanoke," 9; William C. Campbell, Roanoke, VA, to Anna Campbell, Harper's Ferry, WVA, 18 June 1883, Campbell Papers.

116. *Roanoke Saturday Evening News,* 20 May 1882, in Shenandoah Valley Railroad Scrapbook no. 5, N&WRA (hereafter cited as SVRS5). The *Roanoke Saturday Evening News* began as *The Big Lick News* in 1877 and later changed its name to the *Roanoke Saturday Review.* It continued operations until 1885, when a fire destroyed its headquarters and it never reopened. See Cappon, *Virginia Newspapers, 1821–1935,* 196–97; Warren, *History of Newspapers Published in 23 Counties of Southwest Virginia,* 8.

117. *Roanoke Saturday Evening News,* 3 June 1882, in SVRS5.

118. *Roanoke Commercial Advertiser,* June 1882, in SVRS5.

119. *The Philadelphia Press,* 11 Aug. 1882, in SVRS5.

120. *Philadelphia Ledger,* qtd. in *The Roanoke Leader,* 14 June 1883.

121. *Baltimore Sun,* qtd. in *The Roanoke Leader,* 21 June 1883.

122. William C. Campbell, "The First Circus in Roanoke," TMs, no date, Campbell Papers.

123. *The Roanoke Leader,* 21 Sept. 1882.

124. For information about RL&IC carrying out Herring's plan, see Second Annual Report of the Roanoke Land & Improvement Company, 5 December 1883, published in *The Roanoke Leader,* 17 Jan. 1884; for Roanoke rejecting the plan, see *The Roanoke Leader,* 5 Oct, 16 Nov. 1882.

125. *The Roanoke Leader,* 21 Sept, 19 Oct. 1882; 11 Jan. 1883.

126. For the composition of local government, see Barnes, *History of Roanoke,* 98.

127. Roanoke Town Council Minutes, 7 June 1882.

128. *The Roanoke Leader,* 7 Sept. 1882.

129. Ibid., 21 Sept. 1882.

130. *Philadelphia Ledger,* qtd. in *The Roanoke Leader,* 14 June 1883.

131. *American Volunteer,* 31 Oct. 1883.

132. Letter to *Richmond Dispatch,* rpt. in *The Roanoke Leader,* 7 June 1883.

133. *The Roanoke Leader,* 16 Nov. 1882.

134. *Roanoke Saturday Review,* 11 Nov. 1882, in SVRS6.

135. *The Roanoke Leader,* 16 Nov. 1882.

136. See for example, references to "our town" in First Annual Report of the Roanoke Land & Improvement Company, 6 December 1882, published in *The Roanoke Leader,* 7 Dec. 1882; and Second Annual Report of the Roanoke Land & Improvement Company, 5 Dec. 1883, published in *The Roanoke Leader,* 17 Jan. 1884.

137. *The Roanoke Leader,* 30 Nov. 1882.

138. Ibid., 23 Nov. 1882

139. *Roanoke Saturday Review,* 16 Dec. 1882, in SVRS6.

140. Trout's position with the Roanoke Land & Improvement Company at the time is noted in *The Roanoke Leader,* 24 July 1886; delay of vote and quotes are from the *Roanoke Saturday Review,* 27 Jan. 1883, in SVRS6.

141. *Roanoke Saturday Review,* 10 Feb. 1883, in SVRS6.

142. Ibid.

143. *The Roanoke Leader,* 1 Mar. 1883, in SVRS6.

144. Ibid., 5 Apr. 1883.

145. Ibid., 31 May 1883.

146. For similar appearance and community ethos in the "camp phase" of development, see C. Eric Stoehr, *Bonanza Victorian: Architecture and Society in Colorado Mining Towns* (Albuquerque: University of New Mexico Press, 1975), 10–17, 61; for additional commentary on those factors, see Gunther Barth, *Instant Cities: Urbanization and the Rise of San Francisco and Denver* (New York: Oxford University Press, 1975), 5–6, 142–51; Gary W. Malamud, *Boomtown Communities,* Environmental Design Series, vol. 5 (New York: Van Nostrand Reinhold Co., 1984), 9–22, 42–50.

147. For the "corporate town" analogy and characteristics of a "company town," see John S. Garner, *The Model Company Town: Urban Design through Private Enterprise in Nineteenth-Century New England* (Amherst: University of Massachusetts Press, 1984), 5–7, 9, 14–16, 62–68, 77–84.

148. Data derived from United States Bureau of the Census, U.S. Census of 1880, 1880 Schedule of Population, Town of Big Lick, County of Roanoke, State of Virginia; Town Council of Roanoke, "Census of the Town of Roanoke, December 1883," vols. 1 and 2, VR-RCPL; United States Bureau of the Census, *Report on Population of the United States at the Eleventh Census: 1890, Part 1* (Washington, DC.: Government Printing Office, 1895), 389; 1892 statistics compiled from data in *Sholes' Directory of the City of Roanoke, November 1st, 1892,* rpt. in *The Roanoke Times,* 20 Oct. 1892.

149. Malamud, *Boomtown Communities,* xi, 1–5.

150. Ibid.

151. Barth, *Instant Cities,* 132.

Chapter 2

1. For the history of Republican and Readjuster Parties in Southwest Virginia, see McKinney, *Southern Mountain Republicans, 1865–1900,* 12–104; Alan W. Moger, *Virginia: Bourbonism to Byrd, 1870–1925* (Charlottesville: University Press of Virginia, 1968), 5–39; and Virginius Dabney, *Virginia: The New Dominion* (Garden City, NJ: Doubleday and Co., 1971), 375–92; for information on black support for the Readjusters, see Jane Daily, *Before Jim Crow: The Politics of Race in Postemancipation Virginia*

(Chapel Hill: University of North Carolina Press, 2000), 50–69; and James T. Moore, "Black Militancy in Readjuster Virginia, 1879–1883," *Journal of Southern History* 41 (May 1975), 169–71; 1882 election results from *The Roanoke Leader* 9 Nov. 1882; description of black support in Roanoke for Wise from Richmond *Dispatch* 11 Nov. 1882, rpt. in *The Roanoke Leader* 23 Nov. 1882; Big Lick newspaper quote from *Roanoke Saturday Evening News*, 5 Nov. 1881. (Although the Town of Roanoke did not yet officially exist, *The Big Lick Weekly News* had by the fall of 1881 already changed its name to the *Roanoke Saturday Evening News*.)

2. Information on "Danville Riot" from McKinney, *Southern Mountain Republicans*, 106–7; Daily, *Before Jim Crow*, 103–30; Moore, "Black Militancy in Readjuster Virginia," 184–86; election results from *The Roanoke Leader*, 8 Nov. 1883.

3. See letter from Zachariah Hunt in *The Roanoke Leader*, 29 Nov. 1884.

4. For presidential vote, see *The Roanoke Leader*, 6 Nov. 1884; for information on the various newspapers, see Cappon, *Virginia Newspapers, 1821–1935*, 195–98; and Warren, *History of Newspapers Published in 23 Counties of Southwest Virginia*, 8–17. There are no known copies of *The Roanoke Telegram* or John Davis's *Press*. The three extant copies of *The Roanoke Weekly Sun* are in VR-RCPL.

5. *The Roanoke Leader*, 11 July 1885.

6. Ibid., 22 Aug. 1885.

7. Ibid., 26 Sept. 1885. For Wise's campaign for Governor, see Curtis Carroll Davis, "Very Well Rounded Republican: The Several Lives of John S. Wise," *Virginia Magazine of History and Biography* 71, no. 4 (Oct. 1963): 472–78.

8. *The Roanoke Leader*, 3 Oct. 1885. For more on Lee's campaign in Southwest Virginia, see McKinney, *Southern Mountain Republicans*, 114–15.

9. For election results and turning away black voters, see *The Roanoke Leader*, 7 Nov. 1885. Wise even lost in black majority counties. Democrats gained control of the Virginia's election apparatus in 1884 by passing the Anderson-McCormick Election Law, which placed election boards under the control of the Democratic controlled General Assembly. For more on this, see McKinney, *Southern Mountain Republicans*, 107–8; Dabney, *Virginia: The New Dominion*, 393–94; for accusations of fraud, see Moger, *Virginia: Bourbonism to Byrd*, 59–61; and Daily, *Before Jim Crow*, 156.

10. For Southwest Virginians favoring the protective tariff, see Allen W. Moger, "Industrial and Urban Progress in Virginia from 1880 to 1900," *Virginia Magazine of History and Biography* 66 (July 1958), 333; information on Mahone, the N&W, and the 1889 campaign are from McKinney, *Southern Mountain Republicans*, 99–100, 116–17; Moger, *Virginia: Bourbonism to Byrd*, 62–68, 98–99, 112–21; and Dabney, *Virginia: The New Dominion*, 396–99. Travel writer Thomas Clayton noticed this unique dynamic at play in Roanoke during the fall 1883 political season. See his *Rambles and Reflections: From Biscay to the Black Sea and from Aetna to the North Cape with Glimpses of Africa, America and the Island of the Sea* (Chester, PA: Press of the Delaware County Republican, 1893), 321.

11. William C. Sproul, *David F. Houston* (Philadelphia: Press of A. H. Strickler & Co., 1890), 11.

12. William A. Pattie, Roanoke City, to Dr. G. R. Gilmer, "Near Richmond," 9 Sept. 1889, George Kooglar Gilmer Papers, VHS.

13. Vote total is in *Roanoke Daily Times,* 8 Nov. 1889; quote is from *The Roanoke Leader,* 7 Nov. 1889.

14. *The Roanoke Leader,* 6 Dec. 1883.

15. Ibid., 27 Dec. 1883.

16. For draft of city charter, see *The Roanoke Leader,* 14 Feb. 1884.

17. Town Council of Roanoke, "Census of the Town of Roanoke, December 1883," vols. 1 and 2, VR-RCPL; Edward L. Stone, "Through Fifty Eventful Years," *Stone's Impressions* 3, new series, no 4 (July, Aug, Sept, 1933), 1, in author's collection. According to A. E. Dick Howard, in *Commentaries on the Constitution of Virginia,* vol. 2 (Charlottesville: University Press of Virginia, 1974), 793–97, the Virginia legislature did not formalize the distinction between towns and cities until 1887, when it defined cities as having a population over 5,000. All contemporary and secondary sources, however, suggest that Roanoke's Town Council believed they needed 5,000 residents to become a city. See, for example, Barnes, *History of Roanoke,* 132; White, *Roanoke: 1740–1982,* 71.

18. *The Roanoke Leader,* 3 Apr. 1884.

19. See Dunstan campaign ad in *The Roanoke Leader,* 3 Apr. 1884; Dunstan's association with the Roanoke Gas Company is noted in *The Roanoke Leader,* 21 May 1883.

20. For a similar transition in Greensboro, North Carolina, see Samuel M. Kipp III, "Old Notables and Newcomers: The Economic and Political Elite of Greensboro, North Carolina, 1880–1920," *Journal of Southern History* 43, No 3 (Aug. 1977): 373–94.

21. *The Roanoke Leader,* 29 May 1884; see also WPA, *Roanoke: Story of County and City,* 135.

22. *The Roanoke Leader,* 3 July 1884.

23. City of Roanoke, Virginia, *General Ordinances of the City of Roanoke, Together with other Ordinances and Contracts Affecting the Rights and Interests of the City of Roanoke* (Roanoke: Bell Printing, 1884), 51–52, 56–57, 70–71.

24. *The Roanoke Leader,* 24 July 1884.

25. For Roanoke's rate of 31.2 deaths per thousand, see statistics published in *The Roanoke Leader,* 11 July 1885; for New York's 1885 rate of 25 deaths per thousand, see Carl L. Erhardt and Joyce E. Berlin, eds., *Mortality and Morbidity in the United States* (Cambridge: Harvard University Press, 1974), 2.

26. Julia F. (Harris) Via to "Mother," Nancy F. Harris, 13 Oct. 1885, Harris Family Papers, VHS.

27. *The Roanoke Leader*, 17 Apr. 1886.

28. Bruce, *Southwest Virginia*, 147.

29. *The Roanoke Leader*, 7 Aug. 1884.

30. Ibid., 28 Aug. 1884. Nearly 84 percent of voters approved the bonds.

31. See Daniel C. Moomaw letter in *The Roanoke Leader*, 4 Sept. 1884.

32. *The Roanoke Leader*, 21 Aug. 1884.

33. Ibid., 7 Feb. 1885.

34. Ibid., 11, 25 Apr. 1885.

35. Ibid., 4 July 1885.

36. Ibid., 9 May 1885.

37. Ibid., 6 Dec. 1885. Dunstan eventually ended up in South Carolina before returning to Roanoke in 1892. For notice of his return, see *The Roanoke Times*, 15 Apr. 1892.

38. Election results and quote are in *The Roanoke Leader*, 30 May 1885.

39. Election results are in *The Roanoke Leader*, 29 May 1886; blacks endorsing Democrats in available in *The Roanoke Leader*, 15 May 1886.

40. *Roanoke Daily Times*, 27 Aug. 1890.

41. Ibid., 28 Aug. 1890.

42. Ibid., 29 June 1890.

43. Ibid., 1 Aug. 1890.

44. Ibid., 2 Aug. 1890.

45. Goldfield, *Cotton Fields and Skyscrapers*, 92.

46. *Roanoke Daily Times*, 19 Nov. 1889.

47. Ibid., 11, 18 May 1890.

48. Ibid., 5 July 1890.

49. Ibid., 30 July 1890.

50. *The Roanoke Times*, 19 Nov. 1890.

51. Ibid., 29 Jan. 1891.

52. Information on the 1888 jail is from *The Roanoke Times*, 9 July; 20 Nov. 1890.

53. *The Roanoke Times*, 5 Feb. 1891.

54. For local press endorsing issues, see *The Roanoke Times*, 3 Mar. 1891; for the first meeting at High Street Baptist led by P. W. Oliver, Rev. R. R. Jones, Willis W. Brown, Rev. Daniel W. Harth, John H. Davis, T. T. Henry, and Roanoke's only black lawyer, Andrew Jackson Oliver, see *The Roanoke Times*, 21 Feb. 1891.

55. See the council's reaction in *The Roanoke Times*, 25 Feb. 1891.

56. For the second meeting at A. M. E. Church, see *The Roanoke Times*, 3 Mar. 1891.

57. See voter registration statistics published in *The Roanoke Times*, 28 Oct. 1890; 12 May 1892.

58. See the council's reaction to the advisory board in *The Roanoke Times*, 25 Feb. 1891; for business leaders opinions, see *The Roanoke Times*, 3 Mar. 1891.

59. *The Roanoke Times*, 18 Mar. 1891.

60. Ibid., 7 Aug. 1892.

61. See election results in *The Roanoke Times*, 30 May 1891; councilmen Woodward, McCahan, and Scott had all spoken against the board in *The Roanoke Leader*, 25 Feb. 1891.

62. *The Roanoke Times* 18, 26 May; 9, 15 June 1892.

63. Ibid., 2 July; 17 Sept. 1892.

64. See appointments of Charles Bright, John Davis, and A. J. Oliver as delegates in *The Roanoke Times*, 30 Apr. 1892; for coverage of the Republican Convention, see *The Roanoke Leader*, 5, 6 May 1892.

65. *The Roanoke Times*, 25 May 1892.

66. Ibid., 25, 26 May 1892; the "policemen who do not police" is a reference to stories carried in *The Roanoke Times* on 30 Oct. 1890; 3 Oct. 1891; 23 Apr.; 18, 24 May 1892. "Tammany-aping" quote is from the 26 May 1892 edition of *The Roanoke Times*.

67. *The Roanoke Times*, 26 May 1892.

68. Ibid., 27 May 1892.

69. Ibid., 30 May 1892.

70. Ibid., 2 July 1892.

71. Ibid., 7 Aug.; 30 Oct. 1892.

72. William C. Campbell, "1885 Anniversary Sermon," Heritage Room, First Presbyterian Church, Roanoke, rpt. in Brenda McDaniel, "Dr. Campbell's Big Lick," *The Roanoker* (Sept. 1981): 79. Barroom portion of quote is from William C. Campbell, Roanoke, to Editor of *The Central* (location unknown), 12 Mar. 1886, Campbell Papers.

73. Information on the murder is from William C. Campbell, "Roanoke's Tragedies. Part of its earlier History. The death of a young Girl. The Terror that filled the city. Thaxton Wreck. The Great Riot. Nine men killed and Thirty wounded in a moment. The Lynching. A terrible lesson. Tragic death of one of the City's best Citizens." 1–2, TMs, no date, Campbell Papers. Quote is from *The Roanoke Leader*, 6 November 1884; see also Barnes, *History of Roanoke*, 146.

74. The council noted the six hundred dollars it spent on the detectives in *The Roanoke Leader*, 7 Feb. 1885; information about the reward and citizens' group is from *The Roanoke Leader*, 6, 13 Nov. 1884.

75. Information on the Wilsons is from Town Council of Roanoke, "Census of the Town of Roanoke, December 1883," vol. 2, VR-RCPL; Campbell, "Roanoke's Tragedies," 1–2; *The Roanoke Leader*, 6 Nov. 1884; Barnes, *History of Roanoke*, 146.

76. Campbell, "Roanoke's Tragedies," 1.

77. *The Roanoke Leader,* 20 Nov. 1884.

78. Quote is from Bruce, *Southwest Virginia,* 138; information about the posses is from Campbell, "Roanoke's Tragedies," 2 and *The Roanoke Leader,* 13 Nov. 1884.

79. *The Roanoke Leader,* 20 Dec. 1884.

80. Ibid., 25 Apr., 9 May 1885. After the arrests, Roanoke's city council was confident enough in a guilty verdict to withdraw its reward for information about the killers. See Roanoke City Council Minutes, 6 June 1885, Clerk's Office, Roanoke City Municipal Building.

81. *The Wytheville Enterprise,* qtd. in *The Roanoke Leader,* 21 Nov. 1885.

82. Quote and black protection from *The Lynchburg Advance,* rpt. in *The Roanoke Leader,* 13 Feb. 1886.

83. Information about the jury is from *The Roanoke Leader,* 2 Jan; 13 Feb. 1886; information about the outcome of the trail is from Campbell, "Roanoke's Tragedies," 2; and Barnes, *History of Roanoke,* 146.

84. See listings for fifteen saloons on Railroad Avenue between Henry and Holiday Streets in *Haddock & Baily's Roanoke City Directory 1888,* 145–46; and *Haddock's Roanoke Va. City Directory 1890* (Richmond: T. M. Haddock, 1890), 256–57.

85. Stories about crime in the district appear regularly throughout the early and mid-1880s; for early examples, see *The Roanoke Leader,* 21 Dec. 1882; 6, 27 March; 21 Aug. 1884.

86. See black-owned bars and snack houses, along with "hell's half acre" appellation, in *The Roanoke Times,* 23 Dec. 1890.

87. *Roanoke Daily Times,* 1 Feb. 1890.

88. Ibid., 4 Feb. 1890.

89. Ibid., 19 April; 11 July 1890.

90. Ibid., 22 July; 25 Sept. 1890.

91. Ibid., 2, 30 Oct. 1890.

92. Ibid., 9 Dec. 1890.

93. Information about the Massie murder is from William C. Campbell, "Roanoke's Tragedies," 5; *The Roanoke Times,* 23, 24 Dec. 1890 (quote from 24 Dec).

94. *The Roanoke Times,* 24, 27 Dec. 1890 (quote from 27 Dec).

95. Ibid., 28 Dec. 1890.

96. Ibid., 30 Dec. 1890.

97. Ibid., 30 Dec. 1890.

98. Ibid., 1 Jan. 1891.

99. Ibid., 14 Jan; 13, 14 Feb. 1891.

100. Campbell, "Roanoke's Tragedies," 5.

101. William C. Campbell, "1891 Sermon," Heritage Room, First Presbyterian Church, Roanoke, rpt. in McDaniel, "Dr. Campbell's Big Lick," 79.

102. *The Roanoke Times,* 21 Jan. 1891.

103. Ibid., 24 Jan. 1891.

104. Ibid., 25 Jan. 1891.

105. See examples in *The Roanoke Times,* 12, 14, 21, 25 February 1891 (quotes from 12, 25 Feb).

106. *The Roanoke Times,* 10 Mar. 1891.

107. Ibid., 21 Apr. 1891.

108. Ruth Rosen, *The Lost Sisterhood: Prostitution in America, 1900–1918* (Baltimore: Johns Hopkins University Press, 1982), 137–68.

109. Information on brothel operators and prostitutes is from *Roanoke Daily Times,* 14 Nov.; 5, 8, 10, 12 Dec. 1889; 23 Jan.; 2 Feb.; 6 June 1890; *The Roanoke Times,* 25 Sept; 1 Oct; 12, 28 Nov.; 23 Dec. 1890; 29 Jan. 1891.

110. Rosen, *The Lost Sisterhood,* 3–6, 69–79; Joel Best, *Controlling Vice: Regulating Brothel Prostitution in St. Louis, 1865–1883* (Columbus: Ohio State University Press, 1998), 3–6, 18–20, 24–34.

111. See, for example, the story of Estelle King's "Narrow Escape from Ruin" in *The Roanoke Times,* 22 Nov. 1890.

112. *The Roanoke Times,* 7 Feb. 1893.

113. *Roanoke Daily Times,* 10, 11, 12 Dec. 1889.

114. Ibid., 14 Jan. 1890.

115. *The Roanoke Times,* 13 Nov. 1890.

116. See letter from "Many Citizens" in *The Roanoke Times,* 6 July 1892.

117. See story in *The Roanoke Times,* 6 July 1892.

118. *The Roanoke Times,* 7 July 1892.

119. See, for example, *The Roanoke Times,* 13 Sept. and 3 Nov. 1892.

120. The process began in early 1892, when the chief of police ordered five bordello operators in "Pot Liquor Flats," an especially impoverished area of the southeast, to move and suggested that they relocate to "Bunker Hill" in Gainesborough. See *The Roanoke Times,* 24 May 1892. "Pot Liquor Flats," according to Barnes, was the section of the southeast east of Campbell Avenue, north of Tazewell Avenue, and mainly on Randolph and Holiday Streets. "Pot Liquor," according to Barnes, was the juice left in a pot after boiling meat or vegetables and was a pejorative intended to indicate that those who survived on such juice were especially poor. See his *History of Roanoke,* 176–77.

121. Rosen, *The Lost Sisterhood,* 79–80; Best, *Controlling Vice,* 17–18.

122. Numbers with regard to declines in arrests, evictions, and raids on brothels are based on the disappearance of newspaper stories from roughly 1893 to the early 1900s.

123. *Roanoke Saturday News,* 10 June 1882; quote from *Roanoke Commercial Advertiser,* June 1882, both in SVRS5.

124. *The Roanoke Leader,* 27 Dec. 1883.

125. All the information about the volunteer fire brigades comes from William L. Schilling, "Roanoke City Fire Department History, 1882–1983," 1–3, TMs (1983), VR-RCPL; Warren L. Moorman, "Roanoke's First Fire Station," *Journal of the Roanoke Valley Historical Society* 11, no 2 (1982): 32–37; and *The Roanoke Times,* 20 Feb. 1893.

126. Details about the fair are available in *The Roanoke Times,* 19, 24 Apr. and 4 May 1892.

127. Tompkins, "Medical Annals of Roanoke," 8–11 (quote from pages 8–9).

128. See *Roanoke Daily Times,* 14, 18 Jan; 2, 15 Mar.; 10 Apr.; 6, 12 May; 29 June; 1, 22, 29 Aug. 1890; *The Roanoke Times,* 7, 31 Oct.; 18 Nov. 1890 (first quote from 18 Jan.; second quote from 2 Mar.; third quote from 29 June; fourth quote from 22 Aug.; fifth quote from 1 Aug.; sixth quote from 29 Aug.; last quote from 7 Oct.).

129. *Roanoke Daily Times,* 27 Feb. 1890.

130. Ibid., 16 Apr. 1890.

131. Ibid., 15 June 1890; *The Roanoke Times,* 4, 5 Oct. 1890. Ironically, that autumn the drama "After Dark" announced its arrival in town with ads featuring a train bearing down on a pedestrian who had fallen on the tracks. "The Great Railroad Scene" was, the ad promised, all part of "The Funniest Act in Existence." See ad announcing upcoming play in *Roanoke Daily Times,* 28 Aug. 1890.

132. Tompkins, "Medical Annals of Roanoke," 11–12 (quote is from page 12); Moorman, "Roanoke Valley Medicine," 32. The King's Daughters kept their Home for the Sick open by holding charity entertainments. In early 1893, for example, they presented a "series of living charades" and raised four hundred dollars, and in May that year, they staged an elaborate "Columbian Bazaar" that netted another three hundred and fifty dollars. See *The Roanoke Times,* 4, 7 Feb. and 14, 24 May 1893

133. Bond vote published in *The Roanoke Times,* 19 Feb. 1890.

134. *Roanoke Daily Herald,* 28 June 1890.

135. For Roanoke Hospital Association and donations, see *Roanoke Daily Times,* 21 Aug. 1890.

136. *The Roanoke Times,* 5 Oct. 1890.

137. Tompkins, "Medical Annals of Roanoke," 12–13; Moorman, "Roanoke Valley Medicine," 32–33; *The Roanoke Times,* 31 May and 30 June 1893.

138. See *The Roanoke Times,* 7, 9 June 1893. For railroad support for Democrats and opposition to regulation, see Moger, *Virginia: Bourbonism to Byrd,* 95–121.

Chapter 3

1. *The New York Times*, 21 Jan. 1887.

2. Information on production is from *The Roanoke Leader*, 3 July and 7 Aug. 1884; details of wage cut available in *The Roanoke Leader*, 4 Sept. 1884; information about the hour cuts is in Altoona, PA *Tribune*, qtd. in *The Roanoke Leader*, 30 Oct. 1884. For layoffs, see Mayor John Dunstan's address to the city council in *The Roanoke Leader*, 7 Feb. 1885.

3. *The Fidelity Insurance, Trust and Safe Deposit Company, vs. The Shenandoah Valley Railroad Company* (n.p.: Privately printed, 1886), 1–18; Striplin, *The Norfolk & Western*, 51. William Hicks Travers was the SVR's counsel for the court case.

4. See Daniel C. Moomaw letter to editor of *The Roanoke Leader*, 29 Nov. 1884.

5. William C. Campbell, "A Trip to Missouri," 1, TMs, no date, Campbell Papers.

6. The information on Rorer and Waid is from Barnes, *History of Roanoke*, 148–49.

7. See Mayor John Dunstan's address to the city council in *The Roanoke Leader*, 7 Feb. 1885; Bruce, *Southwest Virginia*, 138.

8. Information on both contracts is from *The Roanoke Leader*, 2 Jan. 1886; Bruce, *Southwest Virginia*, 138; and Victor S. Clark, *History of Manufacturers in the United States, 1860–1914* (Washington, DC: Carnegie Institution of Washington, 1928), 339–40.

9. *The Virginian*, 6 Dec. 1885, in SVRS4.

10. William Hicks Travers, Diary Number Eight, 11 Oct. 1886, William Hicks Travers Papers, VHS.

11. For locomotive and car construction in the 1880s, see *Roanoke Daily Times*, 19 Aug. 1890.

12. *Roanoke Daily Times*, 18 May 1890; *The Roanoke Times*, 9 Dec. 1892.

13. *Roanoke Daily Times*, 11 Jan. 1890.

14. Information about the N&W is from Jacobs, *History of Roanoke City*, 146–47, 150–51, 163–64; Striplin, *The Norfolk & Western*, 62.

15. Norfolk & Western Railroad Company, *Reference Book of the Norfolk & Western Railroad Co. Outlining the Condition of Progress in Mining, Manufacturers and Agriculture and the Undeveloped Resources of those Portions of the State of Virginia Traversed by its Line* (New York: Giles, [1889]).

16. Clark, *History of Manufacturers*, 212.

17. See interview with Charles G. Eddy in *The New York Times*, 20 Sept. 1890.

18. *Roanoke Daily Times*, 7 May 1890. For additional examples, see *The Roanoke Leader*, 31 May 1883 and *Roanoke Daily Times*, 23 Nov.; 4 Dec. 1889.

19. Woodward, *Origins of the New South, 1877–1913*, 111–41; Ayers, *Promise of a New South*, 103–31; Gaston, *The New South Creed*, 189–204; Goldfield, *Cotton Fields and Skyscrapers*, 80–132.

20. Woodward, *Origins of the New South*, 152–60; Doyle, *New Men, New Cities, New South*, xi–xiii, 87–95; Flamming, *Creating the Modern South*, 36–51; Carlton, *Mill and Town in South Carolina*, 13–26; Tom Lee, *The Tennessee-Virginia Tri-Cities: Urbanization in Appalachia, 1900–1950* (Knoxville: University of Tennessee Press, 2005), 34–36, 63–69.

21. For Southwest Virginia boosterism, see guides cited in Lester J. Cappon, *Bibliography of Virginia History Since 1865* (Charlottesville: University of Virginia, 1930), 193–257; for description of New South rhetoric, see Gaston, *New South Creed*, 47–114; for industrial boom in Appalachia, see Eller, *Miners, Millhands, and Mountaineers*, 41–59; Shifflett, *Coal Towns*, 3–21; Henry D. Shapiro, *Appalachia on our Mind: The Southern Mountains and Mountaineers in the American Consciousness, 1870–1920* (Chapel Hill: University of North Carolina Press, 1978), 157–85; Lee, *The Tennessee-Virginia Tri-Cities*, 29–52; for results of boom in Virginia, see Moger, *Virginia: Bourbonism to Byrd*, 124–37.

22. For the colonialist and exploitive model, see Eller, *Miners, Millhands, and Mountaineers;* John Gaventa, *Power and Powerlessness: Quiescence and Rebellion in an Appalachian Valley* (Urbana: University of Illinois Press, 1980), 258–60; Helen M. Lewis and Edward Kniper, "The Colonialism Model: The Appalachian Case," in Helen Lewis, Linda Johnson, and Donald Atkins, eds., *Colonialism in Modern America: The Appalachian Case* (Boone, NC: Appalachian Consortium Press, 1978), 22–23. For a counterargument, see Shifflett, *Coal Towns*, 3–12, chap. 1.

23. The best example of this thesis is Eller, *Miners, Millhands, and Mountaineers*, 45–85. Eller, for example, argues "Almost overnight the quiet valley town of Big Lick became the booming industrial town of Roanoke, as the N&W planners used that community as the headquarters for their assault on the nearby mountains" (quote from p. 70); for a counterargument, see Edward L. Ayers, "Northern Business and the Shape of Southern Progress: The Case of Tennessee's 'Model City,'" *Tennessee Historical Quarterly* 39, no. 2 (Summer 1980): 208–22, especially 218.

24. *Roanoke Daily Times*, 10 Jan. 1890; for Atlanta example, see Goldfield, *Cotton Fields and Skyscrapers*, 119–20.

25. Bruce, *Southwest Virginia*, 141.

26. Allen W. Moger, "The Rebuilding of the Old Dominion: A Study in Economic, Social, and Political Transition from 1880 to 1902," Ph. D. diss., Columbia University, 1940, 31–32.

27. *Manufacturers' Record*, 22 Dec. 1888.

28. *The New York Times*, 21 Jan. 1887.

29. See notices of arrival in *Roanoke Daily Times*, 10, 12, 25 Jan.; 14 May 1890.

30. Biographical information on Trout and Terry is from: *The Roanoke Leader*, 24 July 1886; Jacobs, *History of Roanoke City*, 168–71; McCauley, *History of Roanoke County, Salem, Roanoke City*, 383–84; WPA, *Roanoke: Story of County and City*, 85, 132, 135; Barnes, *History of Roanoke*, 19, 73, 75, 89, 92, 96, 98–99, 100, 103, 112, 125–26, 130, 163–64, 170, 186, 207, 212–13, 231–32, 235, 322; White, *Roanoke 1740–1982*, 53, 58, 63, 65, 75.

31. Doyle, *New Men, New Cities, New South,* 19, 87–95, 136–53, 268.

32. *The Roanoke Times,* 16 Oct. 1890; for Midland Iron Company, see *The Roanoke Leader,* 19 Nov. 1890.

33. *Baltimore Sun,* qtd. in *Roanoke Daily Times,* 27 Nov. 1889.

34. For similarity to Birmingham labor supply, see Gordon B. McKinney, "The Blair Committee Investigation of 1883: Industrialization in the Appalachian Mountains," *Appalachian Journal: A Regional Studies Review* 26, no. 2 (Winter 1999): 158–59.

35. For push of countryside and pull of cities in Appalachia, see Shifflett, *Coal Towns,* 3–12, chap. 1; John Alexander Williams, *Appalachia: A History* (Chapel Hill: University of North Carolina Press, 2002), 218; for attraction of cities in South and similar labor paradigm, see Louis M. Kyriakoudes, *The Social Origins of the Urban South: Race, Gender, and Migration in Nashville and Middle Tennessee, 1890–1930* (Chapel Hill: University of North Carolina Press, 2003), 47–48, 96–98, 102–23; for cyclical poverty of tenant farming or sharecropping in rural Virginia as well as the pull of nearby cities as a way out, see Crandall A. Shifflett, *Patronage and Poverty in the Tobacco South: Louisa County, Virginia, 1860–1900* (Knoxville: University of Tennessee Press, 1982), 39–56, 84–103.

36. United States Bureau of the Census, *Historical Statistics of the United States, I* (Washington, DC: Government Printing Office, 1976), 36; John L. Androit, ed., *Population Abstract of the United States* (McLean, VA: Androit Associates, 1980), 854–55.

37. *Roanoke Daily Times,* 19 July 1890.

38. Data compiled from United States Bureau of the Census, U.S. Census of 1880, Schedule of Population, Town of Big Lick, County of Roanoke, State of Virginia; Town Council of Roanoke, "Census of the Town of Roanoke, December 1883," vol. 1 and 2, VR-RCPL; U.S. Bureau of the Census, *Report on Population of the United States at the Eleventh Census: 1890, Part 1,* 389, 483; *Sholes' Directory of the City of Roanoke, November 1st, 1892,* data rpt. in *The Roanoke Times,* 20 Oct. 1892.

39. Quote and information on the Development Company are from *The Roanoke Times,* 12 Sept. 1891; see also *The Roanoke Leader,* 25 Nov. 1892. The Norwich Company had relocated from Connecticut and was at the time the only lock manufacturing plant in the South.

40. Quote is from *The Roanoke Times,* 14 Nov. 1891.

41. Information on the gas and water companies comes from *The Roanoke Leader,* 21 May 1883; Roanoke Land & Improvement Company, Second Annual Report, rpt. in *The Roanoke Leader,* 17 Jan. 1884. The RL&IC already operated a small gas plant to light the hotel, depot, and railroad offices but had no plans to offer its services to the rest of town.

42. *The Roanoke Leader,* 15 Nov. 1883.

43. William Hicks Travers, Diary Number Nine, 22 Apr. 1887, William Hicks Travers Papers, VHS.

44. Jacobs, *History of Roanoke City*, 121–22; Barnes, *History of Roanoke*, 163. A *New York Times* correspondent thought the water monopoly was dangerous and observed that it was possible "Roanoke will find herself paying dearly for the mistake." See 21 Jan. 1887 edition.

45. Raymond P. Barnes, "Roanoke Valley's Early Iron Mines," *Journal of the Roanoke Historical Society* 3, no. 2 (Winter 1967): 25–26.

46. For details about the mule railway and "hay burner" quote, see Recollections of Henry S. Trout in *The* (Roanoke) *World News*, 8 May 1913; see also, WPA, *Roanoke: Story of County and City*, 194–95; for problems and improvements, see *The Roanoke Times*, 15 June and 15 July 1892 (quote is from 15 June); for eventual expansion of the line, see all above plus Roanoke Street Railway schedule dated 10 Sept. 1894, J. Ambler Johnston Papers, VHS; for absorbing the electric company and becoming The Roanoke Street Railway and Electric Company, see Jacobs, *History of Roanoke City*, 113–14.

47. Information on the early history of the Roanoke & Southern comes from *The Roanoke Leader*, 6 Feb. and 3, 24, Apr. 1886; freeholder vote on purchasing stock is in *The Roanoke Leader*, 29 Apr. 1886.

48. *Roanoke Daily Times*, 22 Nov. 1889; see also 11 Dec. 1889; 9 Jan. 1890.

49. Ibid., 11 Jan. 1890.

50. Ibid., 19 Feb. 1890. The vote on bonds for the hospital was 312 to 178, 2 percent below the 66 percent required. The vote on bonds for the police building was 120 to 333.

51. N&W lease is from *The Roanoke Times*, 17 Mar. 1892, in Norfolk & Western Scrapbook no. 16, N&WRA; Jacobs, *History of Roanoke City*, 97, 151–52; reason for lease is from Lambie, *From Mine to Market*, 44.

52. Qtd. in *Roanoke Daily Times*, 5 Jan. 1890.

53. *Roanoke Daily Times*, 27 May 1890. Trout and Terry were charter members and on the Board of Directors, as were Joseph Sands, James Simmons, E. H. Stewart, James Gambill, and Dr. J. A. Gale.

54. *The Roanoke Times*, 28 Sept. 1890.

55. Ibid., 16 Oct. 1890.

56. Ibid., 20 Nov. 1890. Helper was apparently in good enough health to make several land deals in Petersburg in the days after he resigned. Additional details about the "scandal" are available in *The Roanoke Times*, 22, 29 Nov. 1890. Helper, the (in)famous author of *The Impending Crisis of the South: How to Meet It* (1857), eventually continued work on his longtime scheme to link Canada, the United States, and South America with a railroad before ending up utterly impoverished and mentally unstable. He committed suicide in a Washington DC boarding house in 1909. See Hugh C. Bailey, *Hinton Rowan Helper: Abolitionist-Racist* (Tuscaloosa: University of Alabama, 1965), 174–96; see also David Brown, *Southern Outcast: Hinton Rowan Helper and "The Impending Crisis of the South"* (Baton Rouge: Louisiana State University Press, 2006).

57. *The Roanoke Times*, 2, 3 Dec. 1890. Eventually the Roanoke Real Estate Exchange took over the lease on the Club's rooms.

58. Frank H. Taylor, *The City of Roanoke, Virginia: Containing an Outline of its Environment, Resources, Development, Prospects and Substantial Inducements to Capital in the Year 1890* (New York City: The Giles Company, 1890), 1–47. (First quote page 28; second and third quotes page 3; fourth, fifth, and sixth quotes page 12; seventh quote pages 12, 14; eighth, ninth, tenth, eleventh quotes page 9; twelfth and thirteenth quotes page 14.) The Club mailed out 350 copies of the pamphlet in October 1890 alone. See *The Roanoke Times*, 16 Oct. 1890. This was apparently Roanoke's first booster guide.

59. F. P. Smith, *A Synopsis of Roanoke and Her Wonderful Prosperity* (Roanoke: W. M. Yeager & Co., Real Estate Brokers, 1891), 1–50. (First quote page 23; second quote page 4; third and fourth quotes page 5; fifth quote page 8; sixth quote page 22.) Using humble origins and amazing growth to sell the future was a common booster tactic. See Stuart Seely Sprague, "The Great Appalachian Iron and Coal Town Boom of 1889–1893," *Appalachian Journal* 4, numbers 3 and 4 (Spring–Summer 1977), 218.

60. Terry & Pope, *Roanoke, Virginia, in 1891. Its investment opportunities. Its manufacturing advantages. Its transportation services. Its trade facilities. Its home attractions* (Roanoke: Hammond Printing Works, 1891).

61. See full-page ad in *The Roanoke Times*, 22 Jan. 1891; for Roanoke being commonly known by the appellation, see Bruce, *Southwest Virginia*, 132. Throughout the South, boosters created memorable epithets for their towns to aid in selling the place to investors. Birmingham, Alabama, Middlesborough, Kentucky, and Kingsport, Tennessee, also frequently used "Magic City." Locals continued to bill Roanoke as the Magic City well into the twentieth century. The city dubbed athletic teams from its Jefferson High School "The Magicians," and today Magic City continues to appear in the names of a few local businesses.

62. For *The Iron Belt*, see Cappon, *Virginia Newspapers, 1821–1935*, 196; Warren, *History of Newspapers Published in 23 Counties of Southwest Virginia*, 14; as well as the only two extant copies of the journal known to be in existence (February and Apr. 1892), housed in VR-RCPL.

63. Roanoke Booster Speech, TMs circa 1890, author unidentified, Jordan-Stabler Family Papers, VHS.

64. Doyle, *New Men, New Cities, New South*, 189–225; Flamming, *Creating the Modern South*, 36–51; Carlton, *Mill and Town*, 8–13.

65. See RL&IC ad in *The Roanoke Leader*, 9 Oct. 1884.

66. For lot costs and sale prices, see "Unsold Lots—Land Agents Value of Property at Roanoke, Apr. 15, 1884," 1–17, Roanoke Land & Improvement Company Records, HMHSWV.

67. Strategy recounted in *The New York Times*, 21 Jan. 1887.

68. Price increase is from Reverend William C. Campbell's, "1885 Anniversary Sermon," Heritage Room, First Presbyterian Church, Roanoke, rpt. in McDaniel, "Dr. Campbell's Big Lick," 78.

69. William C. Campbell, Roanoke, to Editor of *The Central* (location unknown), 12 Mar. 1886, Campbell Papers.

70. Jacobs, *History of Roanoke City,* 96.

71. Recollections of Henry S. Trout in *The* (Roanoke) *World News,* 8 May 1913.

72. *The New York Times,* 21 Jan. 1887.

73. *Manufacturers' Record,* 22 Dec. 1888.

74. Gordon Blair, "Memories of the Land Boom in the Western Part of Virginia," 1–8, TMs (July 1958), VHS; Moger, "Rebuilding of the Old Dominion," 34–42; Sprague, "The Great Appalachian Iron and Coal Town Boom," 216–22; Stuart Seely Sprague, "Investing in Appalachia: The Virginia Valley Boom of 1889–1893," *Virginia Cavalcade* (Winter 1975), 134–43; Robert Weise, "Big Stone Gap and the New South, 1880–1900," in *The Edge of the South: Life in Nineteenth-Century Virginia,* ed. Edward L. Ayers and John C. Willis (Charlottesville: University Press of Virginia, 1991), 173–93.

75. *The Salem Times-Register,* 26 Nov. 1889 "Supplement Edition" and 13 Dec. 1889 edition, both in Norfolk & Western Scrapbook no. 10, N&WRA.

76. Blair, "Memories of the Land Boom," 4.

77. Moger, "Rebuilding of the Old Dominion," 38–40.

78. Blair, "Memories of the Land Boom," 2.

79. Moger, "Rebuilding of the Old Dominion," 40–41; Sprague, "Great Appalachian Iron and Coal Town Boom," 220.

80. Henry Watterson of the *Louisville Courier-Journal,* qtd. in *Roanoke Daily Times,* 3 May 1890.

81. Bruce, *Southwest Virginia,* 140.

82. McCauley, *History of Roanoke County, Salem, Roanoke City, Va.,* 158.

83. Moger, "Rebuilding of the Old Dominion," 31–32, 38.

84. See Gray & Boswell ad in *Roanoke Daily Times,* 22 Feb. 1890.

85. For first quote, see James S. Simmons & Co. ad in *Roanoke Daily Times,* 20 Feb. 1890; for other quotes, see ads in *Roanoke Daily Times,* 20 Apr. and 21 Mar. 1890.

86. See Dyer & Wingfield ad in *Roanoke Daily Times,* 21 Mar. 1890.

87. This sales tactic was repeated throughout the region. See Moger, "Rebuilding of the Old Dominion," 38; Sprague, "Great Appalachian Iron and Coal Town Boom," 219–21.

88. Information on the various land companies comes from Recollections of Henry S. Trout in *The* (Roanoke) *World News,* 8 May 1913; Bruce, *Southwest*

Virginia, 140. Numerous Roanoke neighborhoods today bear the name of these and other long forgotten land firms.

89. Information on the West End is from *Roanoke Daily Times,* 21 Mar. and 3 May 1890 and *The Roanoke Times,* 14 June 1892; "Reminiscences of Martha Tinsley Taylor," in Sydney Taylor Alexander, *Elmwood of Roanoke* (Washington, DC: By the author, 1958), 15; quote is from Taylor, *The City of Roanoke, Virginia,* 11.

90. Information about the company and quotes are from *Roanoke Daily Times,* 21 Mar. 1890.

91. Information on the company comes from "1890 Buena Vista Land Company Map and Brochure," VR-RCPL.

92. *Roanoke Daily Times,* 21 Feb. 1890.

93. Ibid., 4 Mar. 1890.

94. "Roanoke Land & Improvement Company Sales Book June 1889–May 1906," 58, 44, 53, 84, Roanoke Land & Improvement Company Records, N&WRA.

95. Details about the Woodland Park sale and "Kimball Tower" are available in "Roanoke Land & Improvement Company Sales Book June 1889–May 1906," 62; *The Roanoke Times,* 16, 17, 18 Oct. 1890; Barnes, *History of Roanoke,* 213–14; and Carolyn Hale Bruce, *Roanoke: A Pictorial History* (Norfolk: Donning Co.,1976), 74.

96. *The Roanoke Herald,* 16 Oct. 1890, in Norfolk & Western Scrapbook no. 12, N&WRA.

97. *The Roanoke Times,* 5 May 1901. In the end, the city gave up its claim to the land, and eventually the park became a residential neighborhood. Roanoke moved the development's long-hidden "Kimball Tower" to Elmwood Park in 1982.

98. For the land boom in Roanoke reaching its height in the fall of 1890, see Blair, "Memories of the Land Boom in the Western Part of Virginia," 7–8; and see number of transactions per month and total value of sales in 1890 in *The Roanoke Times,* 1 Jan. 1891; for the December blizzard, see *The Roanoke Times,* 24 Dec. 1890; for the storm's effect on speculation and Trout's quote, see Recollections of Henry S. Trout in *The* (Roanoke) *World News,* 12 May 1913, as well as Jacobs, *History of Roanoke,* 97. The blizzard also chilled local investments in boomtowns nearby; see Sprague, "Investing in Appalachia," 142.

99. *The Roanoke Times,* 22 Jan. 1891.

100. For real estate assessments, see McCauley, *History of Roanoke County, Salem, Roanoke City,* 159; for additional evidence of the overall decline in sales, see "Roanoke Land & Improvement Company Sales Book June 1889–May 1906," 1–125. The first hundred pages of the sales book represent transactions in 1889 and 1890, while the following twenty-five pages cover all sales for the ensuing ten years.

101. See Recollections of Henry S. Trout in *The* (Roanoke) *World News,* 8, 12 May 1913 (quote is from 12 May edition); see also Gordon Blair, "Memories of the Land Boom in the Western Part of Virginia," 8.

102. Sprague, "Investing in Appalachia," 142.

103. Information on the company is from "1890 Janette Land Company Stock Certificate," in Richard Singleton Paulett Papers, VHS; quote is from "Report of the President of the Janette Land Company," 26 May 1891, in Alfred J. Morrison Papers, LVA (hereafter cited as Morrison Papers).

104. Information and 1892 quote are from "Report of the President of the Janette Land Company," 24 May 1892, Morrison Papers; the 1899 stock call and quote are from "Call in Stock by the Secretary of the Janette Land Company," 25 July 1899, Morrison Papers.

105. Morrison's stock coupon receipts are in the receipts file of his Papers at the Library of Virginia; quote is from John M. Hart, "Hart & Hart Attorneys at Law," Terry Building, Roanoke, to Alfred J. Morrison, Esquire, Long Island, NY, 9 Aug. 1904, Morrison Papers. See also Richard A. Irving, 31 Nassau St., New York City, to Alfred Morrison, Esquire, 120 West 49th Street, New York City, 28 May 1904, Morrison Papers.

106. Quote and information from "Report of the Secretary of the Janette Land Company," 25 May 1905, Morrison Papers.

107. For statistics on growth of Roanoke compared to the entire U.S. and Virginia, see Larsen, *The Rise of the Urban South*, 155, 157; for comparison to production elsewhere in Virginia, see statistics in Moger, "Industrial and Urban Progress in Virginia," 311–23; for most southern cities relying on agricultural processing, see Goldfield, *Cotton Fields and Skyscrapers*, 90–91.

Chapter 4

1. U.S. Bureau of the Census, *Report on the United States at the Eleventh Census 1890*, 389, 483, 823; employment statistics and pay from Smith, *A Synopsis of Roanoke and her Wonderful Prosperity*, 12, 28; railroad worker pay is from "N. & W. Accounting Department Personal Records No. 1 Feb. 1874 to December 1901," N&WRA.

2. William C. Campbell, Roanoke, to Editor, *Central*, 12 Mar. 1886, Campbell Papers.

3. Malcolm W. Bryan, Roanoke, to C. M. Zink, Roanoke, 10 Aug. 1895, Malcolm W. Bryan Papers, VR-RCPL (cited hereafter as Bryan Papers).

4. Margaret Mary Myer, "Father Lynch Founder," 3–8, TMs (1941), Emma B. Lynch Papers, VHS.

5. Julia F. (Harris) Via, Roanoke, to "Sister," Susan M. (Harris) Ward, Albemarle County, Virginia, 10 Apr. 1893, Harris Family Papers, VHS.

6. "From a Son of Old Virginia," Roanoke, to William C. Campbell, Roanoke, 3 May 1884, Campbell Papers.

7. For an explanation of the role and culture of the late-nineteenth-century saloon, see Roy Rosenzweig, *Eight Hours for What We Will: Workers and Leisure in an Industrial City, 1870–1920* (Cambridge: Cambridge University Press, 1983), chap. 2;

McKiven, *Iron and Steel*, chap. 4; Ted Ownby, *Subduing Satan: Religion, Recreation, and Manhood in the Rural South, 1865–1920*. The Fred W. Morrison Series in Southern Studies (Chapel Hill: University of North Carolina Press, 1990), 38–41; Philip Thomason, "The Men's Quarter of Downtown Nashville," *Tennessee Historical Quarterly* 41, no. 1 (Spring 1982): 48–55.

8. See statistics published in *The Roanoke Times*, 6 May 1893.

9. See saloon ads in *Roanoke Daily Times*, 20 Apr. 1890; *The Roanoke Leader*, 11 July 1885; *Roanoke Daily Times*, 11 May 1890; *The Roanoke Times*, 8 Apr. 1892. For descriptions of typical late-nineteenth-century barrooms, see Jon M. Kingsdale, "The 'Poor Man's Club': Social Functions of the Urban Working-Class Saloon," *American Quarterly* 25, no. 4 (Oct. 1973): 472–86.

10. *The Roanoke Times*, 16 Mar. 1891.

11. Ibid., 17 Apr. 1892.

12. For the larger crusade by Evangelicals against the saloon, see Kingsdale, "The 'Poor Man's Club,'" 487–89; Ownby, *Subduing Satan*, 14–15, 167–74; Thomason, "The Men's Quarter," 55–64.

13. *The Roanoke Leader*, 17 May 1883; additional information on the band is from *The Roanoke Times*, 17 Nov. 1892.

14. *The Roanoke Leader*, 24 July 1884.

15. *The* (Roanoke) *Daily Bee*, 6 July 1892; for the role of parks in defusing class tensions, see Rosenzweig, *Eight Hours for What We Will*, chap. 5.

16. *The Roanoke Leader*, 2 Jan. 1886.

17. *Roanoke Daily Times*, 31 Aug. 1890.

18. Ibid., 27 May 1890.

19. Steve Goodson, *Highbrows, Hillbillies, and Hellfire: Public Entertainment in Atlanta, 1880–1930* (Athens: University of Georgia Press, 2002), 56–76; see also Lawrence Levine, *Highbrow/Lowbrow: The Emergence of Cultural Hierarchy in America* (Cambridge: Harvard University Press, 1988).

20. *The Roanoke Times*, 29 Nov. 1890.

21. *Roanoke Daily Times*, 18 May 1890.

22. Ibid., 11 July 1890.

23. *The Roanoke Times*, 26 Oct. 1890.

24. Ibid., 16 Mar. 1891.

25. See story about slag dumped on "colored tramp" in *The Roanoke Times*, 31 Oct. 1893.

26. Background on Bryan is from Malcolm W. Bryan III, "The Early Days at Hotel Roanoke," 1–5, TMs, Bryan Papers; undated Raymond Barnes article on Bryan in *The Roanoke Times*, in Bryan Papers; and Town Council of Roanoke, "Census of Town of Roanoke, December 1883," vol. 2, VR-RCPL, which lists Bryan along with

railroad executives W. W. Coe and Joseph Sands as residing at the Hotel Roanoke; Malcolm W. Bryan, Hotel Roanoke, to Ann DeHaven, Philadelphia, 16 Sept. 1885, qtd. in Bryan III, "Early Days at Hotel," 2.

27. Malcolm W. Bryan, Hotel Roanoke, to Ann DeHaven, Philadelphia (Fall 1885), qtd. in Bryan III, "Early Days at Hotel," 2.

28. *The Roanoke Leader,* 29 May; 17 July 1886; WPA, *Roanoke: Story of County and City,* 262.

29. WPA, *Roanoke: Story of County and City,* 263–65; Barnes, *History of Roanoke,* 159.

30. *The Roanoke Times,* 20 Feb. 1893.

31. Ibid., 4 June 1893.

32. See courses listed on Virginia College for Young Ladies, Official Report Card of Miss Bessie Linkous, Oct. 1893, Linkous Family Papers, VHS.

33. Malcolm W. Bryan, Roanoke, to C. D. Epes, Crewe, Virginia, 13 Mar. 1894, Bryan Papers.

34. *The Roanoke Leader,* 2 Aug. 1883.

35. Ibid., 16 Aug. 1883.

36. Origins of the society are from Roanoke German Club, *Roanoke German Club Golden Anniversary Ball 1884–1934* (Roanoke: Privately printed, 1934), in HMHSWV; *The Roanoke Leader,* 27 Dec. 1883.

37. *Roanoke Daily Times,* 9 Nov. 1889.

38. Roanoke German Club, *Roanoke German Club Golden Anniversary Ball.*

39. Occupation and addresses of active members derived from cross-listing names in Roanoke German Club, *Constitution and By-Laws of the Friday German Club of Roanoke, Virginia* (Roanoke: Stone Printing & Mfg. Co, 1892), 17–18, with *Williams' City Directory of Roanoke, Virginia, 1891–1892* (Binghamton, NY: J. E. Williams, 1891); rules are from *Constitution and By-Laws,* 3–18 (first quote is from 3; second is from 15).

40. *The Roanoke Times,* 31 Jan. 1893.

41. Ibid., 4 Feb. 1893.

42. See letters of recommendation in Notice of Eligibility—Special Examination, U. S. Civil Service Commission, Washington, D. C., 10 Dec. 1888, in letters to William Churchill Noland, Noland Family Papers, UVA (cited hereafter as Noland Family Papers).

43. William C. Noland, Hotel Roanoke, to Mrs. Mary E. Noland, Hanover County, Virginia, 7 Jan. 1891, William Churchill Noland Papers, VHS (cited hereafter as William C. Noland Papers).

44. William C. Noland, Roanoke, to Mrs. Mary E. Noland, Hanover County, Virginia, 12 Jan. 1891, William C. Noland Papers.

45. Ibid., 18 Jan. 1891, William C. Noland Papers.

46. Ibid., 25 Jan. 1891, William C. Noland Papers.

47. Ibid., 15 Feb. 1891, William C. Noland Papers.

48. Ibid., 1 Mar. 1891, William C. Noland Papers.

49. Ibid., 8 Mar. 1891, William C. Noland Papers.

50. Ibid., 5, 12 Apr. 1891, William C. Noland Papers.

51. Roanoke Hospital Memoranda Book, Memoranda Books of William C. Noland, Noland Family Papers; see also ad for Noland that lists the Roanoke Hospital as one of his buildings in *Sholes' Directory of the City of Roanoke, November 1, 1892* (Roanoke: Stone Printing & Mfg. Co., 1892), inside front cover.

52. William C. Noland, Roanoke, to Mrs. Mary E. Noland, Hanover County, Virginia, 10 May 1891, William C. Noland Papers.

53. Ibid., 19 Apr. 1891, 21 June 1891, William C. Noland Papers.

54. Ibid., 31 May 1891, William C. Noland Papers.

55. Ibid., 7 June 1891, 29 June 1891, William C. Noland Papers.

56. Ibid., 5 July 1891, William C. Noland Papers.

57. Roanoke was in the center of the "springs region" of Virginia. Each catered to an upper-class clientele and offered lodging, food, and entertainment in addition to baths in the spring water. See Bruce, *Southwest Virginia*, 135.

58. William C. Noland, Roanoke, to Mrs. Mary E. Noland, Hanover County, Virginia, 5 July 1891, William C. Noland Papers.

59. Ibid., 10 Aug. 1891, William C. Noland Papers.

60. William C. Noland, Alleghany Springs, to Mrs. Mary E. Noland, Hanover County, Virginia, 16 Aug. 1891, William C. Noland Papers.

61. William C. Noland, Roanoke, to Mrs. Mary E. Noland, Hanover County, Virginia, 6 Sept. 1891, William C. Noland Papers.

62. Ibid., 13 Sept. 1891, William C. Noland Papers.

63. Ibid., 25 Oct. 1891, William C. Noland Papers.

64. Ibid., 6 Dec. 1891, William C. Noland Papers.

65. See architecture credit given in *The Roanoke Times*, 8 Oct. 1892.

66. See assorted articles and photos in William Churchill Noland, News clippings and Printed Material File, Noland Family Papers.

67. For an analysis of upper classes in New South cities, see Doyle, *New Men, New Cities, New South*, chap. 8; Goodson, *Highbrows, Hillbillies, and Hellfire*, 1–11, 109–26.

68. *The Roanoke Leader*, 17 July 1886.

69. *Roanoke Daily Times*, 12 Feb. 1892.

70. *The Roanoke Leader*, 4 Sept. 1884.

71. Ibid., 10 Oct. 1885.

72. *The Roanoke Times*, 7 July 1892.

73. Contract between Roanoke Gas & Water Co. and F. D. Booth to Build Mill Mtn Observatory, 25 Aug. 1891, HMHSWV; Contract between Roanoke Gas & Water Co. and F. D. Booth to Build Mill Mtn Tavern, 25 Aug. 1891, HMHSWV.

74. *The Roanoke Times*, 4 May 1892.

75. Ibid., 1 June 1892.

76. See ads in *The Roanoke Leader*, 4 Jan. and 3 May 1883.

77. See Sun's ad in *Roanoke Daily Times*, 6 Nov. 1889.

78. *The Roanoke Times*, 3 Dec. 1890; 15 Feb. 1891; 8 Oct. 1892.

79. For significance of "Opera House" construction in Appalachia, see William Fairfax Condee, *Coal and Culture in Appalachia* (Athens, OH: Ohio University Press, 2005), 14–23.

80. *The Roanoke Times*, 29 Apr. 1892.

81. Roanoke Street Railway 1894 Schedule, J. Ambler Johnston Papers, VHS.

82. *The Roanoke Times*, 29 Nov. 1892.

83. For an analysis of the popularity and criticism of vaudeville and burlesque in the South, see Goodson, *Highbrows, Hillbillies, and Hellfire*, 63–76.

84. *The Roanoke Times*, 12 Dec. 1890.

85. James E. Porter, *1895 Roster of Secret Societies of Roanoke, Virginia* (Roanoke: Hammond Printing Works, 1895), 129.

86. *The Roanoke Times*, 12 Dec. 1890.

87. Ibid., 29 Nov. 1892.

88. Ibid., 9 Apr. 1892.

89. Ibid., 25 Nov. 1892.

90. Ibid., 29 Nov. 1892.

91. Tompkins, "Medical Annals of Roanoke," 10.

92. *Roanoke Daily Times*, 23 Feb. 1890; Tompkins, "Medical Annals," 8.

93. Tompkins, "Medical Annals," 10; "Minutes and Proceedings of the Roanoke Valley Medical Association, Organized in Roanoke, Va. at the Office of Dr. Gordon Simmons, June 10, 1891," VR-RCPL (cited hereafter as RVMA Minutes).

94. RVMA Minutes, 31, 33.

95. Ibid., 17.

96. For examples, see History Committee, First Baptist Church, *An Adventure in Faith: A History of the First Baptist Church of Roanoke, Virginia, 1875–1955* (Roanoke: First Baptist Church of Roanoke, 1955), 135–38; Eugenia M. Keen and Gladys D. Hughes, *History of Christ Episcopal Church, Roanoke, Virginia* (Roanoke:

Christ Episcopal Church of Roanoke, 1961), 7, 33–34; Margaret Mary Maier, "Father Lynch Founder," 7–8, TMs (Apr. 1941), Emma B. Lynch Papers, VHS.

97. *The Roanoke Leader,* 17 July 1884.

98. Ibid., 18 Sept. 1884.

99. *The Roanoke Times,* 14 Jan. 1893.

100. Ibid., 20, 21 Jan. 1893 (first quote is 21 Jan; second is 20 Jan).

101. Ibid., 21 Jan. 1893.

102. See examples in *The Roanoke Times,* 22, 26 Jan. 1893.

103. *The Roanoke Times,* 22, 24 Jan. 1893 (quote is from 22 Jan).

104. Ibid., 27 Jan. 1893.

105. Ibid., 29 Jan. 1893.

106. *Roanoke Daily Record,* 10 Feb. 1893.

107. U.S. Bureau of the Census, *Eleventh Census 1890,* 389, 483, 823; *Haddock's Roanoke Va. City Directory 1890,* 270–333; Barnes, *History of Roanoke,* 188, 263; Baratta, "Gainesboro Neighborhood, 1890–1940," 40; George R. Heller, *A Narrative for the Proposed Historic Gainesboro Preservation District,* ed. Helen Davis and Evelyn Davis Bethel (Roanoke: Privately printed, 1991), 17. For similar housing and segregation patterns in the rest of the South, see Howard N. Rabinowitz, *Race Relations in the Urban South, 1865–1890* (New York: Oxford University Press, 1978), 98–124; Thomas W. Hanchett, *Sorting Out the New South City: Race, Class, and Urban Development in Charlotte, 1875–1975* (Chapel Hill: University of North Carolina Press, 1998), 14–45, 116–22.

108. U.S. Bureau of the Census, *Eleventh Census 1890,* 823; Smith, *A Synopsis of Roanoke,* 12; Rabinowitz, *Race Relations,* 61–71; McKiven, *Iron and Steel,* chap. 3.

109. *Haddock & Baily's Roanoke Va. City Directory 1888,* 132, 138–39, 146; Heller, *Proposed Historic Gainesboro Preservation District,* 17.

110. *Haddock's Roanoke Va. City Directory 1890,* 247–57; Rabinowitz, *Race Relations,* 78–82.

111. *Roanoke Daily Times,* 10 Jan. 1890.

112. Ibid., 10 May 1890.

113. Ibid., 27 Dec. 1889.

114. Daily, *Before Jim Crow,* chaps. 3 and 4.

115. See raid on Morton's saloon reported in *The Roanoke Times,* 18 Oct. 1892.

116. *The Roanoke Times,* 9 Nov. 1890.

117. PPFA, *History of the Roanoke Police Department,* 173.

118. *Roanoke Daily Times,* 12, 13, 14, 16 Nov. 1889.

119. PPFA, *Roanoke Police Department,* 174–75.

120. *The Roanoke Times,* 19 Oct. 1890.

121. Ibid., 22 Oct. 1890.

122. Ibid., 18 Nov. 1890.

123. Ibid., 20 Nov. 1890.

124. Rabinowitz, *Race Relations*, 78–96.

125. Biographical information on Oliver is from Reginald Shareef, *The Roanoke Valley's African American Heritage: A Pictorial History* (Virginia Beach: Donning Company, 1996), 63; Baratta, "Gainesboro Neighborhood," 43; *Haddock's Roanoke Va. City Directory 1890*, 165, 310.

126. Information on Boland and Burrell is from Shareef, *Roanoke Valley's African American Heritage*, 41; Baratta, "Gainesboro Neighborhood," 43.

127. Shareef, *Roanoke Valley's African American Heritage*, 13–14; Baratta, "Gainesboro Neighborhood," 43.

128. WPA, *Roanoke: Story of County and City*, 282–83, 285; Rabinowitz, *Race Relations*, 181.

129. *The Roanoke Leader*, 17 July 1886.

130. *The* (Roanoke) *Daily Bee*, 6 July 1892, in LVA.

131. WPA, *Roanoke: Story of County and City*, 285.

132. Rabinowitz, *Race Relations*, 225; Alison Dorsey, *To Build Our Lives Together: Community Formation in Black Atlanta, 1875–1906* (Athens: University of Georgia Press, 2004), 54–81.

133. Information on the city's black churches is from *Haddock's Roanoke Va. City Directory 1890*; Heller, *Proposed Historic Gainesboro Preservation District*, 12–14; Shareef, *Roanoke Valley's African American Heritage*, 74–75, 81–89; Baratta, "Gainesboro Neighborhood," 44–45. Information on the festivals held by First Baptist is from *The Roanoke Leader*, 2 Jan. 1886.

134. *The Roanoke Leader*, 2 Jan. 1886.

135. *The Roanoke Times*, 21 Feb. 1891.

136. Ibid., 14, 30 Oct. 1892.

137. Ibid., 9 Nov. 1892.

138. See coverage of the event in *The Roanoke Times*, 3 Jan. 1893, as well as a description in Daniel B. Williams, *Emancipation Address: Our Duties and How to Discharge Them, Delivered in the Town Hall of Salem, Va., January 2, 1893, Under the Auspices of the Emancipation Club of Salem, which was joined by the Emancipation Club of Roanoke, Va.* (n.p.: by the author, 1893), 7–10 (quote about Davis is from 7).

139. See, for example, Robert H. Gudmestad, "Baseball, The Lost Cause, and the New South in Richmond, Virginia, 1883–1890," *Virginia Magazine of History and Biography* 106, no. 3 (Summer 1998): 267–300.

140. *The Roanoke Leader*, 17 May 1883.

141. Ibid., 19 Apr. 1883.

142. Gudmestad, "Baseball, The Lost Cause, and the New South in Richmond," 297.

143. *The Roanoke Leader*, 30 Aug. 1883.

144. Ibid., 16 Aug. 1883. Background information on the Roanoke Baseball Association is from *The Roanoke Leader*, 17 July 1886.

145. *The Roanoke Leader*, 15 May 1884.

146. Gudmestad, "Baseball, The Lost Cause, and the New South in Richmond," 298.

147. *Roanoke Daily Times*, 2, 4 May 1890.

148. Ibid., 18 May 1890.

149. Ibid., 21 June 1890.

150. Ibid., 11 May 1890.

151. Ibid., 18 May 1890.

152. William Hicks Travers, Diary Number Nine, 3 June 1887, in William Hicks Travers Papers, VHS.

153. Coverage of the circus, which appears to have been the first one held in the city, is from *The Roanoke Leader*, 21 Aug. 1884; Campbell's observations are from William C. Campbell, "The First Circus in Roanoke," TMs, no date, Campbell Papers.

154. *Roanoke Daily Times*, 20 May 1890.

155. *The Roanoke Times*, 29 Oct. 1890.

156. *Roanoke Daily Times*, 13 Nov. 1889.

157. Ibid., 23 July 1890.

158. Anna (Crickenberger) Brown, Riverside, Tazewell County, Virginia, to "Pa and Sister," Levi Crickenberger and Mollie Crickenberger, Salem, Virginia, 26 Nov. 1888, Crickenberger Family Papers, VHS (cited hereafter as Crickenberger Family Papers).

159. Ibid., (7) Mar. (1889), Crickenberger Family Papers.

160. Ibid., 2 Feb. (1889), Crickenberger Family Papers.

161. Ibid., 19 Apr. (1889), Crickenberger Family Papers.

162. See encouragement in *The Roanoke Leader*, 26 Oct. 1882. Founding of association and membership is from "Minute Book A, The Roanoke Association for the Exhibition and Sale of Live Stock from Virginia and other States," 15 May and 22 Oct. 1883, VR-RCPL (cited hereafter as "Minute Book A, Roanoke Fair Association").

163. Donnie Caffery, Roanoke College, Salem, Virginia, to Donelson Caffery, Franklin Louisiana, 10 Oct. 1883, Caffery Family Papers, Louisiana State University, Special Collections, Hill Memorial Library, Baton Rouge. (The date on this transcribed version of Caffery's handwritten letter is incorrect. The date on the original is likely either 16 or 19 Oct., not 10 Oct. as misread by the typist. The fair occurred between Oct. 16 and 19.)

164. *The Roanoke Leader*, 18 Oct. 1883.

165. *American Volunteer*, 31 Oct. 1883, qtd. in *The Roanoke Leader*, 8 Nov. 1883.

166. Roanoke Land & Improvement Company, Second Annual Report, November 1882–November 1883, rpt. in *The Roanoke Leader*, 17 Jan. 1884.

167. "Minute Book A, Roanoke Fair Association," 22 Oct. 1883.

168. Ibid., 8 July and 18 Sept. 1884.

169. *The Roanoke Leader*, 9 Oct. 1884.

170. "Minute Book A, Roanoke Fair Association," 6 Nov. 1884; 29 May 1885.

171. Ibid., 19 Mar. 1886; *The Roanoke Leader*, 20 Mar. 1886.

172. Ibid., 6 May; 28 Sept.; 15 Oct. 1886. For the new exhibits, see *The Roanoke Leader*, 29 May 1886.

173. *The Roanoke Leader*, 5 July 1883.

174. *Roanoke Daily Times*, 5 July 1890.

175. *The Roanoke Times*, 19 Apr. 1892.

176. Ibid., 20 Apr. 1892.

177. *The Iron Belt* 3, no. 4 (Apr. 1892).

178. *The Roanoke Times*, 1 June 1892.

179. Ibid., 9 June 1892.

180. Ibid., 14 June 1892. The spoons did not sell out and were still being offered for sale in September. See *The Roanoke Times*, 7 Sept. 1892.

181. *The Roanoke Times*, 19 June 1892; "Recollections of Henry S. Trout," in *The (Roanoke) World News*, 12 May 1913.

182. Roanoke Decennial Committee, *A Souvenir of the Decennial Celebration of Roanoke, Virginia* (Roanoke: Hammond Printing Works, 1892), 1–13 (quote is from 13).

183. *The Roanoke Times*, 19 June 1892

184. Ibid., 21 June 1892.

185. Decennial Committee, *A Souvenir of the Decennial Celebration*, 1–32 (first quote is from 9; second is from 8).

Chapter 5

1. Black migrants to Roanoke from 1883 to 1890 exceeded whites by almost 200 percent. For population statistics, see Town Council of Roanoke, "Census of the Town of Roanoke, December 1883," vol. 1 and vol. 2, VR-RCPL; U.S. Bureau of the Census, *Report on the United States of the Eleventh Census: 1890*, 483; and figures from *Sholes 1892 Roanoke City Directory* rpt. in *The Roanoke Times*, 20 Oct. 1892.

2. For the same situation elsewhere in the South, see Joel Williamson, *The Crucible of Race: Black and White Relations in the American South Since Emancipation*

(New York: Oxford University Press, 1984), 58–59, 111–14; Doyle, *New Men, New Cities, New South*, 261–62; Rabinowitz, *Race Relations in the Urban South*, 22–30, 46–57.

3. This was common in most southern cities at the time according to Doyle, *New Men, New Cities, New South*, 262.

4. *Roanoke Daily Record*, 24 June 1893, in VR-RCPL.

5. Daily, *Before Jim Crow*, 98–111; Rabinowitz, *Race Relations*, 182–97, 333–39.

6. This was a common practice throughout the South, according to Rabinowitz. See *Race Relations*, 43–44; see also Dorsey, *To Build Our Lives Together*, 149–50. For crime figures, see City of Roanoke, *Department Reports of the City of Roanoke for the Year Ending June 30, 1893* (Roanoke: Stone Printing & Mfg. Co., 1893), 24–26. For black male population (3,447 in 1892), see statistics in *The Roanoke Times*, 20 Oct. 1892.

7. McKinney, *Southern Mountain Republicans*, 131–38. Dorsey argues that it was the success of the local African American community in emulating Victorian ideals that fomented the 1906 Atlanta Riot. See her *To Build Our Lives Together*, 122–46.

8. Williamson, *Crucible of Race*, 186–87.

9. Goldfield, *Cotton Fields and Skyscrapers*, 94.

10. Barnes, *History of Roanoke*, 244.

11. *The Roanoke Times*, 10 Feb. 1892.

12. Ibid., 11 Feb. 1892.

13. *The Salem Times-Register*, 12 Feb. 1892.

14. Identification is from *The Roanoke Times*, 12 Feb. 1892; Lavender's police record is from *The Roanoke Times*, 13 Feb. 1892. According to *The Roanoke Times*, 24 Jan. 1891, when police raided "negro dives" along Railroad Avenue, they found Lavender sleeping near a stove in Wilmeth's barroom.

15. *The Roanoke Times*, 12 Feb. 1892.

16. Ibid.

17. Ibid., 13 Feb. 1892.

18. Ibid., 19 Feb. 1892.

19. Ibid., 16, 17, 18, Feb. 1892 (quote is from 18 Feb).

20. Barnes, *History of Roanoke*, 249.

21. *The Roanoke Times*, 12 Mar. 1892.

22. Ibid., 20, 24 Mar. 1892.

23. Ibid., 3 Feb. 1893.

24. Ibid., 13 May 1893.

25. Ibid., 14 May 1893.

26. Ibid., 7, 17 June; 9 July 1893 (quote is from 9 July).

27. Information on the effects of the 1893 depression is from Jacobs, *History of Roanoke*, 153–55; Pat Striplin, *The Norfolk & Western*, 62–64; account of Roanoke

Machine Works Relief Association in *The Roanoke Times,* 28 Nov. 1893; description of bank failures by James P. Woods in "Personal Biographical Sketches and Reminiscences of James Pleasant Woods," rpt. in Roy H. Hippert Jr., "Col. James P. Woods, Lawyer, Congressman," *Journal of the Roanoke Valley Historical Society* 11, no. 1 (1982): 32.

28. Keen and Hughes, *History of Christ Episcopal Church,* 9.

29. Roanoke City Council Minutes, 18 Sept. 1893, Clerk's Office, Roanoke City Municipal Building.

30. Barnes, *History of Roanoke,* 275, 278.

31. Gordon McKinney, "Industrialization and Violence in Appalachia in the 1890s," in J. W. Williamson, ed., *An Appalachian Symposium: Essays Written in Honor of Cratis D. Williams* (Boone, NC: Appalachian State University Press, 1977), 134–39. According to Joel Williamson, in the South, the depression also created confusion and anxiety among white men, who, unable to wholly fulfill their role as family providers, turned to protecting their wives and daughters from imagined black rapists. See his *Crucible of Race,* 115–17.

32. *Winston* (NC) *Sentinel,* qtd. in *The Roanoke Times,* 30 Apr. 1892.

33. *The Roanoke Times,* 5 May 1892.

34. Ibid., 6 May 1892.

35. Ibid., 10 May 1892.

36. Ibid., 11 May 1892.

37. Ibid., 15 May; 7, 14 June 1892.

38. Quote is from McCauley, *History of Roanoke County, Salem, Roanoke City,* 380; Campbell helped organize various temperance groups in the late 1880s. By 1891, he and his congregation had already begun pushing for local option vote. For his involvement in temperance or prohibition activities, see *Roanoke Daily Times,* 6 Dec. 1889; Barnes, *History of Roanoke,* 229.

39. *Words and Works,* 22 Oct. 1892, in Campbell Papers.

40. *The Roanoke Times,* 31 Jan.; 1 Feb. 1893.

41. Ibid., 30 June; 19, 30 July 1893.

42. Rosenzweig presents an argument for this point in his *Eight Hours for What We Will,* 93–102.

43. *The Roanoke Times,* 1 Sept. 1893.

44. Ibid., "Extra Edition," 5 Sept. 1893. For national WCTU reaching out to black voters, see Glenda E. Gilmore, *Gender and Jim Crow: Women and the Politics of White Supremacy in North Carolina, 1896–1920* (Chapel Hill: University of North Carolina Press, 1996), 46–56; Anastatia Sims, *The Power of Femininity in the New South: Women's Organizations and Politics in North Carolina, 1880–1930* (Columbia: University of South Carolina Press, 1997), 55–66. For black ministers elsewhere in the South speaking out against the dangers of alcohol for the African American community, see Dorsey, *To Build Our Lives Together,* 154–58.

45. *The Roanoke Times*, "Extra Edition," 5 Sept. 1893; 10 Mar. 1894.

46. Ibid., 7, 8 Sept. 1893. The "wets" lost in the local Hustings Court in February 1894, but in March they won an appeal in Circuit Court based on the argument that not enough previously registered voters had signed the local option petition. See *The Roanoke Times*, 1, 13, 14, 15 Feb; 10 Mar. 1894.

47. *The Roanoke Times*, 16 Sept. 1893.

48. Accounts of Bishop's assault are available in *Roanoke Daily Record*, 20 Sept. 1893, in Norfolk & Western Scrapbook No. 18, N&WRA (cited hereafter as N&WS18). Quotes are from *The Roanoke Times*, 21 Sept. 1893. For widespread rumors that Bishop had been murdered, see William C. Campbell, "Roanoke's Tragedies," TMs, no date, in Campbell Papers.

49. *Roanoke Daily Record*, 20 Sept. 1893, in N&WS18; *The Roanoke Times*, 21 Sept. 1893. In the 1890s, Baldwin, a native of Tazewell County, Virginia, teamed with Thomas Felts of Galax, Virginia, to create the Baldwin-Felts Detective Agency which later became notorious for its participation in breaking up strikes at Virginia and West Virginia coal fields.

50. *Roanoke Daily Record*, 20 Sept. 1893, in N&WS18; quotes are from *The Roanoke Times*, 21 Sept. 1893.

51. For chief being dismissed, see Roanoke City Council Minutes, 12 Oct. 1892, Clerk's Office, Roanoke Municipal Building; for problems with the force, see *The Roanoke Times*, 18, 24 May; 10, 15 June; 7, 8 Oct. 1892.

52. The changes in the police force granted by the 1892 charter are noted in PPFA, *History of the Roanoke Police Department*, 92; Trout's address is in Roanoke City Council Minutes, 22 July 1892; information on Terry and Griffin is from *The Roanoke Times*, 23 July 1892.

53. For size of force, see *The Roanoke Times*, 8 July 1892; for Griffin's observation, see PPFA, *Roanoke Police Department*, 96. The force, nevertheless, made close to three thousand arrests in the year after Trout's request. By the summer of 1893, W. H. Turner, the city's Police Justice, proclaimed the department "in excellent condition" and declared the "general order" of the town "now better than ever before." See *Department Reports of the City of Roanoke for the Year Ending June 30, 1893*, 24–27.

54. W. Fitzhugh Brundage, *Lynching in the New South: Georgia and Virginia, 1880–1930* (Urbana: University of Illinois Press, 1993), 166.

55. Hancock's account is from Jack W. Hancock, "Eyewitness Account of the Roanoke Riot of 1893," 1–2, TMs (1893), HMHSWV; see also *The Roanoke Times*, 21 Sept. 1893. According to Hancock's "Clarification Notes" in the same file, he wrote his "Eyewitness Account" immediately following the Roanoke Riot of 1893.

56. Hancock, "Eyewitness Account of the Roanoke Riot of 1893," 3–4; *The Roanoke Times*, 21 Sept. 1893; *Roanoke Daily Record*, 21 Sept. 1893, in N&WS18.

57. Tompkins, "Medical Annals of Roanoke," 18.

58. Campbell, "Roanoke's Tragedies."

59. Hancock, "Eyewitness Account of the Roanoke Riot of 1893," 4–5.

60. *Report of the Acting Adjutant General of the State of Virginia for the Year 1893* (Richmond: Superintendent of Public Printing, 1922), 63.

61. *Roanoke Daily Record*, 21 Sept. 1893, in N&WS18.

62. Hancock, "Eyewitness Account of the Roanoke Riot of 1893," 4–5.

63. *The Roanoke Times*, 21 Sept. 1893.

64. Tompkins, "Medical Annals," 18.

65. *Roanoke Daily Record*, 21 Sept. 1893, in N&WS18.

66. Ibid.

67. Campbell, "Roanoke's Tragedies."

68. Tompkins, "Medical Annals," 19; Hancock, "Eyewitness Account of the Roanoke Riot of 1893," 5.

69. *Roanoke Daily Record*, 21 Sept. 1893, in N&WS18; *The Roanoke Times*, 21 Sept. 1893. Settles's description from *The Roanoke Times*, 22 Sept. 1893; bullet descriptions from *The Roanoke Times*, 26 Sept. 1893.

70. Hancock, "Eyewitness Account of the Roanoke Riot of 1893," 5; *The Roanoke Times*, 21, 23 Sept. 1893.

71. Tompkins, "Medical Annals," 20.

72. Campbell, "Roanoke's Tragedies."

73. *The Roanoke Times*, 24 Sept. 1893.

74. Ibid., 21 Sept. 1893.

75. See testimony in *The Roanoke Times*, 26 Nov.; 11, 12, 17 Dec. 1893 (both quotes are from 17 Dec). George Gordon was later pardoned by the Governor of Virginia for assisting the police in their attempt to hide Smith. See *The Roanoke Times*, 4 Oct. 1893.

76. *Roanoke Daily Record*, 21 Sept. 1893, in N&WS18.

77. H. V. Lineback Photography Studio, Aftermath of Thomas Smith Lynching, Photograph (21 Sept. 1893), HMHSWV. Lineback operated a studio at 23 Salem Avenue and in advertisements boasted "Nothing but first class work turned out." See ad in *Words & Works*, vol. 1, no. 24, Dec. 1892, in Campbell Papers. (According to the HMHSWV, the individual who donated the Smith photograph stipulated that it never be reprinted.) Commercial photographs and postcards of lynching scenes were both common and readily available in the late nineteenth and early twentieth centuries. See James Allen, et al., *Without Sanctuary: Lynching Photography in America* (Santa Fe, NM: Twin Palms Publishers, 2000). Such photos, according to Allen, "played as significant a role in the ritual as torture and souvenir grabbing" and facilitated "the endless replay of anguish." See Allen, 204–5. For a similar analysis and argument, see also Dora Apel, *Imagery of Lynching: Black Men, White Women, and the Mob* (New Brunswick, NJ: Rutgers University Press, 2004), 1–46.

78. See Leon F. Litwack, "Hellhounds," in Allen, et al., *Without Sanctuary,* 10–11; Williamson, *Crucible of Race,* 185–89.

79. *The Roanoke Times,* 22 Sept. 1893.

80. Campbell, "Roanoke's Tragedies"; for another description of Campbell's stand, see McCauley, *History of Roanoke County, Salem, Roanoke City,* 378–80; first quote is from *The Roanoke Times,* 22 Sept. 1893; second quote is from *Roanoke Daily Record,* 21 Sept. 1893, in N&WS18.

81. *The Lynchburg News,* 23 Sept. 1893, in N&WS18.

82. City of Roanoke, "To The People of Roanoke! Sept. 21st, 1893," broadside in Hancock, "Eyewitness Account"; see also *Roanoke Daily Record,* 21 Sept. 1893, in N&WS18.

83. Sands's address and information about the Masons and Odd Fellows is from *Roanoke Daily Record,* 22 Sept. 1893, in N&WS18; reaction of Confederate and Union veterans groups is noted in *The New York World,* 28 Sept. 1893, in N&WS18. Their joint statement is available in part in an unidentified newspaper article on the 28 Sept. 1893 page of N&WS18.

84. "Headquarters of Vigilant Committee," Roanoke, to Jack Hancock, City, 22 Sept. 1893, in Hancock, "Eyewitness Account."

85. *Richmond Dispatch,* 24 Sept. 1894, in N&WS18.

86. Tompkins, "Medical Annals," 20.

87. See coverage of the Coroner's jury in *Roanoke Daily Record,* 22, 23 Sept. 1893, in N&WS18; *The Roanoke Times,* 23, 24, 26, 27 Sept. 1893. Both papers also referred to Walter Davis as Will Davis.

88. *The Richmond Dispatch,* 24 Sept. 1893.

89. *The Roanoke Times,* 26 Sept. 1893.

90. Brundage, *Lynching in the New South,* 168–69. The first and second quotes are from *Journal of the Senate of the Commonwealth of Virginia, 1893–1894* (Richmond: Superintendent of Public Printing, 1894), 45–46; third quote from *Journal of the House of Delegates of the State of Virginia for the Session of 1893–1894* (Richmond: Superintendent of Public Printing, 1893), 52–54.

91. John Anderson Waits II, "Roanoke's Tragedy: The Lynch Riot of 1893" (M.A. thesis, University of Virginia, 1972), 53.

92. *New York Herald,* 23 Sept. 1893, in N&WS18.

93. *Evening Post* and *Telegraph* both rpt. in *The Lynchburg News,* 23 Sept. 1893, in N&WS18.

94. *New York World,* 23 Sept. 1893, in N&WS18.

95. *Richmond Dispatch,* 24 Sept. 1893, in N&WS18; *Richmond Planet,* 30 Sept. 1893.

96. *The Lynchburg News,* 24 Sept. 1893, in N&WS18.

97. Petersburg *Index-Appeal*, 24 Sept. 1893, in N&WS18.

98. Norfolk *Landmark*, 26 Sept. 1893, in N&WS18.

99. *Evening Star* rpt. in *The Lynchburg News*, 23 Sept. 1893, in N&WS18.

100. *The Roanoke Times*, 21 Sept. 1893; *Roanoke Daily Record*, 22 Sept. 1893, in N&WS18.

101. *Words and Works*, 23 Sept. 1893, in Campbell Papers.

102. *The Roanoke Times*, 28 Sept. 1893; Waits, "Roanoke's Tragedy," 49.

103. Ibid., 29 Sept. 1893.

104. Ibid.

105. Ida B. Wells, *A Red Record: Tabulated Statistics and Alleged Causes of Lynching in the United States, 1892–1893–1894* (Chicago: Donohue & Henneberry, 1895), 48.

106. Cleveland *Gazette*, 14 Oct. 1893.

107. "Clarification Notes," in Hancock, "Eyewitness Account." For Griffin's rise to Chief of Police in 1912, see Barnes, *History of Roanoke*, 493.

108. *The Crisis: A Record of the Darker Races* (Oct. 1916), 300.

109. *The Roanoke Times*, 30 Sept. 1893.

110. Ibid., 3 Oct. 1893.

111. Ibid., 24 Oct. 1893.

112. Roanoke City Council Minutes, 10 Oct. 1893; *The Roanoke Times*, 11 Oct. 1893.

113. *The Roanoke Times*, 27 Oct. 1893.

114. Ibid., 16 Nov. 1893.

115. Ibid., 18, 21, 22, 23 Nov. 1893.

116. Ibid., 26 Nov. 1893.

117. Petersburg *Index-Appeal*, 25 Nov. 1893, in N&WS18.

118. Philadelphia *Public-Ledger* qtd. in *The Roanoke Times*, 26 Nov. 1893.

119. *The Roanoke Times*, 26 Nov. 1893.

120. Roanoke City Council Minutes, 12 Dec. 1893.

121. See coverage of trials in *The* (Roanoke) *Evening World*, 11 Dec. 1893, in Campbell Papers; *The Roanoke Times*, 12, 17, Dec. 1893; for firing and demotion, see *The Roanoke Times*, 13, 19 Dec. 1893.

122. See, for example, *The Roanoke Times*, 16 Jan. 1893; 8 Feb. 1894; for Virginia Governor Charles T. O'Ferrall's pardoning of Walter Davis, see *The Roanoke Daily Times*, 24 May 1895.

123. *The Roanoke Times*, 3, 11, 13 Feb. 1894.

124. See petition in *The Roanoke Times*, 27 Jan. 1894.

125. *The Roanoke Times*, 16 Jan. 1894.

126. There is no mention of the riot in the city's first official history, published twenty years later. Indeed, the only reference to the riot appears in the biographical section in a single sentence detailing Reverend William Campbell's stand against men who wanted to drag "a negro who had been lynched" through the streets. See Jacobs, *History of Roanoke City*, 171–72.

127. Douglass quote is from Litwack, "Hellhounds," 29; *The Roanoke Times*, 17 Jan. 1894. According to the *Times*, there were "many prominent people in the audience."

128. See, for example, clippings from the riot in a scrapbook in William C. Campbell's Papers; and in "Valuable Clippings from the Roanoke Riot," another scrapbook compiled by an unidentified resident, located at the HMHSWV. Lineback's photo of Smith's lynching is also available in the scrapbook. Such folk preservation of lynchings was common. See Allen, et al., *Without Sanctuary*; and Bruce E. Baker, "North Carolina Lynching Ballads," in W. Fitzhugh Brundage, ed., *Under Sentence of Death: Lynching in the South* (Chapel Hill: University of North Carolina Press, 1997), 219–45. Although in the immediate aftermath many whites did what they could to preserve memories of the riot and lynching, in the century that followed, the events all but faded from local memory. There are no historical markers denoting the events of September 20 and 21, 1893, nor do local museums include the events of that day in their general exhibits on the city's history. Such neglect, according to Bruce Baker, is common in the South, where whites tend to downplay or erase episodes of racial violence and the African American community typically maintains those memories so as not to forget the longtime history of racial injustice. See his "Under the Rope: Lynching and Memory in Laurens County, South Carolina," in W. Fitzhugh Brundage, ed., *Where These Memories Grow: History, Memory, and Southern Identity* (Chapel Hill: University of North Carolina Press, 2000), 319–45. On the hundredth anniversary of Smith's lynching, the local newspaper published an overview of the Riot, and in subsequent months, followed up with related stories. See *Roanoke Times & World News*, 20 Sept. 1993 and 18 Jan. 1994.

129. For details about the actual tree's demise and removal, see *The Roanoke Times*, 18, 31 Oct. 1893; for persistence of the legend that it lived on, see *The Roanoke Times*, 28 Mar. 2001.

130. *The Roanoke Times*, 31 Oct. 1893.

131. Ibid., 14 Nov. 1893.

132. Lyrics compiled from cross reference of "The Roanoke Riot," ballad lyrics in the collection of Southwest Virginia Tragedy Ballads in the Blue Ridge Institute, Ferrum College, Ferrum, Virginia; and "The Roanoke Outrage," rpt. in *The Roanoke Times & World News*, 18 Jan. 1994.

133. Baker, "Lynching Ballads," 221.

134. Wells, *A Red Record*, 16–19.

135. Thomas Nelson Page, "The Lynching of Negroes—Its Cause and Its Prevention," *The North American Review* 178 (1904): 33–48.

136. Wells, *A Red Record*, 45.

137. Ibid., 46.

138. Ibid., 45, 47, 48.

139. Nathaniel Burwell (hereafter cited as N. B.) Johnston, Roanoke, to Rev. Benjamin Tucker Tanner, Philadelphia, Pa., 29 July 1895, in Nathaniel Burwell Johnston Letterbook, 1894–1895, Nathaniel Burwell Johnston Papers, VHS (cited hereafter as Johnston Letterbook).

140. N. B. Johnston, Roanoke, to N. Ward, Editor, *Independent*, New York City, 11 Aug. 1894, in Johnston Letterbook. See also, N. B. Johnston, Roanoke, to N. Ward, Editor, *Independent*, New York City, 2 Aug. 1894, in Johnston Letterbook.

141. Brundage, *Lynching in the New South*, 169, 282 (O'Ferrall quote is from 169).

142. For concerns about order over racial sympathy, see William A. Link, *The Paradox of Southern Progressivism, 1880–1930* (Chapel Hill: University of North Carolina Press, 1992), 61–70; Dewy W. Grantham, *Southern Progressivism: The Reconciliation of Progress and Tradition* (Knoxville: University of Tennessee Press, 1983), 231; for the conservative nature of anti-lynching in Virginia, see Raymond H. Pulley, *Old Virginia Restored: An Interpretation of the Progressive Impulse* (Charlottesville: University Press of Virginia, 1968), 52–53; Brundage, *Lynching in the New South*, 169–78.

143. Brundage, *Lynching in the New South*, 169, 282 (O'Ferrall quote is from 169).

144. Historians who have analyzed the Roanoke riot have done so primarily to determine its causes and impact. In the most comprehensive study, Ann Field Alexander argues that the city's growing black population, incompetent police force, frontier ethos, and economic recession combined to foster the tragic response to the assault on Bishop. In the aftermath, Alexander contends, the violence and mayhem in Roanoke was the main factor behind the state's dramatic turn toward preventing lynchings. See, Ann Field Alexander, "'Like an Evil Wind': The Roanoke Riot of 1893 and the Lynching of Thomas Smith," *The Virginia Magazine of History and Biography* vol. 100, no. 2 (Apr. 1992): 173–206. Gordon B. McKinney, by contrast, claims that workers and formerly rural residents resented the rationalization and discipline efforts of the city's new professionals and middle classes, and that when the 1893 depression hit Roanoke, its lower classes reacted by blaming business leaders and civic authorities. He argues that such antiauthoritarianism combined with a raw, boomtown atmosphere, large population of former "mountain men who accepted personal revenge as a routine practice," and atypical number of black residents for Appalachia made the riot almost inevitable. McKinney, however, also contends that such episodes of violence were not endemic to Appalachia, but were typical responses to modernization, industrialization, and loss of personal control. See, McKinney, "Industrialization and Violence in Appalachia," 131–41 (quote is from 140); and McKinney, *Southern Mountain Republicans*, 128–31. W. Fitzhugh Brundage notes similarly that the high incidence of lynching in Southwest Virginia, the region most sparsely populated with African Americans, "reflected the desperation of whites to define the status of blacks in a region where blacks were still uncommon and furious

social and economic change was taking place." Moreover, he points out, mob violence against blacks tended to occur in the region's few towns and cities, where population growth, industrialization, and modernization were happening most rapidly. According to Brundage, the riot became a "clarion call for strong action against mob violence" and "a catalyst for widespread demands for the suppression of social disorder" throughout the remainder of the 1890s and early twentieth century. See Brundage, *Lynching in the New South*, 143, 145, 167–90 (quotes are from 143, 169, 172); and W. Fitzhugh Brundage, "Racial Violence, Lynchings, and Modernization in the Mountain South," in John C. Inscoe, ed., *Appalachians and Race: The Mountain South from Slavery to Segregation* (Lexington: University Press of Kentucky, 2000), 302–16.

145. *The Roanoke Times*, 31 Jan. 1904.

146. Ibid.

147. Ibid., 2 Feb. 1904.

148. Ibid., 5 Feb. 1904.

149. Ibid., 4 Feb. 1904.

150. Ibid., 5 Feb. 1904.

151. Ibid., 13 Feb. 1904.

152. Ibid., 4 Feb. 1904.

153. Ibid., 3 Mar. 1901.

154. Ibid., 26 May 1901.

155. Ibid., 2 June 1901.

156. Ibid., 4 Feb. 1904.

157. James Hurd Davis, Roanoke, to Annie H. Woods, Ferrum, VA, 3 Feb. 1904, Davis Family Papers, VHS.

158. *The Roanoke Times*, 6 Feb. 1904.

159. Ibid., 7 Feb. 1904.

160. Ibid., 6 Feb. 1904.

161. Ibid., 7 Feb. 1904.

162. Ibid.

163. Ibid., 9 Feb. 1904.

164. See notices published in *The Roanoke Times*, 9, 10, 11 Feb. 1904 (quote is from the Car Department, Roanoke Machine Works, in 11 Feb).

165. "Proclamation to Colored People," published in *The Roanoke Times*, 11 Feb. 1904.

166. *Richmond Times-Dispatch*, 13 Feb. 1904; *The Roanoke Times*, 13 Feb. 1904.

167. *The Roanoke Times*, 14 Feb. 1904.

168. William Larsen, *Montague of Virginia: The Making of a Southern Progressive* (Baton Rouge: Louisiana State University Press, 1965), 122.

169. *The Roanoke Times*, 16 Feb. 1904.

170. Ibid., 17 Feb. 1904.

171. *Richmond Planet*, excerpts rpt. in *The Roanoke Times*, 17 Feb. 1904.

172. Larsen, *Montague of Virginia*, 122–23.

173. *The Roanoke Times*, 18 Feb. 1904.

174. Ibid., 25 Feb. 1904.

175. Ibid., 1 Mar. 1904.

176. Ibid., 2, 3 Mar. 1904.

177. Ibid., 18 Feb; 2 Mar. 1904.

178. Ibid., 4, 12, 15 Mar. 1904.

179. Ibid., 18 Mar. 1904.

180. Ibid., 19 Mar. 1904.

181. Ibid.

182. Ibid., 20 Mar. 1904.

183. Ibid., 22 Mar. 1904.

184. Ibid., 6, 7, 28 Feb. 1904 (quote is from 28 Feb).

185. *Washington Post*, 25 Feb. 1904, qtd. in *The Roanoke Times*, 26 Feb. 1904.

186. *The Roanoke Times*, 22 Mar. 1904; *Richmond Planet*, qtd. in *The Roanoke Times*, 6 Apr. 1904.

187. *Salem Times-Register & Sentinel*, qtd. in The Roanoke Times, 9 Apr. 1904. See also John D. Long, *South of Main: The History of the Water Street Community of Salem Virginia* (Salem: Virginia Foundation for the Humanities and Public Policy, 2000), 34. Long questions the validity of the story and downplays its significance if true, arguing that "the benign relations of the Salem community prevailed." One wonders, however, where such "benign relations" were during the whipping of Taylor Fields by an enraged Salem mob only a couple of months earlier.

188. R. R. Jones, Washington, D. C., to "The City Council of Roanoke," Roanoke, 26 July 1904, VR-RCPL.

189. *The Roanoke Times*, 28 July 1904.

190. Ibid., 16 Feb. 1905.

191. Ibid., 3 Mar. 1905.

192. Ibid., 11 Mar. 1905.

193. Ibid., 16, 23 March; 16 Sept. 1905; see also Barnes, *History of Roanoke*, 395–96.

194. *The Roanoke Times*, 28 Dec. 1906.

195. Michel Foucault, *Discipline and Punish: The Birth of the Prison* (New York: Vintage, 1995), especially 1–104.

Chapter 6

1. Campbell's sermon to the mechanics, rpt. the following day in *The* (Roanoke) *Evening World,* 11 Dec. 1893, Campbell Papers.

2. Barnes, *History of Roanoke,* 279.

3. *The Roanoke Times,* 15 Mar. 1894.

4. M. W. Bryan, Roanoke, to Richard J. Morris, Philadelphia, PA, 9 Nov. 1895, in Malcolm W. Bryan Papers.

5. Ibid., 23 Nov. 1895, Malcolm W. Bryan Papers.

6. Robert H. Angell, M. W. Bryan, and S. W. Jamison were the local businessmen who bought the building. They sold it the same year for twenty-five thousand dollars to investors interested in turning the plant into a cotton mill.

7. See city directory and U.S. Census data published in *The Roanoke Times,* 20 Oct. 1892; *The Roanoke Daily Times,* 19 July 1895.

8. For the Machine Works Relief Association, see *The Roanoke Times,* 28 Nov. 1893; for the Ladies Union Benevolent Society, see *The Roanoke Times,* 1 Feb; 13, 14, 15 Mar. 1894.

9. John M. Payne Jr., Chairman of Committee, Roanoke Athletic Club, to Miss Edith Browning, care of B. W. Browning, Esq., N&W Railroad, Roanoke, 28 Feb. 1894, in HMHSWV.

10. For examples, see *The Roanoke Daily Times,* 25 April; 6 June; 17 July 1895 (first quote from 6 June; second from 17 July).

11. Charlie Burgess, Roanoke, to "My own dear wife" (Marie Wohlbruck Burgess, Baltimore, MD), 17 Oct. 1895, Wohlbruck and Burgess Family Papers, UVA.

12. Ibid., 18 Oct. 1895, Wohlbruck and Burgess Family Papers, UVA.

13. See reprint of ad in *The Roanoke Times,* 31 Oct. 1893.

14. Stromquist, *A Generation of Boomers,* 144.

15. *The Roanoke Time,* 23 Feb. 1893.

16. Ibid., 28 Feb. 1893, in Norfolk & Western scrapbook no. 17, N&WRA (cited hereafter as N&WS17).

17. *Roanoke Daily Record,* 1 Mar. 1893, in N&WS17.

18. *The* (Roanoke) *Evening World,* 1 Mar. 1893, in N&WS17.

19. *Manufacturers' Record,* 1 Dec. 1893, in N&WS18; *The Roanoke Times,* 17 Nov. 1893.

20. See, for example, accounts and interviews in *The Roanoke Times,* 2 Dec. 1893, in N&WS18; *Roanoke Daily Record,* 2 Dec. 1893, in N&WS18.

21. *Roanoke Daily Record,* 17 Nov. 1893, in N&WS18.

22. Ibid., 21, 30 Nov. 1893, in N&WS18 (quote is from 30 Nov.).

23. Ibid., 6 Dec. 1893, in N&WS18.

24. Ibid.

25. For letters to regional officials about the B&O and C&O, see June and July letters in Johnston Letterbook. Johnston was also active in soliciting new manufacturers. In July 1894, for example, he promised a Petersburg tin-can factory owner that Roanoke companies alone would consume one hundred thousand cans per year if the firm relocated to the city. Later in the year, he notified a Pennsylvania mill operator that the town was surrounded by a huge stock of oak and chestnut tress ready to be harvested. Tin-can factory letter is N. B. Johnston, Roanoke, to Simon Seward, Petersburg, VA, 24 July 1894, in Johnston Letterbook; mill letter is N. B. Johnston, Roanoke, to H. M. Gist, Hanover, PA, 18 Sept. 1894, in Johnston Letterbook.

26. N. B. Johnston, Roanoke, to Peyton L. Terry, Roanoke, 30 Aug. 1894, in Johnston Letterbook.

27. *The Roanoke Times*, 1 Feb. 1894.

28. Information about the demise of the Norfolk & Western Railroad Company is from Jacobs, *History of Roanoke City*, 153–55, 163–64; Striplin, *The Norfolk & Western*, 62–64; Piedmont, "The Railroad Offices,"19; Schilling, "Roanoke City Fire Department History, 1882–1983," 4.

29. Malcolm W. Bryan, Roanoke, to T. W. Neil, Washington and Roanoke Land & Improvement Company, Washington, DC, 12 Jan. 1894, rpt. in Bryan III, "Boom and Bust," 1, Bryan Papers.

30. Malcolm W. Bryan, Roanoke, to T. Roney Williamson, Esq., Philadelphia, 14 May 1894, rpt. in Bryan III, "Boom and Bust," 5, Bryan Papers.

31. Malcolm W. Bryan, Roanoke, to Hon. W. H. Sims, Washington, DC 19 Oct. 1895, Bryan Papers.

32. *The Roanoke Daily Times*, 28 Aug. 1895.

33. For the plight of Terry's Roanoke Trust, Loan & Safe Deposit Company, see Barnes, *History of Roanoke*, 289–90, 301, 322; White, *Roanoke: 1740–1982*, 81–84.

34. For similar advertising of tractable labor in the South, see Woodward, *Origins of the New South*, 307–19; Kyriakoudes, *The Social Origins of the Urban South*, 126–27; for Virginia examples, see Lee, *The Tennessee-Virginia Tri-Cities*, 53–78.

35. A similar pro-railroad stance by municipal leaders in western railroad towns also forestalled strikes. See Stromquist, *A Generation of Boomers*, 145–47.

36. *The Roanoke Leader*, 22 May 1886.

37. *The Roanoke Times*, 5 Oct. 1890.

38. Ibid., 22 Oct. 1890.

39. Ibid., 1 Jan. 1891.

40. For Birmingham unions, see discussion in McKiven, *Iron and Steel*, chap. 2.

41. *The Roanoke Times*, 27 Nov. 1890.

42. Ibid., 11 Dec. 1890.

43. Ibid., 25, 26 Feb. 1891.

44. Bruce, *Southwest Virginia*, 142–43.

45. For a discussion of industrialists' lack of power in small factory-towns in the North, see Herbert G. Gutman, *Work, Culture, and Society in Industrializing America: Essays in American Working-Class and Social History* (New York: Vintage, 1977), chap. 5. Gutman notes a similar respect of workers' power in factory-towns. See page 257. See also Thernstrom, *Poverty and Progress*, chap. 7.

46. McKiven, *Iron and Steel*, 69–71.

47. *Roanoke Daily Times*, 31 Aug. 1890.

48. Ibid., 2 Sept. 1890.

49. *The Roanoke Times*, 19 Apr. 1900.

50. Ibid., 31 Aug. 1902.

51. Virginia State Federation of Labor, *Virginia State Federation of Labor Directory with Historical Sketches of Richmond, Roanoke, Norfolk and Portsmouth*, ed. W. H. Mullen (Richmond: Frank Baptist Printing Co., 1902), 3–5.

52. Information about *The Labor Unionist*, for which there are no known extant copies, is available in *The Roanoke Times*, 7, 25 Apr. 1903; coverage of the VSFL convention is from *The Roanoke Times*, 22, 23 May 1902.

53. *The Roanoke Times*, 3 Sept. 1901. For similar Labor Day celebrations, see *The Roanoke Times*, 24 July 1900, 2 Sept. 1902, 8 Sept. 1903.

54. For early information about The Virginia Brewing Company, see *Roanoke Daily Times*, 13, 23 Nov. 1889.

55. *Roanoke Daily Times*, 9 Jan. 1890.

56. Ibid., 19 Jan., 12 Feb., 21 June 1890.

57. Ibid., 3 May 1890.

58. Ibid., 19 Aug. 1890.

59. *The Roanoke Times*, 13 Nov. 1890.

60. See ad in *The Roanoke Times*, 3 Mar. 1891.

61. Ibid., 7 July 1891.

62. See details of "Beer War" and subsequent lawsuit against Anheuser-Busch by its local distributor for losses incurred during the campaign in *The Roanoke Times*, 27 Dec. 1893. Such cutthroat tactics were the norm for Adolphus Busch's company, which waged a relentless campaign against local breweries throughout the East in 1892. See Philip Van Munching, *Beer Blast: The Inside Story of the Brewing Industry's Bizarre Battles for Your Money* (New York: Times Books, 1997), 16–18.

63. *The Roanoke Times*, "Extra Brewery Fire Edition," 8 Mar. 1892; *The Roanoke Times*, 9 Mar. 1892.

64. See description of improvements in *Roanoke Daily Record*, 4 Nov. 1893, in N&WS18.

65. Schilling, "Roanoke City Fire Department History, 1882–1983," 3.

66. See bock ad in *The Roanoke Times,* 22 Apr. 1892; see decennial ad in *The Roanoke Times,* 16 June 1892; see Wuerzburger ad in *The Roanoke Times,* 15 July 1892 (quote is from 15 July).

67. *Headlight: Special Edition of the Magic City Roanoke, Va., and Scenes Along the Norfolk & Western Railroad* (Chicago: Beard & Collier, 1898), 30, in VR-RCPL; see also Stanford Insurance Map of Roanoke, Virginia, 1907, VR-RCPL.

68. *The Roanoke Times,* 14 Mar. 1901; *The Roanoke Times,* 22 Dec. 1904.

69. *The Roanoke Times,* 16 Apr. 1905; sales stats from *The Roanoke Times,* 2 Jan. 1906. See also Roanoke Chamber of Commerce, *Roanoke: The Magic City of Virginia* (Roanoke: Stone Printing & Mfg. Co., 1904), 83, in VR-RCPL.

70. The U.S. Health Bulletin analysis is from *New York Evening Journal,* 5 June 1902, rpt. in *The Roanoke Times,* 13 July 1902; ads and quotes are from *The Roanoke Times,* 25 Feb. 1903; 24 May and 5 July 1904 (first set of quotes from 5 July; second quote from 24 May).

71. *The Roanoke Times,* 28 Sept. 1905.

72. See VBC ad on back cover of "1906–1907 Roanoke Academy of Music Program," in Edward L. Stone—Borderland Coal Company Papers, Roanoke Memorabilia Collection, UVA (cited hereafter as Edward L. Stone—Borderland Coal Company Papers).

73. VBC ad is in *The Roanoke Times,* 2 July 1905; Portner ad is in *The Roanoke Times,* 12 July 1905; the Anti-Saloon League's claims are from Stanley Baron, *Brewed In America: A History of Beer and Ale in the United States* (Boston: Little, Brown and Co., 1962), 291–92.

74. *The Roanoke Times,* 4 Sept. 1906.

75. Ibid., 13 Nov. 1907.

76. *The Industrial Era,* 14 Oct. 1910, in HMHSWV.

77. Jacobs, *History of Roanoke City,* 136–37.

78. See, for example, accounts of the VBC in *Headlight: Special Edition of the Magic City,* 30; RCOC, *Roanoke: The Magic City,* 83; Jacobs, *History of Roanoke City,* 136–37.

79. According to Stanley Baron, prohibition destroyed over half of all breweries in the United States. The survivors tended to be large corporations that could diversify their assets until they began brewing again rather than small enterprises like the Virginia Brewing Company, which depended on beer sales for the vast majority of income. See his *Brewed In America,* 331.

In 1924, a local fruit cannery purchased the VBC brew house to use as a storage facility. Four years later, in 1928, a varnish manufacturer bought the structure. In 1933, when prohibition ended, Louis Scholz revived the Virginia Brewing Company. His brother Henry had died by then, and in the spring of 1936, only months before the new VBC beer—"Scholz Pilsner"—was slated to hit the market, Louis Scholz passed away too. Scholz's heirs sold the VBC shortly thereafter, and from 1936 to 1954, another beer manufacturer operated the plant. In 1954, S. B. Huff, a longtime Roanoke resident and former local policeman, rented the brewery, once again revived the Virginia Brewing Company name, and began production of "Old Virginia" beer. The brewery changed hands again in 1958, with the Mountain Brewing Company of North Carolina taking over operations and brewing its trademark "Dixie" beer. The following year, however, the company closed its Roanoke branch, and in 1964, the owners of the Scholzes' 1893 brewhouse had it torn down to make way for industrial development. The VBC's bottling plant next door survived, and in the early 1980s was being used by a janitor supply company. For the VBC's post-prohibition history, see *The Roanoke Times & World News*, 17 Oct. 1982; Barnes, *History of Roanoke*, 630, 687, 763.

80. Early history of the Stone Printing & Manufacturing Company is from Jacobs, *History of Roanoke City*, 178; McCauley, *History of Roanoke County, Salem, Roanoke City*, 364–65; Stone Printing & Manufacturing Company, *Stone's Impressions* 1, no. 1 (July 1913): 13–22, in VR-RCPL; Stone Printing & Manufacturing Company, *Stone's Impressions* 3, new series, no. 4 (July–Sept, 1933): 1, in author's collection; Roanoke Century Club, *Eighth Annual Dinner—Century Club—Apr. 17, 1914* (Roanoke: Stone Printing & Mfg. Co., 1914), 21–22, in VR-RCPL.

81. SP&MC, *Stone's Impressions* 1, no. 1, 13–22; McCauley, *History of Roanoke County, Salem, Roanoke City*, 364–65.

82. SP&MC, *Stone's Impressions* 1, no. 1, 13–22; McCauley, *History of Roanoke County, Salem, Roanoke City*, 364–65; Jacobs, *History of Roanoke City*, 178; quotes about the business are from ad in *The Roanoke Times*, 27 Aug. 1893; information on new building is from *The Roanoke Times*, 13 Apr. 1905; information about J. B. Fishburn is from Norma Lugar, "The Life and Times of J. B. Fishburn," *The Roanoker* 5, no. 6 (Nov.–Dec. 1978): 14–16, 18, 20, 86.

83. *The Roanoke Times*, 5 July 1902.

84. Ibid., 5 Jan. 1893.

85. Stone Printing & Manufacturing Company, *First Annual Outing of the Employees of The Stone Printing and Manufacturing Company, of Roanoke, Virginia, Tuesday, August 11th, 1896, at Elliston, Virginia* (Roanoke: Stone Printing & Mfg. Co., 1896), in Edward L. Stone–Borderland Coal Company Papers, box 274, correspondence folder 1896–1900, UVA.

86. Jacobs, *History of Roanoke City*, 178; quote from *The Roanoke Times*, Dec. 1904.

87. *The Roanoke Times*, 14 Sept. 1905.

88. Ibid., 16 Sept. 1905.

89. Ibid., 17 Sept. 1905.

90. Ibid., 13 Oct. 1905.

91. Ibid., 19 Nov. 1907.

92. Quote and rehiring of strikers is from "Guide to the Edward L. Stone–Borderland Coal Company Papers," 9, UVA.

93. Edward L. Stone, Roanoke, to H. W. E. Storey, London, England, 22 Feb. 1908, Edward L Stone–Borderland Coal Company Papers, box 354, 1904–1908 Storey Correspondence file.

94. Petition by Democratic Voters, 13 Mar. 1896, in Edward L. Stone–Borderland Coal Company Records, box 274, 1896–1900 Correspondence file.

95. Edward L. Stone, Roanoke, to "The Voters of the Second Ward," Roanoke, 3 Apr. 1902, Edward L. Stone–Borderland Coal Company Papers, box 274, 1896–1900 Correspondence file; rpt. in *The Roanoke Times*, 4 Apr. 1902.

96. See Stone's reference to twenty years of "patriotic" investments in local companies in Edward L. Stone, Roanoke, to E. A. Schubert, Vice-President, Acme Match Company, Roanoke, 25 Nov. 1908, Edward L. Stone–Borderland Coal Company Papers, box 375, 1908–1911 Correspondence file.

97. Stone Printing & Manufacturing Company, *Picturesque Roanoke / Being a Series of Reproductions from Photographic Views, Taken in the City of Roanoke, Virginia, and the Vicinity Thereof, Especially for this Work*, 2d ed. (Roanoke: Stone Printing & Mfg. Co., 1902).

98. White, *Roanoke: 1740–1982*, 84; Barnes, *History of Roanoke*, 329.

99. Century Club, *Eighth Annual Dinner*, 9–10.

100. Information on the Roanoke Cotton Mill is from RCOC, *Roanoke: The Magic City of Virginia*, 40; Stone's business activity is from Jacobs, *History of Roanoke City*, 178; "A Guide to the Edward L. Stone–Borderland Coal Company Papers," 2.

101. During the 1920s at Stone's behest, Borderland hired a private militia of Baldwin-Felts agents and spent hundreds of thousands of dollars fighting efforts by the United Mine Workers of America to unionize its mines. Due in part to its battle against the UMWA, the Borderland Coal Company went bankrupt in 1934. For information about Stone and Borderland, see Shifflett, *Coal Towns*, 119–34; "Guide to the Edward L. Stone–Borderland Coal Company Papers," 2–7.

102. "Guide to the Edward L. Stone–Borderland Company Coal Papers," 2, 8; Jacobs, *History of Roanoke City*, 119–20, 178; Roanoke German Club, Roanoke, to Edward L. Stone, Roanoke, 15 Nov. 1899, Edward L. Stone–Borderland Coal Company Papers, box 435, 1902–1909 Roanoke file.

103. *The Roanoke Times*, 2 Oct. 1903; see also letter from Stone and Fishburn from "the famous famine district, somewhere between Calcutta and Bombay" in *The Roanoke Times*, 5 Feb. 1905. In that dispatch, the men reported that they were "in the best of health and spirits."

104. Edward L. Stone, "Through Fifty Eventful Years," *Stone's Impressions* 3, new series, no. 4 (July–Sept. 1933): 1. Stone died in 1938. Stone Printing & Manufacturing continued business until 1977, when its owners sold the business to another printing firm.

105. *The Roanoke Times*, 17 Sept. 1899.

106. H. D. Lafferty, President, Roanoke Country Club, Roanoke, to Edward L. Stone, Roanoke, 23 June 1900, in Edward L. Stone–Borderland Coal Company Papers, box 398, Roanoke Country Club file; see additional correspondence in ibid. for memberships and stock purchases.

107. *The Roanoke Times*, 23 Apr. 1905; Roanoke Country Club, *Roanoke Country Club* (Roanoke: Privately printed, 1969), 1–2.

108. Roanoke Country Club, *Roanoke Country Club, 1906–07* (Roanoke: Stone Printing & Mfg. Co., 1906), in Edward L. Stone–Borderland Coal Company Papers, box 398, Roanoke Country Club file.

109. *The Roanoke Times*, 6 Apr. 1905.

110. Century Club, *Eighth Annual Dinner*, 9, 17–25 (quote from page 9).

111. *The* (Roanoke) *Evening World*, 8 Apr. 1912.

112. Century Club, *Eighth Annual Dinner*, 16.

113. *The Roanoke Times*, 14 June 1892

114. Ibid., 4, 5 Jan. 1893 (quote is from 5 Jan).

115. Ibid., 29 Mar. 1893. Although the 1893 mill project never materialized, in 1901, the Roanoke Cotton Mill, an entirely different entity, began operations in the former Norwich Lock Works building.

116. Roanoke Board of Trade, *Roanoke, Virginia 1894: Pluck, Push and Progress Illustrated* (Roanoke: Stone Printing & Mfg. Co., 1894), 1–17, in Edward L. Stone–Borderland Coal Company Papers, box 383, Roanoke file (first, second, third and fourth quotes from page 13; fifth quote from page 17).

117. *Headlight: Special Edition of the Magic City*, 2–30 (first quote is from page 2; second quote is from page 3).

118. RCOC, *Roanoke: The Magic City of Virginia*, 1–83 (first quote is from pages 30–31; second quote is from page 13; third quote is from page 11).

119. See account of the article along with advertising information in *The Roanoke Times*, 9 June 1906.

120. Details of the RCOC's Industrial Securities Company and Jamestown campaign are in the 9 Jan. 1910 address of RCOC President R. H. Angell, rpt. in *The Roanoke Times*, 10 Jan. 1908.

121. Roanoke Chamber of Commerce, *Roanoke, Virginia: Its Location, Climate and Water Supply, Its Manufacturing, Commercial and Educational Advantages and General Desirability as a Place of Residence. Issued by the Chamber of Commerce. Compiled and Edited Under the Auspices of the Jamestown Exposition Committee by Edward Boyle Jacobs, Secretary, Chamber of Commerce*, ed. Edward Boyle Jacobs (Roanoke: Stone Printing & Mfg. Co., 1907), 1–32, especially 2–4 (quotes from page 3).

122. Roanoke Chamber of Commerce, *Busy Facts for the Busy Man about the Busy "Magic City," Roanoke, Va., U. S. A.* (Roanoke: Stone Printing & Mfg. Co., 1910), front cover.

123. Industrial growth figures from George Raymond Stevens, *An Economic and Social Survey of Roanoke County*, vol. 15, no. 1 (Charlottesville: University of Virginia, 1930), 64; real estate values from Jacobs, *History of Roanoke City*, 111.

124. Androit, ed., *Population Abstract of he United States*, 854–55.

125. RCOC, *Busy Facts*, inside front cover.

126. Barnes, *History of Roanoke*, 397, 412, 424–25, 449, 455.

127. In 1910, the company reopened as the Roanoke Twine Mill. See Barnes, *History of Roanoke*, 361, 459, 465, 477. Most cotton mill owners claimed their investment was philanthropic as well as profit driven. See Hall, et al., *Like a Family*, 30–32.

128. RCOC, *Roanoke: The Magic City of Virginia*, 40; Jacobs, *History of Roanoke City*, 122, 124, 131, 134–36.

129. Jacobs, *History of Roanoke City*, 112.

130. *The Roanoke Times*, 25, 29 Nov. 1905 (quote is from 25 Nov.); for dangerous and difficult conditions in cotton mills, see Hall, et al., *Like a Family*, 80–85.

131. Information on Brick Row from Barnes, *History of Roanoke*, 114, 176–77, 328.

132. See real estate assessments in *The Roanoke Times*, 21 June 1900; 4 Dec. 1903; 26 May 1905.

133. See details in story titled "A Big Scheme: Plan Afoot to Open the Mill Mountain Hotel" in *The Roanoke Times*, 30 Mar. 1901.

134. *Virginia College Rattler*, 18 Dec. 1902, in HMHSWV.

135. Information on initial investors and Stone's commitment is from 1909 and 1910 company records and correspondence in Edward L. Stone–Borderland Coal Company Papers, box 442, Mill Mountain Incline file.

136. Edward L. Stone, Roanoke, to L. E. Johnson, Pasadena, CA, 12 Nov. 1909, Edward L. Stone–Borderland Coal Company Papers, box 442, Mill Mountain Incline file.

137. Edward L. Stone, Roanoke, to L. E. Johnson, Roanoke, 7 Dec. 1909, Edward L. Stone–Borderland Coal Company Papers, box 442, Mill Mountain Incline file.

138. For Stone's appointment, see Mill Mountain Incline Incorporated (MMII), Stockholders' Minutes, 2 Mar. 1910, in Edward L. Stone–Borderland Coal Company Papers, box 442, Mill Mountain Incline file; for quote and recommendation, see Edward L. Stone, Roanoke, to S. A. Cooney, care of John A. Roeblings Sons Co., Trenton, NJ, 3 Jan. 1910, Edward L. Stone–Borderland Coal Company Papers, box 442, Mill Mountain Incline file.

139. MMII, Stockholders' Meeting Notice, 3 Mar. 1910, Edward L. Stone–Borderland Coal Company Papers, box 442, Mill Mountain Incline file.

140. MMII, *Mill Mountain Incline*, promotional brochure in Edward L. Stone–Borderland Coal Company Papers, box 442, Mill Mountain Incline file; see also Barnes, *History of Roanoke*, 473.

141. See form letters to all MMII stockholders from Edward Stone, dated 30 July 1910, in Edward L. Stone–Borderland Coal Company Papers, box 442, Mill Mountain Incline file.

142. Louis A. Scholz, President, Virginia Brewing Company, Roanoke, to Edward L. Stone, Roanoke, 24 Aug. 1910, in Edward L. Stone–Borderland Coal Company Papers, box 442, Mill Mountain Incline file; Edward L. Stone, Roanoke, to Louis A. Scholz, Roanoke, 25 Aug. 1910, in Edward L. Stone–Borderland Coal Company Papers, box 442, Mill Mountain Incline file.

143. See various correspondence related to the sales in July, Aug, Sept. 1910 letters to Stone in Edward L. Stone–Borderland Coal Company Papers, box 442, Mill Mountain Incline file.

144. Frank Gravely Payne Diary, 1904–1960, years 1904–1910 excerpted in Neal Payne, "How a Railway Clerk Saw the New Century," *Journal of the Roanoke Valley Historical Society* 11, no. 2 (1982): 46.

145. Information about opening day and quotes are from MMII, *Mill Mountain Incline.*

146. Barnes, *History of Roanoke,* 473; MMII, Annual Statement—1911, in Edward L. Stone–Borderland Coal Company Papers, box 442, Mill Mountain Incline file.

147. Edward L. Stone, Roanoke, to John Hartman Marsteller, Roanoke, 22 Aug. 1910, in Edward L. Stone–Borderland Coal Company Papers, box 442, Mill Mountain Incline file.

148. Edward L. Stone, Roanoke, to Albin B. Hammond, Roanoke, 25 Oct. 1910, in Edward L. Stone–Borderland Coal Company Papers, box 442, Mill Mountain Incline file; see also, Barnes, *History of Roanoke,* 465.

149. In 1941, Roanoke City acquired the summit when J. B. Fishburn, who bought the property from Washington & Lee University for fifty thousand dollars, donated the land to the municipality with the stipulation that it be turned into a public park.

150. MMII, Statement Showing Income by Months from Incline and Observatory—Aug. 14, 1910 to Dec. 31, 1911, in Edward L. Stone–Borderland Coal Company Papers, box 442, Mill Mountain Incline file.

151. *The* (Roanoke) *Evening World,* 2 May 1911; "Views about Mill Mountain and the Incline Railway," extension postcard (Roanoke: Stone Printing & Mfg. Co., 1910), in author's collection.

152. *The* (Roanoke) *Evening World,* 6 May 1911.

153. Eleanor Bowles Armistead, Lewis-Gale Hospital, Roanoke, to James H. Anderson, Richmond, 10 Oct. 1911, in Anderson Family Papers, VHS.

154. MMII, Statement Showing Income by Months from Incline and Observatory—Aug. 14, 1910 to Dec. 31, 1911, in Edward L. Stone–Borderland Coal Company Papers, box 442, Mill Mountain Incline file; MMII, Statement of Earnings—1912, in Edward L. Stone–Borderland Coal Company Papers, box 442, Mill

Mountain Incline file. Information about the destruction of the 1910 observatory is from Roanoke Times & World News Corporation, *Roanoke: 100, A Centennial Edition Reprint* (Roanoke: Roanoke Times & World News Corporation, 1982), 58.

155. MMII, Annual Statement—1911, in Edward L. Stone–Borderland Coal Company Papers, box 442, Mill Mountain Incline file.

156. H. D. Vickers, Secretary and Treasurer, MMII, Roanoke, to Edward L. Stone, Roanoke, 29 Mar. 1912, in n Edward L. Stone–Borderland Coal Company Papers, box 442, Mill Mountain Incline file.

157. MMII, Statement of Earnings—1912, in Edward L. Stone–Borderland Coal Company Papers, box 442, Mill Mountain Incline file.

158. Correspondence between the Roanoke Chamber of Commerce and the Roanoke Gas & Water Company rpt. in *The* (Roanoke) *Evening World,* 31 May 1912. Ironically, thirty-seven years later, the Roanoke Chamber of Commerce, along with the Roanoke Merchants' Association, spent $25,000 to erect the eight-story neon star that now adorns the summit of Mill Mountain.

159. Stone's appointment is from H. D. Vickers, Secretary and Treasurer, Mill Mountain Incline Incorporated, Roanoke, to Edward L. Stone, Roanoke, 30 Mar. 1912, in Edward L. Stone–Borderland Coal Company Papers, box 442, Mill Mountain Incline file.

160. Edward L. Stone, Roanoke, to J. W. Hancock, President, Mill Mountain Incline Incorporated, 10 Sept. 1912, in Edward L. Stone–Borderland Coal Company Papers, box 442, Mill Mountain Incline file.

161. Barnes, *History of Roanoke,* 561, 563, 722.

Chapter 7

1. See, for example, Robert H. Wiebe, *The Search for Order, 1877–1920* (New York: Hill and Wang, 1967), 111–32, 153–63; Richard Hofstadter, *The Age of Reform: From Bryan to F. D. R.* (New York: Vintage, 1955), 176–85, 216–18; Grantham, *Southern Progressivism,* xvi–xviii, 4–34, 158, 275–88; Link, *The Paradox of Southern Progressivism,* xi–xiii, 322–24.

2. *The Roanoke Times,* 6, 7 Nov. 1901. Although the local election went to the Democratic candidates, the 1,502 ballots cast for local Republican Robert H. Angell combined with ballots from Roanoke County to give him a majority of votes for the House of Delegates.

3. Woods, "Personal Biographical Sketches and Reminiscences of James Pleasants Woods," 33.

4. *The Roanoke Times,* 10 Apr. 1900.

5. Ibid., 24 May 1900.

6. Ibid., 26 May and 7 June 1900. The number of Republicans who endorsed the constitution convention is derived from the total ballots cast against the convention (640) subtracted from total ballots cast for the Republican candidate for mayor

(1,094); 26 May election results on constitution were incomplete—see 7 June for final count.

7. *The Roanoke Times*, 24 May 1901. The vote was 1,017 for the Democratic delegate, 124 for the Independent delegate, and 40 for the Socialist-Labor delegate.

8. Ibid., 6 Aug. 1902.

9. McKinney, *Southern Mountain Republicans*, 196–97.

10. *The Roanoke Times*, 2 Oct. 1902.

11. Ibid., 5 Nov. 1902.

12. Ibid., 16 Jan. 1904.

13. Ibid., 11 Aug. 1905.

14. Woods, "Personal Biographical Sketches and Reminiscences," 35.

15. Details of law from *The Roanoke Times*, 6 June 1900.

16. *The Roanoke Times*, 7 Aug. 1900.

17. See details of streetcar law in *The Roanoke Times*, 14 June 1906; for editors' opposition, see *The Roanoke Times*, 7, 13 Mar. 1902 (first three quotes from 13 March; fourth quote from 7 March). For enactment of the law in Roanoke and fifth quote, see *The Roanoke Times*, 22 June 1906.

18. *The Roanoke Times*, 13 Sept. 1903.

19. Electric Parlor ad from *The Roanoke Times*, 19 May 1907; "colored day" and Mountain Park from *The* (Roanoke) *Evening World*, 31 Aug. 1911.

20. *The* (Roanoke) *Evening World*, 16 Sept. 1911.

21. First example from *The Roanoke Times*, 28 July 1900; second example from *The Roanoke Times*, 26 July 1904.

22. Baratta, "Gainesboro Neighborhood, 1890–1940," 40–41.

23. *The Roanoke Times*, 29 July 1900.

24. Ibid., 12 Apr. 1905.

25. Ibid., 14 Mar. 1905.

26. Ibid., 21 Mar. 1905.

27. Ibid., 28 Mar. 1905.

28. For this same "progressive reform" throughout Virginia, see J. Douglas Smith, *Managing White Supremacy: Race, Politics, and Citizenship in Jim Crow Virginia* (Chapel Hill: University of North Carolina Press, 2002), 19–39; Pulley, *Old Virginia Restored*, 66–151; for similar intensification of segregation in Charlotte, North Carolina the 1890s and early 1900s, see Hanchett, *Sorting Out the New South City*, 116–34; for the rest of the South, see Grantham *Southern Progressivism*, 10–34, 116–25; Link, *Paradox of Southern Progressivism*, 70–85, 322.

29. Malcolm W. Bryan, Roanoke, to Roanoke City Council, 23 Oct. 1894, rpt. in Bryan, III, "Humor—1890s Variety," TMs (1995), Bryan Papers.

30. *The Roanoke Daily Times,* 26 April; 14 May; 21 June; 14 Aug. 1895.

31. Martha Tinsley Taylor, a resident of Campbell Avenue in the 1890s, re-counted seeing "boys drive cows up the Avenues to the suburbs to graze each morn-ing and back home again in the evenings." See "Reminiscences of Martha Tinsley Taylor," in Alexander, *Elmwood of Roanoke,* 15.

32. See cattle count by Ward published in *The Roanoke Times,* 14 Sept. 1902. White residents of the First Ward owned 254 cows; white residents of the Fourth owned 148 cows; white residents of the Fifth owned 188 cows; and black residents of the Third owned 31 cows.

33. *The Roanoke Times,* 12 June 1902.

34. Ibid., 10 Sept. 1902.

35. Ibid., 11 Sept. 1902.

36. Ibid., 14 Sept. 1902.

37. Ibid., 16 Sept. 1902.

38. Ibid., 19 Sept. 1902.

39. Ibid., 24 Sept. 1902.

40. Ibid., 1 Oct. 1902.

41. Ibid., 4 Oct. 1902.

42. Ibid., 9 Oct. 1902.

43. Ibid., 8 Oct. 1902.

44. Ibid., 19 Oct. 1902.

45. Ibid., 22 Oct. 1902.

46. Ibid., 25 Oct. 1902. Crumpecker, a fifty-five-year-old native of Franklin County, was, like his nemesis Blair Antrim, a University of Virginia trained lawyer.

47. Ibid., 29 Oct. 1902.

48. Ibid., 30 Oct. 1902.

49. Ibid., 4 Nov. 1902.

50. Ibid., 5 Nov. 1902.

51. *The Richmond News,* 5 Nov. 1902, qtd. in *The Roanoke Times,* 7 Nov. 1902; see also *The Richmond Dispatch,* 5 Nov. 1902, also qtd. in *The Roanoke Times,* 5 Nov. 1902.

52. *The Newport News Times-Herald,* qtd. in *The Roanoke Times,* 27 Nov. 1902; see also *The Norfolk Landmark,* also qtd. in *The Roanoke Times,* 27 Nov. 1902.

53. *The Roanoke Times,* 12 Nov. 1902.

54. Ibid., 13 Aug. 1903.

55. Ibid., 15 Aug. 1903.

56. Ibid., 18 Aug. 1903.

57. Ibid., 19 Aug. 1903.

58. Ibid., 20 Aug. 1903.

59. Ibid.

60. Ibid., 9 Sept. 1903.

61. Ibid., 9 Oct. 1903.

62. Ibid., 6 July 1904.

63. Ibid., 15, 16 July 1904 (quote from 16).

64. See reprint of the ordinance in *The Roanoke Times*, 25 Aug. 1904.

65. Ibid., 18 Aug. 1904.

66. Ibid., 20 Aug. 1904.

67. Ibid., 31 Mar. and 30 June 1905.

68. Ownby, *Subduing Satan*, 14–15, 167–74.

69. *The Roanoke Times*, 3 Apr. 1900.

70. Ibid., 5 Feb. 1902.

71. Virginia Anti-Saloon League, *Temperance Handbook of Virginia* (Richmond: Anti-Saloon League of Virginia, 1910), 17.

72. *The Roanoke Times*, 16 Feb. 1902.

73. For membership increases, see *The Roanoke Times*, 11, 21 Mar. 1902; for law against women in saloons, see *The Roanoke Times*, 20, 26 May 1903.

74. *The Roanoke Times*, 14 June 1903.

75. Ibid., 30 Sept. 1903. Biographical information on Fishburn is from HC, FBCR, *An Adventure in Faith*, 47–50.

76. *The Roanoke Times*, 22 Nov. and 2 Dec. 1903 (quote is from 22 Nov).

77. Ibid., 6 Dec. 1903.

78. Ibid., 8 Dec. 1903.

79. Ibid.

80. Ibid., 20 Dec. 1903; in 1904, E. B. Jacobs helped found the Roanoke Chamber of Commerce. He served as its secretary until 1910.

81. Ibid., 22 Dec. 1903.

82. *The* (Roanoke) *Evening World*, clipping in Campbell Papers (dated December, no day or year given, but it is from 1903, the only year a local option vote occurred on New Year's Eve).

83. Both rallies covered in *The Roanoke Times*, 29 Dec. 1903.

84. For official vote of 1,823 opposed to prohibition, 841 in favor of prohibition, see *The Roanoke Times*, 1 Jan. 1905.

85. For examples of Anti–Saloon League speakers, see address by president of Virginia ASL and address by national ASL representative in *The Roanoke Times*, 12 July 1905.

301

86. VASL, *Temperance Handbook,* 17–19; Moger, *Virginia: From Bourbonism to Byrd,* 297–305.

87. VASL, *Temperance Handbook,* 4; Moger, *Virginia: From Bourbonism to Byrd,* 297–305.

88. Roanoke Anti–Saloon League, *To The Voters of Roanoke / Brothers, Sons, Husbands, Fathers / We Have No Protectors But You* (Roanoke: Union Printing & Mfg. Co., 1908), in Edward L. Stone–Borderland Coal Company Papers, box 276, 1908 Anti-Saloon League file; for national prohibitionists' consistent use of "appetite," "avarice," women, and boys in their campaign literature, see Gaines Foster, *Moral Reconstruction: Christian Lobbyists and the Federal Legislation of Morality, 1865–1920* (Chapel Hill: University of North Carolina, 2002), 2–5, 79–81.

89. Edward L. Stone, Roanoke, to Small-Grain Distilling, Louisville, KY. 12 Nov. 1908, in Edward L. Stone–Borderland Coal Company Papers, box 444, 1909–1910 Small Grain Distilling Co. file.

90. "Agreement—between the undersigned Liquor dealers of the City of Roanoke, Va., in the one part, and the Business Men's League of the City of Roanoke of the other part," in Edward L. Stone–Borderland Coal Company Papers, box 276, 1908 Anti-Saloon League file. Stone's involvement is evident from his notes and instructions on attached sheets of paper as well as by the inclusion of the contract in his personal files.

91. Barnes, *History of Roanoke,* 454–55, 457–58; Frank Payne Diary, 1904–1960, 45.

92. Barnes, *History of Roanoke,* 458, 465. The vote was 1,644 against prohibition and 1,575 in favor of it.

93. *The* (Roanoke) *Evening World,* 27 Nov. 1911.

94. Ibid., 27 Feb. 1912.

95. Hart's vote against the bill is from *The* (Roanoke) *Evening World,* 4 Mar. 1912; the defeat of the bill is from Moger, *Virginia: From Bourbonism to Byrd,* 306–7; editorial is from *The* (Roanoke) *Evening World,* 5 Mar. 1912.

96. Moger, *Virginia: From Bourbonism to Byrd,* 308–13; Barnes, *History of Roanoke,* 536.

97. Link, *Paradox of Southern Progressivism,* 96–112; Grantham, *Southern Progressivism,* 160–76. For civic boosters in Southwest Virginia and East Tennessee supporting prohibition, see Lee, *The Virginia-Tennessee Tri-Cities,* 108 and Ayers, "Northern Business and the Shape of Southern Progress," 214–15.

98. Sims, *The Power of Femininity in the New South,* 1–5, 80–114; Marsha Wedell, *Elite Women and the Reform Impulse in Memphis, 1875–1915* (Knoxville: University of Tennessee Press, 1991), 77–126; Joan Marie Johnson, *Southern Ladies, New Women: Race, Region, and Clubwomen in South Carolina, 1890–1930* (Gainesville: University Press of Florida, 2004), 145–95; Valeria G. Lerda, "'We were no class at all': Southern Women as Social Reformers," in Melvyn Stokes and Rick Halpern, eds., *Race and Class in the American South Since 1890* (Oxford, UK: Berg Publishers, 1994), 121–38.

99. *The Roanoke Times,* 1 Mar. 1904.

100. Ibid., 10 Aug. 1905.

101. See Cutchin's address to the council in Roanoke City Council Minutes, 7 July 1903, Clerk's Office, Roanoke City Municipal Building.

102. *The Roanoke Times,* 22, 23 Sept. 1905.

103. Biographical material is from Ann Field Alexander, "Joel Holleman Cutchin," in Sara Bearss, ed., *The Dictionary of Virginia Biography: Volume 3* (Richmond: The Library of Virginia, 2006), 643–44.

104. *The Roanoke Times,* 30 Nov. and 13 Dec. 1905 (quote from 30 Nov).

105. Ibid., 22, 24 Mar. 1906.

106. Ibid., 22, 23 Mar. 1906.

107. Ibid., 24 Mar. 1906.

108. Ibid., 1 Apr. 1906.

109. Ibid., 11 Mar. 1906.

110. Ibid., 6 Apr. 1906.

111. Ibid., 8 Apr. 1906.

112. Ibid., 11 Apr. 1906.

113. Ibid., 12 April; 9, 12, 18 May 1906.

114. Ibid., 26 Apr. 1906.

115. Ibid., 3, 6 May 1906 (quote from 6 May).

116. Ibid., 9, 15 May 1906.

117. Ibid., 6 June 1906.

118. Ibid., 22, 25, 30 Sept.; 4 Oct. 1906 (first quote from 25 Sept; second quote from 4 Oct).

119. Ibid., 9, 10 Nov. 1906 (quote from 10 Nov).

120. Ibid., 7 Dec. 1906.

121. Ibid., 22 Nov. 1906.

122. Ibid., 8 Dec. 1906.

123. Ibid., 13 Dec. 1906.

124. Woman's Civic Betterment Club of Roanoke, *The Year Book of the Woman's Civic Betterment Club / Roanoke, Virginia 1910* (Roanoke: Hammond Printing Works, 1910), 5, in WCBC file, VR-RCPL.

125. WCBC, *Year Book of the Woman's Civic Betterment Club,* 2, 7–11; for female clubwomen, see Anne Firor Scott, *Natural Allies: Women's Voluntary Associations in America* (Urbana: University of Illinois Press, 1992).

126. WCBC, *Year Book of the Woman's Civic Betterment Club,* 2, 7–11; husbands' professions from city directories as well as Barnes, *History of Roanoke.*

127. Biographical information on Sarah Johnson Cocke (Mrs. Lucian Cocke) from *The Roanoke Times*, 29 Sept. and 31 Oct. 1903; 21 Jan. 1944 (obituary); Sarah Johnson Cocke, "From Hoopskirts to Airplanes," 1–98, TMs (1933), VR-RCPL; information on Howell Cobb from William W. Freehling, *The Road to Disunion Volume I: Secessionists at Bay, 1776–1854* (New York: Oxford University Press, 1990), 5–6, 479, 523–24. Sarah Johnson Cocke later received national acclaim for her *Bypaths in Dixie* (New York: E. P. Dutton, 1911), a collection of "negro folktales."

128. Cocke, "From Hoopskirts to Airplanes," 99–104 (first two quotes from 99); Mrs. Lucian H. Cocke, "The Woman's Civic Betterment Club of Roanoke," *The Virginia Realtor* (Sept. 1926): 35 (third quote from 35).

129. Biographical information on Mrs. M. M. (Willie) Caldwell from *The Roanoke Times*, 3 Mar. and 5 Oct. 1907; 22 Mar. 1946 (obituary); attendance at school funding meeting and quote are from *The Roanoke Times*, 8 Apr. 1906.

130. For examples, see Cutchin's speeches to the council in Roanoke City Council Minutes, 4 Feb. 1907; 9 Mar. 1908; 8 Feb. and 10 Aug. 1909; 6 June, 7 Nov, 17 Dec. 1910, Clerk's Office, Roanoke City Municipal Building.

131. *The Roanoke Times*, 15 Dec. 1906.

132. Ibid., 18 Dec. 1906.

133. See running column in *The Roanoke Times* beginning 13 Jan. 1907 and appearing at least weekly thereafter until 1912.

134. *The Roanoke Times*, 26, 30 Jan.; 3 Feb. 1907 (quote from 30 Jan).

135. Ibid., 26 Jan.; 3 Feb.; 14 May 1907 (first quote from 14 May; second quote from 3 Feb).

136. Ibid., 10 Feb. 1907.

137. Ibid., 21, 22 Feb. 1907.

138. Ibid., 12, 14 May 1907.

139. *The Roanoke Times*, 23 Feb.; 21 Apr.; 11 May; 8, 9 Nov.; 6, 10 Dec. 1907; 11, 25, 26 Jan. 1908; Barnes, *History of Roanoke*, 432–33.

140. *The Roanoke Times*, 19 Mar. 1907. For WCBC invitation to city councilors to attend McFarland's lecture, see Roanoke City Council Minutes, 12 Feb. 1907.

141. *The Roanoke Times*, 7 Apr. 1907.

142. See letters to WCBC in its column in *The Roanoke Times*, 10, 17 Feb.; 3, 10, 24, 31 Mar.; 7, 21 Apr.; 12, 21 May; 2 June 1907 (first quotes from 24 March; last quote from 12 May).

143. *The Roanoke Times*, 7 Apr. 1907.

144. Advisory board information from Willie Walker Caldwell, Chairman Ways & Means Committee, WCBC, Roanoke, to Ed Stone, Roanoke, 10 Apr. 1907, Edward L. Stone–Borderland Coal Company Papers, box 354, 1907–1908 Civic Betterment file; Edward L. Stone, Roanoke, to Mrs. M. M. Caldwell, Roanoke, 11 Apr. 1907, ibid.

145. For meetings, see Taylor Gleaves, Chairman, Roanoke, to Edward L. Stone, Roanoke, 3, 12 June; 16 Aug.; 3 Oct. 1907, Edward L. Stone–Borderland Coal Company Papers, box 354, 1907–1908 Civic Betterment file; quote is from Edward L. Stone, Roanoke, to Mrs. M. M. Caldwell, Roanoke, 11 Apr. 1907, ibid.

146. Male support of female reform groups is discussed in James L. Leloudis II, "School Reform in the New South: The Woman's Association for the Betterment of Public School Houses in North Carolina, 1902–1919," *The Journal of American History* 69, no. 4 (Mar. 1983): 889.

147. See Cocke's speech to the Virginia Federation of Women's Clubs rpt. in *The Roanoke Times*, 20 May 1937.

148. *The Roanoke Times*, 30 Apr. 1907; Hanchett, *Sorting Out the New South City*, 154–56; Nolen's 1906 Hollins Institute campus design is noted in John L. Hancock, "John Nolen and the American City Planning Movement: A History of Culture Change and Community Response, 1900-1940" (Ph.D. diss., University of Pennsylvania, 1964), 45.

149. See details of advisory board's involvement in Taylor Gleaves, Roanoke, to Edward L. Stone, Roanoke, 27 Apr. 1907, Edward L. Stone–Borderland Coal Company Papers, box 354, 1907–1908 Civic Betterment file.

150. Taylor Gleaves, Chairman, Roanoke, to Edward L. Stone, Roanoke, 3 June 1907, Edward L. Stone–Borderland Coal Company Papers, box 354, 1907–1908 Civic Betterment file. See also references to loaning the club money in Taylor Gleaves, Chairman, Roanoke, to Edward L. Stone, Roanoke, 8 Oct; 2, 3, Dec. 1907, ibid.

151. Cocke, "Woman's Civic Betterment Club," 36; *The Roanoke Times*, 25 Sept. 1907.

152. *The Roanoke Times*, 25 Sept. 1907.

153. Ibid., 26, 29 Sept. 1907.

154. Ibid., 27 Sept. 1907; for a stream of stories about the Fall Festival, see *The Roanoke Times*, 28, 29 Sept.; 1, 3, 4, 5, 6, 8, 9, 10, 12, 13, 16, 17, 18, 19, 22, 26, 27 Oct.; 5, 6, 7, 8, 9, 10, 12 Nov. 1907.

155. Ibid., 6 Oct. 1907.

156. See coverage of speech by Sarah Cocke and Willie Caldwell to Virginia Federation of Women's Clubs rpt. in *The Roanoke Times*, 20 May 1937.

157. *The Roanoke Times*, 10, 26, 27 Oct. 1907 (quote from 27 Oct).

158. Ibid., 19 Oct. 1907.

159. Ibid., 13 Nov. 1907.

160. See coverage in *The Roanoke Times*, 13–26 Nov. 1907; *Festival Facts and Fancies*, 12–23 Nov. 1907, in VR-RCPL.

161. Woman's Civic Betterment Club of Roanoke, *The Roanoke Cook Book: Favorite Recipes by Some of Roanoke's Good Housekeepers*, compiled by Mrs. Albert A. Stone (Roanoke: Stone Printing & Mfg. Co., 1907), 1.

162. *Festival Facts and Fancies,* 12 Nov. 1907.

163. Pedigo and WCTU opinions from *Festival Facts and Fancies* 14 Nov. 1907; Stone's, 15 Nov. 1907; Scholz's, 19 Nov. 1907; Campbell's, 20 Nov. 1907.

164. Speech by Sarah Johnson Cocke, President WCBC, to the Civic Betterment Club of Virginia, TMs (ca. 1908), WCBC file, VR-RCPL.

165. For Stone and advisory board's supervision, see Edward L. Stone, Roanoke, to Taylor Gleaves, Roanoke, 19, 21 Dec. 1907; 20 Jan. 1908, Edward L. Stone–Borderland Coal Company Papers, box 354, 1907–1908 Civic Betterment file.

166. John Nolen, *Remodeling Roanoke: Report to the Committee on Civic Improvement* (Roanoke: Stone Printing & Mfg. Co., 1907), 38; Debra L. Alderson, "John Nolen, City Planner: The Roanoke Plans" (M.A. thesis, University of Virginia, 1992), 21–57.

167. C. E. Emerson Jr., and Ezra B. Whitman, *Sanitary Roanoke: Report to the Committee on Civic Improvement* (Roanoke: Stone Printing & Mfg. Co., 1907), 5–21.

168. Goldfield, *Cotton Fields and Skyscrapers,* 101–2; for Nolen's work in Charlotte, North Carolina, see Hanchett, *Sorting Out the New South City,* 167–81, 218–21.

169. Paul S. Boyer, *Urban Masses and Moral Order in America, 1820–1920* (Cambridge, MA: Harvard University Press, 1978), vii, 251–54; William H. Wilson, *The City Beautiful Movement* (Baltimore: Johns Hopkins University, 1989), 80–92; Alderson, "John Nolen, City Planner: The Roanoke Plans," 8–19; Hancock, "John Nolen and the American City Planning Movement," 2–51, 157–73, 233–50.

170. Nolen, *Remodeling Roanoke,* 10–11, 40 (first two quotes 10–11; third quote 40); see also John Nolen, *Replanning Small Cities: Six Typical Studies* (New York: B. W. Huebsch, 1912), chap. 2, "Roanoke: A Small City of the New South"; Frances J. Niederer, "John Nolen's Roanoke City Plan of 1907," *Journal of the Roanoke Historical Society* 2, no. 2 (Winter 1965–66): 1–8.

171. *The Roanoke Times,* 18 Jan. 1908.

172. For reception of Nolen's Roanoke plans, see letter to WCBC from American Civic Association published in *The Roanoke Times,* 26 Jan. 1908; Speech by Sarah Johnson Cocke, President WCBC, to the Civic Betterment Club of Virginia; Cocke, "Woman's Civic Betterment Club," 36.

173. Roanoke City Council Minutes, 8 Feb. and 10 Aug. 1909 (quote from 10 Aug.).

174. Speech by Sarah Johnson Cocke, President WCBC, to the Civic Betterment Club of Virginia.

175. Approval of the bonds is in Roanoke City Council Minutes, 4 Apr. 1910; Cutchin's remarks are in Roanoke City Council Minutes, 6 June 1910.

176. Cocke, "Woman's Civic Betterment Club," 36. Nolen returned nearly twenty years later, invited by the Roanoke Planning Commission, which was headed by Edward L. Stone, to draw up yet another comprehensive plan for the city. Nolen's 1928 plan, while never implemented in full, guided municipal development through subsequent decades. See WPA, *Roanoke: Story of County and City,* 253–54; John

Nolen, *Comprehensive City Plan: Roanoke, Virginia, 1928* (Roanoke: Stone Printing & Mfg. Co., 1928).

177. *The Roanoke Times*, 19 Dec. 1907; Speech by Sarah Johnson Cocke, President WCBC, to the Civic Betterment Club of Virginia; Cocke, "Woman's Civic Betterment Club," 36.

178. City of Roanoke, *Annual Report of the Official Departments of the City of Roanoke for the Fiscal Year Ending December 31, 1910* (Roanoke: Stone Printing & Mfg. Co., 1911), 145–53.

179. City of Roanoke, *An Ordinance, Approved January 18, 1911, To define the Duties of the Dairy and Food Inspector, and to provide for the Inspection of Milk, Meat and other Food Supplies brought into, or offered for sale in the City of Roanoke, and to prohibit the sale of Adulterated or Impure Milk, Meat and other Food Supplies within the City of Roanoke* (Roanoke: City of Roanoke, 1911), in HMHSWV.

180. *The* (Roanoke) *Evening World*, 13 May 1911. Cutchin was indicted on March 29, 1911.

181. Ibid., 6, 8, 9, 10, 12 May 1911 (WCBC quote from 6 May; Cutchin's quote from 8 May).

182. Rosen, *The Lost Sisterhood*, 4–5, 69–79; Best, *Controlling Vice*, 15–34.

183. *The Roanoke Times*, 14 Dec. 1905. Campbell's leadership of the group is noted in *The Roanoke Times*, 9 Jan. 1906.

184. Cutchin's speech was reprinted in *The Roanoke Times*, 16 Dec. 1905; the ministers' response is in *The Roanoke Times*, 19 Dec. 1905.

185. Alexander, "Joel Holleman Cutchin," 643–44.

186. Rosen, *The Lost Sisterhood*, 14–49, 112–35; Link, *The Paradox of Southern Progressivism*, 121–23.

187. *The* (Roanoke) *Evening World*, 23 Mar. 1911.

188. Ibid., 17, 18, 19 May 1911.

189. Ibid., 27 May 1911.

190. Ibid., 1, 2 June 1911.

191. Ibid., 8, 27 June; 3, 17 July 1911.

192. Ibid., 3 Jan. 1912.

193. Ibid., 28 Mar.; 18 Apr. 1912.

194. Ibid., *The* (Roanoke) *Evening World*, 6, May 1912; quote from *The* (Roanoke) *Evening World*, 21 May 1912.

195. Ibid., 14 June 1912. After his impeachment, Cutchin returned to practicing law full time before voters elected him as a trial justice in 1913. In 1916, he ran for mayor again but lost in a close race after receiving about 43 percent of ballots cast. He died of a stroke the following year. See Alexander, "Joel Holleman Cutchin," 643–44.

196. *The* (Roanoke) *Evening World*, 18 Nov. 1911.

197. Ibid., 9 Jan. 1912; Sims, *The Power of Femininity in the New South*, 68–79; Goodson, *Highbrows, Hillbillies, and Hellfire*, 85–89.

198. *The* (Roanoke) *Evening World*, 27 Mar. 1912. See also listing of fifteen WCBC members elected to the board of censorship in *The Evening World*, 2 Apr. 1912.

199. *The* (Roanoke) *Evening World*, 20 June 1912; for revival of the Board of Police Commissioners, see *The Evening World*, 15 June 1912; PPFA, *History of the Roanoke Police Department*, 94–96.

200. *The* (Roanoke) *Evening World*, 4 May 1912; Mrs. M. M. [Willie] Caldwell, "Nationwide Work for Civic Betterment," *The American City* 11, no. 6 (June 1912): 841–42.

201. History of the WCBC from Stevens, *An Economic and Social Survey of Roanoke County*, 118–19; Iva J. Geary, "The Woman's Club of Roanoke," 1–2, TMs (1936), Federal Writers' Project, District No. 5, Project No. 65-1700, WCBC file, VR-RCPL; drop in typhoid death rate from Roanoke City, *Official Reports of the City of Roanoke, Virginia, with Tables of General and Special Statistical Information of the Several Departments for the Fiscal Year Ending December 31, 1905* (Roanoke: Stone Printing & Mfg. Co., 1906), 73; PPFA, *History of the Roanoke Police Department*, 182–84. In 1997, relatives of WCBC members teamed up with Roanoke's PBS affiliate to produce a documentary about the group, somewhat misleadingly titled "The Hand that Rocked the Cradle, Pulled the Strings." The film, which unfortunately contains several factual errors, traces the history of WCBC only through its 1907 city plan campaign, includes no mention of the Club's male advisory board, and offers no indication of Mayor Joel Cutchin's inspiration or support. See "Transcript of 'The Hand that Rocked the Cradle, Pulled the Strings,'" TMs (1997), WCBC file, VR-RCPL.

202. Wiebe, *The Search for Order*, 45–60, 111–32, 153–54; 170; Gabriel Kolko, *The Triumph of Conservatism: A Reinterpretation of American History, 1900–1916* (New York: The Free Press, 1963), 1–10. Far less apparent in Roanoke are the "reformers" Richard Hofstadter contends were the "old rich" reacting to a "status upheaval" caused by the social and economic dislocation of the period. Moreover, Hofstadter's argument that "progressives" wanted an end to "trusts" and an expansion of democracy runs entirely counter to the aims of the city's "reformers," many of whom worked for the monopolistic N&W and supported disenfranchisement of blacks and poor whites. There was no "status upheaval" in Roanoke, mainly because the city lacked a long-established wealthy class. Nor was there any sort of merger between Roanoke's "progressives" and Populists from the countryside, as Hofstadter suggests happened elsewhere. See, Hofstadter, *The Age of Reform*, 135–66.

203. Link, *The Paradox of Southern Progressivism*, xiii, 268–94.

204. Ownby, *Subduing Satan*, 210–11.

205. Pulley, *Old Virginia Restored*, ix, 18–151.

206. Grantham, *Southern Progressivism*, xvi–xviii; 70–75, 275–88; Kipp III, "Old Notables and Newcomers," 382–84.

Epilogue

1. William J. Cooper Jr. and Thomas E. Terrill, *The American South: A History*, vol. 2 (New York: McGraw-Hill Inc., 1991), 501–4; Howard N. Rabinowitz, "Continuity and Change: Southern Urban Development, 1860–1900," in *The City in Southern History: The Growth of Urban Civilization in the South*, ed. Blaine A. Brownwell and David R. Goldfield (Port Washington, NY: Kennikat Press, 1977), 105–39; Brownwell and Goldfield, "Southern Urban History," in *The City in Southern History*, ed. Brownwell and Goldfield, 8–10; Larsen, *Rise of the Urban South*, 116–58 (quote from 143); David Goldfield, *Region, Race, and Cities: Interpreting the Urban South* (Baton Rouge: Louisiana State University Press, 1997), 63–68; Woodward, *The Origins of the New South*, 111–41; Goldfield, *Cotton Fields and Skyscrapers*, 80–132.

Bibliography

Manuscripts

Baton Rouge, Louisiana

Special Collections, Hill Memorial Library, Louisiana State University.

Caffery Family Papers.

Blacksburg, Virginia

Norfolk & Western Railway Archives, Special Collections, Carol M. Newman Library, Virginia Tech.

Norfolk & Western Scrapbooks, numbers 10, 12, 16, 17, 18.

"N. & W. Accounting Department Personal Records No. 1 Feb 1874 to December 1901."

Shenandoah Valley Railroad Scrapbooks, numbers 3, 4, 5, 6.

Roanoke Land & Improvement Company Records.

"Roanoke Land & Improvement Company Sales Book June 1889–May 1906."

Roanoke Machine Works Records.

"The Roanoke Machine Works—Agreement of Corporation and Certificate of Incorporation."

Shenandoah Valley Railroad Records.

"Minute Book Shenandoah Valley Railroad, 1870–1881."

Charlottesville, Virginia

Manuscripts Department, Special Collections, Alderman Library, University of Virginia.

Noland Family Papers.

Norman-Lewis Family Papers (microfilm).

Edward L. Stone–Borderland Coal Company Papers.

Wohlbruck and Burgess Family Papers.

Ferrum, Virginia

Southwest Virginia Tragedy Ballads Collection, Blue Ridge Institute, Ferrum College.

"Roanoke Riot" (ballad lyrics).

Richmond, Virginia

Archives Department, Library of Virginia.

Alfred J. Morrison Papers.

Virginia Historical Society.

Anderson Family Papers.

Gordon Blair, "Memories of the Land Boom in the Western Part of Virginia" (1958 typescript).

Crickenberger Family Papers.

Davis Family Papers.

George Kooglar Gilmer Papers.

Harris Family Papers.

Nathaniel Burwell Johnston Papers.

J. Ambler Johnston Papers.

Jordan-Stabler Family Papers.

Linkous Family Papers.

Anna Clayton Logan, "Recollections of My Life" (1917 typescript).

Emma B. Lynch Papers.

William Churchill Noland Papers.

Richard Singleton Paulett Papers.

William Hicks Travers Papers.

Roanoke, Virginia

History Museum and Historical Society of Western Virginia.

William Creighton Campbell Papers.

"The First Train into Big Lick" (1927 typescript).

Jack W. Hancock, "Eyewitness Account of the Roanoke Riot of 1893" (1893 typescript).

H. V. Lineback Photography Studio, Aftermath of Thomas Smith Lynching (1893 photograph).

Roanoke Gas & Water Company Records.

Contract between Roanoke Gas & Water Co. and F. D. Booth to Build Mill Mtn Observatory, 25 Aug 1891.

Contract between Roanoke Gas & Water Co. and F. D. Booth to Build Mill Mtn Tavern, 25 Aug 1891.

Roanoke Land & Improvement Company Records.

John C. Moomaw Letters.

H. L. Moore Letters.

"Proposition and Contract—Julius G. Holmes—To erect 8 houses for colored people, 10 March 1882."

Roanoke Land & Improvement Company Housing Contracts.

"Unsold Lots—Land Agents Value of Property at Roanoke, April 15, 1884."

Virginia Room, Roanoke City Public Library.

"1890 Buena Vista Land Company Map and Brochure."

Malcolm W. Bryan Papers.

Sarah Johnson Cocke, "From Hoopskirts to Airplanes" (1933 typescript).

Sarah Johnson Cocke, "1908 Speech to the Civic Betterment Club of Virginia" (1908 typescript).

Richard R. Jones Letter.

"Minutes and Proceedings of the Roanoke Valley Medical Association, Organized in Roanoke, Va. at the Office of Dr. Gordon Simmons, June 10, 1891."

"Minute Book A. Roanoke Association for the Exhibition and Sale of Live Stock from Virginia and Other States."

John M. Payne Jr. Letter.

Stanford Insurance Map of Roanoke, Virginia, 1907.

E. P. Tompkins, "Medical Annals of Roanoke" (1922 typescript).

Roanoke Newspapers and Periodicals

Big Lick Weekly News, 1881.

The Daily Bee, 1892.

The Evening World, 1893, 1911–13.

Festival Facts and Fancies, 1907.

The Industrial Era, 1910.

The Iron Belt, 1892.

Roanoke Commercial Advertiser, 1882.

Roanoke Daily Herald, 1890.

Roanoke Daily Record, 1893.

Roanoke Daily Times, 1889, 1890, 1892, 1895.

The Roanoke Leader, 1882–86.

Roanoke Saturday Evening News, 1882.

Roanoke Saturday Review, 1882, 1883.

The Roanoke Times, 1890–1908.

The Roanoke Weekly Sun, 1888, 1889.

Stone's Impressions, 1913, 1933.

Virginia College Rattler, 1902.

The World News, 1913.

Words and Works, 1892, 1893.

Other Newspapers or Periodicals

Baltimore Sun, 1883.

Bulletin of the Bureau of Immigration and Mining Intelligence, 1882.

The Crisis: A Record of the Darker Races, 1916.

The (Cleveland) Gazette, 1893.

The Industrial South, 1882.

The (Petersburg, VA) Index-Appeal, 1893.

The (Norfolk) Landmark, 1893.

The Lynchburg News, 1893.

The Manufacturers' Record, 1888.

The New York Herald, 1893.

The New York Times, 1881, 1883, 1887, 1890.

The New York World, 1893.

The Philadelphia Press, 1882.

The Richmond Dispatch, 1882, 1893.

The Richmond Planet, 1893.

The Richmond Times-Dispatch, 1904.

The Salem Register, 1881.

The Salem Times-Register, 1892.

The Virginias, 1883.

Virginia Free Press, 1881.

Government Documents

City Council of Roanoke, Virginia. Roanoke City Council Minutes, 1885, 1891, 1892, 1893, 1903, 1907, 1908, 1909, 1910. Clerk's Office, Roanoke City Municipal Building.

City of Roanoke, Virginia. *An Ordinance, Approved January 18, 1911, To define the Duties of the Dairy and Food Inspector, and to provide for the Inspection of Milk, Meat and other Food Supplies brought into, or offered for sale in the City of Roanoke, and to prohibit the sale of Adulterated or Impure Milk, Meat and other Food Supplies within the City of Roanoke.* Roanoke: City of Roanoke, 1911.

————. *Annual Report of the Official Departments of the City of Roanoke for the Fiscal Year Ending December 31, 1910.* Roanoke: Stone Printing & Mfg. Co., 1911.

————. *Department Reports of the City of Roanoke for the Year Ending June 30, 1893.* Roanoke: Stone Printing & Mfg. Co., 1893.

————. *General Ordinances of the City of Roanoke, Together with other Ordinances and Contracts Affecting the Rights and Interests of the City of Roanoke.* Roanoke: Bell Printing, 1884.

————. *Official Reports of the City of Roanoke, Virginia, with Tables of General and Special Statistical Information of the Several Departments for the Fiscal Year / Ending December 31, 1905.* Roanoke: Stone Printing & Mfg. Co., 1906.

————. "To the People of Roanoke! Sept 21st, 1893." Roanoke: City of Roanoke, 1893.

Journal of the House of Delegates of the State of Virginia for the Session of 1893–1894. Richmond: Superintendent of Public Printing, 1893.

Journal of the Senate of the Commonwealth of Virginia, 1893–1894. Richmond: Superintendent of Public Printing, 1894.

Report of the Acting Adjutant General of the State of Virginia for the Year 1893. Richmond: Superintendent of Public Printing, 1922.

Town Council of Big Lick, Virginia. Big Lick Town Council Minutes, 1881. Clerk's Office, Roanoke City Municipal Building.

Town Council of Roanoke, Virginia. "Census of the Town of Roanoke, December 1883." Volumes 1 and 2. Virginia Room, Roanoke City Public Library.

———. Roanoke Town Council Minutes, 1882. Clerk's Office, Roanoke City Municipal Building.

United States Bureau of the Census. *Historical Statistics of the United States, I.* Washington, DC: Government Printing Office, 1976.

———. *Report in Population of the United States at the Eleventh Census: 1890. Part 1.* Washington, DC: Government Printing Office, 1895.

———. U.S. Census of 1880, Schedule of Population, Town of Big Lick, County of Roanoke, State of Virginia.

Published Primary Works

Boyd, Charles R. *Resources of South-West Virginia, Showing the Mineral Deposits of Iron, Coal, Zinc, Copper, and Lead.* New York: John Wiley & Sons, 1881.

Bruce, Thomas. *Southwest Virginia and Shenandoah Valley.* Richmond: J. L. Hill, 1891.

Buena Vista Land Company. *1890 Map and Brochure of the Buena Vista Land Company.* N.p., 1890.

Caldwell, Mrs. M. M. [Willie]. "Nationwide Work for Civic Betterment." *The American City* 11, no. 6 (June 1912): 841–42.

Clayton, Thomas J. *Rambles and Reflections: From Biscay to the Black Sea and from Aetna to the North Cape with Glimpses of Asia, Africa, America and the Islands of the Sea.* Chester, PA: Press of the Delaware County Republican, 1893.

Cocke, Mrs. Lucian H. (Sarah Johnson Cocke). "The Woman's Civic Betterment Club of Roanoke." *The Virginia Realtor* (Sept.1926): 35–36.

Cocke, Sarah Johnson. *Bypaths in Dixie.* New York: E. P. Dutton, 1911.

Emerson, C. E., and Ezra B. Whitman. *Sanitary Roanoke: Report to the Committee on Civic Improvement.* Roanoke: Stone Printing & Mfg. Co., 1907.

Fidelity Insurance, Trust & Safe Deposit Company, Vs. The Shenandoah Valley Railroad Company. N.p.: privately printed, 1886.

Haddock & Baily's Roanoke, Va., City Directory, 1888. Richmond: Haddock & Baily, 1888.

Haddock's Roanoke, Va. City Directory 1890. Richmond: T. M. Haddock, 1890.

Headlight: Special Edition of the Magic City of Roanoke, Va., and Scenes Along the Norfolk & Western Railroad. Chicago: Beard & Collier, 1898.

Ingersol, Earnest. *To the Shenandoah and Beyond: A Chronicle of a Leisurely Journey Through the Uplands of Virginia and Tennessee, Sketching their Scenery, Noting their Legends, Portraying Social and Material Progress, and Explaining Routes of Travel.* New York: Leve & Alden Printing Company, 1885.

Jack, George S. *History of Roanoke County.* Roanoke: Stone Printing & Mfg. Co., 1912.

Jacobs, Edward B. *History of Roanoke City and History of the Norfolk & Western.* Roanoke: Stone Printing & Mfg. Co., 1912.

McCauley, William. *History of Roanoke County, Salem, and Roanoke City, Va., and Representative Citizens.* Chicago: Bibliographical Publishing Co., 1902.

Mill Mountain Incline Incorporated. *Mill Mountain Incline.* Roanoke: Privately printed, n.d.

———. "Views about Mill Mountain and the Incline Railway." Extension postcard. Roanoke: Stone Printing & Mfg. Co. 1910.

Nolen, John. *Comprehensive City Plan: Roanoke, Virginia, 1928.* Roanoke: Stone Printing & Mfg. Co., 1928.

———. *Remodeling Roanoke: Report to the Committee on Civic Improvement.* Roanoke: Stone Printing & Mfg. Co., 1907.

———. *Replanning Small Cities: Six Typical Studies.* New York: B. W. Huebsch, 1912.

Norfolk & Western Railroad Company. *Reference Book of the Norfolk & Western Railroad Co. Outlining the Condition of Progress in Mining, Manufacturers and Agriculture and Undeveloped Resources of those Portions of the State of Virginia Traversed by its Lines.* New York: Giles Co., 1889.

Page, Thomas Nelson. "The Lynching of Negroes—Its Causes and Its Prevention." *The North American Review* 178 (1904): 33–48.

Porter, James E. *1895 Roster of Secret Societies of Roanoke, Virginia.* Roanoke: Hammond Printing Works, 1895.

Roanoke Anti–Saloon League. *To The Voters of Roanoke / Brothers, Sons, Husbands, Fathers / We Have No Protectors But You.* Roanoke: Union Printing & Mfg. Co., 1908.

Roanoke Board of Trade. *Roanoke, Virginia 1894: Pluck, Push and Progress Illustrated.* Roanoke: Stone Printing & Mfg. Co., 1894.

Roanoke Century Club. *Eighth Annual Dinner—Century Club—April 17, 1914.* Roanoke: Stone Printing & Mfg. Co., 1914.

Roanoke Chamber of Commerce. *Busy Facts for the Busy Man about the Busy "Magic City," Roanoke, Va., U. S. A.* Roanoke: Stone Printing & Mfg. Co., 1910.

———. *Roanoke, Virginia: Its Location, Climate and Water Supply, Its Manufacturing, Commercial and Educational Advantages and General Desirability as a Place of Residence. Issued by the Chamber of Commerce. Compiled and Edited Under the Auspices of the Jamestown Exposition Committee by E. B. Jacobs, Secretary, Chamber of Commerce.* Edited Edward B. Jacobs. Roanoke: Stone Printing & Mfg. Co., 1907.

Roanoke City, *Official Reports of the City of Roanoke, Virginia, with Tables of General and Special Statistical Information of the Several Departments for the Fiscal Year Ending December 31, 1905.* Roanoke: Stone Printing & Mfg. Co., 1906.

———. *Roanoke: The Magic City of Virginia.* Roanoke: Stone Printing & Mfg. Co., 1904.

Roanoke Country Club. *Roanoke Country Club, 1906–07.* Roanoke: Stone Printing & Mfg. Co. 1906.

Roanoke Decennial Committee. *A Souvenir of the Decennial Celebration of Roanoke, Virginia.* Roanoke: Hammond Printing Works, 1892.

Roanoke German Club. *Constitution and By-Laws of the Friday German Club of Roanoke, Virginia.* Roanoke: Stone Printing & Mfg. Co., 1892.

———. *Roanoke German Club Golden Anniversary Ball 1884–1934.* Roanoke: n.p., 1934.

Roanoke Police Pension Fund Association. *History of the Roanoke Police Department.* Roanoke: Union Printing, 1916.

Sholes' Directory of the City of Roanoke, November 1st, 1892. Roanoke: Stone Printing & Mfg. Co., 1892.

Smith, F. P. *A Synopsis of Roanoke and her Wonderful Prosperity.* Roanoke: W. M. Yeager & Co., Real Estate Brokers, 1891.

Sproul, William C. *David F. Houston.* Philadelphia: Press of A. H. Strickler & Co., 1890.

Stone Printing & Manufacturing Company. *First Annual Outing of the Employees of The Stone Printing & Manufacturing Company, of Roanoke, Virginia, Tuesday, August 11th, 1896, at Elliston, Virginia.* Roanoke: Stone Printing & Mfg. Co. 1896.

———. *Picturesque Roanoke / Being a Series of Reproductions from Photographic Views, Taken in the City of Roanoke, Virginia, and the Vicinity Thereof, Especially for this Work.* Second edition. Roanoke: Stone Printing & Mfg. Co., 1902.

Terry & Pope. *Roanoke, Virginia, in 1891. Its investment opportunities. Its manufacturing advantages. Its transportation services. Its trade facilities. Its home attractions.* Roanoke: Hammond Printing Works, 1891.

Taylor, Frank H. *The City of Roanoke, Virginia: Containing an Outline of its Environment, Resources, Development, Prospects and Substantial Inducements to Capital in the Year 1890.* New York: Giles Co., 1890.

Virginia Anti–Saloon League. *Temperance Handbook of Virginia.* Richmond: Anti-Saloon League of Virginia, 1910.

Virginia State Federation of Labor, *Virginia State Federation of Labor Directory with Historical Sketches of Richmond, Roanoke, Norfolk and Portsmouth.* Ed. W. H. Mullen. Richmond: Frank Baptist Printing Co., 1902.

Wells, Ida B. *A Red Record: Tabulated Statistics and Alleged Causes of Lynching in the United States, 1892–1893–1894.* Chicago: Donohue & Henneberry, 1895.

Williams' City Directory of Roanoke, Virginia, 1891–1892. Binghamton, NY: J. E. Williams, 1891.

Williams, Daniel B. *Emancipation Address: Our Duties and How to Discharge Them, Delivered in the Town Hall of Salem, Va., January 2, 1893, Under the Auspices of the Emancipation Club of Salem, which was joined by the Emancipation Club of Roanoke, Va.* N.p.: by the author, 1893.

Woman's Civic Betterment Club of Roanoke. *The Roanoke Cook Book: Favorite Recipes by Some of Roanoke's Good Housekeepers.* Compiled by Mrs. Albert A. Stone. Roanoke: Stone Printing & Mfg. Co., 1907.

———. *The Year Book of the Woman's Civic Betterment Club / Roanoke, Virginia 1910.* Roanoke: Hammond Printing Works, 1910.

Published Secondary Works

Allen, James, et al. *Without Sanctuary: Lynching Photography in America.* Santa Fe, NM: Twin Palms Publishers, 2000.

Alexander, Ann Field. "Joel Holleman Cutchin." In *The Dictionary of Virginia Biography, Vol. 3,* ed. Sara B. Bearss, 643–44. Richmond: The Library of Virginia, 2006.

———. "Like an Evil Wind: The Roanoke Riot of 1893 and the Lynching of Thomas Smith." *Virginia Magazine of History and Biography* 100, no. 2 (Apr. 1992): 173–206.

Alexander, Sydney Taylor. *Elmwood of Roanoke.* Washington, DC: By the author, 1958.

Androit, John L. ed. *Population Abstract of he United States.* McLean, VA: Androit Associates, 1980.

Apel, Dora. *Imagery of Lynching: Black Men, White Women, and the Mob.* New Brunswick, NJ: Rutgers University Press, 2004.

Ayers, Edward L. "Narrating the New South." *Journal of Southern History* 61, no. 3 (Aug. 1995): 555–66.

———. "Northern Business and the Shape of Southern Progress: The Case of Tennessee's 'Model City.'" *Tennessee Historical Quarterly* 39, no. 2 (Summer 1980): 208–22.

———. *The Promise of a New South: Life after Reconstruction.* New York: Oxford University Press, 1992.

Baker, Bruce E. "North Carolina Lynching Ballads." In *Under Sentence of Death: Lynching in the South,* ed. W. Fitzhugh Brundage, 219–45. Chapel Hill: University of North Carolina Press, 1997.

———. "Under the Rope: Lynching and Memory in Laurens County, South Carolina." In *Where These Memories Grow: History, Memory, and Southern Identity,* ed. W. Fitzhugh Brundage, 319–45. Chapel Hill: University of North Carolina Press, 2000.

Bailey, Hugh C. *Hinton Rowan Helper: Abolitionist—Racist.* Tuscaloosa, AL: University of Alabama Press, 1965.

Baratta, Erin. "Gainesboro Neighborhood, 1890–1940." *The Journal of the History Museum and Historical Society of Western Virginia* 14, no. 1 (1999): 40–50.

Barnes, Raymond P. *A History of Roanoke.* Radford, VA: Commonwealth Press, 1968.

———. "Roanoke Valley's Early Iron Mines." *Journal of the Roanoke Historical Society* 3, no. 2 (Winter 1967): 24–27.

Baron, Stanley. *Brewed in America: A History of Beer and Ale in the United States.* Boston: Little, Brown and Co., 1962.

Barth, Gunther. *Instant Cities: Urbanization and the Rise of San Francisco and Denver.* New York: Oxford University Press, 1975.

Best, Joel. *Controlling Vice: Regulating Brothel Prostitution in St. Paul, 1865–1883.* Columbus: Ohio State University Press, 1998.

Boyer, Paul S. *Urban Masses and Moral Order in America, 1820–1920.* Cambridge, MA: Harvard University Press, 1978.

Brownwell, Blaine, and David Goldfield, eds. *The City in Southern History: The Growth of Urban Civilization in the South.* Port Washington, NY: Kennikat Press, 1977.

Bruce, Carolyn Hale. *Roanoke: A Pictorial History.* Norfolk and Virginia Beach: Donning Company, 1976.

Brundage, W. Fitzhugh. *Lynching in the New South: Georgia and Virginia, 1880–1930.* Urbana: University of Illinois Press, 1993.

———. "Racial Violence, Lynchings, and Modernization in the Mountain South." In *Appalachians and Race: The Mountain South from Slavery to Segregation,* ed. John C. Inscoe, 302–16. Lexington: University of Kentucky Press, 2000.

Burton, Vernon, and Robert C. McMath Jr., eds. *Towards a New South? Studies in Post–Civil War Southern Communities.* Westport, CT: Greenwood Press, 1982.

Cappon, Lester J. *Bibliography of Virginia History Since 1865.* Charlottesville: University of Virginia, 1930.

———. *Virginia Newspapers, 1821–1935: A Bibliography with Historical Introduction and Notes.* Guide to Virginia Historical Materials Part I. New York: D. Appleton–Century Co. for the Institute for Research in the Social Sciences at the University of Virginia, 1936.

Carlton, David. *Mill and Town in South Carolina.* Baton Rouge: Louisiana State University Press, 1982.

Clark, Victor S. *History of Manufacturers in the United States, 1860–1914.* Washington DC: Carnegie Institution of Washington, 1928.

Coleman, Elizabeth Dabney. "The Night Ride That Made Roanoke." *Virginia Cavalcade* 4 (Summer 1954): 9–13.

Condee, William Fairfax. *Coal and Culture in Appalachia.* Athens, OH: Ohio University Press, 2005.

Corbin, David. *Life, Work, and Rebellion in the Coalfields: The Southern West Virginia Miners, 1880–1922.* Urbana: University of Illinois Press, 1981.

Dabney, Virginius. *Virginia: The New Dominion.* Garden City, NJ: Doubleday and Co., 1971.

Daily, Jane. *Before Jim Crow: The Politics of Race in Postemancipation Virginia.* Chapel Hill: University of North Carolina Press, 2000.

Davis, Carroll Curtis. "Very Well Rounded Republican: The Several Lives of John S. Wise." *Virginia Magazine of History and Biography* 71, no. 4 (Oct. 1963): 461–87.

Dixon, Kelly J. *Boomtown Saloons: Archaeology and History in Virginia City.* Reno and Las Vegas: University of Nevada Press, 2005.

Dorsey, Allison. *To Build Our Lives Together: Community Formation in Black Atlanta, 1875–1906.* Athens: University of Georgia Press, 2004.

Doyle, Don H. *New Men, New Cities, New South: Atlanta, Nashville, Charleston, Mobile, 1860–1910.* Chapel Hill: University of North Carolina Press, 1990.

———. *Nashville in the New South, 1880–1930.* Knoxville: University of Tennessee Press, 1985.

Eller, Ronald. *Miners, Millhands, and Mountaineers: Industrialization of the Appalachian South, 1880–1930.* Knoxville: University of Tennessee Press, 1982.

Erhardt, Carl L., and Joyce E. Berlin, eds. *Mortality and Morbidity in the United States.* Cambridge: Harvard University Press, 1974.

First Baptist Church of Roanoke—History Committee. *An Adventure in Faith: A History of the First Baptist Church of Roanoke, Virginia, 1875–1955.* Roanoke: First Baptist Church of Roanoke, 1955.

Flamming, Douglas. *Creating the Modern South: Millhands and Managers in Dalton, Georgia, 1884–1984.* Chapel Hill: University of North Carolina Press, 1992.

Foster, Gaines M. *Moral Reconstruction: Christian Lobbyists and the Federal Legislation of Morality, 1865–1920.* Chapel Hill: University of North Carolina Press, 2002.

Foucault, Michel. *Discipline and Punish: The Birth of the Prison.* New York: Vintage, 1995.

Freehling, William W. *The Road to Disunion Volume I: Secessionists at Bay, 1776–1854.* New York: Oxford University Press, 1990.

Garner, John S. *The Model Company Town: Urban Design through Private Enterprise in Nineteenth-Century New England.* Amherst: University of Massachusetts Press, 1984.

Gaston, Paul M. *New South Creed: A Study in Southern Mythmaking.* Baton Rouge: Louisiana State University Press, 1976.

Gaventa, John. *Power and Powerlessness: Quiescence and Rebellion in an Appalachian Valley.* Urbana: University of Illinois Press, 1980.

Gilmore, Glenda E. *Gender and Jim Crow: Women and the Politics of White Supremacy in North Carolina, 1896–1920.* Chapel Hill: University of North Carolina Press, 1996.

Goldfield, David. *From Cotton Fields to Skyscrapers: Southern City and Region, 1607–1980.* Baton Rouge: Louisiana State University Press, 1982.

———. *Region, Race, and Cities: Interpreting the Urban South.* Baton Rouge: Louisiana State University Press, 1997.

Goodson, Steve. *Highbrows, Hillbillies, and Hellfire: Public Entertainment in Atlanta, 1880–1930.* Athens: University of Georgia Press, 2002.

Grantham, Dewy W. *Southern Progressivism: The Reconciliation of Progress and Tradition.* Knoxville: University of Tennessee Press, 1983.

Gudmestad, Robert H. "Baseball, The Lost Cause, and the New South in Richmond, Virginia, 1883–1890." *Virginia Magazine of History and Biography* 106, No. 3 (Summer 1998): 267–300.

Gutman, Herbert G. *Work, Culture, and Society in Industrializing America: Essays in American Working-Class and Social History.* New York: Vintage, 1977.

Hall, Jacquelyn Dowd, James Leloudis, Robert Korstad, Mary Murphy, Lu Ann Jones, and Christopher B. Daly. *Like a Family: The Making of a Southern Cotton Mill World.* Chapel Hill: University of North Carolina Press, 1987.

Hanchett, Thomas W. *Sorting Out the New South City: Race, Class, and Urban Development in Charlotte, 1875–1975.* Chapel Hill: University of North Carolina Press, 1998.

Harris, Carl. V. *Political Power in Birmingham, 1871–1921.* Knoxville: University of Tennessee Press, 1977.

Heller, George R. *A Narrative for the Proposed Historic Gainesboro Preservation District,* ed. Helen Davis and Evelyn Davis Bethel. Roanoke: Privately printed, 1991.

Hippert, Jr., Roy H. "Col. James P. Woods, Lawyer, Congressman." *Journal of the Roanoke Valley Historical Society* 11, no. 1 (1982): 23–39.

Hofstadter, Richard. *The Age of Reform: From Bryan to F. D. R.* New York: Vintage, 1955.

Howard, A. E. Dick. *Commentaries on the Constitution of Virginia,* vol. 2. Charlottesville: University Press of Virginia, 1974.

Jackson, Joy L. *New Orleans in the Gilded Age: Politics and Urban Progress, 1880–1896.* Baton Rouge: Louisiana State University Press, 1969.

Johnson, Joan Marie. *Southern Ladies, New Women: Race, Region, and Clubwomen in South Carolina, 1890–1930.* New Perspectives on the History of the South. Gainesville: University Press of Florida, 2004.

Kagey, Deedie. *When Past is Prologue: A History of Roanoke County, Salem, and Roanoke City.* Roanoke: Roanoke County Sesquicentennial Committee, 1988.

Kasson, John F. *Amusing the Million: Coney Island at the Turn of the Century.* New York: Hill & Wang, 1978.

Kegley, Frederick B. *Virginia Frontier: The Beginnings of the Southwest, The Roanoke of Colonial Days, 1740–1783.* Roanoke: Southwest Virginia Historical Society, 1938.

Keen, Eugenia M., and Gladys D. Hughes. *History of Christ Episcopal Church, Roanoke, Virginia.* Roanoke: Christ Episcopal Church of Roanoke, 1961.

Kingsdale, Jon M. "The 'Poor Man's Club': Social Functions of the Urban Working-Class Saloon." *American Quarterly* 25, no. 4 (Oct. 1973): 472–89.

Kipp, Samuel M. III. "Old Notables and Newcomers: The Economic and Political Elite of Greensboro, North Carolina, 1880–1920." *Journal of Southern History* 43, no. 3 (Aug. 1977): 373–94.

Kolko, Gabriel. *The Triumph of Conservatism: A Reinterpretation of American History, 1900–1916.* New York: The Free Press, 1963.

Kyriakoudes, Louis M. *The Social Origins of the Urban South: Race, Gender, and Migration in Nashville and Middle Tennessee, 1890–1930.* Chapel Hill: University of North Carolina Press, 2003.

Lambie, Joseph T. *From Mine to Market: The History of Coal Transportation on the Norfolk and Western Railway.* New York: New York University Press, 1954.

Larsen, Lawrence H. *The Rise of the Urban South.* Lexington: University of Kentucky Press, 1985.

———. *The Urban South: A History.* Lexington: University Press of Kentucky, 1990.

Larsen, William. *Montague of Virginia: The Making of a Southern Progressive.* Baton Rouge: Louisiana State University Press, 1965.

Lee, Tom. *The Tennessee-Virginia Tri-Cities: Urbanization in Appalachia, 1900–1950.* Knoxville: University of Tennessee Press, 2005.

Leloudis, James L. II. "School Reform in the New South: The Woman's Association for the Betterment of Public School Houses in North Carolina, 1902–1919." *The Journal of American History* 69, no. 2 (Mar. 1972): 886–907.

Lerda, Valeria G. "'We were no class at all': Southern Women as Social Reformers." In *Race and Class in the American South Since 1890,* ed. Melvyn Stokes and Rick Halpern, 121–38. Oxford: Berg Publishers, 1994.

Levine, Lawrence. *Highbrow/Lowbrow: The Emergence of Cultural Hierarchy in America.* Cambridge: Harvard University Press, 1988.

Lewis, Helen, and Edward Kniper. "The Colonialism Model: The Appalachian Case." In *Colonialism in Modern America: The Appalachian Case,* ed. Helen Lewis, Linda Johnson, and Donald Atkins, 9–31. Boone, NC: Appalachian Consortium Press, 1978.

Lewis, Ronald. *Transforming the Appalachian Countryside: Railroads, Deforestation, and Social Change in West Virginia, 1880–1920.* Chapel Hill: University of North Carolina Press, 1998.

Link, William A. *The Paradox of Southern Progressivism, 1880–1930*. Chapel Hill: University of North Carolina Press, 1992.

Long, John D. *South of Main: The History of the Water Street Community of Salem, Virginia*. Salem, VA: Virginia Foundation for the Humanities and Public Policy, 2000.

Lugar, Norma. "The Life and Times of J. B. Fishburn." *The Roanoker* (Nov.–Dec. 1978): 14–16, 18, 20, 86.

McDaniel, Brenda. "Dr. Campbell's Big Lick." *The Roanoker* (Sept. 1981): 35–36, 78–82.

McKinney, Gordon B. "The Blair Committee Investigation of 1883: Industrialization in the Appalachian Mountains." *Appalachian Journal: A Regional Studies Review* 26, no. 2 (Winter 1999): 150–67.

———. "Industrialization and Violence in Appalachia in the 1890s." In *An Appalachian Symposium: Essays Written in Honor of Cratis D. Williams*, ed. J. W. Williamson, 131–44. Boone, NC: Appalachian State University Press, 1977.

———. *Southern Mountain Republicans, 1865–1900: Politics and the Appalachian Community*. Chapel Hill: University of North Carolina Press, 1978.

McKiven, Jr., Henry M. *Iron and Steel: Class, Race, and Community in Birmingham, Alabama, 1875–1920*. Chapel Hill: University of North Carolina Press, 1995.

Malamud, Gary W. *Boomtown Communities*. Environmental Design Series, vol. 5. New York: Van Nostrand Reinhold, Co., 1984.

Mann, Harold W. "Economic Development in Southwest Virginia." *Journal of the Roanoke Valley Historical Society* 11, no. 2 (1982): 66–81.

Middleton, Norwood. *Salem: A Virginia Chronicle*. Salem, VA: Salem Historical Society, 1986.

Moger, Alan W. "Industrial and Urban Progress in Virginia from 1880 to 1900." *Virginia Magazine of History and Biography* 66 (July 1958): 307–36.

———. "Railroad Practices in Virginia after the Civil War." *Virginia Magazine of History and Biography* 59, no. 4 (Oct. 1951): 423–57.

———. *Virginia: Bourbonism to Byrd, 1870–1925*. Charlottesville: University Press of Virginia, 1968.

Moore, James T. "Black Militancy in Readjuster Virginia, 1879–1883." *Journal of Southern History* 41 (May 1975): 167–86.

Moorman, Warren L. "Roanoke's First Fire Station." *Journal of the Roanoke Valley Historical Society* 11, no. 2 (1982): 32–37.

———. "Roanoke Valley Medicine." *Journal of the Roanoke Valley Historical Society* 9, no. 1 (1973–74): 21–40.

Niederer, Frances J. "John Nolen's Roanoke City Plan of 1907." *Journal of the Roanoke Historical Society* 2, no. 2 (Winter 1965–66): 1–8.

Noe, Kenneth W. *Southwest Virginia's Railroad: Modernization and the Sectional Crisis*. Urbana: University of Illinois Press, 1994.

Ownby, Ted. *Subduing Satan: Religion, Recreation, and Manhood in the Rural South, 1865–1920*. The Fred W. Morrison Series in Southern Studies. Chapel Hill: University of North Carolina Press, 1990.

Payne, Neal. "How a Railway Clerk Saw the New Century." *Journal of the Roanoke Valley Historical Society* 11, no. 2 (1982): 38–46.

Peiss, Kathy. *Cheap Amusements: Working Women and Leisure in Turn of the Century New York*. Philadelphia: Temple University Press, 1986.

Piedmont, Donlan. *Peanut Soup and Spoonbread: An Informal History of Hotel Roanoke*. Roanoke: Virginia Tech Real Estate Foundation, 1994.

———. "The Railroad Offices." *Journal of the Roanoke Valley Historical Society* 13, no. 2 (1996): 18–22.

Pulley, Raymond H. *Old Virginia Restored: An Interpretation of the Progressive Impulse*. Charlottesville: University Press of Virginia, 1968.

Rabinowitz, Howard N. "Continuity and Change: Southern Urban Development, 1860–1900." In *The City in Southern History: The Growth of Urban Civilization in the South*, ed. Blaine A. Brownwell and David R. Goldfield, 105–39. Port Washington, NY: Kennikat Press, 1977.

———. *Race Relations in the Urban South, 1865–1890*. New York: Oxford University Press, 1978.

Roanoke Country Club. *Roanoke Country Club*. Roanoke: Privately printed, 1969.

Roanoke Times & World News Corporation. *Roanoke: 100, A Centennial Edition Reprint*. Roanoke: Roanoke Times & World News Corporation, 1982.

Rosen, Ruth. *The Lost Sisterhood: Prostitution in America, 1900–1918*. Baltimore: Johns Hopkins University Press, 1982.

Rosenzweig, Roy. *Eight Hours for What We Will: Workers and Leisure in an Industrial City, 1870–1920*. Cambridge: Cambridge University Press, 1983.

Russell, James M. *Atlanta, 1847–1890: City Building in the Old South and New South*. Baton Rouge: Louisiana State University Press, 1988.

Sante, Luc. *Low Life: Lures and Snares of Old New York*. New York: Farrar Straus Giroux, 1991.

Scott, Anne Firor. *Natural Allies: Women's Voluntary Associations in America*. Urbana: University of Illinois Press, 1992.

Shapiro, Henry D. *Appalachia on our Mind: The Southern Mountains and Mountaineers in the American Consciousness, 1870–1920*. Chapel Hill: University of North Carolina Press, 1978.

Shareef, Reginald. *The Roanoke Valley's African American Heritage: A Pictorial History*. Virginia Beach, VA: Donning Company, 1996.

Shifflett, Crandall A. *Coal Towns: Life, Work, and Culture in Company Towns of Southern Appalachia, 1880–1960*. Knoxville: University of Tennessee Press, 1991.

———. *Patronage and Poverty in the Tobacco South: Louisa County, Virginia, 1860–1900.* Knoxville: University of Tennessee Press, 1982.

Sims, Anastatia. *The Power of Femininity in the New South: Women's Organizations and Politics in North Carolina, 1880–1930.* Columbia: University of South Carolina Press, 1997.

Smith, J. Douglas. *Managing White Supremacy: Race, Politics, and Citizenship in Jim Crow Virginia.* Chapel Hill: University of North Carolina Press, 2002.

Smith, Robert H. *General William Mahone, Frederick J. Kimball and Others: A Short History of the Norfolk & Western Railway.* New York: Newcomen Society in North America, 1949.

Sprague, Stuart Seely. "The Great Appalachian Iron and Coal Town Boom of 1889–1893." *Appalachian Journal* 4, nos. 3–4 (Spring and Summer 1977): 216–23.

———. "Investing in Appalachia: The Virginia Valley Boom of 1889–1893." *Virginia Cavalcade* (Winter 1975): 134–43.

Stevens, George Raymond. *An Economic and Social Survey of Roanoke County.* Vol. 15, no. 1. Charlottesville: University of Virginia, 1930.

Stoehr, Eric. *Bonanza Victorian: Architecture and Society in Colorado Mining Towns.* Albuquerque: University of New Mexico Press, 1975.

Stoner, Robert D. *A Seed-Bed of the Republic: Early Botetourt.* Roanoke: Roanoke Valley Historical Society, 1962.

Striplin, E. F. Pat. *The Norfolk & Western: A History.* Forest, VA: Norfolk & Western Historical Society, 1997.

Stromquist, Shelton. *A Generation of Boomers: The Pattern of Railroad Labor Conflict in Nineteenth-Century America.* Urbana: University of Illinois Press, 1987.

Thernstrom, Stephen. *Poverty and Progress: Social Mobility in a Nineteenth Century City.* Cambridge, MA: Harvard University Press, 1964.

Thomason, Philip. "The Men's Quarter of Downtown Nashville." *Tennessee Historical Quarterly* 41, no. 1 (Spring 1982): 48–66.

Trotti, Michael A. "When Coney Island Arrived in Richmond: Leisure in the Capital at the Turn of the Century." *Virginia Cavalcade* 51, no. 4 (Autumn 2002): 168–79.

Van Munching, Philip. *Beer Blast: The Inside Story of the Brewing Industry's Bizarre Battles for Your Money.* New York: Times Books, 1997.

Waller, Altina L. *Feud: Hatfields, McCoys, and Social Change in Appalachia, 1860–1900.* The Fred W. Morrison Series in Southern Studies. Chapel Hill: University of North Carolina Press, 1988.

Watts, Anne DeWitt. "Cities and Their Place in Southern Appalachia." *Appalachian Journal* 8, no. 2 (Winter 1981): 105–17.

Warren, I. M. *History of Newspapers Published in 23 Counties of Southwest Virginia.* Roanoke: Works Progress Administration, 1937.

Wedell, Marsha. *Elite Women and the Reform Impulse in Memphis, 1875–1915.* Knoxville: University of Tennessee Press, 1991.

Whisnant, David E. *All that is Native and Fine: The Politics of Culture in an American Region*. Chapel Hill: University of North Carolina Press, 1983.

White, Clare. *Roanoke 1740–1982*. Roanoke: Roanoke Valley Historical Society, 1982.

Wiebe, Robert H. *The Search for Order, 1877–1920*. New York: Hill and Wang, 1967.

Weise, Robert. "Big Stone Gap and the New South, 1880–1900." In *The Edge of the South: Life in Nineteenth-Century Virginia,* ed. Edward L. Ayers and John C. Willis, 173–93. Charlottesville: University Press of Virginia, 1991.

Williams, John Alexander. *Appalachia: A History*. Chapel Hill: University of North Carolina Press, 2002.

Williamson, Joel. *The Crucible of Race: Black and White Relations in the American South Since Emancipation*. New York: Oxford University Press, 1984.

Wilson, William H. *The City Beautiful Movement*. Baltimore: Johns Hopkins University, 1989.

Woodward, C. Vann. *Origins of the New South*. Baton Rouge: Louisiana State University Press, 1951.

Woodman, Harold. "How New was the New South?" *Agricultural History* 58, no. 4 (Oct. 1984): 529–45.

Works Projects Administration in the State of Virginia. *Roanoke: Story of County and City*. Roanoke: Roanoke City School Board, 1942.

Unpublished Secondary Works

Alderson, Debra Lynn. "John Nolen, City Planner: The Roanoke Plans (1907, 1928)." M.A. thesis, University of Virginia, 1992.

Geary, Iva J. "The Woman's Club of Roanoke." TMs (1936). Federal Writers' Project, District No. 5, Project No. 65-1700. Virginia Room, Roanoke City Public Library.

Hancock, John Loretz. "John Nolen and the American City Planning Movement: A History of Culture Change and Community Response." Ph.D. diss. University of Pennsylvania, 1964.

Moger, Alan W. "The Rebuilding of the Old Dominion: A Study in Economic, Social, and Political Transition from 1880 to 1902." Ph.D. diss. Columbia University, 1940.

Schilling, William L. "Roanoke City Fire Department History, 1882–1983." TMs, 1983. Virginia Room, Roanoke City Public Library.

Town of Gainesborough, 1834–1874 Map. Virginia Room, Roanoke City Public Library.

"Transcript of 'The Hand that Rocked the Cradle, Pulled the Strings,'" TMs (1997). Virginia Room, Roanoke City Public Library.

Waits, John Anderson II. "Roanoke's Tragedy: The Lynch Riot of 1893." M.A. thesis, University of Virginia, 1972.

Index

Crystal Spring Land Company, 66, 76, 185

Cutchin, Joel H. (mayor): biography of, 218, 306n195; and civic improvement, 218–19, 221, 224, 226, 229, 230, 232–33, 238; dismissed from office, 233–36; during Shields episode, 152–53, 155, 157, 158, 159–60; municipal leadership of, 209–10, 215–16

Danville, VA: Race Riot, 32–33

Daughters of the American Revolution, 222, 223, 224

Daughters of the Confederacy, 222

Davis, James Hurd, 154–55

Davis, John H., 33, 36, 38, 111, 112

Davis, Walter, 143, 148

Davis Hall, 111, 131, 203

decennial celebration. *See* Roanoke Decennial Celebration

Democratic Party: newspapers, 33; of Roanoke, xvi; 31–34, 36, 38, 44, 56, 97, 111, 182–83, 200–202, 204, 234–36; of Virginia, 34, 56, 201–2, 255n9

Depression of 1873, 4–5

Depression of 1883: impact on business, 27, 38, 60–61, 247n33; charity during, 104; impact on land speculation, 60, 73; impact on municipal government, 38, 68

Depression of 1893: attempts to mitigate, 165–67, 187–88, 197; charity during, 164–65; impact on business, xviii, 129–30, 163–64, 167–68, 169, 187; impact on municipal improvements, 55, 129; impact on race relations, xviii, 279n31; impact on real estate speculation, 79, 168–69; impact on residents, 129–30, 164–65, 285n144; impact on Virginia, 152

Derr, Rush U., 23, 25–27

disfranchisement, 200–202, 211

Dooley, Jeff, 125, 128

Douglass, Frederick, 148

Downing, Lylburn Liggins, 111

Dunstan, John H. (mayor), 257n37; businesses of, 16, 35, 68; and civic improvement, 35–36, 119; municipal leadership of, 36–38

Duval Engine Woks, 68

E. H. Stewart & Company Furniture, 16

Early, Jubal, 33

education: African American schools, 36, 42, 110–11, 131, 154; Catholic schools, 84; during 1893 Depression, 164; private schools, 91–92, 122; public schools, 20, 25, 36, 42, 45, 110, 191; and Woman's Civic Betterment Club, 199, 219–20, 224, 232–33, 236–37. *See also* Hollins Institute; Roanoke College; Virginia College for Young Ladies

Elmwood, 12, 65, 99; purchased by Enoch W. Clark & Company, 11; purchased by Roanoke, 233

Enoch W. Clark & Company, 5, 38, 61, 65–66, 91, 93, 185; credited with creation of Roanoke, 23–24; development of Atlantic, Mississippi & Ohio Railroad, 5; development of Big Lick, 8–10; development of Norfolk & Western Railroad, 5, 6–8; development of Roanoke, 28; development of Shenandoah Valley Railroad, 5, 6–8; development of Southwest Virginia coal industry, 6, 62; during Depression of 1883, 60; sale of Norfolk & Western Railroad, 168. *See also* Clark, Clarence; Hotel Roanoke; Kimball, Frederick J.; Norfolk & Western Railroad; Roanoke Land & Improvement Company; Roanoke Machine Works; Shenandoah Valley Railroad

Mill Mountain Star, 241–42, 297n158;
earlier idea for, 196
Montague, Andrew Jackson (governor),
156–59
Moomaw, Daniel C., 37
Moomaw, John C., 7–8, 10, 69
Moorman, Robert, 140
Morning Star Saloon, 21
Morton, Charlie, 138
Morton's Saloon, 47, 49–50, 108
Mount Zion African Methodist Episco-
pal Church, 110
Mountain Park, 202
Mountain View Land Company, 76

narrow gauge railroad bridge, 141
National Business College, 92
National Exchange Bank, 43, 55, 183,
212
Needles, Arthur, 186
New South: Roanoke as example of, xv,
xx–xxi, 1, 15, 59–60, 63, 71–72,
80–81, 188–89, 240
New South creed, xv, xx, 63, 217, 237
"New Town," xvi, 13, 30, 31
newspapers, 253n116; African American, 33, 110, 255n4; support for
lynching, 127–29; political stance
of, 33; racist views of, 107–8, 122,
203. *See also individual newspaper
names*
Newton, John B., 186
Noland, William C., 94–98
Nolen, John, 228, 230–33, 305n176
Norfolk & Western Railroad (N&W):
depot, 8, 12, **48**, 107–8, 210; during
Depression of 1883, 27, 38; during
Depression of 1893, 129, 167–68;
during Roanoke Riot of 1893, 141;
economic impact on Southwest
Virginia, 59, 62–64, 74; employees,
18, 54, 80, 83 **89**, 113, 190; general
offices, 12–13, 19, **48**, 168, 169;
growth of, 5–6, 28, 61–62, 240–41;

initial development of Roanoke, xvi,
xx, 1, 8–9, 10–15; lease of Roanoke
& Southern Railroad, 70; origins of,
5; purchased by Norfolk & Western
Railway Company, 168; political
involvement of, 34, 55–56; purchase
of Shenandoah Valley Railroad,
60; rail monopoly of, xviii, 70,
165–67, 185, 190; in reorganization
receivership, 129; route of tracks
in 1880s, **14**; segregation by, 108;
volunteer fire company, 53. *See also*
Clark, Clarence; Enoch W. Clark
& Company; Kimball, Frederick J.;
Shenandoah Valley Railroad
Norfolk & Western Railway Company
(N&W): depot, 206–7, 210, 242;
general offices, 169; merger with
Southern Railway, 241; origins of,
168; political involvement, 206–7,
210–11; and Woman's Civic Betterment Club, 222–23, 226, 228
Norwich Lock Works, 68, 84, 95, 96,
97, 264n39; during Depression of
1893, 129, 164; and Roanoke Cotton Mill, 190, 294n115

O'Ferrall, Charles T. (governor), 152,
283n122
Oak Ridge Land Company, 75
Oliver, Andrew Jackson, 110, 112,
257n54, 258n64
Opera House, **39**, 131; entertainment at,
101, 102; origins of, 101; patrons
of, 72–73, 101, 121
organized labor. *See* labor unions

Page, Edward, 147
Page, Thomas Nelson, 102, 151
patent medicines. *See* con artists
Pattie, James, 56
Pattie, William A., 34
Payne, Frank G., 193, 215–16

Payne, John, 97
Peach Road, 107, 109
pedestrians struck by trains, 54–56
Pedigo, L. G., 224, 230
Perry, Alice: assault on, 125–27, 139
Philadelphia, PA: residents in Roa-
    noke, 68, 91–93, 222; newspaper
    accounts of Roanoke, 23–25, 144,
    147. *See also* Enoch W. Clark &
    Company; Clark, Clarence; Bryan,
    Malcolm W.; Kimball, Frederick J.;
    Noland, William C.
Phoenix Land Company, 76
Pleasant Valley Land Company, 77
Pocahontas, VA, 6, 247n23
Ponce de Leon Hotel, **139**; construc-
    tion of, 72; during Roanoke Riot of
    1893, 136, 137, 138, 142
population of Roanoke, 1, 17, 29, 67,
    189, 239, 241; in 1883, 35; in 1890,
    40, 67–68; in 1895, 164; and popu-
    lation of Big Lick, 4
post office building, 96, 97; used in
    boosterism campaigns, 72, 75, 165,
    190
Poteet's & Company Saloon, 87
progressive reform: advocates of, xix,
    199; and city beautification,
    218–19, 221; and "City Beautiful"
    movement, 221; and disfranchise-
    ment, 200–202; and education,
    219–20; goals of, xix–xx, 199–200,
    212, 217–18, 237–38; and livestock
    restrictions, 205–11; and New
    South creed, 237; and prohibition
    of alcohol, 211–17; and prostitu-
    tion, 233–36; and pure milk and
    food, 220–21; in Roanoke and
    nationally, 307n202; and segre-
    gation, 202–5. *See also* Cutchin,
    Joel H.; Stone, Edward L.; Wom-
    an's Civic Betterment Club
prohibition of alcohol: campaigns for,
    50, 88, 130–32, 178, 199, 211–17;
    as catalyst for Roanoke Riot of

1893, 130–32, 152; opposition to,
124, 131–32, 152, 176–77, 211,
212–14, 215, 217; role of African
Americans in, 131–32, 211; role of
women in, 130–31, 214–15, 216;
in Virginia, 211, 214, 216. *See also*
Campbell, William C.; Roanoke
Anti-Saloon League; Woman's
Christian Temperance Union
prostitution, 1, 44, 45, 49, 115, 135; in
brothels, 50–52; campaigns against,
51–52, 88, 215–16, 234–35; and
red light district, 31, 52, 234–35; in
saloon district, 22, 87, **88**

railroads. *See names of individual rail-
    roads or railways*
Railroad Avenue, 13, **48**, **87**; crime
    on, 22, 47, 50, 234; criticism of,
    40, 47–48, 49–50, 88, 124–25,
    130, 221; housing on, 18–19, **28**,
    77; map of, 85; saloon district on,
    21–22, 47, 86–87, 107, 108, 241
Randolph Street Bridge, 45, 133
Randolph Street Market, 225
Readjuster Party, 32–34, 204
real estate speculation: and Depression
    of 1883, 38; and Depression of
    1893, 168–69; in Roanoke, 16–18,
    59–60, 71–72, 73–81, 94, 95, 97,
    168–69; in Southwest Virginia,
    xvii, 59, 74–75. *See also names of
    individual land companies*
Red Row, 21, 109
Red Sulfur Springs Quadrille, 92
Reid, W. Lawrie, 168
Republican Party, 125; newspapers, 33;
    of Roanoke, xvi–xvii, 31–34, 36,
    38, 44, 56, 111, 172, 200–202, 204,
    224; of Virginia, 32, 33, 34, 44, 56
Richardson, James G., 147
Richlands, VA, 74, 129
Richmond Planet, 144, 156, 159
River View Land Company, 76

130; first locomotive built by, **61**; operation of, 18, 28, 60–61, 80, 240–41; origins of, 1, 8, 10–11; paternalism by, 20, 55, 170, 172; volunteer fire company, 52, 53. *See also* Enoch W. Clark & Company; Roanoke Machine Works Band

Roanoke Machine Works Band, 53, 88, 92, 93, 99, **101**, 117, 119

Roanoke Marble and Granite Works, 190

Roanoke Medical Society, 103–4

Roanoke Merchants' and Manufacturers' Association, 188, 241, 297n158

Roanoke Police Department: management of, 43, 44, 126, 134–35, 148, 152, 280n53; officers of, 135. *See also* gambling; lynching; Massie, Thomas; Perry, Alice; prostitution; Roanoke Riot of 1893; Shields episode; Wilson, Lizzie

Roanoke Real Estate Exchange, **xix**, 42

Roanoke Riot of 1893: and assault on Sallie A. Bishop, 132; ballad of, 149–51; community memories of, 148–51, 284n126, 284n128; community responses to, xviii, 148, 151–52, 160–61, 163, 165, 204; contributing causes of, xviii, 123, 124–32; and evidence of Thomas Smith's innocence, 134, 145–46; historiography of, 285–86n144; and impact on Virginia, 123–24, 144, 152, 156–57, 160–61; investigation of, 143, 146–48; legacy of, 156–57, 160–61; and lynching of Thomas Smith, 139–40; mob rule during, 138–43; and municipal stance against lynch mob, 134–38; press coverage of, 143, 144–45, 147; and progressive reform, 237; and Thomas Smith, 133–34, 138; victims of, 137–38

Roanoke River, 1–2, 10, 230; boating on, 99; entertainment near, 89, 113;

housing near, 126, 165; industry near, 68, 126, 190; and Roanoke Riot of 1893, 138, 140–41

Roanoke Star. *See* Mill Mountain Star

Roanoke Street Railway, 69, 76, 84, 102; segregation of, 202

Roanoke Stockyards Company, 65, 90–91

Roanoke & Southern Railroad, 66, 69–70, 75, 76, 166

Roanoke Trust, Loan & Safe Deposit Company, 66, 72, 169

Robert Portner Brewing Company, 175, 177

Robertson, William Gordon, 131, 173

Rockledge Inn: closure of, 191–92; origins of, 72, 100; patronage of, 100, **101**, 195; reopening of, 194

Rogers, Mortimer M., 76

Rorer, Ferdinand, 16, 56, 60, 69, 99, 179

Rorer Hall, 100

Rorer Park, 113

Rorer Park Hotel, 92, 112, 251n83

Rorer Park Literary Society, 102

Rustic Saloon, 87

Saint Andrew's Catholic Church, 20, 84

Saint Andrew's Society, 102

Saint James Hotel, 138

Saint John's Episcopal Church, 111

Saint Mark's Lutheran Church, 66

Saint Paul United Methodist Church, 110

Salem Avenue, 13, 16, 19, 33, 39, 40, 69, 89, 99

Salem, VA: campaign for rail junction by, 6–8, 247–48n34; during Roanoke Riot of 1893, 143; during Shields episode, 155, 159, 287n187; Emancipation Proclamation anniversary celebration in, 111–12; land speculation in, 74; and Roanoke & Southern Railroad, 69; selected as Roanoke County seat, 2